CVV

D0214312

Modeling and Analysis of Computer Communications Networks

Applications of Communications Theory
Series Editor: R. W. Lucky, *Bell Laboratories*

A Continuation Order Plan is available for this series. A continuation order will bring delivery of each new volume immediately upon publication. Volumes are billed only upon actual shipment. For further information please contact the publisher.

Modeling and Analysis of Computer Communications Networks

Jeremiah F. Hayes
Concordia University
Montreal, Quebec, Canada

PLENUM PRESS • NEW YORK AND LONDON

Library of Congress Cataloging in Publication Data

Hayes, Jeremiah F., 1934–
    Modeling and analysis of computer communications networks.

    (Applications of communications theory)
    Bibliography: p.
    Includes index.
    1. Computer networks — Mathematical models. 2. Local area networks (Computer networks) — Mathematical models. I. Title. II. Series.
TK5105.5.H39   1984   384   84-16107
ISBN 0-306-41782-0

First Printing — November 1984
Second Printing — February 1986

© 1984 Plenum Press, New York
A Division of Plenum Publishing Corporation
233 Spring Street, New York, N.Y. 10013

Printed in the United States of America

**Dedicated to James and Mary Hayes
from Glandore and Drinagh
in the West of County Cork
the Republic of Ireland**

Preface

In large measure the traditional concern of communications engineers has been the conveyance of voice signals. The most prominent example is the telephone network, in which the techniques used for transmission multiplexing and switching have been designed for voice signals. However, one of the many effects of computers has been the growing volume of the sort of traffic that flows in networks composed of user terminals, processors, and peripherals. The characteristics of this data traffic and the associated performance requirements are quite different from those of voice traffic. These differences, coupled with burgeoning digital technology, have engendered a whole new set of approaches to multiplexing and switching this traffic. The new techniques are the province of what has been loosely called computer communications networks.

The subject of this book is the mathematical modeling and analysis of computer communications networks, that is to say, the multiplexing and switching techniques that have been developed for data traffic. The basis for many of the models that we shall consider is queueing theory, although a number of other disciplines are drawn on as well. The level at which this material is covered is that of a first-year graduate course. It is assumed that at the outset the student has had a good undergraduate course in probability and random processes of the sort that are more and more common among electrical engineering and computer science departments. (For the purpose of review, but not first introduction, the required background material is given in a pair of appendices.) The material in the text is developed from this starting point. The objective is to develop in the student the ability to model and analyze computer communication networks. We also seek to impart a critical appreciation of the literature in the field.

In a book at this level, it is inevitable that the choice of the particular material to be included in the text is heavily influenced by the author's own research and professional experience. However, as the book evolved, the work of others assumed a more and more prominent role. In fact, one of the most rewarding aspects of writing the book was learning and appreciating the fine work that others have done, and getting a sense of how the field has progressed. We hope that we have conveyed some of this to the reader. Our appreciation of a good deal of the material outside our immediate interests was gained to a significant degree through a number of first-rate survey papers in the field. We shall gratefully acknowledge these papers at the appropriate points in the text.

The level of the course for which this book is intended places certain limitations on the material that could be covered. In several instances important work could not be included simply because students could not be expected to have the appropriate mathematical training. In other cases the analysis was simply too involved. In spite of these difficulties, we derive great satisfaction from the fact that we were able to include almost all of the work which we consider to be seminal in the field. We tried very hard to present this work in a form that would be palatable to the serious though inexperienced student. A number of exercises illustrating the material are included.

Since the focus is on modeling and analysis, somewhat less attention is given to the details of implementation and operation. However, we attempted to include enough of this material so as to place the mathematical models in the proper context. In the course of the discussion we direct the reader to a number of authoritative sources on implementation and operation.

There is more material in the text than can be covered in an ordinary graduate course. In order to assist the instructor in selecting material, we point out several natural groupings. Chapters 1, 2, and 3 serve as an introduction to the rest of the text. After completing Chapter 3 one could go on to Chapter 4 or to Chapter 10. The main results in Chapters 4, 5, and 6 are obtained through the imbedded Markov technique, thereby providing a unifying theme for the three chapters. The results in Chapters 6, 7, 8, and 9 are pertinent to the modeling of a particular form of computer communication network—the local area network. In fact, all of the well-known accessing techniques are considered. In order to cover Chapters 6 through 9, some material on the imbedded Markov chain is also necessary.

Chapters 10, 11, and 12 also provide a convenient grouping. Chapters 10 and 11 rely heavily on Jackson network theory. The linkage between Chapters 11 and 12 is that they treat the so-called "higher-level" protocols, in particular flow control and routing. Although the final chapter on network layout stands somewhat apart from the others, there are points of contact between network layout and routing. This latter is the subject of Chapter 12.

In concluding these opening remarks we would like to express our deep gratitude to a number of people for their contributions to this work.

Jerry Foschini and John Silvester read an earlier version of the text and made a number of valuable suggestions for its improvement. Their diligent effort and encouragement were significant contributions. Thelma Hyland typed the manuscript. She was the soul of patience through the numerous revisions. A picture is worth a thousand words, and a thousand thanks are due to Miao Duen-Zhi for her assistance with the figures. The book evolved from notes of a course taught at McGill University over the period 1979–1983. A number of students suffered through the earlier (and later) versions of the notes. For their forbearance we express our deep gratitude. As mentioned earlier, the material in the book reflects our research. Our interest in computer communications began at Bell Labs, and was stimulated by Bob Lucky and Jack Salz. We would also like to acknowledge our first collaborator in the field, Dave Sherman. Finally, the author would like to pay tribute to his wife, Florence, and to his children, Mary, Ann, Jemmy, and Martin. They endured his absence and preoccupation during the long writing process.

JEREMIAH F. HAYES
Concordia University
Montreal, Quebec

Contents

Basic Orientation

1.1. Modeling and Analysis of Computer Communications Networks

Computer communications has recently emerged from its origins—the fields of computers and communications—as a separate, distinct area of study. We hope a complete picture of the field will become apparent in the course of the book; however, a useful short-term definition is that computer communications is the study of networks that are designed for the transmission of digital data. Such networks allow users to communicate with computers and computers to communicate with one another. The advent of distributed processing has been the great impetus to the development of computer communications. As we shall see in the course of our discussion, the properties of data signals are significantly different for voice signals. Because of this difference techniques employed in designing and operating computer communication networks are fundamentally different from those that have been used in the traditional voice network. However, these techniques are so well suited to digital technology that there is, at this writing, a full-scale effort to integrate voice traffic into the same networks.

The term "computer communications" encompasses a great range of activities and concepts. The immediate impression is that of daunting complexity as one is faced with the task of modeling and analysis. Nevertheless workers in the field have developed mathematical models which have provided a great deal of insight into the design and performance of systems. The fundamental aim of this book is to present these models and to develop the basic tools for their analysis. To a large extent the models are based on queueing theory. Since it plays such a large role in computer communications, much of this book is concerned with queueing theory, beginning with its basic principles. Other disciplines have also had varying degrees of application, in particular, optimization theory, information theory, and statistical communication theory.

The basic objective of the mathematical modeling of computer communications system is the prediction of performance. In the generic queueing theory model, customers randomly arrive at a facility with service requirements that may be random in duration. The theory attempts to find probabilistic descriptions of such quantities as the sizes of waiting lines, the delay experienced by an arrival, and the availability of a service facility.

Queueing theory began with the work of the danish mathematician A. K. Erlang (1–3) on telephone switching systems. Although queueing finds wide use as one of the basic components of operations research, telecommunications remains its most successful application. In the voice telephone network, demands for service take the form of subscribers initiating a call. Erlang found that given a sufficiently large population, the random rate of such calls can be described by a Poisson process.† In this application the server is the telephone line. The analog of the service time of a customer is the duration of the call, which was found to have an exponential distribution. An important result obtained by Erlang, which is still used in engineering the telephone network, is the probability of a busy signal as a function of the traffic level and the number of lines that have been provided.

Although queueing theory was developed for voice traffic, it is applicable to computer communications. The generation of data messages at a computer terminal corresponds to the initiation of voice calls to the network. The time required to transmit the message over a communications facility corresponds to the required time of service. We shall deal exclusively with digital data; accordingly the transmission time is a function of the number of bits in the message and the data rate of the line. We shall consider digital transmission exclusively.

1.2. Computer Communications Networks

Broadly speaking, the function of a communications network is the transmission of information through shared transmission facilities. As we shall see in the course of the book, a large array of techniques are used to effect this sharing. In this introductory section we shall sketch them.

For purposes of explanation we may classify computer communication networks in two basic categories: local area networks and wide area networks. Local area networks have a limited geographical extent, typically within a kilometer. In a widely encountered example of a local area network the users are sitting at terminals accessing a main frame computer. A number of users share a common transmission line. Because of the localized nature

---

†Terms such as "Poisson process" and "exponential distribution" will be defined in Chapter 3.

of the network, the network can have relatively simple topologies such as the ring, the bus, or the star (see Figure 2.20a, 2.20b, and 2.20c, respectively). A number of accessing techniques can be employed in conjunction with these topologies. For example, with the ring and the bus, token passing grants access to one user at a time. Users having access simply transmit data messages. The protocol governing the technique provides means for passing exclusive access from one user to another. In a contrasting technique used with the bus topology, users contend for the line by transmitting messages in a random fashion. The controlling protocol provides a mechanism for resolving conflict. In the modeling of these protocols we shall be concerned with quantities such as the time required to gain access and the overhead required by the protocol. The overhead has a large effect on throughput, which is the volume of traffic that can go through the network.

For networks covering a wider area the mesh configuration shown in Figure 2.19 is typical. User data are encapsulated in entities which we shall call packets. Since packets contain source and destination addresses, transmission lines can be shared in a flexible manner. Packets may travel from source to destination through a number of intermediate nodes. At each of these nodes the packet is processed. The addressing indicates the route to be followed. Further, at the intermediate nodes the packet may be checked for errors which were incurred in transmission.

In wide area networks we are interested in performace at a number of levels. We shall consider the means of sharing the links between network nodes among a number of users. The total time required by a packet to travel through the network is of considerable interest. Because of the dispersed nature of the control of store-and-forward networks, congested spots can appear within the network. This phenomenon necessitates protocols for the control of flow into and within the network. Hand-in-hand with flow control protocols are routing protocols, which choose the sequence of nodes a packet must follow. Again the focus of the modeling is on throughput and delay.

1.3. Summary of Text

In this section we shall summarize the text. Before doing so, a general comment is in order. As mentioned above, the primary subject of the text is mathematical modeling and analysis of computer communications networks. Accordingly, we shall not be concerned with details of implementation. We shall present only the detail required to place a problem in context and to carry out the modeling and analysis.

Let us now proceed to consider the remaining chapters of the book in sequence. In order to smooth the flow in this first exposure, several terms are defined only implicitly or not at all. For definitions the reader is referred to the section of the book under discussion.

Chapter 2: Protocols and Facilities

Chapter 2 is mainly descriptive in tone. The idea is to establish the framework under which the modeling and analysis is carried out. For purposes of explanation we consider the basic components of a computer communication system to be what we shall call facilities and protocols, corresponding roughly to hardware and software in computer systems. The facilities are the communications systems. The flow of information on the facility is controlled by protocols. Under facilities we shall consider the telephone network, satellite systems, local area networks, mobile radio, and CATV. Now, given the means of communication, protocols shape the flow of information. For example, protocols translate electrical impulses into binary digits. In making this dichotomy there is something of a pedagogical artifice since the operation of the communication facilities involves control. However, in our discussion we shall focus on protocols only as they relate to data transmission.

We shall set out discussion of protocols in the framework of a system of protocols called open systems interconnection (OSI). This system is composed of seven entities called layers or levels. Each level contains a closely related set of functions. Careful attention is paid to the interface between levels, where information is exchanged between the sets of functions that make up the different layers. As part of the discussion of the protocols, we consider both baseband and passband data transmission techniques. In general terms we also consider packetizing, flow control, and routing. These subjects are treated from the aspect of an overview since they will be dealt with in detail in the remainder of the text. Protocols that are used in local area networks are treated in the same way since they are given a great deal of attention in the rest of the book.

Chapter 3: Pure Birth and Birth–Death Processes

Chapter 3 begins the work of establishing the mathematical models for the networks. The properties of the Poisson arrival process are derived from first principles. This is generalized to the pure birth process and then to the birth–death process. This process leads directly to queueing theoretic models. We develop the principles of the $M/M/S$ queue with infinite and finite storage capacity. By Little's formula the average delay can be related to the average number of messages in the system. The departure process from the $M/M/S$ queue is shown to be Poisson by means of Burke's theorem, a result which has considerable implications when we consider networks of queues in Chapters 10 and 11. In the final section of the chapter nonexponentially distributed service times are dealt with by means of Erlang's method of stages.

Chapter 4: Imbedded Markov Chains: The M/G/1 Queue

Messages with a general length distribution are considered under the assumption of Poisson arrival to a single server. The analysis is carried out by means of the imbedded Markov chain—a far simpler technique than the method of stages considered in the previous chapter. The results of the analysis are in the form of transforms of probability distributions of queue sizes and message delay. From these transforms averages and higher-order moments can be readily obtained. Also considered are methods for finding probability distributions of queue size and delay.

Chapter 5: Time-Division Multiplexing

The imbedded Markov chain approach is applied to the study of synchronous and asynchronous time-division multiplexed (TDM) systems. Bulk departure in TDM systems is analyzed by application of Rouche's theorem. As in Chapter 4, the results of analysis are queue size and message delay. Automatic repeat-request protocols are considered in the same general framework of the imbedded Markov chain.

In the Chapters 6, 7, 8, and 9, accessing techniques for local area networks are analyzed. All of these techniques can be viewed as ways of sharing a server, the transmission line among a number of message sources. Since the locations of these sources are different from one another, part of the capacity of the channel must be used to coordinate the flow of traffic. This overhead plays an important role in the analytical results on accessing techniques. In fact, the objective of the design of access protocols is the balancing of overhead and performance.

Chapter 6: Priority Queues and Ring Systems

As we have indicated, a prominent class of local area network has the ring topology. Certain of the accessing techniques used on ring systems can be viewed as giving one class of messages priority over another. The imbedded Markov chain technique is used to analyze systems with two or more priority classes. Again performance is measured in terms of queue size and message delay.

Chapter 7: Polling and Token Passing

An important accessing technique is polling, which can be viewed as a server visiting queues cyclically, giving equal service to each. The polling technique is appropriate to systems with a tree topology. The same basic model applies as well to an accessing technique called token passing. This technique is used on both ring and bus systems. The salient result of performance studies is the strong sensitivity to overhead. In this case overhead is the time required to pass channel access from one message source to another either by polling or by passing a token.

Chapter 8: Random Access Systems

The results of the previous chapter show the deleterious effect of overhead on performance, particularly at light loading. Random access techniques seek to minimize overhead by minimizing coordination between sources. As shown by the analysis presented in Chapter 8, random access systems are characterized by performance that is good at light loading, but which deteriorates rapidly with increasing load. The results of analysis also show that these systems also exhibit unstable behavior as the load increases. A comparison is made between two contending techniques for accessing in local area networks: token passing and carrier sense multiple access.

Chapter 9: Probing and Tree Search Techniques

In response to the effect of overhead in polling systems and instability in random access systems, a class of adaptive techniques, based on tree search, have been devised. The basic idea of the techniques is to minimize the overhead at light loading and, through adaptivity, to allow graceful degradation as the loading increases. Analysis of the tree search technique based on a Markov chain model of the system shows that the desired results have been obtained. The throughput is increased and the system is stable.

In Chapters 10, 11, and 12, the general subject under study is networks of queues. The application is the mesh network encountered in wide area networks. The particular aspect of these networks that is considered is the performance of higher-level protocols, routing, and flow control.

Chapter 10: Networks of Queues

Under certain assumptions networks whose nodes contain queues can be analyzed in a manner similar to birth–death processes. These networks of queues are the so-called Jackson networks. The importance of these networks lies in the fact that the steady-state probability distribution for the network assumes a particularly simple form of the product of the marginal probability distributions. This product form permits the computation of quantities of interest. In order to apply Jackson network theory to computer communications networks certain assumptions are necessary, one of which is Kleinrock's often quoted (and much abused) independence assumption. The main results of analysis is the calculation of message delay. This result is applied to the allocation of transmission capacity within the network so as to minimize cost while maintaining a certain standard of performance in terms of message delay.

Chapter 11: Congestion and Flow Control

Because of the random nature of traffic flow, it is possible for points of congestion to build up in the interior of a network. In this chapter techniques for controlling the flow into networks are modeled and analyzed. Flow control is studied by means of extended classes of Jackson networks with the objective of exploring both subjects. Both link and network levels are treated by means of closed networks of queues. Of particular interest are computational methods for closed networks of queues. Finally, Jackson theory is applied to the study of networks in which blocking due to limited storage capacity is possible.

Chapter 12: Routing–Flow Allocation

In general a message may take more than one path through a network in traveling from source to destination. In large measure the algorithms used to determine the route of a message are based on shortest-path routing. Classical algorithms of this sort which are traffic independent are given. This is followed by the consideration of techniques for minimizing the average delay of a message, taking into account queueing as well as other factors. These algorithms may be centralized or distributed. In a final section flow control and routing are considered in the same general context.

Chapter 13: Network Layout and Reliability

The final chapter of the text is something of a departure from the preceding from the points of view of both the subject matter and the mathematical foundations. The first subject taken up is minimum spanning trees. We begin with an algorithm which does not take capacity contraints into account. This is followed by the branch and bound technique, which finds minimum spanning trees under capacity constraints. While this technique is optimum, it requires too much computation for reasonable size networks. The Esau–Williams algorithm is suboptimum with the same objective.

The layout of mesh networks is the next topic of discussion. The complexity of the problem is such that only suboptimum techniques are feasible. One such technique which is based on certain graph theoretic ideas is considered.

In the final section of the text the reliability of networks is treated. Bounds for connectability are found under the assumption that network links fail independently of one another. A brief survey of other approaches to reliability is made as well.

References

1. E. Brockmeyer, H. L. Halstrom, and A. Jensen, "The Life and Works of A. K. Erlang" *Transactions of the Danish Academy of Technical Science ATS*, No. 2 (1948).
2. A. K. Erlang, "The Theory of Probabilities and Telephone Conversations," *Nyt Tidsskrift Matematik B*, **20**, 33–39 (1909).
3. A. K. Erlang, "Solution of Some Problems in the Theory of Probabilities of Significance in Automatic Telephone Exchanges," *Electroteknikeren*, **13**, 5–13 (1917) [in English: *PO Electrical Engineering Journal*, **10**, 189–197 (1917–1918).

Protocols and Facilities

2.1. Introduction

In this chapter the general framework for the mathematical models to be presented in the remainder of the text is constructed. In consonance with the objectives of this book, only limited detail is presented. We wish to model and analyze rather than to build and operate. If we realize our objective, considerable assistance will be given to the task of building and operating.†

For purposes of explanation, we consider computer communication systems to consist of two parts: *protocols* and *facilities*. As part of the facilities we include the architecture of the computer communications network. Roughly speaking, the facilities are the physical means for conveying information while the protocols are the means of organizing and controlling the flow of data traffic on the facilities. We make this distinction in full recognition of the fact that the operation of what we call facilities requires procedures that are properly called protocols. An example of this is circuit switching, a topic we shall consider in connection with our discussion of the telephone network. Our way of treating the material is in line with the goals of the book: We simply want to put the analytical models in context. There is also some justification from a historical perspective. The sort of protocols that we consider were originally created just for data communication. With the success of the concept and the growth of technology, the protocols were broadened to include other classes of traffic.

---

†Good books giving details on the design and operation of computer communications networks have been written. References 1–4 are those that we can recommend from personal experience.

2.2. Properties of Data Traffic

The development of facilities and protocols for data traffic has been shaped by data traffic's unique characteristics. These characteristics are very different from those of voice traffic. This comparison is pertinent since the most important facility for data traffic has been and continues to be the telephone network, which was designed for voice. This background has had a strong influence on the facilities and protocols which have been used in computer communication networks.

The properties of data traffic may be summarized by the acronym BAD, meaning that data traffic is

1. Bursty
2. Asymmetric
3. Delicate

The statement that data is "bursty" means that in many applications the traffic is characterized by short periods of activity interspersed with long idle periods. Moreover, unlike voice traffic, the idle periods have no contextual meaning. The burstiness of data traffic is illustrated by a study which is venerable with age as measured by the pace of development in the field.[5,6] Nevertheless, the results are still relevant, particularly when human interaction is involved. The traffic on a two-way line when a user interacts with a computer is shown in Figure 2.1. Computer and user burst segments are interleaved and are separated by idle times and by think times as shown. Within these burst segments there are significant periods of idle time, shown as user and computer interburst times. The percentage of time in which a user transmits data has been measured to be less than 5%. The percentage of time claimed by the computer is less than 30%.

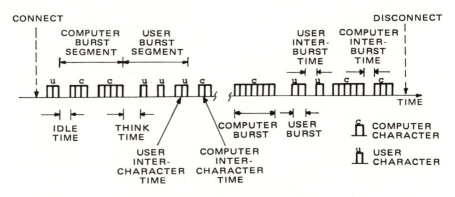

Figure 2.1. The data stream model (Ref. 5).

There are two implications to the bursty nature of data traffic. First of all, the fact that the long-term average usage by a single source is small would suggest that the dedication of facilities to a single source is not economical and that some sort of sharing is appropriate. The second aspect of burstiness is that sources transmit at a relatively high instantaneous rate. This is, in effect, a requirement on the form that this sharing of facilities can take. In fact, the techniques packet and message switching, which we shall study presently, were developed in response to the bursty nature of data traffic.

The second significant attribute of data traffic is the asymmetric nature of the flow. In many applications the volume and speeds are greatly different in one direction from the other. For example, the rule of thumb in interactive computing and in airline reservation systems is that the traffic volume from the computer is ten times the traffic volume to the computer.

It may be stretching a point, but we may also speak of asymmetries in performance requirements. In applications such as credit checking or interactive computing, the response of the system should be of the order of seconds or even milliseconds, whereas in applications such as the bulk transfer of records, the delivery time of messages can be in the order of hours. These asymmetries in volume, speed, and performance have no counterpart in voice traffic.

The final distinguishing property of data, "delicacy," denotes its vulnerability to errors. In many applications, a single bit error would be enough to spoil an entire message. (Consider financial transactions, for example.) This vulnerability stands in contrast to human speech which, by virtue of human perception, is very robust. In order to give the transfer of data a similar robustness, redundancy in the form of parity check bits are added to data messages, thus enabling the detection and/or the correction of transmission errors. As we shall see, these parity check bits part a key role in link control procedures.†

2.3. Protocols

In computer communications a great deal of effort has gone into the study of protocols. The reason for this is that, to a far greater degree than the voice network, computer communications networks operate without human intervention. In many applications the calling and the called parties are processors and the function of the human operator is, at most, starting and monitoring the process. In order to establish, maintain, and terminate a call, either voice or data, a number of tasks must be carried out. Several

†For a discussion of error correcting and detecting codes see Section 2.5.3.3.

of these tasks are implicit in the ordinary voice call. Dial tone tells us that a line is available. A ringing or busy tone indicates the state of the called party. Once the call has been set up, the parties can take the appropriate action if transmission quality deteriorates. Finally the termination of a call is a well-defined procedure. For computer communications all of the actions associated with call establishment, maintenance, and termination must be carried out by machine. The situation is further complicated by the fact that computer communications networks carry out many more tasks than the voice network. The protocols in computer communications networks are not unlike the software of a computer system. One of the similarities is burgeoning complexity. In order to deal with this complexity, the idea of imposing a structure, in which tasks are compartmentalized, has been introduced in both cases. In computer communications protocols this structure takes the form of layering, with similar tasks residing at the same level. The interface between levels is carefully controlled and standardized. The interfaces should be independent of implementation within the levels. As technology evolves the implementation within a layer may change without affecting the interface.

Currently the prime example of a layered system of protocols is *open systems interconnection* (OSI), which has been established by the International Standards Organization† to provide a framework for the development of protocols. OSI consists of the seven layers depicted in Figure 2.2a.‡ In Figure 2.2b the portions of the network controlled by each of these layers are illustrated. The functions of each of these layers along with the interfaces between layers have been standardized.[7] In the remainder of this section we outline the functions of each of the layers and give simple examples of their operation. In connection with out later discussion of facilities, we shall give more complete examples of the operation of protocol layers.

Before discussing the OSI levels, however, a small caveat is appropriate. Like all systems of classification, OSI is an ideal. It attempts to impose uniformity in a complex, diverse situation. Uniformity has economic benefit, particularly in the short term. For example, a standard set of protocol eases VLSI implementation. While it seems that future systems will be heavily influenced by standardized, layered protocols such as OSI, there will inevitably be other pressures. As the technology advances, economics may compromise the strictures of OSI. In any case OSI is an excellent guide to the protocols in a computer communications network.

What is termed the lowest layer in OSI, the *physical* level, is the tradiational realm of communication theory. At this level the electrical or

---

† As its name implies, the International Standards Organization (ISO) is an international body composed of the national standards organizations of its member countries.
‡ In Ref. 3 leading experts give detailed descriptions of each of these protocols.

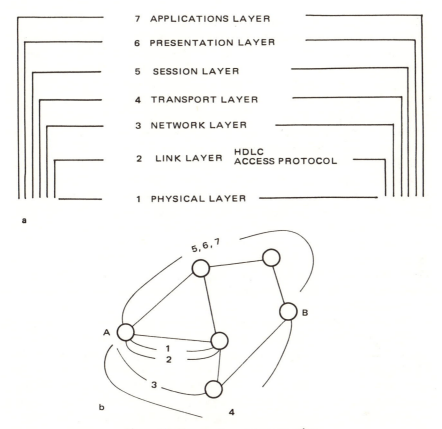

Figure 2.2. Open systems interconnection.

optical signals on the physical medium are translated into a sequence of zeros and ones that can be handled by a processor. We shall consider examples of the physical level later in this chapter when we discuss baseband and passband transmission.

The next highest layer, the *link*, provides structure for the flow of bits over a link between nodes of a network. At this level, for example, parity check bits would be used to detect transmission errors in the link. Control of the flow of traffic over a link takes place at the link level.

In general a network consists of more than one link. The flow of messages over tandem links is dealt with at the next level, the *network* level. An example of a function at this level would be routing, whereby the sequence of links from source to destination nodes is found.

These first three levels of OSI are concerned with components of the path from the origin node to the destination node of the network. The next layer, the *transport* level, exercises end-to-end control. Among other tasks, flow into the network is controlled at the transport level. Also complete data messages are reassembled from packets in packet switched networks.

The four lowest-level protocols form what is called the *transport service.* The transport service ensures the conveyance of bits from source to destination during a data call or session. The remaining three levels in the hierarchy are referred to as the *higher-level protocols.* The lowest of the higher levels is the *session* level. As its name implies, it is at this level that users initiate and terminate calls. Next we have the *presentation* level, which deals with the form in which information is encoded. For example ASCII characters may be translated into EBCDIC characters at this level. Data encryption may also take place at the presentation level. The final layer of OSI is the *applications* level. This layer concerns the management of files and data bases and is very much under the control of the user.

In terms of studies of performance, not much work has been done at the higher levels of OSI. Consequently the models that we shall be considering are confined to the transport service, i.e., the first four levels of OSI. Many of the models that we shall consider are concerned with the access protocols for local area networks. Opinions vary, but these protocols are usually categorized in level 2.

Although OSI provides a useful framework for studying protocols and will strongly influence future developments, other systems of protocols are more widely implemented at present. Foremost among these is the *systems network architecture* (SNA), which was developed by IBM for its product line. The objective of SNA is to provide an architecture allowing products to act as system components in a uniform fashion. As in OSI there is a concept of layering; however, the assignment of functions to different layers is different. These same general remarks apply to the architecture *digital network architecture* (DNA) developed by the Digital Equipment Corporation. For comparisons among OSI, SNA, and DNA, the reader is directed to Refs. 2 and 3.

2.4. The Telephone Network

To a large extent the techniques of computer communications have been shaped by the facilities that have been available. It is appropriate then to review the properties of these facilities with particular emphasis on application to computer communications. As we have indicated earlier, the most important facility for the transmission of data has been and continues to be the telephone network. The fact that the telephone network was originally designed for voice traffic has had considerable impact on the development of the field of computer communications, for, as we have seen, voice and data traffic have very different characteristics.

We consider the telephone network to consist of three basic components, local loops, carrier systems, and switching.† In all three of these are aspects that relate to computer communications.

2.4.1. Local Loops

An important component of the telephone network is the loop plant,‡ which consists mainly of twisted pairs of copper wires connecting station equipment on the user's premises, e.g., a telephone, to local telephone end offices. All but a small minority of loops are less than 4 km long and consist of 26 gauge wire. Typical loops are equipped with loading coils, which are useful for efficient voice transmission but which impair data signals. When the loading coils are removed, data can be transmitted without amplification at a rate of 56 kbps for distances of 4 km or more. In the usual case of transmission over the voice network, the local loop accesses the end office through protective transformers, thus preventing the passage of signals with dc components beyond the local office.

2.4.2. Carrier Systems

In all but very localized calls the voice or data signal is conveyed by means of a carrier system whereby a number of channels are multiplexed onto a common transmission medium. There are several categorizations that can be used to describe carrier systems currently in operation.§ According to the distances involved we have short- and long-haul carrier systems. The fomer is designed for distances of from 15 to 40 km, while long-haul systems convey intercity traffic over longer distances.

Classification according to the means of conveying signals is also relevant. A number of different physical media have been used to carry signals in carrier systems. Carrier systems began with open wire and cable pairs. Today the vast bulk of long-haul traffic is carried on coaxial cable systems and microwave radio. For distances of less than 400 km terrestrial digital radio is of growing importance.[13] The bulk of short-haul traffic is carried on twisted pairs equipped with digital repeaters, as exemplified by the T1 carrier system in North America. Optical fiber seems to be destined to carry an increasing share of short-haul, intracity traffic.[14] Satellites will be considered in a separate category later, but it should be noted at this point that they play an important role in long-distance telephone

---

†For an alternate discussion of telephone facilities as they relate to data communications, see the chapter by R. W. Lucky in Ref. 8.

‡Detailed descriptions on all aspects of the loop plant may be found in Ref. 9.

§For a description of the evolution of telephone carrier systems as well as the recent state of such systems, see Ref. 10, which has been reproduced in Refs. 11 and 12.

transmission. For transoceanic transmission, satellites[15-17] and submarine coaxial cable[18] share the traffic.

2.4.2.1. Analog Carrier Systems

From the point of view of data transmission, the most relevant characterization of carrier systems is the form in which information is conveyed—digital or analog. Within each type a different multiplexing technique is used to create a number of communications channels from the physical medium. Analog systems use *frequency-division multiplexing* (FDM), in which an analog signal, e.g., voice, modulates the amplitude of a sinusoid, the carrier. This modulation places the signal in a frequency band adjacent to the carrier. The characteristics of the media are such that each has a particular frequency band that is appropriate for transmission. In the telephone network, bandwidth is at a premium, therefore a particular technique called *single-sideband* modulation is used. This technique employs half the bandwidth of that used in standard AM broadcasting, but requires the tracking of a carrier phase in order to recover the signal.

Multiplexing is carried out in stages, thereby forming a multiplexing hierarchy (see Figure 2.3, reproduced from Ref. 10). The first stage of the hierarchy involves multiplexing 12 voice channels, each with a nominal bandwidth of 4 kHz, into a group band from 60 to 108 kHz. Five of these group bands are multiplexed to form a supergroup, 312–552 kHz. The

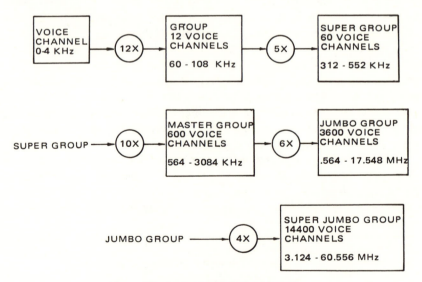

Figure 2.3. Analog multiplexing hierarchy.

hierarchy goes on like this to form larger and larger bands of frequencies, as shown. Each of these bands forms a standard building block in the modulation scheme used in a particular carrier system. The earliest systems carried a single group, while today, for example, the Bell System's L5 coaxial cable system carries 18 mastergroups in the band 3.124–51.532 MHz. The TD radio system carries three mastergroups in the band 0.564–8.524 MHz.

2.4.2.2. Digital Carrier Systems

As its name implies, the signal format in a digital system is digital. Inherently analog signals, such as voice, are converted into digital form upon entering the system. In the Bell System's T1 carrier system, for example, the analog voice signal is converted into binary form by sampling at a rate of 8000 times per second and quantizing these samples into seven binary digits. To these binary digits is added one bit, which is used for signaling, e.g., setting up calls. The result is that the voice signal is represented by a 64-kbps digital sequence.† In digital systems *time-division multiplexing* (TDM) is used to share the physical medium among a number of sequences. In TDM binary digits modulate the amplitudes of pulses that are transmitted over the medium. Groups of pulses representing different channels are interleaved in time. Again the T1 carrier system serves as an appropriate example. In this system 24 digital sequences, each representing a voice channel, are combined. Eight pulses‡ from each of the 24 channels are interleaved to form a frame which is repeated 8000 times a second. With the addition of a framing bit, the total length of the frame is 193 bits (see Figure 2.4) and the total volume of the T1 digital stream is 1.544 Mbps.

The origin of the T1 carrier system is the effort to use existing facilities more efficiently. A vast number of twisted pairs lay under city streets. Before T1, each pair carried a single conversation. However the use of what are called regenerative repeaters allows the 1.544-Mbps T1 stream to be transmitted reliably over these same twisted pairs. As a pulse travels down the pair it tends to be dispersed and corrupted by noise. If this continued long enough, all information would be lost. Periodically spaced repeaters detect pulses and regenerate new ones thereby wiping the slate clean of noise and dispersion. As in the case of analog systems, there is a multiplexing hierarchy for digital carrier systems (see Figure 2.5). TDM is the mechanism for building this hierarchy. Four T1 streams together with signaling bits form the T2 stream, 6.312 Mbps. The remaining levels in the digital hierarchy

---

†Until quite recently, 64 kpbs was required to represent a single voice channel in the telephone system. However, recently predictive encoding techniques, which take advantage of the inherent redundancy of the speech signal, have reduced this to 32 kbps.

‡In connection with our discussion of data transmission later in this chapter, we shall consider the form of this pulse modulation.

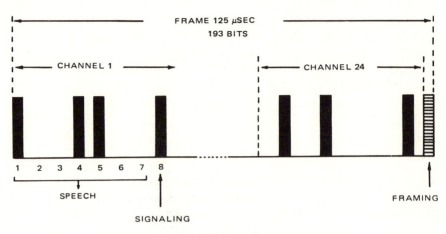

Figure 2.4. T1 frame format.

are as shown in Figure 2.5. We have the T3 level at 44.736 Mbps and the T4 level at 274.176 Mbps.†

In both analog and digital carrier systems transmission is four-wire, i.e., the FDM or TDM channel conveys information in only one direction. However, in the usual voice network the connection between the station equipment and the local office is two-wire. The interface between the two- and four-wire parts of the network is formed by a hybrid coupler (see Figure 2.6). Ideally flow of signal energy is exclusively as shown in Figure 2.6 (A to B, A′ to B′, C to A, and C′ to A′). However, because of hybrid imbalance, there is leakage, so signals transmitted at A and received at C′ leak into B′ and are subsequently received at C as an echo. This is particularly annoying for voice calls. The classic remedy is an echo suppressor, which

†We have chosen to illustrate digital multiplexing by means of the system used in North America and Japan. Elsewhere a different standard, that of the Committee Consultative Téléphonique et Télégraphique (CCITT), prevails. Although the rates at the different levels in the hierarchy are different, the basic principle is the same.

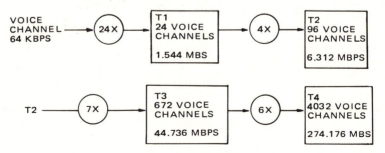

Figure 2.5. Digital multiplexing hierarchy.

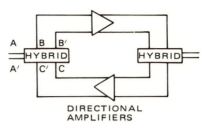

Figure 2.6. Hybrid coupler.

opens the path in one direction of transmission when there is energy only in the other direction. A recent development in this area is echo cancellation. This solution is particularly appropriate for satellite communications since long delays are involved.

2.4.3. Switching

A key motivating factor in the development of the techniques of computer communications is switching. As in the case of transmission, the focus in switching has been voice service. Dialing information sets up a closed path or circuit between the calling and the called party. Although the signal may travel over several analog and digital carrier systems in the same call, the user is aware of a continuous two-wire connection for the duration of the call. The term *circuit switching* has been associated with this technique.

During call setup, dialing information is processed by a switching machine to route a call over the most direct available path. If the called party is at another central office, the call is routed over interoffice trunks, which in contrast to local loops, are shared among many customers. The seminal work of Erlang, which we alluded to in Chapter 1, was concerned with the problem of choosing the proper number of trunks for a given level of traffic between offices. Even within the same city there may not be a trunk between every pair of central offices. Calls may be routed through intermediate facilities called *tandem offices*. Intercity calls are called *toll calls* and are routed through toll offices. There is a four-level hierarchy within the switching system (see Figure 2.7). The route of a call is chosen to stay at the lowest possible level. In periods of light traffic calls are routed through toll centers if direct connections exist. Otherwise calls are routed through *primary centers* as the next choice. The final two levels are the *sectional center* and the *regional center*. As traffic conditions warrant, high-usage trunks can be established between parts of the hierarchy.

In connection with computer communications, an important measure of performance is the time required to set up a call. This call-connect time depends upon the number of switching offices in a circuit, which is in turn

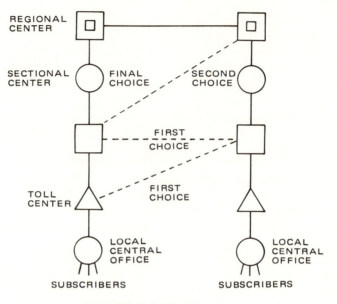

Figure 2.7. Switching hierarchy.

correlated with distance. Figures published in 1971 show that the average connect time ranged from 11 sec for short distances to almost 18 sec for long connections.[19] In view of the bursty nature of data traffic in many applications, this call setup time was simply too long. The time to establish a call was often longer that the time required to transmit the message. A second problem for data traffic was that the minimum duration of a call was 3 min, the standard for voice.

Later developments have considerably reduced the time required to set up a circuit. An example of these developments is called *common channel interoffice signaling* (CCIS).[20] In this system all of the dialing and call setup information flowing between offices is on the same channel rather than on the channel to be used during the call. This establishes a network in parallel to the voice network. Traffic on this parallel network can be given priority. A second improvement relates to the switches themselves. Until recently all switches, even those with stored program control, had electromechanical components; however, int the recently developed digital switching, analog signals are converted to digital form and processed as in a digital computer.[22,23] Digit computer processing speeds should be attainable for switching.

Even with rapid call setup, traditional circuit switching is still not suited to many of the kinds of traffic encountered in computer communications applications. As we have noted earlier, data traffic is asymmetric with respect to speed and volume. But in traditional circuit switching there is no provision for converting speeds; nor is there provision for translation between users employing different codes. Furthermore, the channel that is dedicated to a user after call setup may be too slow to meet the needs of bursty sources. Such sources do not require a channel very often, but when they do it should be high speed. In the following, we shall be considering alternatives which answer these objections, viz., packet switching and message switching.

2.5. Data Transmission

In this section we summarize the techniques that are used to transmit data over both the baseband and the voiceband channels.† In terms of an OSI system of protocols, the techniques used to transmit data are classified in the physical level. In both cases, the device that does this transmission is commonly called a *modem*, a contraction of the words "modulate" and "demodulate." In the case of baseband transmission this is something of a misnomer, since modulation and demodulation are not involved. The proper term for both bands is *data set*.

2.5.1. Baseband Data Transmission

In a number of applications data are transmitted by means of baseband signaling, i.e., the power density spectrum of the signal extends from dc to higher frequencies. In the T1 carrier system, for example, digital information is transmitted over twisted pairs by modulating the amplitudes of a sequence of pulses. In the following we shall be considering local area networks in which baseband transmission occurs over various media such as twisted pairs, coaxial cable, or optical fiber. Baseband techniques are also a building block in passband data transmission such as voiceband data transmission.

In general a data sequence is encoded into a sequence of pulses. In order for the receiver to be easily implementable, the sequence should have certain properties.† First of all, for reasons of safety and reliability, transformer coupling is used in the transmitter and receiver. This would require that the signal have no dc component and little low-frequency energy. A second requirement involves timing. At the receiver, the sequence of pulses is sampled and their amplitude is detected. The sampling must be in synchronism with the pulse sequence, and timing should be derived from the sequence itself. In practice, timing is derived by passing the signal

---

†For full, detailed discussions of data transmission see Refs. 24–26.
†Surveys on baseband rechniques are contained in Refs. 27 and 28.

through a nonlinear device. If there is a strong signal component at half the timing frequency, timing can be recovered. Finally, it is desirable that the sequence have some form of redundancy so that system failures can be detected.

A technique with the desired properties is *bipolar signaling,* illustrated in Figure 2.8 A binary zero is encoded into a zero level pulse and binary ones are encoded into alternating positive and negative pulses. A typical sequence is shown in Figure 2.8. Suppose that $P(f)$ is the Fourier transform of the transmitted pulse. The power density spectrum of the modulated pulse train is

$$M(f) = |P(f)|^2(\sin^2 \pi f T)/T \qquad (2.1)$$

This spectrum is plotted in Figure 2.9 for the case of a square pulse. Notice that there is little energy at low frequencies and that there is a peak at $1/2T$ Hz. There is also redundancy in the encoding since, under normal operations, the next nonzero pulse after a positive must be negative and vice versa. If two successive nonzero pulses of the same sign are received, there is an error.

The problem with bipolar coding is that long strings of zeros can occur, thereby causing problems with timing recovery. One solution is to pass the digital sequence through a device called a scrambler. Essentially the scrambler substitutes another sequence for the all-zero sequence. Another approach is to encode binary zeros and ones into a diphase pulse which has a transition from -1 to $+1$ or vice versa in the middle of a symbol interval (see Figure 2.10). A common technique using diphase pulses is the *Manchester code.* The power spectral density of the Manchester code is similar to that of bipolar coding in that there is a null at dc and a strong component at $f = 1/2T$. A variation on the Manchester code which is obtained by reducing the number of transitions in a binary sequence is the *Miller code.* The Miller code has a spectrum which is shifted downward compared to the Manchester code, but still has no dc component.

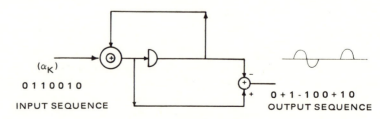

Figure 2.8. Bipolar encoder.

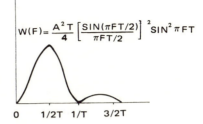

$$W(F) = \frac{A^2 T}{4} \left[\frac{SIN(\pi FT/2)}{\pi FT/2} \right]^2 SIN^2 \pi FT$$

Figure 2.9. Spectrum bipolar signaling.   0   1/2T 1/T   3/2T

2.5.2. Nyquist Pulses

Bipolar, Manchester, and Miller coding are appropriate to situations where bandwidth is not severely limited. For example, for coaxial cable, attenuation increases only in proportion to $f^{1/2}$. However, for certain other applications such as high-speed voiceband data transmission the limiting resource is bandwidth. An efficient technique for transmitting data in the form of a baseband signal is by modulating the amplitude of *Nyquist pulses*, which are defined by the following relation:

$$x(nT) = \begin{cases} 0, & n \neq 0 \\ 1, & n = 0 \end{cases} \tag{2.2}$$

where T is a parameter. If these pulses are transmitted at intervals spaced by T seconds and sampling is correctly synchronized, the amplitude of only one pulse is seen at a time (see Figure 2.11). The transmitted data sequence is given by

$$S(t) = \sum_{n=-\infty}^{\infty} a_n x(t - nT) \tag{2.3}$$

As we shall see presently, in modern voiceband data transmission, this baseband signal is then modulated into the voiceband.

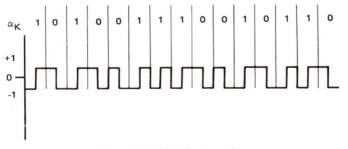

Figure 2.10. Manchester code.

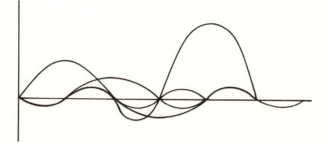

Figure 2.11. Sequence of Nyquist pulses.

A form of Nyquist pulse commonly used in data transmission is the so-called "raised cosine pulse," the time and frequency characteristics of which are shown in Figures 2.12a and 2.12b, respectively. The parameter α in Figure 2.12 is called either excess bandwidth or rolloff. The value of α has significant effect on intersymbol interference (ISI), which is energy from one symbol interval spilling over into another. ISI is caused by sampling at the wrong time or by channel distortion which changes the pulse shape away from the Nyquist shape. By increasing the value of α the tails of the pulses fall more rapidly, thus reducing the effect of ISI. The cost of increasing α is increased bandwidth. The bandwidth occupied by the sequence of Nyquist pulses spaced by T seconds is $(1 + \alpha)/T$ Hz (see Figure 2.12.).

We turn now to the consideration of the relationships between channel bandwidth signal-to-noise ratio and performance. If the pulse amplitudes

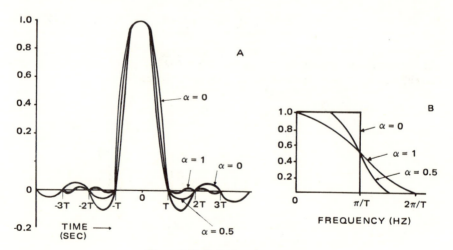

Figure 2.12. Raised cosine pulses.

can assume L levels, the number of bits transmitted in a symbol interval is $\log_2(L)$ where $\log_2$ indicates the logarithm to the base z. Since there are $1/T$ symbols per second, the bit rate is $(1/T)\log_2(L)$ bits per second. The number of levels that can be transmitted is limited by the noise in the channel. This is illustrated in Figure 2.13, where probability of error is shown as a function of the ratio of average signal power to average noise power in the channel for several values of L. As shown, increasing L without a compensating increase in signal-to-noise ratio causes a deterioration of performance.

Nyquist pulses trade bandwidth for immunity to intersymbol interference. Another approach is to trade immunity to noise for immunity to ISI. This is done by introducing a controlled amount of intersymbol interference. The generic term for the technique is *partial response*. The technique is also called *correlative level encoding*. The advantage of partial response signaling is that the bandwidth of the signal is the same bandwidth as a minimum bandwidth Nyquist pulse, $1/T$ Hz, but it has far less ISI. In order to have the same performance with respect to noise as Nyquist pulses, the energy of partial response pulses must be increased by a couple of dB relative to the noise. For the voiceband channel this is an advantageous trace since it is relatively quiet, but limited in bandwidth.

2.5.3. Voiceband Data Transmission

2.5.3.1. Characteristics of the Voice Channel

The components of the telephone system, local loop, carrier systems, and switching, all leave their imprint on the voice channel.[29] The characteristics of the voice channel have a significant impact on the way data signals are transmitted. The attenuation and delay characteristics of the channel are shown in Figures 2.14a and 2.14b. Recall that a transformer terminating the local loop blocks dc. The filtering necessary to achieve a

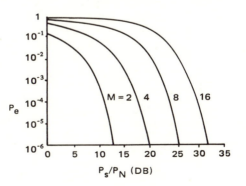

Figure 2.13. Probability of error vs. signal-to-noise ratio.

4-kHz bandwidth for carrier systems attenuates high-frequency signals. As shown in Figure 2.14, the useful bandwidth of the voice channel is approximately from 200–3100 Hz. As is indicated in Figure 2.14, this low- and high-pass filtering introduces attenuation and delay distortion in that they are not flat across the band.

In addition to attenuation and delay distortion, other impairments are introduced by the channel. As we shall see presently, data signals are transmitted over the voiceband channel by modulating a carrier. Analog carrier systems introduce frequency offset and phase jitter of this carrier. In certain digital carrier systems nonlinearities are introduced. Improper hybrid termination causes echoes. Transients in switching cause impulse noise. Finally, as in any physical circuit, there is thermal noise. With respect to this last impairment, it turns out that the telephone channel is relatively quiet and the other impairments have a greater effect on performance. The cumulative effect of these impairments has been to limit the speed and performance of voiceband data transmission. In commercial systems, the traditional upper limit on speed has been 9600 bps. The standard of performance is stated as a probability of bit error of 10^{-5}. This figure gives an incomplete picture since errors tend to cluster in time and on a subset of poor circuits.

The results quoted in the preceding paragraph are generally true for circuits in what is called the *switched network*, i.e., circuits obtained by ordinary dialing. Improved performance can be obtained by leasing private lines. These lines are a permanent connection. They can be conditioned to decrease attenuation and delay distortion. The circuit can also be established in such a way that certain troublesome facilities are avoided.

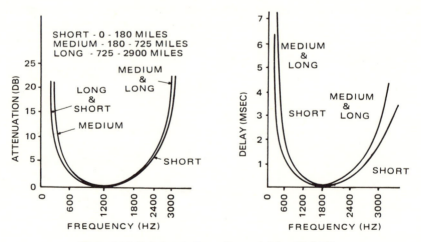

Figure 2.14. Voiceband attenuation and delay (Ref. 29).

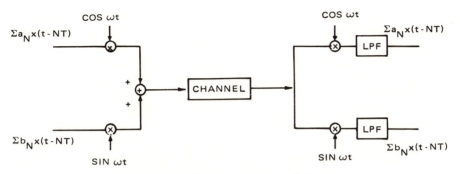

Figure 2.15. Passband data transmission.

2.5.3.2. Passband Signaling

As indicated in Figure 2.14, the voiceband channel is bandpass in that there is no dc. In current practice, two kinds of modulation techniques are used to convey data over this channel. At rates up to 1200 bps frequency shift keying (FSK) is used. FSK consists of transmitting one of two frequencies for each bit. For example, in the international standard for 300 bps transmission, the two frequencies 980 and 1180 Hz are used. The advantage of FSK is that it is simple and reliable. However, it is not efficient in terms of utilization of channel bandwidth, since no use is made of phase information.

For higher data speeds, the so-called "linear modulation techniques" are used. These techniques can be described as frequency multiplexing a baseband data signal into the passband by allowing weighted Nyquist pulses to modulate a carrier. In terms of international standards, the most prevalent techniques are forms of double-sideband which are called *quadrature amplitude modulation* (QAM). In this method two Nyquist pulse sequences are modulated by an in-phase and a quadrature carrier, respectively. The two signals are added to form the bandpass signal

$$B(t) = \sum_{n=-\infty}^{\infty} a_n x(t - nT) \cos \omega_c t + b_n x(t - nT) \sin \omega_c t \qquad (2.4)$$

The data sequences a_n and b_n, $n = 0, \pm1, \pm2, \ldots$, can be recovered from the passband signal if the phase of the carrier is known at the receiver. This operation is shown in Figure 2.15.

The double-sideband signal can also be written in polar coordinate form:

$$B(t) = \sum_{n=-\infty}^{\infty} R_n x(t - nT) \cos (\omega_c t + \theta_n) \qquad (2.5)$$

where $R_n = (a_n^2 + b_n^2)^{1/2}$ and $\theta_n = \arctan(a_n/b_n)$. For the intermediate speeds of 2400 bps and 4800 bps, all of the information to be transmitted is expressed by the phase, θ_n, and R_n is set to a constant value. The technique is called *phase-shift keying* (PSK). In order to eliminate the need to track the absolute phase of the carrier, data are encoded into the difference of the phases in successive symbol intervals. The technique is then called *differential phase-shift keying* (DPSK). In CCITT† recommendation V.24 for 2400 bps transmission, four phase angles are used, giving two bits per symbol. For 4800-bps transmission, recommendation V.27 calls for eight equally spaced angles or three bits per symbol. In order to transmit at 9600 bps over voiceband lines, data must be encoded into amplitude as well as phase. The technique is then called quadrature amplitude modulation. CCITT recommendation V.29 specifies 16 combinations of phase and amplitude. The spectra of three CCITT recommended modems, V.24, V.27, and V.29,

†International standards for telecommunications are formulated by the CCITT which is part of the International Telecommunications Union (ITU). Standards for voiceband transmission are contained in the so-called "V-series" recommendations.

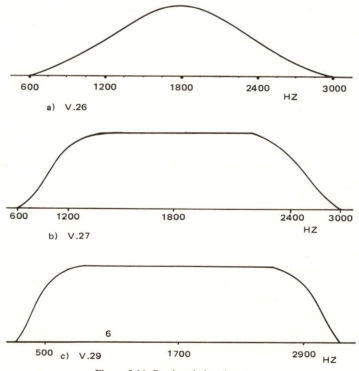

Figure 2.16. Passband signal spectra.

are shown in Figures 2.16a, 2.16b, and 2.16c, respectively. Notice that for the higher data rates the rolloff is less and the signals are more vulnerable to intersymbol interference. A more complex receiver is required to counter this tendency.

In order to transmit reliably, there must be compensation for channel distortion so that the original Nyquist pulse shape is retained. Departure from the Nyquist pulse shape introduces ISI. The procedure for compensating for channel distortion is called equalization. In order to transmit at speeds of 4800 bps and 9600 bps, receivers must be equipped with automatic, adaptive equalizers. These devices automatically adjust to the channel encountered on a particular data call and adapt to changes in the channel while the call is in progress.

For all of the voiceband modems there is a startup period before data transmission can begin. During this period the phase of the carrier must be acquired. So that the received signals are sampled at the right time, the timing of the transmitted pulses must also be obtained. For the higher-speed modems, automatic equalizers must be adjusted to the channel during the startup period. In order to initialize a session, the transmitter sends a training sequence prior to the transmission of data. The duration of the startup period can range from 20 msec for 2400-bps modems to over 300 msec for 9600-bps modems. This startup time plays a role in the operation of polling systems, discussed in Chapter 7.

We have concentrated on the transmission of data over voiceband circuits. The same techniques can be used to transmit data over other analog bands in the telephone network. For example, CCITT recommendation v.50 deals with transmission at a rate of 50 Kbps over the group band, 60–108 kHz.

2.5.3.3. Error-Detecting and -Correcting Codes

In many applications the signal-to-noise ratio in the facility leads to unacceptably high error rates. For example, on the voice channel the rate of one error in 10^5 bits is too high a rate for printed text. However, the error rate can be reduced by adding redundant bits to the data stream by means of error-detecting and -correcting codes. These codes fall into two basic classes: *block codes* and *convolutional codes.*†

An (n, k) binary block code is composed of a set of n-bit code words. In each of the code words there are k binary digits which carry the data to be transmitted and $n - k$ binary digits containing redundancy in the form of *parity checks.* In order to perform a parity check modulo 2 sum is taken over a subset of the k information bits and one of the $n - k$ parity check

---

†For surveys of error-detecting and -correcting codes see Refs. 30 and 31.

bits. The parity check bit is set so that this sum is equal to 0 (mod 2). The *Hamming distance* between a pair of code words is the number of places that the pair words differ. For example, the code words 0011 and 1110 have Hamming distance 3. The error-detecting and -correcting capability of a code depends upon the Hamming distance. For example, a code which has minimum distance three between all of its codewords can detect up to two bit errors or correct a single bit error. In Figure 2.17a (6, 3) code, which is an example of such a code, is given. In general, a code can detect up to S bit errors and correct up to T bit errors if D, the minimum distance between codewords, is such that

$$D \geq 2T + S + 1 \tag{2.6}$$

By adding (redundant) parity check bits in the right way, the distance between codewords can be increased. Clearly there is a trade of bandwidth for performance since the data stream is augmented by the parity check bits.

A convolutional code is generated by feeding the data stream into a linear sequential circuit and sampling the output at a higher rate than the input. In Figure 2.18 this is demonstrated for a rate 1/2 code. A convolutional code is characterized by its constraint length, which is the number of output bits that are affected by a single input bit. If, as in Figure 2.18, the circuit is a binary shift register, the constraint length is simply the length of the shift register.

On terrestrial links the codes are used in the error-detecting mode. Data are encapsulated in blocks to which parity check bits are added. If an error is detected at the receiver the block is retransmitted. The transmitter becomes aware of the error either through a negative acknowledgment (NACK) or the absence of a positive acknowledgement (ACK). Forms of this technique, known as automatic repeat-request (ARQ), will be analyzed in Chapters 4 and 11. Because of the block nature of the flow, it is more natural to use block code in this application.

C1	C2	C3	C4	C5	C6	
0	0	0	0	0	0	
0	0	1	1	0	1	
0	1	0	0	1	1	INFORMATION BITS: C1, C2, and C3
0	1	1	1	1	0	
1	0	0	1	1	0	PARITY BITS: C4 = C1 $\oplus$ C3
1	0	1	0	1	1	C5 = C1 $\oplus$ C2
1	1	0	1	0	1	C6 = C2 $\oplus$ C3
1	1	1	0	0	0	

Figure 2.17. A (6, 3) block code.

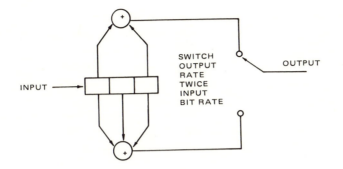

Figure 2.18. Convolutional encoder.

The error-correcting mode is of limited value in the great majority of terrestrial telephone links. For typical error rates, the redundancy that is required for error detection leads to lower throughput than ARQ. The situation is different for satellite links because of the large delays that are involved.† For these links, a moderate error rate considerably reduces the throughput for the ARQ technique. This has given rise to a resurgence of interest in error-correcting codes. Since such codes act in the forward direction they are called (perhaps redundantly) *forward error-correcting codes* (FEC). Because of the propagation delays that are involved, these codes have played an important role in deep space communications. In these applications convolutional codes yield better performance primarily because of the signal processing that can be used in the receiver. An example of such techniques is the Viterbi algorithm used with soft decisions.

2.6. Data Networks

2.6.1. All-Digital Systems

Voiceband modems modulate a carrier so that a digital sequence fits into the analog voiceband. Recall that the voiceband circuit may include digital transmission facilities. There is a kind of circularity here since inherently digital information is put into an analog form for transmission over digital facilities. It is not surprising then that it is difficult to obtain good performance for data transmission. This situation has led to the development of purely digital networks which are dedicated to the transmission of data. An example of such a system is the Bell System's Digital Data Systems (DDS).[32] In DDS, transmission over local loops is by means of baseband pulse transmission at speeds of 2.4, 4.8, 9.6, and 56 kbps. At the end office, the digital sequence is digitally multiplexed onto digital

†See Section 2.8 below for a discussion of satellite transmission.

carrier systems. Short-haul transmission is by means of the T1 carrier system. A microwave band under the normal voiceband in the radio carrier system is used for long-haul transmission.

Purely digital systems for data transmission are precursors of what is called the "all digital network." In this network whose complete development lies somewhere in the future, all traffic is digital. The telephone handset converts the voice signal to digital form for transmission over the local loop. At the end office the digital stream is multiplexed onto long- and short-haul carrier facilities. All switching is digital as well.

2.6.2. Packet- and Message-Switched Networks

As we have seen there are several problems associated with the use of traditional circuit switching for data traffic in many applications. These problems have engendered the growth of the technique of *packet switching*.[33,34] The essential idea of packet switching is to encapsulate data messages into fixed length blocks. Addressing as well as other overhead information is added to these blocks to form a packet. This other overhead would include information on message length and sequencing necessary to reconstruct the original message. Finally, in order to detect the presence of transmission errors, parity check bits are added to the packet. As far as switching is concerned these packets are self-contained entities. The packetizing technique allows a number of bursty sources to share the same transmission line. At the receiving end a processor can distinguish packets from different sources on the basis of these addresses.

The packet multiplexing technique is seen to best advantage when there are a large number of bursty sources sharing the same transmission facility. For the usual multiplexing techniques, i.e., FDM and TDM, each source is allocated a small fraction of the total capacity, whereas in packet switching the entire line capacity of the line is available when it is needed. The price paid for this increase in flexibility is an increase in the overhead due to the addressing that accompanies each packet.

A packet-switched network is illustrated in Figure 2.19. Since it is the first large-scale network of this kind, we use the ARPANET as an example of a packet-switched network.† The nodes of this network, called *interface message processors* (IMPs), are connected by full-duplex links. In early versions of the network these links were 50 kbps, attained using group band modems. Terminal and HOST computers are connected to the network through the IMPs. HOST computers have the facility to form packets, but for simple terminals this can be done in the IMP. In any case packets from the source connected to an IMP are multiplexed on lines leading out of

---

†There are other packet-switched networks in operation, e.g., TYMNET (Ref. 35), the Cigal network (Ref. 36), TELENET (Ref. 37), and DATAPAC (Ref. 38).

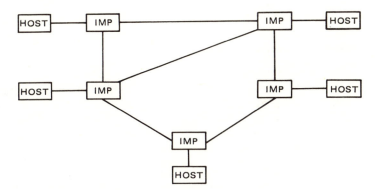

Figure 2.19. Packet-switched network.

the IMP. Also multiplexed on these lines are packets generated by other IMPs.

Packets traverse the network in a store-and-forward fashion. After an IMP transmits a message, it waits for a positive acknowledgement (ACK) from the receiving IMP before relinquishing responsibility for the packet. If an IMP does not receive an ACK, the packet is retransmitted after a suitable interval. Upon receipt of a packet, the receiving IMP checks for transmission errors. The IMP also determines whether or not sufficient buffering is available to store the packet. If there is room for the packet and it is error free, the receiving IMP issues an ACK. In this fashion a packet travels over the links between the source and destination IMPs. The store-and-forward technique has an advantage in error control in that the integrity of each link is assured. In terms of the OSI system, the procedure of passing a packet from one node to another is an example of a link level protocol (level 2). At each of the nodes a network level protocol (level 3) would determine the next node in a packet's itinerary.† At destination nodes messages are reassembled from packets and end-to-end acknowledgments are transmitted for the purpose of end-to-end flow control. These last two procedures lie in the transport level (level 4).

While packet switching has the advantage of a certain modularity, there is the inefficiency of partially filled packets and the overhead associated with each packet. An alternative is *message switching*, in which the entire message along with address bits, parity check bits, and bits indicating message length are transmitted. As in the case of packets, there are address and parity check fields. The data field is of variable length. The end of the data message is indicated by a specified sequence of bits called a flag. The data sequence is encoded in such a way that the flag cannot appear in the data sequence.

†Excellent surveys of routing and flow control have been written. See Refs. 39 and 40.

2.7. Local Area Networks

2.7.1. General Considerations

The second major class of networks that we shall consider are *local area networks* (LANs), which are data networks having limited geographical area, usually within a kilometer.† Networks confined to a single office building, shopping center, or university campus are prime examples of LANs. The emergence of this sort of network is part of the general growth of computer and digital technology; however, the introduction of office automation and distributed processing systems has furnished additional impetus. In both of these applications LAN techniques play a significant part.

In the past, local area networks were defined in terms of geographical extent and data rate; however, in view of the rapid growth of the technology, a more useful definition may be in terms of usage and configuration. In providing a common channel for a number of users in a limited geographical area the emphasis is upon ease and flexibility in providing access. Due to the limited geographical area, bandwidth is not the critical commodity that it is in networks covering a wide area. Therefore, access to the network can be simplified at the cost of bandwidth. A second point is that data networks covering a large area require redundancy with respect to connectivity in order to ensure operation in the face of failures. For example, the ARPA net requires at least two paths between source–destination pairs. Because of the limited geographical extent of the typical LAN, it is in something of a protected environment and this sort of redundancy is unnecessary. This simplifies the topology since only a single path need be provided between source–destination pairs.

2.7.2. Topology

In current practice three basic topologies are prevalent in local area networks: the bus, the ring, and the star (see Figures 2.20a–2.20c). A fourth topology, the tree (see Figure 2.20d), is used in related systems and may be considered as a form of the bus configuration.

The bus topology is appropriate to transmission media such as coaxial cable or radio which allow what are, in effect, high-impedance taps. In principle, these taps do not affect the medium, and a large number of stations can be connected. Each of these stations can broadcast simultaneously to the others. The bus topology is particularly appropriate for the random accessing techniques that we shall be discussing presently.

---

†Surveys of LAN techniques are contained in Refs. 41–43. See also Ref. 44.

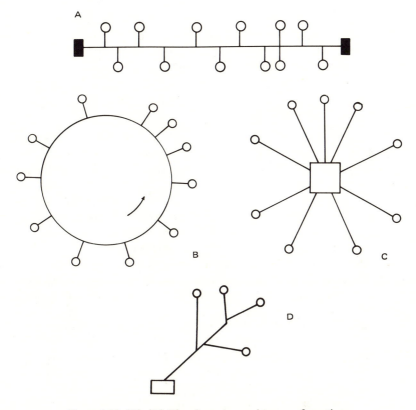

Figure 2.20. (A)–(D) Ring, bus, star, and tree configurations.

The ring topology is a sequence of point-to-point links with flow in one direction around the ring. As we shall see, there are several accessing techniques for the ring system. In all of these there is a delay due to processing at each of the stations. For reasons of reliability, there are provisions to bypass stations if they become inoperative.

In both the bus and the ring topologies the control of traffic is distributed. A topology in which control is concentrated is the star. In this case all of the traffic in the system is switched in a central "hub." The stations access the hub through high-speed lines.

A fourth topology, the tree, has been used to distribute data over a wider area. Typically, in networks using the tree topology, remote stations access a central processor. A ubiquitous example of such a network uses multipoint private lines in common carrier networks. The tree topology would also be relevant for CATV networks used to transmit data, since these sorts of networks are closely related to LANs and the same modeling techniques are relevant.

The four topologies can be the basic building blocks for more complex topologies. For example, a system of interconnected rings has been proposed. In the current standard involving the bus topology a series of connected buses form a kind of rootless tree.

2.7.3. Transmission Media

In the foregoing discussion of topology we alluded to the transmission media used to implement the network. In current practice three kinds of transmission media are used in LANs: twisted pairs, coaxial cable, and optical fiber. The twisted pairs of copper wires are the same as those used in the telephone plant. Because of the readily available technology, there is a strong tendency to operate at the same rates as short-haul digital carrier systems, i.e., the T1 rate 1.544 Mbps. Higher speeds are possible as well. The nature of twisted pairs is such that it is basically a point-to-point medium. As mentioned earlier, coaxial cable can operate as a multiple access medium by use of high impedance taps. Rates of up to 10 Mbps are attained in commercial systems. Optical fiber is the medium with the highest transmission rate currently used in LANs. Data can be transmitted at rates of up to 50 Mbps using light emitting diodes. With Laser transmitters, rates in the range of hundreds of Mbps can be achieved without repeaters over distances compatable with LAN operation. At the present writing optical fiber is basically a point-to-point medium. However, the development of a low-loss optical tap could change this situation.

In the future other transmission media may play a role in LAN and related systems. Radio, for example, would allow more flexible operation than the media we have considered. A radio medium would allow a random accessing technique to be employed. A second widely available medium which could be adapted for two-way data transmission is the CATV network. We shall be considering this medium in some detail in the sequel.

2.7.4. Access Protocols

The fundamental purpose of the local area network is to allow data sources that are dispersed throughout an area to share a common transmission medium. Because of this dispersal, transmission capacity must be expended to coordinate the flow of traffic from each of the sources. The way that this is done is the function of the access protocol. A significant portion of this book is devoted to the modeling and analysis of these access protocols. The objective of the analysis is to evaluate performance in terms of delay, storage, and throughput.

2.7.4.1. Polling

The predecessors to the current local area networks were tree networks,† which provide communications between a number of remote stations and a central processor. Such an arrangement would be appropriate to a bank's credit checking system, for example. The coordination of traffic from the stations is effected by roll call polling. Each station is assigned an address. The central processor polls stations for messages by broadcasting the addresses in sequence. The reception by a station of its address is, in effect, a license to transmit. If a station has a message to transmit, it interrupts the polling cycle.

Polling systems are modeled and analyzed in Chapter 7 of the text. The salient result of this analysis is the effect of overhead on performance. Overhead in this case is the time required to poll all of the stations even if none of the stations has a message to transmit. In many applications a significant portion of the overhead is due to the establishment of communications between the remote stations and the central processor. In the case of voiceband modems, for example, this would require phase and timing recovery and equalizer training for the higher speeds.

An alternate technique, called hub polling, attempts to reduce this overhead. In this case the license to transmit is transferred between stations directly without going through a central processor. This technique is similar to those used in ring systems, which we shall be discussing in the next section.

2.7.4.2. Ring Protocols

From the perspective of current techniques, the first local area network was the ring system built by Farmer and Newhall.[45] This system is shown in Figure 2.21.‡ The flow of data around the ring is organized into the frame

†In Chapter 13 we shall be considering the layout of tree networks.
‡A survey of LANs with the ring topology is given in Ref. 46.

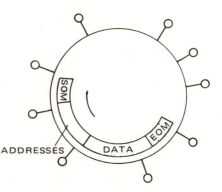

Figure 2.21. Farmer–Newhall loop.

structure shown in Figure 2.21. At any given point in time only one station on the ring is authorized to transmit. Message transmission begins with a start of message (SOM) character. This is followed by source and destination addresses and by the data to be transmitted. Stations along the ring monitor the line flow and read messages which are addressed to them. The transmitting station relinquishes control by appending an end of message (EOM) character to the data. Upon receipt of the EOM character the next station downstream has the opportunity to take control of the ring. If this station has nothing to transmit, the EOM character is passed on to the next station, and so the cycle goes. In later implementations of the ring the term "token" is used to indicate control. Again the bearer of the token has control which he relinquishes by transmitting it. A station with a message to transmit seizes control when it observes a free token on the line. In this case the token can simply be a one-bit field at the beginning of a frame. The mathematical models of the Farmer–Newhall and the token passing rings are basically the same polling model that we have just discussed. In all three systems opportunity to transmit a message is given to a single station at a time. Moreover, this opportunity cycles through all of the stations. For polling systems the opportunity consists of the poll, which, in effect, asks a station "Do you have a message?" In the case of the ring protocols it is the reception of an EOM character or a token.

A drawback to the token passing technique is that only one station may transmit at a time. If traffic is symmetric around the loop, this means that only half of the capacity is used on the average. If bandwidth is not scarce in LANs then this may be an advantageous trade for simplicity of operation. However, there are alternative techniques which allow more than one transmitting station at a time. One of these is what is called *demand multiplexing* and is illustrated in Figure 2.22.[47,48] Flow on the line is segmented into fixed size frames. At the beginning of each of the frames is a one-bit field indicating whether or not the frame is occupied. Stations having data to transmit seize empty frames as they pass. The indicator bit is changed from empty to full and addressing information is transmitted along with the data. Demand multiplexing requires that each frame or packet have addressing, while for token passing a single address would suffice for an entire multipacket message. The demand multiplexing technique is analyzed by means of priority queues in Chapter 6 of the text. Priority queues are appropriate in this context since traffic already on the line has priority over locally generated traffic. Furthermore, the priority is what is called preemptive inasmuch as the transmission of messages consisting of more than one packet can be interrupted by packets already on the line.

A final alternative, called *buffer insertion*, does not allow interruption once the transmission of a messages has begun. Messages arriving on the

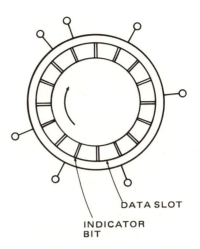

DATA SLOT

INDICATOR
BIT

Figure 2.22. Demand multiplexing.

line from other stations are buffered while the locally generated message is being transmitted. For buffer insertion messages are kept intact and more than one station may transmit at a time. The buffer insertion technique is also analyzed in Chapter 6.

In each of the ring accessing techniques the idea is to cope with the burstines of data sources by giving line access only as it is required. It is useful to compare this kind of technique to one in which transmission capacity is dedicated to particular data sources. In Chapter 5 we study the performance of time-division multiplexing (TDM), in which time slots are dedicated to data sources sharing the same line.†

2.7.4.3. Random Access Protocols

Random access techniques first developed for radio systems[49,50] have been successfully applied to local area networks. The origin of these techniques is the ALOHA protocol, which is a form of completely distributed control. Again it is assumed that several stations are sharing the same transmission line. Furthermore it is assumed that the line is of the bus configuration (see Figure 2.23). When a station generates a fixed-length packet, it is immediately transmitted without coordinating with the other stations. As usual, the packet contains addressing information and parity check bits. If a message is correctly received by a central controller, a positive acknowledgment is returned to the transmitter. Since there is no coordination among the stations, it may happen that two or more stations interfere with one another by transmitting at the same time. If messages

---

†TDM was discussed in connection with the T1 digital carrier system. In the context of a local area network, the TDM concept is called time-division multiple access (TDMA).

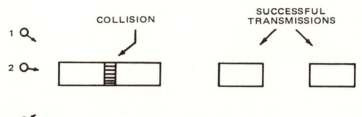

Figure 2.23. The ALOHA technique.

collide, the resulting errors are detected by the central controller, which returns either a negative acknowledgment or nothing. An alternate implementation is to have the transmitting station monitor the line for collisions. After a suitable time-out interval a station involved in a collision retransmits the packet. In order to avoid repeated collisions, the time-out intervals are chosen at random independently at each station. The analysis of the ALOHA technique is presented in Chapter 8. The results show that, because of collisions and the resulting retransmissions, the throughput is no more than 18% of the line capacity. Moreover, there is a basic instability in the system.

The basic ALOHA technique can be improved by rudimentary coordination among the stations. Suppose that a sequence of synchronization pulses is broadcast to all stations. Again assume that the stations generate fixed-length packets. The interval between synch pulses is called a slot and is equal to the time required to transmit a packet. Packets, either new or retransmitted, can only be transmitted at a pulse time. This simple device reduces the rate of collisions by half since only packets generated in the same interval interfere with one another. In pure ALOHA this "collision window" is two slot intervals. This modification is called slotted ALOHA.[51] In Chapter 8 it is shown that there is saturation at approximately 36% of capacity. However, in spite of the increase in throughput, the unstable behavior persists.

An extension of ALOHA that is particularly appropriate for local area networks is *carrier sense multiple access* (CSMA).[52] Before transmitting a newly generated message, a station listens on the common channel for the signal of another station. If the channel is free, the message is transmitted; if not, transmission is deferred. Because of delay in the system, collisions can still occur. As in the basic ALOHA technique, conflict is resolved by random retransmission. Variations in conflict resolution techniques involve the retransmission strategy. The results of anlysis show that for local area networks sensing potential conflict considerably improves performance. The results also indicate the same sort of instability that is present in the ALOHA systems.

2.7.4.4. Tree Search Techniques

The deleterious effect of overhead on polling systems can be lessened by means of an adaptive tree search technique which has been given the name *probing*. A similar technique can be used to eliminate instability in random access systems. The technique is modeled and analyzed in Chapter 9. In the application of the technique to polling systems,[53] a basic assumption is that a central processor can broadcast to all stations simultaneously. The essense of the technique is to poll stations in groups rather than one at a time. If a member of a group being polled has a message to transmit it responds by putting a signal on the line. Upon receiving a positive response, the central processor splits the group in two and polls each subgroup in turn. The process of splitting groups continues until stations having messages are isolated, whereupon the messages are transmitted. Clearly we have a form of tree search. As the process unfolds the probability of stations having messages varies. Accordingly, the sizes of the initial groups to be polled are adapted to the probability of their having messages to transmit. The criterion for choosing the group sizes is the minimization of the time required to grant access to all of the stations. Comparison of the technique with conventional polling shows a considerable improvement in performance at light loading. Moreover, due to the adaptivity there is no penalty at heavy loading.

As mentioned above, the tree search technique is also appropriate to random access systems. Suppose that in response to a signal from a central processor, a station simply transmits any message that it might be harboring. Conflicts between stations responding to the same signal are detected by the processor. In order to resolve the conflict the group is split in two and the subgroups are polled. The process continues until all of the subgroups have only one station with a message to transmit. As in polling systems, optimal initial subgroup sizes can be chosen so as to minimize the time required to read message out of a group of stations. Optimum group sizes are chosen adaptively as the process unfolds.

Control of the adaptive process need not be as centralized as the foregoing implies.[54] As in slotted ALOHA, the transmission process can be synchronized by a sequence of pulses broadcast to all stations. By explicit or implicit feedback, stations are informed of successful transmissions and of collisions. This information determines the response of an individual station to a synchronizing pulse. As in the polling case there is an adaptive algorithm which minimizes the time required to grant access to all stations having messages to transmit. Analysis of the adaptive technique shows that its thoughput is 43% of capacity. This contrasts with slotted ALOHA where the saturation point is 36% of capacity. A possibly greater advantage is that there are no unstable states where the system is saturated by retransmissions and conflicts. In the case of heavy loading each station is assigned a slot and the system reverts to TDMA.

2.7.4.5. Reservation Systems

Related to random access multiplexing are a number of techniques in which stations reserve part of the capacity of a channel when they have messages to transmit.[55,56] The reservation techniques are appropriate to sources which are active infrequently but which transmit a steady stream when active. Traffic from such sources is not bursty; however, the requests for service can be treated as bursty traffic. The random access and the adaptive techniques discussed above would then be appropriate.

2.7.5. Optical Fiber Systems

Optical fiber is suited to local area networks because of the high data rates that it can sustain over the appropriate distances. Moreover, these rates are achieved at relatively low cost. Optical fiber has other advantages for LANs. A typical fiber together with cladding is small and flexible and consequently easy to install. Secondly optical fiber is immune to electromagnetic interference. The network topology most often associated with optical fiber based systems is the star,[57] although a ring based system has been deployed as well. In both the ring and the star systems the fiber is used as a point-to-point medium. A factor that militates toward a star configuration is reliability. By its nature, fiber is nonconducting. Thus, it is not possible to power equipment at a user station through the transmission medium. It is therefore advisable to concentrate essential equipment at one place, as in the star. A second factor that may come into play is processing power. In order to take advantage of the high speed of the fiber, processing speeds should be high. At the speeds with which we are dealing, concentrating computation in one place seems to be the better approach. At this writing optical fiber LANs are at an embryonic stage of development. In the two star systems that have been discussed in the literature, the hub acts as reflector.

2.8. Alternative Facilities: Satellites and Cable Television

At the present writing the vast bulk of data traffic is conveyed by the telephone networks including value added networks such as TYMNET and TELENET. However, the advance of technology in the form of satellites and cable television provides alternative data transmission facilities for end-to-end service. In both of these systems there is the means to bring high data rates directly to the user. Moreover, the service promises to be ubiquitous since the basic facilities are either already in place or can be easily installed.

2.8.1. Satellite Communications†

The commercial use of satellites for telecommunication began in 1965 with the launching of INTELSAT I which provided transatlantic service. Since 1971, when INTELSAT IV[58] was launched, satellites have been a basic component of transoceanic transmission systems. This system provided 6000 voice channels. Later INTELSAT systems provide as many as 18,000 voice circuits. The first domestic system was the Canadian TELSAT which went into service in 1973, since then there has been a rapid sucession of domestic and international communications satellites.

Unlike some of its experimental predecessors, the modern communications satellite is active in that received signals are amplified and retransmitted. In early experimental systems the satellite was simply a passive reflecter. Another standard feature of modern communications satellites is that they are in the geostationary orbit at a distance of 37,000 km from the earth. The geostationary orbit simplifies tracking and ensures that the satellite is always in view. The disadvantage of this orbit is that the link delay of 0.23 sec affects the way in which data may be transferred reliably. For example, this large delay considerably reduces the throughput of the ARQ technique, which is standard on domestic links.

The three frequency bands that have been allocated to communications systems are shown in Table 2.1. For currently operating systems the bulk of the traffic is carried over the 6/4 band. In the 14/12 band the bands 11.7 to 12.2 MHz are designated for domestic use while the remaining bands are for international traffic.

A number of links or channels can be established through the same satellite. This can be accomplished in several ways. For *space-division*

†The material in this section has been distilled from Refs. 15–17.

Table 2.1

Band designation	Bandwidth (MHz)	Transmit (downlink) (GHz)	Receive (uplink) (GHz)
6/4	500	3.7–4.2	5.925–6.425
14/12	250–500	11.7–12.2	14.0–14.5
		10.95–11.2	
		11.45–11.7	
29/19	2500–3500	17.7–21.2	27.5–31.0

multiple access (SDMA) each link is served by a different antenna. In order to provide for several distinct links or channels the antennas must have narrow beam width, hence large size. A second approach is *frequency-division multiple access* (FDMA). In this case each distinct channel between earth stations occupies a different frequency band. The technique is essentially the same as frequency-division multiplexing (FDM), which we have considered earlier (see Section 2.4.2). The baseband signals to be transmitted, whether data or voice, modulate different carriers. Since satellite amplifiers are nonlinear, the large numbers of carriers produce intermodulation products which tend to degrade performance. In order to compensate for this effect, signal levels are reduced to a point where intermodulation noise and background noise are balanced. In order to use FDMA it is necessary to provide a guard band between channels, and the entire band is not available for information transmission. A third method for sharing a satellite is time-division multiple access (TDMA). In this case the corresponding multiplexing technique is time-division multiplexing (TDM) (again see Section 2.4.2). Each channel sharing the satellite is assigned a distinct time slot. Since earth stations must synchronize their transmissions, station complexity is higher in this sort of system. However, performance is improved over FDMA since there are no intermodulation products, and full power can be used. A final technique for providing separate channels is called *code-division multiple access* (CDMA). Pairs of stations using ther same channel spread the spectrum of the signal to be transmitted over the whole satellite band using a pseudorandom code word. The same code word is used to demodulate the signal. This technique is not as efficient as FDMA or TDMA, but it does have the virtue of a built-in encryption capability.

The technology of satellite communications plays a large role in the determination of analog and digital transmission techniques to be used over the satellite channel. Signals are transmitted most efficiently when the amplitude of the carrier is at a constant level. This implies that all information is contained in the phase of the carrier. A common technique for digital transmission is four-phase modulation, in which one of four possible phase angles is transmitted at any instant of time. In order to confine the band occupied by the signal, transitions between these angles are staggered. Rather than allowing 180 degree phase shifts at T-sec intervals, the maximum phase shifts is 90 degrees at $(T/2)$-second intervals.[13]

From the point of view of computer communications, satellite links have unique properties. First of all, widely separated points may be connected as easily as points close together and the costs of satellite links are distance independent. Furthermore, the nature of the satellite transmission link allows great flexibility in the allocation of channel capacity. For example, by use of multiple antenna in the satellite, the channel can be shared among different pairs of ground stations simultaneously. This sharing may be effected by means of FDMA or TDMA. In the former each geographically distinct pair communicates over the same frequency band. In the case of TDMA, access is switched in time among the various pairs of stations.

When a large number of bursty sources access the satellite, the dedication that FDMA or TDMA implies may not be appropriate. In this case accessing techniques similar to those used in local area networks can be employed. The most likely of these is ALOHA, either slotted or unslotted. A number of ground stations share the same channel. After a transmission, the stations can detect a collision by listening on the common channel. In the event of a collision the stations retransmit after a random time out. This process continues until messages are transmitted without impediment.

In the foregoing we alluded to the flexibility that satellites allow. This flexibility is exemplified by the the proposals of Satellite Business Systems Inc. (SBS),[59] by which satellites provide end-to-end service. The novel aspect of the SBS plan is what is called direct access. This is effected by means of a satellite antenna located on the premises of the users. Since operation is in the 14/12 band, these antennas need not be very large.

2.8.2. Cable Television†

The recent development of cable television networks may provide facility for the conveyance of data traffic over intracity distances. One can envision systems in which cable television networks in conjunction with satellites provide end-to-end service over intercity distances. This combination already exists for broadcast television. The technical obstacle to the immediate use of existing systems is that they were originally designed for one-way transmission from a central point to a large number of remote users. As we shall see, there are ways around this difficulty.

The transmission medium in cable television networks is coaxial cable. By use of amplifiers, signals can be delivered at distances up to 13 km. The standard configurations for cable television networks are variations of the tree topology illustrated in Figures 2.24. A high-bandwidth trunk cable carries signals to a hub where it is distributed to cable serving 10,000 to 15,000 subscribers. At intermediate bridges the signal is fed onto feeder cables which serve on the order of hundreds of subscribers by means of taps. In an alternative configuration each subscriber is served by a dedicated line from what is called a minihub. Transmission over the cable is in what is termed the broadband mode in which a number of the channels are placed in a passband by means of frequency-division multiplexing. The number of these channels ranges from 12 for community antenna systems

†For a discussion of cable television systems see Ref. 60.

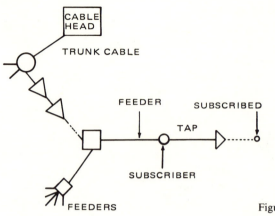

Figure 2.24. Cable television network.

to more than 35 for wideband systems. The standard service lies in the middle of this range, 13–35 channels. The wideband system allows transmission in the range 5–400 MHz. Thus, with Nyquist signaling, wideband cable could transmit data at rates of hundreds of megabits per second. Two-way service can be provided by splitting the frequency band. The band 5–30 MHz can be used upstream, i.e., toward the subscriber, and 50–400 MHz downstream. A salient feature of cable television systems is that a large number of subscribers share the same transmission medium—too many for the dedication of facilities to be viable. As in the case of satellites, sharing may be effected by means of one of the accessing techniques discussed in connection with local area networks. A technique that seems suited to this application is probing or tree search. Groups of subscribers could be polled from a central point over the downstream channel. The subscribers respond over the downstream channel.

References

1. M. Schwartz, *Computer Communication Network Design and Analysis*, Prentice-Hall, Englewood Cliffs, New Jersey (1977).
2. A. S. Tannenbaum, *Computer Networks*, Prentice-Hall, Englewood Cliffs, New Jersey (1981).
3. P. E. Green, editor, *Computer Network Architectures and Protocols*, Plenum Press, New York (1982) [this is a revised version of *IEEE Transactios on Communications*, **Com. 28**(4), April (1980)].
4. D. W. Davies and D. L. A. Barber, *Communications Networks for Computers*, John Wiley and Sons, London (1973).
5. P. Jackson and C. Stubbs, "A Study of Multiaccess Computer Communications," in *AFIPS Conference Proceedings*, **34**, 491–504 (1969).
6. E. Fuchs and P. E. Jackson, "Estimates of Distributions of Random Variables for Certain Computer Communication Traffic Models," *Communications of the ACM*, **13**(12), 752–757 (1970).

7. H. Zimmerman, "A Standard Layer Model," in Ref. 3.

8. N. Abramson and F. Kuo, editors, *Computer Communications Networks*, Prentice-Hall, Englewood Cliffs, New Jersey (1973).

9. *The Loop Plant*, Special Issue of the *Bell System Technical Journal*, **57**(4), April (1975).

10. R. T. James and P. E. Muench "AT & T Facilities and Services," *Proceedings of the IEEE*, **6**(10), 1342–1350, November (1972); in Ref. 11.

11. P. E. Green and R. W. Lucky, editors, *Computer Communications*, IEEE Press, New York (1975).

12. W. W. Chu, *Advances in Computer Communications*, Archtech House, Dedham, Massachusetts (1974).

13. *IEEE Transitions on Communications*, Special Issue on Digital Radio, **Com-27**(12), December (1979).

14. *IEEE Journal on Selected Areas in Communications*, Special Issue on Fiber Optic Systems, **SAC-1**(3), April (1983).

15. H. L. Van Trees, *Satellite Communications*, IEEE Press, New York (1979).

16. J. J. Spilker, Jr. *Digital Communications by Satellite*, Prentice-Hall, Englewood Cliffs, New Jersey (1977).

17. B. K. Bhargava, D. Haccoun, R. Matyas, and P. Nuspl, *Digital Communication by Satellite*, John Wiley and Sons, New York (1981).

18. R. L. Easton, "Undersea Cable—A Survey, or An Explanation to an Unknown Lady in Philadelphia," *IEEE Communications Society Magazine*, **13**(5), 12–15, September (1975).

19. "Data Communications Using the Switched Telecommunications Network," Bell System Technical Reference PUB41005, May (1971) (also reprinted in Ref. 11).

20. R. W. Lucky, "Common Carrier Data Communications," in Ref. 8.

21. *Common Channel Interoffice Signaling*, Special Issue of *Bell System Technical Journal*, **57**(2), February (1978).

22. A. Joel, *Electronic Switching: Central Office Systems of the World*, IEEE Press, New York (1976).

23. *Digital Switching*, Special Issue of *IEEE Transactions on Communications*, **Com.** 27(7), July (1979).

24. R. W. Lucky, J. Salz, and E. J. Weldon Jr., *Principles of Data Communication*, McGraw-Hill, New York (1968).

25. W. R. Bennett and J. R. Davy, *Data Transmission*, McGraw-Hill, New York (1965).

26. J. G. Proakis, *Digital Communications*, McGraw-Hill, New York (1983).

27. N. Q. Duc, "Line Coding Techniques for Baseband Digital Transmission, "*Australian Telecommunications Research*, **9**(1), 3–13 (1975).

28. N. Q. Duc and B. M. Smith, "Line Coding Techniques for Digital Data Transmission," *Australian Telecommunications Research*, **11**(2), 14–27 (1977).

29. F. P. Duffy and T. W. Thacher, "Analog Transmission Performance on the Switched Telecommunications Network," *Bell System Technical Journal*, **50**, 1311–1347, April (1971).

30. V. K. Bhargava, "Forward Error Correction Schemes for Digital Communications," *IEEE Communications Society Magazine*, **21**(1), January (1983).

31. J. G. Proakis, Digital Communications, McGraw-Hill, New York (1983), Chapter 5.

32. *Digital Data System*, Special Issue of *Bell System Technical Journal*, **54**(5), May–June (1975).

33. L. G. Roberts, "Computer Network Development to Achieve Resource Sharing," *Spring Joint Computer Conference Proceedings*, Vol. 37, pp. 543–549 (1970).

34. *Packet Switched Networks*, Special Issue of the *Proceedings of the IEEE*, **66**(11), November (1978).

35. L. Tymes, "TYMNET—A Terminal-Oriented Communication Network," *1971 Spring Joint Computer Conference Proceedings*, Vol. 38 (1971), pp. 211–216.

36. L. Pouzin, "CIGALE, The Packet Switching Machine of the CYCLADES Computer Network," *IFIP Congress*, Stockholm, Sweden, August (1974), pp. 155–159.

37. H. Opderbeck and R. B. Hovey," Telenet—Network Features and Interface Protocols," *Proc. NTG-Conference Datanetworks*, Baden-Baden West Germany, February (1976).
38. W. W. Clipshaw and F. Glave," Datapac Network Review," *International Computer Communications Conference Proceedings*, August (1976), pp. 131–136.
39. M. Schwartz and T. Stern, "Routing Protocols," contained in Ref. 3.
40. M. Gerla and L. Kleinrock, "Flow Control Protocols," contained in Ref. 3.
41. F. A. Tobagi, "Multiaccess Protocols in Packet Communications Systems," in Ref. 3.
42. S. S. Lam, "Multiple Access Protocols," TR-88, Department of Computer Science, University of Texas; to appear in *Computer Communications: The Art and Direction for the Future*, W. Chou, editor, Prentice-Hall, Englewood Cliffs, New Jersey.
43. J. F. Hayes, "Local Distribution in Computer Communications," *IEEE Communications Society Magazine*, **19**(2), 6–14, March (1981).
44. *Local Area Networks*, Special Issue of *IEEE Transactions on Communications*, **Com.-31**(11), November (1983).
45. W. D. Farmer and E. E. Newhall, "An Experimental Distributed Switching System to Handle Bursty Traffic," *Proceedings of the ACM Symposium on Problems of Optimization Data Communication Systems*, Pine Mountain, Georgia, October (1969), pp. 1–34.
46. B. K. Penny and A. A. Baghdadi, "Survey of Computer Communications Loop Networks, Parts 1 and 2," *Computer Communications*, **2**(4), 165–180, August (1979); **2**(5), 224–241, September (1979).
47. J. R. Pierce, "How Far Can Data Loops Go?" *IEEE Transactions on Communications*, **Com-20**, 527–530, June (1972).
48. J. R. Pierce, "Network for the Block Switching of Data," *Bell System Technical Journal*, **51**, 1133–1145, July/August (1972).
49. N. Abramson, "The ALOHA System—Another Alternative for Computer Communications," *Fall Joint Computer Communications Conference Proceedings*, **37**, 281–285 (1970).
50. N. Abramson, "The ALOHA System," *Computer Communication Networks*, N. Abramson and F. Kuo, editors, Prentice-Hall, Englewood Cliffs, New Jersey (1973).
51. L. G. Roberts, "ALOHA Packets System with and without Capture," *Computer Communications Review*, **5**, 28–42, April (1975).
52. R. M. Metcalfe and D. R. Boggs, "Ethernet: Distributed Packet Switching for Local Computer Networks," *Communications of the ACM*, **19**, 395–404, July (1976).
53. J. F. Hayes, "An Adaptive Technique for Local Distribution," *IEEE Transactions on Communications*, **Com-26**, 1178–1186, August (1978).
54. J. Capetanakis, "Tree Algorithms for Packet Broadcasting Channels," *IEEE Transactions on Information Theory*, **IT-25**, 505–515, September (1979).
55. W. R. Crowther, *et al.*, "A System for Broadcast Communication," *Proceedings of the Sixth Hawai International Systems Science Conference*, January (1973).
56. L. Roberts, "Dynamic Allocation of Satellite Capacity Through Reservations," *Proceedings of the AFIPS Conference*, **42**, 711–716, June (1973).
57. E. G. Rawson and R. M. Metcalf, "Fibernet: Multimode Optical Fibers for Local Computer Networks," *IEEE Transactions on Communications*, **Com-20**(7), July (1978).
58. W. L. Pritchard, "Satellite Communications—An Overview of the Problems and Programs," *Proceedings of the IEEE*, **65**, 294–307, March (1977); reproduced in Ref. 15.
59. J. D. Barnla and F. R. Zitman, "Digital Satellite Communication System of SBS," *IEEE Electronics and Aerospace Convention*, September 26–28 (1977), pp. 7.13–7.21; reproduced in Ref. 15.
60. S. B. Weinstein, *Cable Television and Its Competitors*, IEEE Press, New York (1985).

Pure Birth and Birth–Death Processes: Applications to Queueing

3.1. Introduction

Measurements of traffic in voice and in data systems have shown that in a wide range of applications call and message generation can be modeled as a *Poisson process.* In this instance nature is kind to the system analyst since the Poisson process is particularly tractable from a mathematical point of view. We shall examine the Poisson arrival process in some detail. In particular we show that the Poisson arrival process is a special case of the *pure birth* process. This leads directly to the consideration of *birth–death* processes, which model certain queueing systems in which customers having exponentially distributed service requirements arrive at a service facility at a Poisson rate.

3.2. Bernoulli Trials—Markov Chains

A useful heuristic approach to the Poisson process begins with Bernoulli trials. Consider an experiment with two possible outcomes, which we designate as success and failure. The experiment is repeated independently for n trials. The resulting sample space of this compound experiment has 2^n points. An elementary event on this sample space is a specific sequence of successes and failures, preserving order. If the probability of success is P, then the probability of a particular sequence with k successes is $P^k(1 - P)^{n-k}$. A more complex event is the occurrence of k successes in any order. There are

$$\binom{n}{k} = \frac{n!}{k!(n-k)!}$$

49

ways for there to be k successes in n trials, each pattern being a mutually exclusive event. Summing over these disjoint events we have

$$P[k \text{ successes in } n \text{ trials}] = b(k; n, P) \triangleq \binom{n}{k} P^k (1 - P)^{n-k} \qquad (3.1)$$

This is the binomial distribution. The probability-generating function of the binomial distribution is

$$B(z) = E[z^B] \triangleq \sum_{k=0}^{n} b(k; n, P) z^k = [Pz + (1 - P)]^n \qquad (3.2)$$

where B is the number of successes in n trials and $E[\ ]$ denotes expectation. The mean number of successes in n trials is nP. There are two interesting properties of the binomial distribution which we take notice of before going on. Given that there are k successes the distributions of the k successes are uniformly distributed among the n trials. Thus given k successes, the probability that any particular trial is successful is k/n. The second property is lack of memory. If we know the value of P and we are told that there has been a particular pattern of successes, we have no information about future successes. For example, if in ten flips of a fair coin there were ten heads, the probability of a head on the eleventh is one half.

Because of this memoryless property, a sequence of Bernoulli trials is a Markov chain.† A Markov chain is a random sequence which has a finite number of states and which has a certain memoryless property. The probability distribution of a state in the sequence depends only on the immediately preceding state. This is expressed in the following equation for the state at the $(N + 1)$st trial, S_{N+1}:

$$P(S_{N+1} = k_{N+1} / S_1 = k_1, S_2 = k_2, \ldots, S_N = k_N)$$
$$= P(S_{N+1} = k_{N+1} / S_N = k_N) \qquad (3.3)$$

Equation (3.3) states that the probability of the state being k_{N+1} at trial $N + 1$ depends only on the outcome of the Nth trial. For the sequence of Bernoulli trials, the state on the Nth trial is defined to be the accumulated number of successes up to and including the Nth trial. As we noted earlier, the probability of a success of a trial is independent of previous successes.

3.3. The Poisson Process

3.3.1. Introduction

The Poisson distribution can be derived as a limiting case of the binomial distribution. Let us assume that the n Bernoulli trials are carried

---

†A review of Markov chain is given in Appendix B.

out in a one-second interval. Now suppose that the number of trials is increased without limit and the probability of success on any one trial is decreased toward zero in such a way that the average number of successes in a 1-sec interval remains constant at value $\lambda \triangleq nP$. We have

$$\lim_{\substack{n\to\infty \\ P\to 0}} b(0; n, P) = \lim_{\substack{n\to\infty \\ P\to 0}} \left(1 - \frac{\lambda}{n}\right)^n = e^{-\lambda} \qquad (3.4a)$$

and

$$\lim_{\substack{n\to\infty \\ P\to 0}} \frac{b(k; n, P)}{b(k-1; n, P)} = \lim_{\substack{n\to\infty \\ P\to 0}} \frac{n-k+1}{k} \frac{P}{1-P} = \frac{\lambda}{k} \qquad (3.4b)$$

By induction it follows from equations (3.4a) and (3.4b) that the probability of k successes in 1 sec is

$$p(k, \lambda) = e^{-\lambda}\lambda^k/k! \qquad k = 0, 1, 2, \ldots$$

This result is easily extended to any t-second interval. Again we imagine the number of trials to increase without limit and the probability of success to go to zero. The average rate of successes in the t-second interval is taken to be λt. The probability of k successes in the interval is given by

$$P_k(t) \triangleq P[k \text{ successes in } t \text{ seconds}] = \frac{e^{-\lambda t}(\lambda t)^k}{k!}, \qquad k = 0, 1, \ldots \qquad (3.5)$$

The generating function for the number of successes in t seconds is

$$N(z) = E[Z^{X(t)}] = \sum_{k=0}^{\infty} P_k(t)z^k = e^{-\lambda t(1-z)} \qquad (3.6)$$

where $X(t)$ is the number of successes in t seconds. Notice that the parameter of the distribution here is λt. Notice also that the number of successes can be any finite number with a nonzero probability.

We can construct a continuous time Markov chain based on the Poisson distribution. We define the Poisson process to be a point process for which the number of events (successes) in a t-second interval is given by the Poisson distribution of equation (3.5) and where the numbers of events in nonoverlapping intervals are independent random variables.† If we view

†Poisson processes are a member of the class of independent increment processes.

the Poisson process as a limiting case of Bernoulli trials, it is entirely reasonable that the Markov property carries through. Let X_t represent the accumulated number of successes in $(0, t)$ and let $t_1 \leqslant t_2 \leqslant \cdots \leqslant t_N \leqslant t_{N+1}$. In analogy with equation (3.3) we may write

$$
\begin{aligned}
P[X_{t_{N+1}} &= k_{N+1} | X_{t_1} = k_1, X_{t_2} = k_2, \ldots, X_{t_N} = k_N] \\
&= P[X_{t_{N+1}} = k_{N+1} | X_{t_N} = k_N]
\end{aligned}
\tag{3.7}
$$

The Binomial and the Poisson distribution may serve to model a message arrival process. Suppose there are a *finite number* of message sources which may transmit a single message in a 1-sec interval with probability P. The probability of k sources transmitting messages is $b(k; n, P)$ given in equation (3.1). Now suppose that the number of sources, n, approaches infinity and that the probability of an individual source transmitting a message, P, approaches zero in such a way that $nP = \lambda$. The number of sources transmitting messages is given by Poisson distribution. The distinction here is between *finite* source and *infinite* source models. Our queueing results will be obtained for the infinite source model, although many results carry over to the finite source model.

Properties of the Poisson process may be inferred from the Bernoulli trials. For example, given that there are k arrivals in a time interval t, it can be shown that the arrivals are uniformly distributed throughout the interval. Secondly, the Poisson process has the memoryless property, i.e., being given that there were k arrivals in the previous time interval has no bearing on the arrival probabilities for the next time interval, provided the arrivals are at the same known average rate.

Let us now consider an alternative characterization of the Poisson processes, in terms of the time interval between arrivals. Let T denote the random time of the first arrival after some initial time set arbitrarily at $t = 0$. The probability distribution for T is found by the following manipulations:

$$
\begin{aligned}
F_T(t) &\triangleq P[T \leqslant t] = 1 - P[\text{no arrival in } (0, t)] \\
&= 1 - P_0(t) = 1 - e^{-\lambda t}
\end{aligned}
\tag{3.8a}
$$

The probability density function for an arrival is

$$
f_T(t) \, dt \triangleq P[t < T \leqslant t + dt] = \lambda \, e^{-\lambda t} \, dt
\tag{3.8b}
$$

In equations (3.8a) and (3.8b) we have an exponentially distributed random variable. Its mean value is

$$
E(T) = \int_0^\infty t\lambda \, e^{-\lambda t} \, dt = 1/\lambda
\tag{3.8c}
$$

The relation between the Poisson and the exponential distributions is illustrated on Figure 3.1. The Poisson distribution is a discrete random variable, the number of arrivals in a time interval; while the exponentially distributed random variable is a continuous, random variable, the interval between arrivals.

The exponential distribution also has a memoryless property. Suppose we are given the event that there has been an arrival at time $t = 0$ and none in the interval $(0, t)$; what is the probability of an arrival in the interval $(0, t + \tau)$? This is the probability of an arrival in the interval $(t, t + \tau)$ conditioned on no arrival in the interval $(0, t)$. We designate the time of this first arrival as T. From equation (3.8a) we have

$$
\begin{aligned}
P[T &\leq t + \tau / T \geq t] \\
&= P[t < T \leq t + \tau / T \geq t] \\
&= \frac{F_T(t + \tau) - F_T(t)}{1 - F_T(t)} = \frac{1 - e^{-\lambda(t+\tau)} - 1 + e^{-\lambda t}}{e^{-\lambda t}} \\
&= 1 - e^{-\lambda \tau}
\end{aligned}
\tag{3.9}
$$

Equation (3.9) reaffirms the memoryless character of the arrival process. The probability of an arrival in an interval depends only on the duration of the interval and not on previous arrivals. Equations (3.8) and (3.9) provide an alternate characterization of the Poisson process. The Poisson process is one in which the interarrival times are independent and exponentially distributed.

There is yet another fruitful alternative to the foregoing definitions of the Poisson process. From equation (3.5) we have for $\lambda \delta \ll 1$

$$
P_0(\delta) = 1 - \lambda \delta + o(\delta)
\tag{3.10a}
$$

$$
P_1(\delta) = \lambda \delta + o(\delta)
\tag{3.10b}
$$

$$
P_i(\delta) = o(\delta), \qquad i \geq 2
\tag{3.10c}
$$

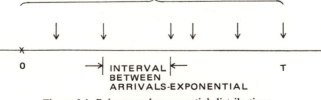

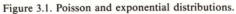

Figure 3.1. Poisson and exponential distributions.

where $o(\delta)$ designate higher-order terms in t such that $\lim_{\delta \to 0}[o(\delta)/\delta] = 0$. The significance of equations (3.10a)–(3.10c) is that for an incremental interval the probability of more than one arrival is negligible and the probability of an arrival is proportional to the duration of the incremental interval, δ.

Although equations (3.10a)–(3.10c) are a consequence of the previous definition of the Poisson process, it can be shown that an independent increment process which is stationary and which satisfies equations (3.10a)–(3.10c) is a Poisson process characterized by equation (3.5). Let $P_n(t)$ denote the probability that there are n arrivals in a time interval t for this process. We examine the change in probability in the incremental interval $(t, t + \delta)$ beginning with $n = 0$. Since the process is independent increment we may write

$P_0(t + \delta)$

$$\triangleq P[\text{no arrivals in } (0, t + \delta)]$$
$$= P[\text{no arrivals in } (0, t)] \, P[\text{no arrivals in } (t, t + \delta)] \qquad (3.11a)$$
$$= P_0(t)[1 - \lambda\delta]$$

For $n > 0$ we have two disjoint events (see Figure 3.2):

$P_n(t + \delta)$

$$= P[n \text{ arrivals in } (0, t + \delta)]$$
$$= P[n \text{ arrivals in } (0, t)]P[\text{no arrivals in } (t, t + \delta)] \qquad (3.11b)$$
$$\quad + P[(n - 1) \text{ arrivals in } (0, t)]P[\text{one arrival in } (t, t + \delta)]$$
$$= P_n(t)(1 - \lambda\delta) + P_{n-1}(t)(\lambda\delta)$$

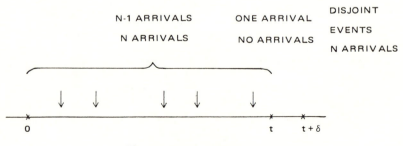

Figure 3.2. Arrivals in $(0, t + \delta)$.

Letting $\delta \to 0$ and rearranging terms in equations (3.11a) and (3.11b) we find the following differential equations:

$$\frac{dP_0(t)}{dt} = -\lambda P_0(t) \tag{3.12a}$$

$$\frac{dP_n(t)}{dt} = \lambda(P_{n-1}(t) - P_n(t)), \qquad n > 0 \tag{3.12b}$$

In equations (3.12a) and (3.12b) we have a set of linear equations with constant coefficients whose solution is an elementary exercise in Laplace transforms. Define the Laplace transform of $P_n(t)$ as

$$L_n(s) = \mathscr{L}(P_n(t)) = \int_0^\infty e^{-st} P_n(t)\, dt$$

From the basic properties of the Laplace transform we have

$$\mathscr{L}\left(\frac{dP_n(t)}{dt}\right) = sL_n(s) - P_n(0), n = 0, 1, 2, \ldots$$

Substituting this into equation (3.12) we find

$$L_0(s) = P_0(0)/(s + \lambda) \tag{3.13a}$$

$$L_n(s) = \frac{P_n(0) + \lambda L_{n-1}(s)}{s + \lambda}, \qquad n > 0 \tag{3.13b}$$

If we assume that the arrival process starts at time $t = 0$ then $P_0(0) = 1$, $P_n(0) = 0$, $n > 0$. Substituting into equations (3.12a) and (3.12b) we have

$$L_0(s) = 1/(s + \lambda) \tag{3.14a}$$

$$L_n(s) = \lambda^n/(s + \lambda)^{n+1} \tag{3.14b}$$

These time domain solutions can be found by application of the following Laplace transform relations:

$$\mathscr{L}(e^{-at}U(t)) = 1/(s + a)$$

$$\mathscr{L}(t^n/n!) = 1/s^{n+1}$$

$$\mathscr{L}(e^{-at}F(t)) = f(s + a)$$

It is a simple exercise to show that the solution is as given in equation (3.5).

3.3.2. Adding and Splitting Poisson Processes

In the preceding section we have shown that if a process is such that the probability of an arrival over an incremental interval δ is proportional to the duration of the interval, i.e., $\lambda\delta$, and independent from interval to interval, then the process is Poisson. This result can be used to prove certain important properties of the Poisson process. For example, consider the sum of two arrival processes consisting of the total number of arrivals in an interval from either process (see Figure 3.3). If the two processes are independent and Poisson with average arrival rates λ_1 and λ_2, respectively, then the sum process is Poisson with average arrival rate $\lambda_1 + \lambda_2$. To prove this consider arrivals in an incremental interval, δ. The probability of an arrival from either source is $(\lambda_1 + \lambda_2)\delta$. The probability of arrivals from both is $\lambda_1\lambda_2\delta^2$, which is vanishingly small. It is easy to show that the conditions of stationary and independent increments hold for the sum process. The sum process has the same properties as before with the average arrival rate $\lambda_1 + \lambda_2$. This same replication of Poisson processes holds for the sum of any finite number of independent Poisson processes.†

This same approach can be applied to the random splitting of bifurcation of a Poisson arrival process. Consider the case depicted in Figure 3.4, where Poisson arrivals are placed in either one of two bins with probabilities

†For an alternate proof see Exercises 3.4 and 3.5.

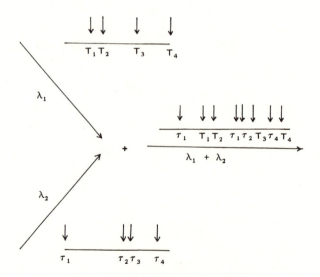

Figure 3.3. Sum of Poisson processes.

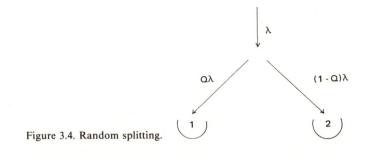

Figure 3.4. Random splitting.

q and $1 - q$, respectively. In an incremental interval the event of an arrival to bin one is the joint event of an arrival to the system and the selection for bin one. Since the subevents are independent the probability of an arrival to bin is the product $q\lambda\delta$. Again the arrival process is a stationary independent process, consequently it is Poisson with average rate $q\lambda$ arrivals/sec. Clearly the arrival process to queue 2 is also Poisson but with average arrival rate $(1 - q)\lambda$. The same basic results hold for any independent random splitting of a Poisson arrival process. For an example of nonrandom splitting see Exercise 3.6.

3.4. Pure Birth Processes

The Poisson process can be generalized by allowing the probability of an arrival in an incremental interval to be a function of the number already in the system. The probability of an arrival in an incremental interval is indicated as $\lambda_n\delta$ if there were n previous arrivals. The general class of processes so obtained are called *pure birth* processes, indicating an application to population dynamics where the rate of increase is a function of the size of the population. The set of differential equations governing pure birth processes can be derived in a fashion very similar to those for Poisson arrival processes. In analogy with equations (3.11a) and (3.11b) we write

$$P_0(t + \delta) = P[\text{no arrivals in } (0, t)]$$
$$\times P[\text{no arrivals in } (t, t + \delta)/\text{no arrivals in } (0, t)] \quad (3.15a)$$
$$= P_0(t)(1 - \lambda_0\delta)$$

$$P_n(t + \delta) = P[n \text{ arrivals in } (0, t)]P[\text{no arrivals in } (t, t + \delta)/n \text{ arrivals in } (0, t)]$$
$$+ P[n - 1 \text{ arrivals in } (0, t)]P[1 \text{ arrival in } (t, t + \delta)/n - 1 \text{ arrivals in } (0, t)] \quad (3.15b)$$
$$= P_n(t)[1 - \lambda_n\delta] + P_{n-1}(t)(\lambda_{n-1}\delta), \quad n > 0$$

Letting $\delta \to 0$ and rearranging terms we find

$$\frac{dP_0(t)}{dt} = -\lambda_0 P_0(t) \tag{3.16a}$$

$$\frac{dP_n(t)}{dt} = -\lambda_n P_n(t) + \lambda_{n-1} P_n(t), \qquad n > 0 \tag{3.16b}$$

These equations can be solved using the same procedure as previously. We take the Laplace transform of both sides of (3.16a) and (3.16b) and solve for $P_n(t)$, $n = 0, 1, \ldots$. We have

$$L_0(s) = \frac{P_0(0)}{s + \lambda_0} \tag{3.17a}$$

$$L_n(s) = \frac{P_n(0)}{s + \lambda_n} + \frac{\lambda_{n-1}}{s + \lambda_n} L_{n-1}(s), \qquad n > 0 \tag{3.17b}$$

where

$$L_n(s) \triangleq \mathcal{L}[P_n(t)]$$

These equations can be solved for the time domain representation by applying the Laplace transform relations that we have seen previously. We also remind the reader that a product in the s domain translates into a convolution in the time domain. Such a product is $1/(s + \lambda_n)$ and $\lambda_{n-1} L_{n-1}(s)$. After some manipulation the following general solution is obtained:

$$P_0(t) = P_0(0) e^{-\lambda_0 t}, \qquad t \geqslant 0 \tag{3.18a}$$

$$P_n(t) = P_n(0) e^{-\lambda_n t} + \lambda_{n-1} \int_0^t e^{-\lambda_n \tau} P_{n-1}(t - \tau) \, d\tau, \qquad t \geqslant 0 \tag{3.18b}$$

Notice that the solution in (3.18a) and (3.18b) $n > 0$ is a function of the initial conditions $P_n(0)$, $n = 0, 1, \ldots$. Solutions to specific problems can be found by determining the initial conditions and the incremental arrival probability $\lambda_n \delta$ for each value of n. In problems of this sort it is helpful to sketch a diagram showing the average flows from one state to another. Such a *state transition flow diagram* is shown in Figure 3.5a. The average flow out of the state where there are n members in the population is λ_n per second.

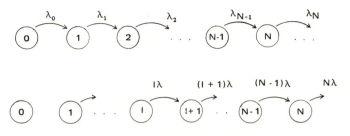

Figure 3.5. State transition flow diagrams.

We now apply these results to a particular problem. We assume that each member of a population gives birth to a new member in an incremental interval with probability $\lambda\delta$. We have then $\lambda_n = n\lambda$. (See Figure 3.5b.) We also specify that there is a nonzero initial population, $P_k(0) = 1$. By substituting into equations (3.18a) and (3.18b) we have

$$P_j(t) = 0, \qquad j < k, \qquad t \geq 0 \tag{3.19a}$$

$$P_n(t) = (n - 1)\lambda \int_0^t e^{-n\lambda\tau} P_{n-1}(t - \tau)\, d\tau \tag{3.19b}$$

An inductive proof can be used to verify that the solution to equations (3.19a)–(3.19c) is

$$P_n(t) = \binom{n-1}{n-k} e^{-k\lambda t}(1 - e^{-\lambda t})^{n-k}, \qquad n \geq k, \qquad t \geq 0 \tag{3.20}$$

For an alternate approach to this problem see Exercise 3.9.

We note that in spite of the fact that the probability of a birth increases with the size of the population, the process in equation (3.20) behaves reasonably in that growth remains stable. This reasonable behavior is not always the case. If the probability of a birth increases quickly enough with the population size, explosive growth takes place; an infinite number of births can take place in a finite time interval. It can be shown that a necessary and sufficient condition for stable growth is for the series $\sum_{n=0}^{\infty} 1/\lambda_n$ to diverge.[1]

3.5. Birth–Death Processes

In the previous section the pure birth process, generalized from the Poisson process, served as a model of an arrival process. In an incremental interval at most one arrival was possible. However, in queueing models we are interested in departures from the system as well as arrivals. This can be handled as an extension of the pure birth process. By allowing the number of members of the population to increase or decrease by at most one in an incremental interval we have a birth–death process. As in the case of the pure birth process we look at the change of state in an incremental time interval $(t, t + \delta)$. Again it is assumed that δ is so small that at most one arrival with probability $\lambda_n \delta$ can occur when the population size is n. The probability of a departure in this same incremental interval is $\mu_n \delta$. The probability of both an arrival and a departure in an incremental interval is of the order of δ^2, and consequently it may be neglected. For the case $n > 0$ we have in analogy to equations (3.11a) and (3.11b)

$P_n(t + \delta) = P[n$ in system at time $t]$

$\quad \times P[$neither arrivals nor departures in $(t, t + \delta)/n$ in system$]$

$\quad + P[n - 1$ in system at time $t]$

$\quad \times P[$one arrival in $(t, t + \delta)/n - 1$ in system$]$ $\quad\quad\quad$ (3.21a)

$\quad + P[n + 1$ in system at time $t]$

$\quad \times P[$one departure in $(t, t + \delta)/n + 1$ in system$]$

$\quad = (1 - \lambda_n \delta - \mu_n \delta) P_n(t) + \lambda_{n-1} \delta P_{n-1}(t) + \mu_{n+1} \delta P_{n+1}(t)$

The state transition flow diagram for the birth–death process is shown in Figure 3.6 where μ_n and λ_n represent average flows. In equation (3.21a) we recognize that $(1 - \lambda_n \delta - \mu_n \delta)$ is the probability of neither an arrival nor a departure. In the case of $n = 0$, no departures are possible and we have

$P_0(t + \delta) = P[0$ in system at time $t]P[$no arrivals in $(t, t + \delta)/0$ in system$]$

$\quad + P[1$ in system at time $t]P[$departure in $(t, t + \delta)/1$ in system$]$

$\quad = (1 - \lambda_0 \delta) P_0(t) + \mu_1 \delta P_1(t)$ $\quad\quad\quad\quad\quad\quad\quad\quad\quad\quad\quad\quad$ (3.21b)

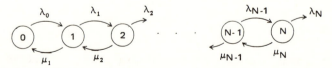

Figure 3.6. General state transition flow diagram—birth–death processes.

Letting $\delta \to 0$ we have the following set of differential equations:

$$\frac{dP_0(t)}{dt} = -\lambda_0 P_0(t) + \mu_1 P_1(t) \tag{3.22a}$$

$$\frac{dP_n(t)}{dt} = -(\lambda_n + \mu_n)P_n(t) + \lambda_{n-1}P_{n-1}(t) + \mu_{n+1}P_{n+1}(t), \qquad n > 0 \tag{3.22b}$$

The solution to the set of equations in (3.22a) and (3.22b) is not as simple as the case of pure birth equations. Indeed the question of the existence and uniqueness of solutions to these equations is not trivial.† However, it can be shown that a positive solution such that $\sum_{n=0}^{\infty} P_n \leq 1$ always exists as long as $\mu_n \geq 0$, $\lambda_n \geq 0$. The case $\sum_{n=0}^{\infty} P_n < 1$ is of theoretical interest; one can draw an analogy with the divergent birth processes discussed earlier. However, for the cases of practical interest solutions may be assumed to be unique and $\sum_{n=0}^{\infty} P_n = 1$.

It is possible to side-step the difficulties inherent in solving equations (3.22a) and (3.22b) by shifting the focus of our attention. A pure birth process is monotonically increasing if $\lambda_n > 0$ for all n since there are no departures. If one waits long enough the population size will surpass any bound. In this case it is natural to seek a transient solution focusing upon such questions as population size at a particular time or the time required to reach a certain level. Now for birth–death processes as applied to queueing we are interested in cases where the population does not increase without bound. Indeed one of our concerns is to find conditions for such stability. Accordingly, our interest is not in transient but in steady-state solutions.‡

In order to find the equilibrium distribution of the population we let $dP_i(t)/dt = 0$; $i = 0, 1, 2, \ldots$, implying that there is no change with time in the probability distribution in equations (3.22a) and (3.22b). The resulting set of equations are

$$\lambda_0 P_0 = \mu_1 P_1 \tag{3.23a}$$

$$(\lambda_n + \mu_n)P_n = \lambda_{n-1}P_{n-1} + \mu_{n+1}P_{n+1} \tag{3.23b}$$

where P_i, $i = 0, 1, 2, \ldots$, indicates the probability that there are i customers in the system at equilibrium. In equations (3.23a) and (3.23b) the time dependence is suppressed. In order to obtain a solution§ to equation (3.23)

---

†For a discussion of this point see Chap. XVII of Ref. 1.

‡For a transient solution to the birth–death equation when $\lambda_n = \lambda$ and $\mu_n = \mu$, see Ref. 2, Chap. 2.

§The precise conditions for a steady-state solution to exist in general are beyond the scope of this text. The interested reader should consult the References at the end of this chapter. However, for the cases of interest, the conditions on μ_i and λ_i are stability in the size of the populations.

the normalizing condition is required:

$$\sum_{n=0}^{\infty} P_n = 1 \tag{3.23c}$$

Equations (3.23a) and (3.23b) are called *equilibrium* equations since they arise from the condition $dP_n(t)/dt = 0$ and the right-hand side is the probability of entering state n while the left-hand side is the probability of leaving state n. This equilibrium is indicated in Figure 3.6.

By a simple rearrangement of the terms in equations (3.23a) and (3.23b), an interesting alternative view of the process is obtained. We have

$$\mu_{n+1} P_{n+1} - \lambda_n P_n = \mu_n P_n - \lambda_{n-1} P_{n-1}, \qquad n = 1, 2, \ldots \tag{3.24a}$$

$$\mu_1 P_1 - \lambda_0 P_0 = 0 \tag{3.24b}$$

The solution to these equations are the *balance* equations:

$$\mu_n P_n = \lambda_{n-1} P_{n-1}, \qquad n = 0, 1, 2, \ldots \tag{3.25}$$

Equation (3.25) states that the flow from state n to state $n - 1$, as represented by the right-hand side, must be balanced by the flow into state n from state $n - 1$.

By a simple iteration on equation (3.25) we find

$$P_n = P_0 \prod_{j=1}^{n} (\lambda_{j-1}/\mu_j) \tag{3.26a}$$

and from the normalizing condition [equation (3.23c)] we have

$$P_0 = \left[1 + \sum_{n=1}^{\infty} \prod_{j=1}^{n} (\lambda_{j-1}/\mu_j) \right]^{-1} \tag{3.26b}$$

3.6. Queueing Models

In general the *birth–death* process models the situation where there is a Poisson arrival of what we shall, for the moment, call customers† at a service facility with each customer requiring an exponentially distributed amount of service. The facility gives to each customer the amount of service

†For most of the text we shall be dealing with data messages arriving at a random rate. In this chapter it is convenient to speak of customers as the arriving entities.

that it requires. The completion of service to a customer results in the departure of the customer from the system. Customers awaiting service form a queue. In terms of the birth–death model, arrivals and departures correspond to births and deaths, respectively. By choosing different values of λ_n and μ_n variations on this basic theme are achieved.

Because the service times are exponentially distributed, the dynamics of the process as measured by the variation of the number of customers in the system do not depend upon the order in which customers are served. This service discipline can be, for example, first-come first-served (FCFS), last-come first-served (LCFS), or even service in random order. Moreover, since the service time is memoryless a server can interrupt service on one customer before completion to serve another without changing the dynamics. Such is the case in round robin service, where the server cycles through all members of the queue, giving each at most a fixed amount of service. As this increment of service decreases we approach a service discipline where the customer with the least required service is served first. The key in all of these cases is that the server is never idle while the queue is not empty. Since service times are exponentially distributed, the probability of a departure in the next incremental interval is $\mu_n\delta$ independent of the amount of service previously given to a customer. As we shall see presently, the value of μ_n depends upon the particular queueing model under consideration.

In connection with queues, a convenient notation has been developed. In its simplest form it is written $A/R/S$, where A designates the arrival process, R the service required by an arriving customer, and S the number of servers. For example, $M/M/1$ indicates a Poisson arrival of customers, an exponentially distributed service discipline and a single server. The M may be taken to stand for memoryless (or Markovian) in both the arrival process and the service time. A further embellishment on this notation indicating the size of the waiting room is denoted by an additional space. Thus, for example, $M/M/S/N$ indicates a system where there is Poisson arrival, exponential service, S servers, and room for N customers including those in service. It is frequently assumed that there is no restriction on the number in the system. In this case the final reference to the waiting room is suppressed.

3.6.1. The $M/M/1$ Queue—Infinite Waiting Room

The first model that we shall consider is the $M/M/1$ queue with an infinite waiting room. In this case customers arrive at a Poisson rate of λ per second on the average and each customer requires an exponentially distributed amount of service with mean $1/\mu$ [see equations (3.8a)–(3.8c)]. From our previous discussion, we have the probability of an arrival in an incremental interval δ as $\lambda\delta$ irrespective of the number in the system. Since the service time is exponentially distributed with mean $1/\mu$, the probability of a completion of service in an incremental interval is $\mu\delta$. Arrivals correspond to births and departures to deaths, therefore the parameters of the process are $\lambda_n = \lambda$ and $\mu_n = \mu$. (See Figure 3.7.) Substituting in equations (3.26a) and (3.26b) we find that the probability of n customers in the system, both in service and enqueued, is given by

$$P_n = (1 - \rho)\rho^n, \qquad n = 0, 1, 2, \ldots \tag{3.27}$$

where $\rho = \lambda/\mu$. We assume here that $\rho < 1$, which is reasonable since it means that the average number of arrivals during the average service time, $1/\mu$, is less than one. Were it otherwise the queue would be unstable. We notice that the distribution of the number of customers in the system is geometric with the probability of an empty system, $P_0 = 1 - \rho$. The generating function is

$$P(z) = \frac{1 - \rho}{1 - \rho z} \tag{3.28a}$$

with mean and variance

$$\bar{n} = \rho/(1 - \rho) \tag{3.28b}$$

$$\text{Var } n = \rho/(1 - \rho)^2 \tag{3.28c}$$

(See Table A.1 in Appendix A.)

In Figure 3.8 the average number in the system, $\bar{n}$, is plotted as a function of ρ. The curve is typical of queueing systems. For low values of ρ, $\bar{n}$ is a linear function of ρ. There is a saturation at $\rho = 1$. At approximately $\rho = 0.6$ there is a characteristic knee. Below the knee $\bar{n}$ increases relatively slowly with increasing load, ρ. For values of ρ greater than 0.6 the system saturates rapidly.

The statistics we have considered thus far lump together customers being served and waiting in line. It is of interest to consider the number in the queue separately. From equation (3.27), the distribution of the number

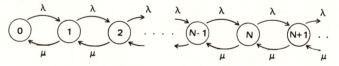

Figure 3.7. State transition flow diagram—$M/M/1$ queue.

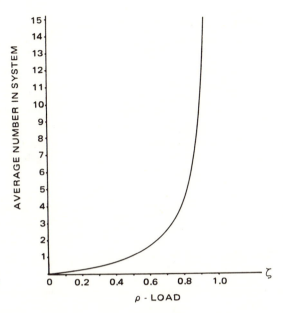

Figure 3.8. Average number of
.customers as a function of load.

in the queue is given by

$$Q_n \triangleq P[n \text{ in queue}] = \begin{cases} (1-\rho)(1+\rho), & n = 0 \\ (1-\rho)\rho^{n+1}, & n = 1, 2, \ldots \end{cases} \qquad (3.29)$$

It follows immediately that the average queue size is given by

$$\bar{q} = \frac{\rho^2}{1-\rho} \qquad (3.30)$$

The quantity ρ is called the traffic intensity or load. We shall follow the convention of measuring the load in *erlangs* with ρ defined as above. An alternative that is common in telephone traffic studies is the call second (CS) according to the portion of a busy hour that is used. The relation between the two units of measurement is $CS = 3600 \cdot \rho$.

3.6.2. The $M/M/1/N$ Queue—Finite Waiting Room

The case of the $M/M/1/N$ queue represents the simplest case of a queue in which the arrival and the departure rates are not constant. Customers arrive at rate λ as long as there are less than N in the system. When the waiting room becomes full, arriving customers are lost to the system. This may be expressed as

$$\lambda_n = \begin{cases} \lambda, & n < N \\ 0, & n \geq N \end{cases}$$

and since the service time of a customer in service is exponentially distributed, the departure rate remains at $\mu_n = \mu$ for all μ. The state transition flow diagram for this case is shown in Figure 3.9. In this case the steady-state distribution of the number in the system length is

$$P_n = \begin{cases} (1 - \rho)\rho^n / (1 - \rho^{N+1}), & n \leq N \\ 0, & n > N \end{cases} \qquad (3.31)$$

The generating function of the number in the system is

$$P(z) = \frac{(1 - \rho)[1 - (z\rho)^{N+1}]}{(1 - \rho^{N+1})(1 - z\rho)} \qquad (3.32)$$

A quantity that is of interest in systems with finite waiting rooms is the probability of a customer arriving to a full waiting room. From equation (3.3) we find this to be given by

$$P_N = \frac{(1 - \rho)\rho^N}{1 - \rho^{N+1}} \qquad (3.33)$$

This blocking probability is shown as a function of the load, ρ, for several values of N in Figure 3.10. As expected, the blocking probability increases with increases in load and decreases as the size of the waiting room increases.

These $M/M/1$ queues can be used to model the arrival of messages at a buffer whose output is a transmission line. The time required to "serve a customer" in this case is the length of the message in bits divided by the transmission rate. The messages may arrive at random from a number of different sources. An infinite waiting room or buffer approximates the case where the probability of too many messages in the buffer is negligible. Since

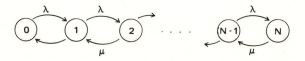

Figure 3.9. State transition flow diagram—$M/M/1$ queue finite waiting room.

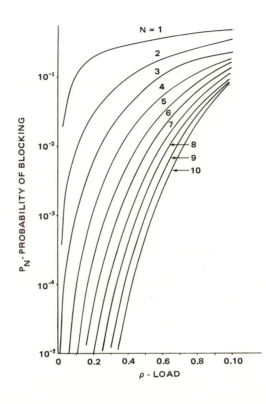

Figure 3.10. Blocking probability as a function of load.

the lengths of messages in the queue are independent of one another, the number of bits required to store the messages is the sum of a random number of independent random variables.

The difficulty with the model is the assumption of the exponential length of messages. This implies that messages have a continuous distribution and can be of any length greater than zero. In both aspects we have an approximation since messages are in bits and messages should contain overhead information. Nevertheless, studies have shown that the exponential distribution is a reasonable approximation in many applications. As we shall see in Chapter 10, the assumption of exponential message length is useful in dealing with networks of queues.

The message arrival model in this application also merits comment. The assumption is that messages arrive at the buffer instantaneously. If the input lines are of the same speed or lower than the output lines this is again an approximation. Processes where arrivals occur over a period of time may be modeled by the theory of dams.[7]

After we have considered queueing models with more than one server, we shall apply these models to a communications example.

3.6.3. The $M/M/S$ Queue—Infinite Waiting Room

As the next variation on the basic theme we shall consider the $M/M/S$ queue with an infinite waiting room in which there are $S \geq 1$ servers. If the number of customers is less than the number of servers all customers receive service simultaneously. If the number of customers is greater than the number of servers a queue forms. In any event, each of the customers receiving service may depart in an incremental interval with probability $\mu\delta$. If there are j customers simultaneously being served, the probability of one departure in an incremental interval is $j\mu\delta$. The probability of more than one departure in an incremental interval is negligible. If the waiting room is infinite the arrival rate is independent of the number of customers in the system. We have

$$\mu_n = \begin{cases} n\mu, & n \leq S \\ S\mu, & n > S \end{cases} \tag{3.34}$$

The state transition flow diagram for this case is shown in Figure 3.11. From equations (3.26a) and (3.26b) we have

$$P_n = \begin{cases} P_0 \rho^n/n!, & n \leq S \\ P_0 \rho^n/(S!S^{n-S}), & n > S \end{cases} \tag{3.35a}$$

where

$$P_0 = \left[\sum_{n=0}^{S-1} \frac{\rho^n}{n!} + \frac{S\rho^S}{S!(S-\rho)} \right]^{-1} \tag{3.35b}$$

In order for this solution to obtain we must have $\lambda/\mu S = \rho/S < 1$. This is essentially the same condition for stability as for the $M/M/1$ queue.

In connection with this model, a quantity of interest is the probability that a customer arrives to find all of the servers busy. From equations (3.35a) and (3.35b) this is seen to be

$$P_c = \sum_{n=S}^{\infty} P_n = \frac{S\rho^S/S!(S-\rho)}{\sum_{n=0}^{S-1}(\rho^n/n!) + [S\rho^S/S!(S-\rho)]} \tag{3.36}$$

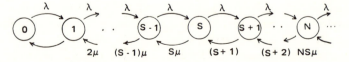

Figure 3.11. State transition flow diagram—$M/M/S$ queue with infinite waiting room.

This is the Erlang C formula (after A. K. Erlang; see Chapter 1), which was obtained in connection with voice traffic on the telephone network. The Erlang C formula is plotted in Figure 3.12, where P_c is shown as a function of ρ with S as a parameter.

3.6.4. The $M/M/S/N$ Queue—Finite Waiting Room

Another widely applicable formula is obtained by considering the model of the $M/M/S$ queue with a finite waiting room. As in the earlier arrival case of a finite waiting room, there can be no new arrival when the waiting room is full, i.e., $\lambda_n = 0$ for $n \geq N$, where N is the total number in the system. The following coefficients describe the system:

$$\mu_n = \begin{cases} n\mu, & n \leq S \\ S\mu, & n > S \end{cases} \tag{3.37a}$$

$$\lambda_n = \begin{cases} \lambda, & n < N \\ 0, & n \geq N \end{cases} \tag{3.37b}$$

The state transition flow diagram in this case is shown in Figure 3.13. Again substituting these coefficients into equations (3.26a) and (3.26b) the solution can be obtained. The general solution is not difficult to find—just messy. We consider only the special case where $N = S$. In this case only the customers in the system are being served. The formula for the $M/M/S/S$ queue is

$$P_n = P_0 \rho^n / n!, \qquad n = 1, 2, \ldots, S \tag{3.38a}$$

$$P_0 = \left(\sum_{n=0}^{S} \rho^n / n! \right)^{-1} \tag{3.38b}$$

A case of interest in connection with equation (3.38) is the case $S = \infty$, the infinite server queue. An arriving customer always has a server available. We have

$$P_0 = \left[\sum_{n=0}^{\infty} \rho^n / n! \right]^{-1} = e^{-\rho} \tag{3.39a}$$

and

$$P_n = e^{-\rho} \rho^n / n!, \qquad n = 1, 2, \ldots \tag{3.39b}$$

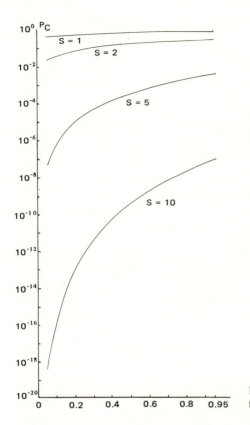

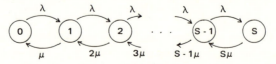

Figure 3.12. Probability of queueing as a function of load.

There are any number of other choices of coefficients which give interesting solutions. Several of the exercises at the end of the chapter illustrate this point.

The historic application of the multiple server queue is in sizing telephone trunks. It is well known that the duration of telephone calls is exponentially distributed and the arrival rate is Poisson. A certain percentage of the arriving calls are toll calls to be carried on toll trunks. The servers in this case are these trunks. The question of interest is to choose the number of trunks for a particular traffic volume. The first model of the infinite waiting room is termed blocked calls held. Equation (3.36) gives the proba-

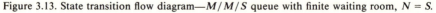

Figure 3.13. State transition flow diagram—$M/M/S$ queue with finite waiting room, $N = S$.

bility that on arriving calls are held in queue until a trunk becomes available. The case where calls cannot be held is modeled by the $M/M/S/S$ queue. The probability of an arriving call finding all trunks busy is given by equation (3.38) with $n = S$. This is the celebrated Erlang B formula. The value of equation (3.38) lies in the fact that it can be shown that the distribution is independent of the service distribution and depends only upon the mean value of the service time. This equation is plotted in Figure 3.14.

3.7. Delay—Little's Formula

In the foregoing we concentrated on the number of messages in the queue and in service. This gives an idea of the size of storage facilities that are necessary. In computer communications networks the size of the queue indicates data buffering that may be required. An alternative measure of performance is delay, i.e., the time elapsing between customer arrival and

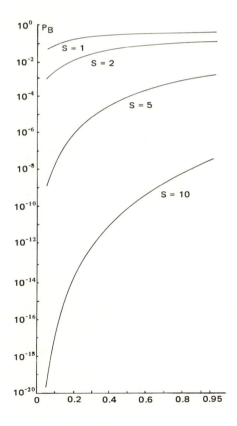

Figure 3.14. Probability of blocking as a function of load.

completion of service. We consider first the $M/M/1$ queue with an infinite waiting room. Equation (3.27) gives the portion of the time that the system has n customers in the queue or in service. But due to the random nature of the Poisson arrival process, the arrival distribution is the same as the distribution seen by an outside observer. Therefore the probability of an arriving customer meeting n customers is given by equation (3.27). If the queueing discipline is first-come first-served, the newly arrived customer must wait until the n customers already in the queue have been served. After this queueing delay he remains in the system for an amount of time required for service. We find first the distribution of the time in the queue. This is the time a customer spends waiting to receive service (see Figure 3.15). The device used to make this calculation is first to decompose events into subsets of disjoint events:

$$Q(t) \triangleq P[\text{queueing time} \leq t]$$

$$= P[\text{empty queue}] \tag{3.40}$$

$$+ \sum_{n=1}^{\infty} P[n \text{ completions in } (0, t)/n \text{ found on arrival}]P_n$$

where P_n is as in equation (3.27). Now since the service time is exponential, hence memoryless, the remaining service time of the customer already in service is also exponentially distributed with mean $1/\mu$. The time required for n service completions is the n-fold convolution of exponential densities with mean value $1/\mu$ given by†

$$f_n(t) = \frac{\mu(\mu t)^{n-1}}{(n-1)!} e^{-\mu t}, \qquad t \geq 0 \tag{3.41}$$

†This can be seen by induction on n. Another approach is Laplace transforms using the same relations used in connection with equations (3.14a) and (3.14b).

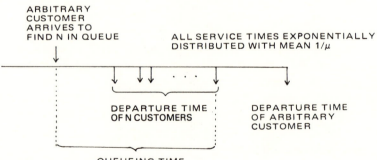

Figure 3.15. Queueing time and total delay.

This is called the Erlang type-n distribution. Substituting into equation (3.40) we have

$$
\begin{aligned}
Q(t) &= (1 - \rho) + (1 - \rho) \sum_{n=1}^{\infty} \rho^n \int_0^t \frac{\mu(\mu x)^{n-1}}{(n-1)!} e^{-\mu x} \, dx \\
&= (1 - \rho) + \rho(1 - \rho) \int_0^t \mu \, e^{-\mu x} \sum_{n=1}^{\infty} \frac{(\mu x \rho)^{n-1}}{(n-1)!} \, dx \\
&= (1 - \rho) + \rho(1 - \rho) \int_0^t \mu \, e^{-\mu x(1-\rho)} \, dx \\
&= 1 - \rho \, e^{-\mu(1-\rho)t}, \qquad t \geqslant 0
\end{aligned}
\tag{3.42}
$$

Notice in equation (3.42) $Q(0) = 1 - \rho$, the probability of the queue being empty. The probability density function of the queueing time is given by the derivative with respect to t

$$
q(t) = \delta(t)(1 - \rho) + \lambda(1 - \rho) \, e^{-\mu(1-\rho)t}, \qquad t \geqslant 0
\tag{3.43}
$$

where $\delta(t)$ is the Dirac delta function. The total delay of a customer is the sum of two independent random variables: the queueing time and the service time of a customer. The probability density of the delay of a customer is found by convolving $q(t)$ with the service time distribution. We find that the delay density is given by

$$
\begin{aligned}
d(t) &= (1 - \rho)\mu \, e^{-\mu t} + \lambda(1 - \rho)\mu \int_0^t e^{-\mu(1-\rho)(t-\tau)} \, e^{-\mu \tau} \, d\tau \\
&= (1 - \rho)\mu \, e^{-\mu t} + \lambda(1 - \rho)\mu \, e^{-\mu(1-\rho)t} \int_0^t e^{-\lambda \tau} \, d\tau \\
&= (1 - \rho)\mu \, e^{-\mu t} + (1 - \rho)\mu \, e^{-(\mu-\lambda)t}(1 - e^{-\lambda t}) \\
&= (\mu - \lambda) \, e^{-(\mu-\lambda)t}, \qquad t \geqslant 0
\end{aligned}
\tag{3.44}
$$

Thus the delay is exponentially distributed with mean

$$
\bar{d} = \frac{1}{\mu - \lambda} = \frac{1}{\lambda} \frac{\rho}{1 - \rho}
\tag{3.45}
$$

which is the mean service time divided by the factor $(1 - \rho)$. From equations (3.28b) and (3.45) we have the relationship

$$
\bar{n} = \lambda \bar{d}
\tag{3.46}
$$

where $\bar{n}$ is the average number of messages in the system. This formula is eminently reasonable. Consider a departing customer; he has spent an average amount of time $\bar{d}$ in the system. While waiting in line new customers arrive so that at departure an average of $\lambda\bar{d}$ remain in the system. For equilibrium the average number at departure should be the same as at arrival.

Equation (3.46) is broadly applicable and is known as *Little's* formula. The formula is true for non-Poisson arrivals and nonexponential distributions of service times. It also holds for arbitrary order of service, not just first-come first-served. Thus given the average number in the system and the average arrival rate, average delay can be found. A general proof is due to Jewel[5] under the following hypotheses:

1. At some point in time the system becomes empty with probability 1.
2. There is a certain stationarity in that an arrival to an empty system begins the queueing process afresh; an arrival is what is termed a renewal point.
3. While the server (or servers) is occupied, the mean delay and the mean time between arrivals is finite.
4. The expected number of customers in the system is finite during a busy period.

Since we have not at this point studied the busy period of queues we must hold in abeyance questions of the applicability of Little's formula. Nevertheless it is safe to say that it is difficult to conceive a physical system in which the conditions necessary for Little's formula do not apply [with the possible exception of condition (2)]. In order to illustrate the generality of Little's formula we shall apply it to queueing delay. We conceive of the queue as a system which the customer departs when he begins service. From equation (3.43) it can be shown that the average queueing time for the $M/M/1$ queue is

$$\bar{d}_Q = \frac{\lambda}{\mu}\frac{1}{\mu(1-\rho)} = \frac{\rho/\mu}{1-\rho} \tag{3.47}$$

From equation (3.30) we have

$$\bar{q} = \lambda\bar{d}_Q$$

We proceed now to prove Little's formula for the case of Poisson arrivals at a single server with a general distribution of service time and a first-come first-served discipline. The probability of n customers in the system when a customer departs is equal to the probability that they arrived while the customer was in the system. Given that the total time spent in the system by a customer is t, the probability of n remaining in the system is

$(\lambda t)^n e^{-\lambda t}/n!$. Averaging over the delay we have

$$P_n = \int_0^\infty \frac{(\lambda t)^n e^{-\lambda t}}{n!} f_D(t)\, dt$$

where $f_D(t)$ is the probability density of delay. There is an interesting relationship between the probability generating function for delay and the Laplace transform of delay. We have for the probability generating function

$$
\begin{aligned}
G_n(z) &= \sum_{n=0}^\infty z^n P_n = \sum_{n=0}^\infty z^n \int_0^\infty \frac{(\lambda t)^n e^{-\lambda t}}{n!}\, d(t)\, dt \\
&= \int_0^\infty e^{-\lambda t}\left[\sum_{n=0}^\infty \frac{(z\lambda t)^n}{(n-1)!} \right] d(t)\, dt \\
&= \int_0^\infty e^{-\lambda t(1-z)} d(t)\, dt \\
&= \mathscr{D}(\lambda(1-z))
\end{aligned}
\tag{3.48}
$$

where $\mathscr{D}(s)$ is the Laplace transform of the delay density, $d(t)$. Notice that equation (3.48) holds irrespective of the form of the probability density of delay. Differentiating both sides of (3.48) and setting $z = 1$, we find Little's formula $\bar{N} = \lambda \bar{D}$.

The preceding argument for Little's formula holds for an arbitrary service time, but it is predicated on the first-come-first-served discipline and Poisson arrivals. We now present, in slightly altered form, a heuristic line of reasoning due to P. J. Burke which justifies the general result. Guests arrive at a certain vacation resort at an average rate of λ per unit time interval. Each guest pays in advance for his stay. Fees depend only on the length of the stay at the resort. The average income over an interval of t time units is then $t\lambda \bar{d}\$$, where $\bar{d}$ is the average duration of a stay and $\$$ is the price of accommodation per guest per unit time interval. It happens that the resort is completely nonprofit and income is balanced by expenses. The cost of keeping a guest for a unit time interval is $\$$ per guest. If $\bar{N}$ is the average number of guests at the resort in a time interval, the average cost of running the resort in an interval t time units in duration is $\$t\bar{N}$. The analogs are obvious and we have over a long time interval, $\lambda \bar{d} = \bar{N}$.

In order to further illustrate the generality of Little's formula, we consider delay in the $M/M/S$ queue. As in the case of the $M/M/1$ queue we start with the amount of work in the system encountered by a newly arriving customer. If the number of customers in the system, n, is less than the number of servers, an arrival is served immediately and there is no queueing time. If $n \geq S$ a new customer must queue until $n - S + 1$ previous customers have departed from the system, having completed service. Since there are S simultaneous servers the departure rate is $S\mu$. The sum of $n - S + 1$ departure intervals has an Erlang type $n - S + 1$ distribution $\mu S(\mu St)^{n-S} e^{-\mu St}/(n - S)!$. The probability distribution of the queueing time is given by

$$Q(t) \triangleq P[\text{queueing time} \leq t]$$

$$= P[\text{queueing time} = 0] + \sum_{n=S}^{\infty} P[\text{queueing time} \leq t/n \text{ customers}]P_n$$

If P_0 is the probability of no customers in the system, from equations (3.35a) and (3.35b) we have

$$Q(t) = P_0 \left[\sum_{n=0}^{S-1} \rho^n/n! + \sum_{n=S}^{\infty} \frac{\rho^n}{S!S^{n-S}} \int_0^t \frac{\mu S(\mu S\tau)^{n-S}}{(n-S)!} e^{-\mu S\tau} d\tau \right]; \qquad t \geq 0$$

$$= 1 - P_0 \left[\frac{S\rho^S}{S!(S-\rho)} - \frac{\rho^S}{(S-1)!} \int_0^t \mu e^{-\mu S\tau} \sum_{n=S}^{\infty} \frac{(\mu\rho\tau)^{n-S}}{(n-S)!} d\tau \right]; \qquad t \geq 0$$

$$= 1 - P_0 \left[\frac{S\rho^S}{S!(S-\rho)} - \frac{\rho^S}{(S-1)!} \int_0^t \mu e^{-\mu\tau(S-\rho)} d\tau \right]; \qquad t \geq 0$$

$$= 1 - P_0 \left[\frac{S\rho^S}{S!(S-\rho)} - \frac{\rho^S(1 - e^{-\mu(S-\rho)t})}{(S-1)!(S-\rho)} \right]; \qquad t \geq 0$$

The density function of the queueing delay is given by

$$q(t) = \left\{ 1 - P_0 \left[\frac{S\rho^S}{S!(S-\rho)} \right] \right\} \delta(t) + \left[\frac{\mu P_0 \rho^S e^{-\mu(S-\rho)t}}{(S-1)!} \right] U(t) \quad (3.49)$$

Again as in the $M/M/1$ queue, queueing delay and service time are independent random variables. The density function of total delay, queueing delay, plus service time is found by convolving the density function for queueing delay with the density function of the service time. We find

$$d(t) = \left\{ 1 - P_0 \left[\frac{S\rho^S}{S!(S-\rho)} \right] \right\} \mu e^{-\mu t} - \frac{\mu P_0 \rho^S [e^{-\mu(S-\rho)t} - e^{-\mu t}]}{(S-1)!(1-S-\rho)}; \qquad t \geq 0$$

$$(3.50)$$

From equations (3.49) and (3.50), Little's formula can be demonstrated. (See Exercises 3.14 and 3.15.)

3.8. Burke's Theorem

The final property of the $M/M/S$ queue with infinite waiting room that we consider in this chapter is the departure process. In particular we shall prove Burke's theorem, which states that the departure process from an $M/M/S$ queue is Poisson. As we shall see in Chapter 10 the departure process is important in the study of tandem queues. We shall carry through a proof of Burke's theorem due to Galliher.[6] We simplify matters somewhat by considering only the case $S = 1$. The proof for $S > 1$ is quite similar. Let the average arrival rate of customers be λ per second and let the mean service time for each of the servers be $1/\mu$ sec. We place departures over the interval $(0, t + \delta)$. Let $D(t_1, t_2), 0 \le t_1, t_2 < \tau$ denote the number of departures in the interval $[t_1, t_2)$ and $N(\tau)$ the number of customers in the system at time $\tau, 0 \le \tau < t + \delta$. Consider the subintervals $(0, \delta)$ and $(\delta, t + \delta)$. (See Figure 3.16.) If, as we have seen in previous sections in connection with birth–death processes, δ is small enough, then in the interval $[0, \delta)$ there can be at most one arrival or departure with probability $\lambda\delta$ or $\mu\delta$, respectively. The probability of neither an arrival nor a departure is $[1 - \lambda\delta - \mu\delta]$. We decompose the event of j departures in the interval $(0, t + \delta)$ into three disjoint events according to events in the interval $[0, \delta]$, an arrival, a departure, or nothing. We also condition on there being k customers in the system at time $t = 0$. Let us assume for the moment that the number of departures is $j > 0$. For $k > 0$ we have

$$P[D(0, t + \delta) = j / N(0) = k]$$

$$= \lambda\delta P[D(\delta, t + \delta) = j / N(0) = k, \text{arrival in } (0, \delta)]$$

$$+ \mu\delta P[D(\delta, t + \delta) = (j - 1) / N(0) = k, \text{departure in } (0, \delta)]$$

$$+ (1 - \lambda\delta - \mu\delta) P[D(\delta, t + \delta) = j / N(0) = k,$$

$$\text{neither arrival nor departure in } (0, \delta)] \qquad (3.51a)$$

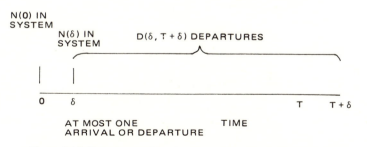

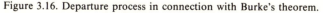

Figure 3.16. Departure process in connection with Burke's theorem.

and for $k = 0$ since we cannot have a departure in $(0, \delta)$ we have

$$P[D(0, t + \delta) = j/N(0) = 0]$$

$$= \lambda \delta P[D(\delta, t + \delta) = j/N(\delta) = 0, \text{arrival in } (0, \delta)] \qquad (3.51b)$$

$$+ (1 - \lambda \delta)P[D(\delta, t + \delta) = j/N(\delta) = 0, \text{no arrival in } (0, \delta)]$$

We point out that in the interval $(\delta, t + \delta)$ there can be any number of arrivals to the system. We can write the right-hand side of equations (3.51a) and (3.51b) in terms of the number in the system at time, $t = \delta$:

$$P[D(0, t + \delta) = j/N(0) = k]$$

$$= \lambda \delta P[D(\delta, t + \delta) = j/N(\delta) = k + 1]$$

$$+ \mu \delta P[D(\delta, t + \delta) = (j - 1)/N(\delta) = k - 1]$$

$$+ (1 - \mu \delta - \lambda \delta)P[D(\delta, t + \delta) = j/N(\delta) = k] \qquad (3.52a)$$

$$P[D(0, t + \delta) = j/N(0) = 0]$$

$$= \lambda \delta P(D(\delta, t) = j/N(\delta) = 1)$$

$$+ (1 - \lambda \delta)P(D(\delta, t + \delta) = j/N(\delta) = 0) \qquad (3.52b)$$

Equations (3.52a) and (3.52b) are another example of equations for the change in a probability distribution in an increment of time. In this case there is a slight difference. We go from a t-second interval $(\delta, t + \delta)$ to a $(t + \delta)$-second interval $(0, t + \delta)$. Again letting $\delta \to 0$ we obtain a set of differential equations:

$$\frac{dP[D(0, t) = j/N(0) = k]}{dt}$$

$$= \lambda P[D(0, t) = j/N(0) = k + 1]$$

$$+ \mu P[D(0, t) = (j - 1)/N(0) = k - 1]$$

$$- (\mu + \lambda)P[D(0, t) = j/N(0) = k] \qquad (3.53a)$$

$$\frac{dP[D(0, t) = j/N(0) = 0]}{dt}$$

$$= \lambda P[D(0, t) = j/N(0) = 1]$$

$$- \lambda P[D(0, t) = j/N(0) = 0] \qquad (3.53b)$$

Assuming the queue is in equilibrium at time $t = 0$, we have from equation (3.27) $P[N(0) = k] = \rho^k(1 - \rho)$, where $\rho = \lambda/\mu$. We have then that

$$P[D(0, t) = j/N(0) = k] = \frac{P[D(0, t) = j, N(0) = k]}{\rho^k(1 - \rho)}$$

Substituting into equations (3.53a)–(3.53b), we obtain, after some manipulation,

$$\frac{dP[D(0, t) = j, N(0) = k]}{dt}$$

$$= \mu P[D(0, t) = j, N(0) = k + 1]$$
$$+ \lambda P[D(0, t) = j - 1, N(0) = k - 1]$$
$$- (\mu + \lambda)P[D(0, t) = j, N(0) = k]; k > 0 \quad (3.54a)$$

$$\frac{dP[D(0, t) = j, N(0) = 0]}{dt}$$

$$= \mu P[D(0, t) = j, N(0) = 1]$$
$$- \lambda P[D(0, t) = j, N(0) = 0] \quad (3.54b)$$

Summing over disjoint events

$$P[D(0, t) = j] = \sum_{k=0}^{\infty} P[D(0, t) = J, N(0) = k]$$

Applying this to equations (3.54a) and (3.54b) we have for $j > 0$

$$\frac{dP[D(0, t) = j]}{dt} = -\lambda\{P[D(0, t) = j - 1] - P[D(0, t) = j]\} \quad (3.55)$$

A similar analysis applies to the case $j = 0$. We write for $k > 0$

$$P[D(0, t + \delta) = 0/N(0) = k]$$

$$= \lambda\delta P[D(\delta, t + \delta) = 0/N(\delta) = k + 1]$$
$$+ (1 - \lambda\delta - \mu\delta)P[D(\delta, t + \delta) = 0/N(\delta) = k] \quad (3.56)$$

For the case $k = 0$, there is no term $\mu\delta$ in the RHS of equation (3.56). If we follow through the same analysis as before, we find

$$\frac{dP[D(0, t) = 0]}{dt} = -\lambda P[D(0, t) = 0] \quad (3.57)$$

If we compare equations (3.55) and (3.57) with equations (3.12a) and (3.12b) we see that the process $P[D(0, t) = j]$ is a Poisson process with average rate λ. We make the identification

$$P[D(0, t) = j] = P_j(t)$$

3.9. Communications Example

We consider in this section an application of some of our queueing theoretic results to a communications problem. Suppose that a 50-Kbps line is available for data transmission. This line can be used in either of two ways. Time-division multiplexing (TDM) can be used to provide five 10-Kbps channels or the full 50-Kbps rate can be used to transmit messages.

Let us assume that messages arrive at a Poisson rate and are exponentially distributed. As we shall see in Chapter 5, if average message lengths are long enough, the transmission line may be treated as a continuously available server in TDM systems. We may assume that this condition applies in the present case. From Little's formula the average message delay is given by

$$\bar{D} = \frac{1}{\mu\rho} \bar{N} \tag{3.58}$$

where $\bar{N}$ is the average number of messages in the system. For the TDM case this can be found from equations (3.35a) and (3.35b) with $S = 5$. The results are plotted as a function of load in Figure 3.17 for average message lengths of 1000 bits and 2000 bits. Also plotted in Figure 3.17 is the average delay when the full 50-Kbps channel is used for all arriving messages. In this case there is a single server but the average time required to transmit a message is one fifth what it is for the TDM case. Then this case may be treated as an $M/M/1$ queue.

The plots show a result which is of particular interest in the computer communications where bursty traffic is a factor. For light loading the delay for TDM is five times what it is for the full channel. For light loading there is little queueing delay and the time required to transmit a message dominates. As the load increases queueing delay becomes more important and delays tend to be equal for both systems. For heavy load all of the channels in TDM are in use and the departure rate of messages is the same as the full channel case.

3.10. Method of Stages

The extension of the birth–death process to multiple dimensions provides a way of analyzing systems where the service time is not exponential

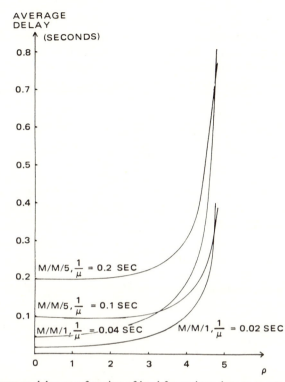

Figure 3.17. Average delay as a function of load for various departure rates, for an $M/M/5$ server queue and an $M/M/1$ server queue with infinite waiting room.

but may be approximated as the sum of independent exponentially distributed random variables. The technique was devised by Erlang himself and is called the method of stages. As the name implies, we imagine the customer service time to be composed of a sequence of stages each of which has an exponentially distributed duration. (See Figure 3.18.)

The state of the system is the number of customers in the system, waiting in line and in service, augmented by the current stage of the customer in service. As in the one-dimensional case, only single events can occur in

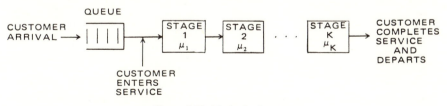

Figure 3.18. Method of stages.

an incremental interval. Since arrivals are Poisson, there can be at most one arrival. Because of the exponential nature of the stages, there can be at most one transition from one stage to another or out of the system. Again we can write a set of equilibrium equations, equating flow out of a state to flow into a state. The state transition flow diagram is shown in Figure 3.19. Define

$$P_{n,i} = P(n \text{ customers, customer in stage } i),$$

$$n = 1, 2, \ldots, \qquad i = 1, 2, , \ldots, K$$

where K is the total number of stages. Let λ be the average arrival rate of customers and let $1/\mu_i$, $i = 1, 2, \ldots, K$, be the average time spent by a customer in stage i. We may write

$$P_{00}\lambda = P_{1K}\mu_K \tag{3.59a}$$

$$P_{11}(\lambda + \mu_1) = P_{00}\lambda + P_{2K}\mu_K \tag{3.59b}$$

$$P_{1i}(\lambda + \mu_i) = P_{1i-1}\mu_{i-1}, \qquad 1 < i \le K \tag{3.59c}$$

$$P_{n1}(\lambda + \mu_1) = P_{n-1,1}\lambda + P_{n+1,K}\mu_K, \qquad n > 1 \tag{3.59d}$$

$$P_{n,i}(\lambda + \mu_i) = P_{n-1,i}\lambda + P_{n,i-1}\mu_{i-1}, \qquad n > 1, 1 < i \le K \tag{3.59e}$$

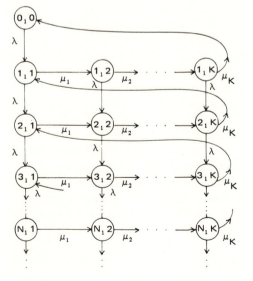

Figure 3.19. State transition flow diagram—method of stages.

Each of these equations is obtained by a straightforward application of the basic principle. In equation (3.59e), for example, the system leaves state (n, i) when a customer arrives or when a customer departs stage i. The state is entered by an arrival or by a transition from stage $i - 1$ to i. In addition to these equations we also have the normalizing condition

$$P_{00} + \sum_{n=1}^{\infty} \sum_{i=1}^{K} P_{ni} = 1$$

Solutions for equations (3.59a)–(3.59e) can be found by simple substitution. For example, consider the case of only two stages, $K = 2$. From equations (3.59a)–(3.59e) we find

$$P_{12} = (\lambda/\mu_2)P_{00}$$

$$P_{11} = [(\lambda + \mu_2)/\mu_1]P_{12}$$

$$P_{22} = [(\lambda + \mu_1)P_{11} - \lambda P_{00}]/\mu_2$$

$$P_{21} = [(\lambda + \mu_2)P_{22} - \lambda P_{12}]/\mu_1$$

$$P_{n+1,2} = [(\lambda + \mu_1)P_{n1} - \lambda P_{n-1,1}]/\mu_2, \qquad n = 2, 3, \ldots$$

$$P_{n1} = [(\lambda + \mu_2)P_{n2} - \lambda P_{n-1,2}]/\mu_1, \qquad n = 2, 3, \ldots$$

We see that everything can be expressed in terms of P_{00}, which can be found from the normalizing condition.

The Laplace transform of the service time for the foregoing is

$$S(s) = \prod_{i=1}^{K} \mu_i/(s + \mu_i) \tag{3.60}$$

When μ_i is the same for all i we have the K stage Erlangian distribution. In this case the queue is called the $M/E^{(K)}/1$ queue.

Extensions of this basic concept are straightforward. For example, a finite waiting room can be handled by making the arrival rate a function of the number in the system. By allowing more than one customer in service at a time, multiple servers can be accommodated. Cox[10] has developed this technique to the point of obtaining service distributions whose Laplace transform is an arbitrary rational function. The idea is illustrated in Figure 3.20. Again there are K exponentially distributed stages, but the customer can enter a stage or depart from the system according to fixed probabilities for each stage. The state of the system is no more complicated than before,

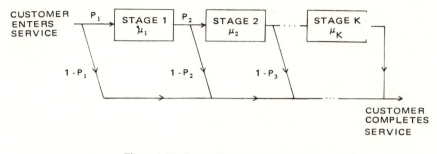

Figure 3.20. Generalized method of stages.

consisting of the number of customers in the system and the stage of the customer in service. The Laplace transform of the service time is

$$\mathcal{M}(s) = 1 - P_1 + \sum_{j=1}^{K} P_1 \cdots P_{j-1}(1 - P_j) \prod_{i=1}^{j} \frac{\mu_i}{s + \mu_i} \quad (3.61)$$

By use of a partial fraction expansion, a rational function with simple roots can be put into the form

$$\mathcal{M}(s) = \alpha_0 + \sum_{i=1} \frac{\alpha_i}{s + \mu_i} \quad (3.62)$$

where the α_i, $i = 0, 1, \ldots, K$, are functions of the μ_i and the P_i. Now given any service time distribution whose Laplace transform can be expressed as a rational function in s,

$$\mathcal{M}(s) = \frac{\mathcal{N}(s)}{\mathcal{D}(s)} \quad (3.63)$$

By means of partial fraction expansions equation (3.63) can be put in the form of equation (3.62) and the service time may be represented by the generalized method of stages.

The obvious problem with the method of stages is computational complexity. However, it does lead to a solution in terms of the probability distribution of the number of customers in the system. In the next chapter we shall look at an imbedded Markov chain approach to the problem of general service time distribution. A solution is obtained in terms of Laplace transforms.

References

1. W. Feller, *An Introduction to Probability Theory and Its Applications*, Vol. I, John Wiley, New York (1957).
2. L. Kleinrock, *Queueing Systems*, Vol. I: *Theory*, John Wiley, New York (1975).
3. R. B. Cooper, *Introduction to Queueing Theory*, Macmillan, New York (1972).
4. H. Kobayashi, *Modeling and Analysis, An Introduction to System Performance Evaluation Methodology*, Addison-Wesley, Reading, Massachusetts (1978).
5. W. S. Jewell, "A Simple Proof of $L = \lambda W$," *Operations Research* **15**(6), 109–116 (1967).
6. H. P. Galliher, *Notes on Operations Research*, M.I.T. Technology Press, Operations Research Center, Cambridge, Massachusetts (1959), Chap 4.
7. P. A. P. Moran, *Theory of Storage*, Methuen, New York (1959).
8. W. Feller, Ref. 1, pp. 407–411.
9. D. R. Cox and W. L. Smith, *Queues*, Methuen, New York (1961).
10. D. R. Cox, "A Use of Complex Probabilities in Theory of Stochastic Processes," *Proceedings of the Cambridge Philosophical Society* **51**, 313–319 (1955).

Exercises

3.1. A gambler bets on the appearance of a 7 in the toss of a pair of dice. After 50 tosses a seven has only appeared once.
(a) Are the dice loaded? (Calculate the probabilities.)
(b) If the dice are not loaded, how many trials would be necessary for the probability of at least one 7 to be 0.99?

3.2. Messages arrive at a telephone exchange at a Poisson rate of 6000 messages in a busy hour on the average. What is the probability of more than 500 calls in a given 3-minute interval? (Just show the proper expression.)

3.3. The duration D of a telephone conversation is distributed according to $P_r[D \leq t] = 1 - e^{-t/3}$, $t \geq 0$.
(a) What is the average duration of the call?
(b) If you are waiting outside a telephone booth (in the wind and rain), how long should you expect to wait assuming you arrived 1 min after the call started?
(c) If you did (a) and (b) right, there is a paradox. Explain.

3.4. In the text we proved that the sum of independent Poisson processes is Poisson. Give an alternate derivation involving probability generating functions.

3.5. As in Exercise 3.4, consider the sum of two independent Poisson processes. Show that the interval between arrivals in the sum process is exponentially distributed. (*Hint:* No arrivals in an interval means no arrival from either process.)

3.6. Suppose that a Poisson message arrival process is split deterministically, i.e., alternate arrivals are placed in one of two different bins.

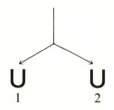

Describe the arrival process at bin No. 2.

3.7. The time between the failures of components in a certain electronic system is exponentially distributed. However, the average of the distribution depends on the number of components that have already failed since component failures put stress on the functioning components.

(a) Sketch the state transition flow diagram for the number of failed components. Assume that the number of failed components is small.

(b) Write down the set of differential equations governing this system.

3.8. Suppose that a buffer holds exactly M fixed length messages. Messages arrive at the buffer at a Poisson rate with an average of λ messages per second. As soon as the buffer is full there are no new arrivals.

(a) Write down the set of differential equations for the probability of m messages in the buffer at time t.

(b) Solve these equations.

3.9. In a pure birth process assume that each member of a population may split in two in the interval $(t, t + \Delta t)$ with the probability $\lambda \Delta t + O(\Delta t)$; one will remain the same with probability $1 - \lambda \Delta t + O(\Delta t)$ as $\Delta t \to 0$. Assume initial condition $P_1(0) = 1$.

(a) Find the differential equation for $P_n(t)$, i.e., probability of population of size n at time t.

(b) Show that the generating function

$$P(z, t) \triangleq \sum_{n=0}^{\infty} z^n P_n(t)$$

satisfies

$$P(z, t) = z\,e^{-\lambda t}/(1 - z + z\,e^{-\lambda t})$$

[Hint: Sum over both sides of the differential equation in (a).]

(c) Find $E[N(t)]$ (expected population at time t).

(d) Solve for $P_k(t)$.

3.10. An undergraduate engineering society holds a beer and pizza party every year. These are enormously successful events and tend to become crowded. Several insightful graduate students notice a rate of change in the arrival pattern.

When there are places to sit in the room the arrival rate is λ_1 students per second. When there is only room to stand the arrival rate is λ_2 students per second ($\lambda_1 < \lambda_2$). When the room becomes so crowded that one cannot get near the bar the arrival rate is zero. Assume the room is empty at the beginning of the party and no one leaves the party until it is over. Assume also that there are n_1 chairs and that bar service ceases when there are n_2 people in the room.

  (a) Write down the set of differential equations for the probability of k people in the room at time t.

  (b) Solve these equations.

3.11. Consider a birth–death process with discouraged arrivals. We have

$$\lambda_n = \frac{\lambda}{n+1} \quad \text{and} \quad \mu_n = \mu$$

Find P_n for all n.

3.12. Suppose customers are drawn from a finite source population. Once a customer is in the queue or in service, there can be no more arrivals from that source. Assuming that there are S servers we have

$$\lambda_n = (N-n)\lambda \quad \text{and} \quad \mu_n = \begin{cases} n\mu, & n \le S \\ S\mu, & n > S \end{cases}$$

Find P_n for all n if $N > S$.

3.13. Customers arrive at a Poisson rate to a single-server queue with infinite waiting room. The average arrival rate is λ per second and the average service time is $1/\mu$. Upon service completion a customer either leaves the system with probability q or rejoins the queue.

  (a) Write down the equilibrium equations.

  (b) Solve equations for the probability distribution for the number of customers in the queue.

3.14. Demonstrate the Little formula for the $M/M/S$ queue by calculating average delay and average number in the system separately for the case $S = 2$.

3.15. Find an expression for the average delay for the $M/M/S$ queue for an infinite waiting room. Do this two ways.

3.16. Customers having exponentially distributed service times arrive at a service facility at a Poisson rate. Assume that the service facility has a waiting room which can hold only two customers in addition to the one being served. Customers arriving to a full waiting room leave the system. When service is completed for a customer, the next customer is the most recent arrival.

  (a) Sketch the state transition flow diagram for this system.

  (b) Write down the equilibrium equations.

  (c) Solve the equilibrium equations.

  (d) Write down an expression for the average amount of time a customer spends in the system.

3.17. In the text it was stated that the $M/M/1$ queue could be used to approximate the situation where randomly arriving messages of variable length are transmitted over a channel. Suppose that the average message length is 128 bytes (8-bit) and the line bit rate is 4800 bits per second. Messages arrive at an average rate of 7500 per busy hour.

(a) What is the probability of the buffer being empty? (Assume that the buffer holds messages being transmitted as well as messages waiting to be transmitted.)

(b) What is the average number of messages in the system?

(c) What is the average number of bits in the buffer?

(d) What is the average delay of a message?

(e) As we have noted, the number of bits in the buffer is a random sum of random variables. Show that the probability generating function of the total number of bits in the buffer is given by $P(M(z))$, where $P(z)$ and $M(z)$ are the generating functions of the number of messages and the number of bits per message, respectively.

3.18. Show that the intervals between departures from an $M/M/1$ queue are exponentially distributed by showing that the Laplace transform of their probability density function is

$$X(s) = \frac{\lambda}{\lambda + s}$$

where λ is the average arrival rate to the queue.

Hint: When the system is empty the interval between departures is the sum of two exponentially distributed random variables, one with mean $1/\lambda$ and the other with mean $1/\mu$; otherwise the interval between departures is exponentially distributed with mean $1/\mu$. In order to prove that the departures are Poisson, it would be necessary to show that the departure intervals are independent.

3.19. Find the probability distribution for the $M/E^{(2)}/1$ queue under the assumption that there can be at most three customers in the system.

Imbedded Markov Chains
The *M*/*G*/1 Queue

4.1. Introduction

The queueing model considered to this point is predicated on exponentially distributed service times. This is appropriate to voice communications where the holding time of a call is exponentially distributed. However, as we have seen in Chapter 2, in computer communications a frequently used technique is *packet* switching, in which data messages are broken up into fixed-size blocks each of which are addressed, thereby forming a packet. Packets are routed through the network as separate entities by means of the addresses. Packet switching allows facilities to be shared among many bursty data sources; each source is given full access to transmission facilities according to immediate need.

Since fixed size packets require a constant transmission time, queueing models predicated upon exponential service times are not relevant. An appropriate queueing model is the *M*/*D*/1 queue, where the arrival rate to a single server is Poisson and the service time is constant or deterministic. The problems in analyzing the behavior of this sort of queue arise because there is an additional component of memory and one cannot say, as in the case of exponential service, that the event of a service completion in the next incremental interval is independent of the past given the number presently in the system. Thus, one cannot calculate delay directly from the number in the system when a message arrives, such as was done in calculating equation (3.44), for example. It is necessary to take into account the fact that the customer has been in service for some time.

As it turns out, the behavior of all service times, deterministic or otherwise, can be studied under the same framework. This is fortuitous since, as we shall see in this and subsequent chapters, a number of service distributions come into play in computer communications. In this chapter we shall study the $M/G/1$ queue, where, in accordance with the notation defined in Section 3.6 of Chapter 3, G stands for general service time.

As we have seen in Section 3.10, it is possible to analyze queues with a general distribution of service time by the method of stages. However, many of the same results can be obtained more simply by means of an analysis based on the imbedded Markov chain. The imbedded Markov chain is a widely used technique in the analysis of probabilistic systems.† It consists of choosing both a sequence of points in time in the evolution of a process and a state so that a Markov chain is formed. Let $t_1 \leq t_2 \leq \cdots \leq t_i$ be the suitably chosen points in time and let $S_1, S_2, \ldots, S_i, \ldots$ be the system states corresponding to these times. Because of the imbedded chain we have

$$
\begin{aligned}
P[S_N = l_N | S_1 = l_1, S_2 = l_2, \ldots, S_{N-1} = l_{N-1}] \\
= P[S_N = l_N | S_{N-1} = l_{N-1}]
\end{aligned}
\tag{4.1}
$$

In the analysis of the $M/G/1$ queue the points that we choose are the instants when there is a service completion and a consequent departure from the queue. We speak of a Markov chain being imbedded at these instants. These points are appropriate because there is no memory of message service times.

As in the case of the $M/M/1$ queue, we are interested in the steady-state distribution of the state after initial transients have died away. For the $M/G/1$ queue it can be shown that the steady-state solution exists if the average message arrival rate during a message transmission is less than one. A discussion of the conditions for the existence of a steady-state distribution is given in Appendix B.

4.2. The $M/G/1$ Queue

4.2.1. Imbedded Markov Chains

We consider messages arriving at a transmitter at a Poisson rate with an average λ per second. The message transmission time has probability distribution function

$$
M(t) \triangleq P[\text{transmission time} \leq t]
\tag{4.2a}
$$

---

†The idea of using the imbedded Markov chain to study the $M/G/1$ queue is due to Kendall.[1]
A review of the relevant concepts in the theory of Markov chains is given in Appendix B.

and probability density function

$$m(t) \triangleq dM(t)/dt \tag{4.2b}$$

Let the Laplace transform of $m(t)$ be denoted by

$$\mathcal{M}(s) = \mathcal{L}[m(t)] = \int_0^\infty m(t)e^{-st}\,dt \tag{4.2c}$$

We focus now upon the number of messages in the queue at departure epochs, i.e., those time instants when a transmission is completed. Given the number of messages in the system at a particular departure epoch, the number of messages in the system at future epochs depends only on new arrivals and not on past occupancies. Thus the succession of message states forms an imbedded Markov chain. Suppose that the ith departing message leaves behind a nonempty system with n_i messages. At this epoch transmission of the $(i + 1)$st message begins. While this is in progress messages continue to arrive. We denote the number of such arrivals by a_{i+1}. The state of the system at the next departure is given by

$$n_{i+1} = n_i - 1 + a_{i+1}, \qquad n_i \geq 1 \tag{4.3a}$$

If the departure of the ith message leaves the system empty, a slightly different equation describes the process. The $(i + 1)$st departing message arrived to an empty queue, consequently he leaves behind only those messages that arrived during his service period. We have

$$n_{i+1} = a_{i+1} \tag{4.3b}$$

Notice that in both equations, (4.3a) and (4.3b), the number of new arrivals is the number of arrivals during a message transmission time. The state dynamics can be summarized in the following equation:

$$n_{i+1} = n_i - U(n_i) + a_{i+1} \tag{4.4}$$

where the unit step

$$U(x) = \begin{cases} 0, & x \leq 0 \\ 1, & x > 0 \end{cases}$$

Consider now the dynamics of the state, i.e., the number of messages in the system at departure epoch. This state changes from epoch to epoch with a single departure and with new arrivals. It is not difficult to show that the probability of a return to any state at any future time is greater than zero provided that the queue is stable, i.e., the average number of departures over a time interval is equal to the average number of arrivals. This will be the case when the average arrival rate of messages during a message transmission is less than one. In this case the probability of return to a state is sufficiently large so that the return is infinitely often. It is also easy to show that the probability of reaching any state is greater than zero. In summation, provided that the queue is stable, the imbedded Markov chain described by equation (4.4) is ergodic and a steady-state probability distribution exists. (See Appendix B.)

Equation (4.3) completely characterizes the evolution of the Markov chain imbedded at the departure epochs. The random element in this equation is the number of arrivals a_i. The probability distribution of this random variable will completely determine the characteristics of the chain. Notice that since a_i is the number of arrivals during a service interval both the arrival distribution and the service distribution come into play here.

For a general service time distribution only the departure epochs are suitable imbedding points for a Markov chain of the number of customers in the system. Only exponentially distributed service times have the memoryless property discussed in Section 3.3 of Chapter 3. Thus, for a point in the midst of a generally distributed service time, the system may not be characterized only by the number in the system. It is necessary also to know how long the particular service has been in progress. This is a very much more complicated model.

We proceed to find this steady-state distribution beginning with a calculation of mean values. We take expectations on both sides of equation (4.4). Under the assumption that a steady-state solution exists,

$$\lim_{i \to \infty} E[n_{i+1}] = \lim_{i \to \infty} E[n_i] = \bar{n},$$

and we have

$$E[U(n_i)] = E[a_{i+1}] \tag{4.5}$$

$E[a_{i+1}]$ is the expected number of arrivals while a single message is being transmitted. There are two random quantities involved in a_{i+1}, the duration of the message and the number of arrivals while a message is being transmitted. We compute $E[a_{i+1}]$ by first conditioning on the message length then averaging over the message length:

$$E[a_{i+1}] = \int_0^\infty E[a_{i+1}/\text{message length} = t]m(t)\,dt$$

$$= \int_0^\infty \lambda t m(t)\,dt = \lambda \int_0^\infty t m(t)\,dt = \lambda \bar{m}$$

where $\bar{m}$ denotes the mean time required to transmit a message. In the analysis of the $M/M/s$ queue $(s \geq 1)$, we had $\bar{m} = 1/\mu$ and $\rho = \lambda/\mu$. Therefore if we define the intensity as $\rho = \lambda\bar{m}$, we are consistent with the definition in the previous chapter. Again ρ is the average number of arrivals during the time a message is being transmitted. Thus the condition $\rho < 1$ is a criterion for system stability.

We return to equation (4.5). The term $U(n_i)$ is the indicator function of the event that the number of messages in the system is greater than 0. Accordingly we have

$$E[U(n_i)] = P[\text{more than zero messages}] = 1 - P_0$$

where P_0 is the probability that the system is empty. Equation (4.5) then becomes

$$P_0 = 1 - \rho \tag{4.6}$$

We have dropped dependence on i here. The justification for this should be evident from the analysis, which has the same result that we have seen in the $M/M/1$ [see equation (3.27) in Chapter 3].

As we shall see in a number of situations in the sequel, the standard techniques for analyzing difference equations such as equation (4.4) is by means of the probability generation function of the system state which we define as

$$P_i(z) \triangleq E[z^{n_i}] = \sum_{k=0}^{\infty} z^k P[n_i = k] \tag{4.7}$$

Taking expectation on both sides of equation (4.4) we have

$$P_{i+1}(z) = E[z^{n_i - U(n_i) + a_{i+1}}] \tag{4.8}$$

The number of arrivals in a message transmission time is independent of the number of messages in the queue and we can write

$$P_{i+1} = E[z^{n_i - U(n_i)}]E[z^{a_{i+1}}]$$
$$= E[z^{n_i - U(n_i)}]A(z) \tag{4.9}$$

where $A(z) = E[z^{a_i}]$. Due to stationarity we suppress the dependence on i.

Now consider the term

$$E[z^{n_i - U(n_i)}] = \left[\sum_{k=0}^{\infty} z^{k-U(k)} \right] P[n_i = k]$$

$$= P_0 + \sum_{k=1}^{\infty} z^{k-1} P[n_i = k]$$

$$= P_0 + z^{-1} \left[\sum_{k=0}^{\infty} z^k P[n_i = k] - P_0 \right]$$

$$= P_0 + z^{-1}[P_i(z) - P_0]$$

(4.10)

From equations (4.8), (4.9), and (4.10) we have

$$P_{i+1}(z) = \{P_0 + z^{-1}(P_i(z) - P_0)\} A(z) \tag{4.11}$$

Assuming that a steady-state solution exists we have

$$\lim_{i \to \infty} P_{i+1}(z) = \lim_{i \to \infty} P_i(z) = P(z)$$

Utilizing equation (4.6) we have

$$P(z) = \frac{(1 - \rho)(1 - z)A(z)}{A(z) - z} \tag{4.12}$$

This generating function allows us to find the moments of the distribution of the number of messages in the queue. Clearing fractions in equation (4.12) and differentiating successively, we have

$$P'(z)[A(z) - z] + P(z)[A'(z) - 1] = (1 - \rho)(-1)A(z) + (1 - \rho)(1 - z)A'(z)$$

$$P''(z)[A(z) - z] + 2P'(z)[A'(z) - 1] + P(z)A''(z)$$

$$= 2(1 - \rho)(-1)A'(z) + (1 - \rho)(1 - z)A''(z)$$

We let $z = 1$; since $A(1) = P(1) = 1$, we have

$$\bar{n} = P'(1) = \frac{(1 - \rho)A'(1)}{1 - A'(1)} + \frac{A''(1)}{2[1 - A'(1)]} \tag{4.13}$$

Recall that we have defined $A(z)$ to be the probability generating function of the number of Poisson arrivals during the random message transmission. The calculation of this quantity illustrates a particular form that we shall see again. We condition on the transmission time, then average over the density of the transmission time

$$A(z) = E[z^a] = \int_0^\infty E[z^a|\text{transmission time} = t]m(t)\,dt$$

$$= \int_0^\infty \sum_{n=0}^\infty z^n \frac{(\lambda t)^n e^{-\lambda t}}{n!}\,m(t)\,dt \tag{4.14}$$

$$A(z) = \int_0^\infty e^{-\lambda t(1-z)}m(t)\,dt = \mathcal{M}(\lambda(1-z)) \tag{4.15}$$

where $\mathcal{M}(s)$ is the Laplace transform of the $m(t)$. Equation (4.15) expresses the relationship between the Laplace transform of the density of the duration of a random interval and the probability-generating function of the number of Poisson arrivals in the interval. Differentiating $A(z)$ with respect to z and setting $z = 1$, we find

$$A'(z)|_{z=1} = -\lambda\mathcal{M}'(0) = \lambda\bar{m} = \rho \tag{4.16a}$$

$$A''(z)|_{z=1} = \lambda^2\mathcal{M}''(0) = \lambda^2\overline{m^2} \tag{4.16b}$$

where $\overline{m^2}$ is the mean square message transmission time. Substituting into equation (4.13) we have

$$\bar{n} = \rho + \lambda^2\overline{m^2}/[2(1-\rho)] \tag{4.17}$$

It can be shown that the distribution of the number of messages in the system at the departure epoch is equal to the distribution of the number at the arrival epoch for Poisson arrivals. It is also equal to the number seen by a random observer.

4.2.2. Message Delay

The Poisson arrival of messages leads to a simple relation between the transform of the distribution of message delay and the generating function of the number of messages in the system. If service is first-come first-served, then all of the messages in the system arrived while at the departing customer was in the system. As in the calculation of $A(z)$ we have a Poisson arrival during a random interval. Again we condition on the duration of the interval, in this case, delay, then we average over the probability density function of delay, $d(t)$:

$$P(z) = E[z^n] = \int_0^\infty E[z^n/\text{delay} = t]d(t)\,dt$$

$$\int_0^\infty \left[\sum_{n=0}^\infty \frac{z^n(\lambda t)^n}{n!} e^{-\lambda t} \right] d(t)\,dt = \int_0^\infty e^{-\lambda t(1-z)}d(t)\,dt$$

$$P(z) = \mathscr{D}(\lambda(1-z)) \tag{4.18}$$

where $\mathscr{D}(s)$ is the Laplace transform of the density function of delay. [The similarity of equations (4.15) and (4.18) is not surprising in view of the similar derivations.] By substituting equations (4.15) and (4.18) into equation (4.12), we have

$$\mathscr{D}(\lambda(1-z)) = \frac{(1-\rho)(1-z)\mathscr{M}(\lambda(1-z))}{\mathscr{M}(\lambda(1-z)) - z}$$

Substituting $s = \lambda(1-z)$, we obtain

$$\mathscr{D}(s) = s(1-\rho)\mathscr{M}(s)/[s - \lambda + \lambda\mathscr{M}(s)] \tag{4.19}$$

By clearing fractions and differentiating, the mean delay can be found. However, from Little's formula [equations (3.46) and (4.17)] we have the same result, the celebrated Pollaczek–Khinchin formula:

$$\bar{d} = \bar{n}/\lambda = \bar{m} + \lambda\overline{m^2}/[2(1-\rho)] \tag{4.20}$$

The form of this equation exhibits the components of total delay. $\bar{m}$ is the average time to transmit a message, and the second term in equation (4.20) is the time spent in the queue waiting for service. When $\lambda \cong 0$, $\bar{d} = \bar{m}$ and queueing delay is negligible. As $\lambda \to 1$ the second component in equation (4.20), which accounts for queueing delay, predominates. As ρ approaches 1 the queueing delay increases without bound. This is the same behavior that we have seen in connection with the $M/M/1$ queue. (See Figure 3.8.)

As seen in the $M/M/1$ queue, the total delay is the sum of service time and queueing delay. Furthermore, these random variables are independent of one another. If $\mathscr{Q}(s)$ is the Laplace transform of the density function of queueing delay then we have

$$\mathscr{D}(s) = \mathscr{M}(s)\mathscr{Q}(s) \tag{4.21}$$

Comparing equations (4.19) and (4.21) we see that

$$\mathscr{D}(s) = \frac{s(1 - \rho)}{s - \lambda + \lambda\mathscr{M}(s)} \tag{4.22}$$

We remind the reader that the transform results for delay hold for first-come-first-served service. Regardless of the service discipline the mean delay and the mean number of messages in the system can be related through Little's formula. We have

$$\bar{n} = \lambda\bar{D}$$

The same result holds when we consider only those in the queue

$$\bar{n}_g = \lambda\bar{D}_Q$$

It is instructive to check these results with those obtained previously for the *M/M/1* queue. For an exponentially distributed service time we have the transform

$$\mathscr{M}(s) = E[e^{-sM}] = \int_0^\infty e^{-st}[\mu\, e^{-\mu t}]\, dt$$
$$= \frac{\mu}{\mu + s} \tag{4.23}$$

Substituting into equations (4.15) and (4.16), we have

$$A(z) = \frac{\mu}{\mu - \lambda(z - 1)} \tag{4.24a}$$

$$A'(z)\big|_{z=1} = \frac{\lambda\mu}{[\mu - \lambda(z - 1)]^2}\bigg|_{z=1} = \rho \tag{4.24b}$$

$$A''(z)\big|_{z=1} = \frac{2\lambda\mu}{[\mu - \lambda(z - 1)]^3}\bigg|_{z=1} = 2\rho^2 \tag{4.24c}$$

From equations (4.19) and (4.23) we have

$$\mathscr{D}(s) = \frac{\mu - \lambda}{s + \mu - \lambda} \tag{4.25}$$

Equation (4.25) is the Laplace transform of an exponentially distributed random variable with mean value $1/(\mu - \lambda)$. This checks with results obtained in Chapter 3. (See equation 3.44).

4.2.3. Application to Data Transmission

An important special case is that of deterministic service—the $M/D/1$ queue. If the service duration is equal to m with probability one, the Laplace transform of the packet length is then $\mathcal{M}(s) = e^{-sm}$. Substituting into equations (4.12), (4.15), and (4.19) we have

$$P(z) = \frac{(1 - \rho)(z - 1) e^{\rho(z-1)}}{z - e^{\rho(z-1)}} \tag{4.26a}$$

and

$$\mathcal{D}(s) = \frac{s(1 - \rho) e^{-sm}}{s - \lambda + \lambda e^{-sm}} \tag{4.26b}$$

The mean square value of the service duration is simply m^2 and the expressions for mean number in the queue and the mean delay found from equations (4.26a) and 4.26b) by differentiation are

$$\bar{n} = \rho + \frac{\lambda^2 m^2}{2(1 - \rho)} = \rho + \frac{\rho^2}{2(1 - \rho)} = \frac{2\rho - \rho^2}{2(1 - \rho)} \tag{4.27a}$$

$$\bar{d} = m + \lambda m^2 / 2(1 - \rho) = \frac{m(2 - \rho)}{2(1 - \rho)} \tag{4.27b}$$

It is interesting to compare the results for the $M/D/1$ queue with those of the $M/M/1$ queue. From equation (3.45), the average delay for the $M/M/1$ queue is given by

$$\bar{d} = \bar{m}/(1 - \rho)$$

where $\bar{m} = 1/\mu$. In Figure 4.1 delays normalized to message length are plotted as a function of load. As is evident in Figure 4.1, the average delay for the $M/M/1$ queue is always larger than that of the $M/D/1$ queue. This difference may be attributed to the variability of the exponential distribution.

As mentioned earlier, in computer communications networks an important application of the $M/D/1$ queue is packet transmission. Quite often it is assumed that fixed-length packets arrive at a node for transmission

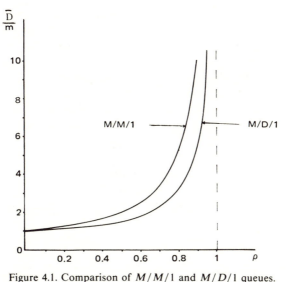

Figure 4.1. Comparison of $M/M/1$ and $M/D/1$ queues.

over a synchronous communications link (see Figure 4.2). If the number of bits in each packet is b bits and if the transmission line rate is R bits/sec, then $m = b/R$. Assuming that the arrival of packets is Poisson, the average number of packets in the transmit buffer and the average delay are described in equations (4.27a) and (4.27b) under the assumption of no retransmission. We shall consider data transmission in considerably more detail in Chapter 5 and in subsequent chapters.

In the description of message switched networks in Chapter 2, the retransmission of messages was described. One way that this may be implemented is the send-and-wait protocol. If a message is received with no error detected and if there is room for the message in the next node of the network, an acknowledgement (ACK) is sent to the transmitting node. If the transmitting node does not receive an acknowledgement within a specified timeout interval, the message is retransmitted. No messages are transmitted during the timeout interval. Until an acknowledgement is received the packet is held in a transmit buffer. This protocol resides in the link layer (see Section 2.3).

Figure 4.2. Data message transmission.

We consider now an analysis of the send-and-wait protocol under the assumption of a random transmission delay in the channel.[2] This random delay may be ascribed to random propagation delay in a physical channel. We model this system as an $M/G/1$ queue. The difficult part is the derivation of the probability distribution of the message transmission time which begins when a message begins transmission and ends when the message has been acknowledged by the receiver. It may include a number of retransmissions. This is depicted in Figure 4.3. Let $B(t)$ denote the probability distribution of acknowledgement delay

$$B(t) \triangleq P[\text{ACK delay} \leq t]$$

The density function is denoted $b(t) = dB(t)/dt$. This delay includes delay in the forward path and processing as well as delay of the ACK in the reverse path. Let Q be the probability that a message is accepted by the receiver. If there is no loss of the ACK in the feedback channel, the probability of receiving an ACK in the time-out interval is

$$G = QB(T) \tag{4.28}$$

In writing equation (4.28) we assume that the ACK delay is independent of the event of a loss. The event of the loss of an ACK can be taken into account simply by modifying Q. If the successive transmissions are independent then the number of transmissions is required to get a message through to the receiver geometrically distributed

$$P[n \text{ transmissions}] = (1 - G)^{n-1}G, \qquad n = 1, 2, \ldots \tag{4.29}$$

Each transmission, except the last, is made up of the packet transmision time and a time-out interval T. In the last transmission the arrival of an ACK terminates the timeout interval.

We calculate the total time required to transmit a message, with retransmissions and time-outs, by first conditioning on the number of transmissions. Notice that successive packet transmissions are of the same length message,

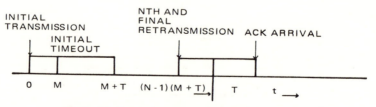

Figure 4.3. Successive retransmission of a message.

therefore the time required for n message transmissions has Laplace transform

$$E[e^{-snm}] = \mathcal{P}(ns) \qquad (4.30)$$

where m is the time required for a single transmission, and where $\mathcal{P}(s)$ is the Laplace transform of the density of the message length. Similarly the time required for $n - 1$ fixed-length timeouts has Laplace transform $e^{-s(n-1)T}$. By definition the final timeout interval is ended by an ACK. For this interval we have

$$P[\text{ACK arrival} \leqslant t/\text{ACK arrival} \leqslant T] = B(t)/B(T), \qquad 0 \leqslant t \leqslant T \qquad (4.31)$$

The Laplace transform of the probability density of this quantity is

$$\mathcal{R}(s) = \int_0^T b(t)\, e^{-st}\, dt / B(T)$$

The message transmission times and the time-out intervals are independent. Thus the Laplace transform of the sum is the product of the individual transforms. Averaging over the number of transmissions we have for the Laplace transform of the density of the total time required to transmit a packet

$$\mathcal{M}(s) = \sum_{n=1}^{\infty} (1 - G)^{n-1} G\mathcal{P}(ns)\, e^{-sT(n-1)}\mathcal{R}(s) \qquad (4.32)$$

This message transmission time may be substituted into equation (4.19) to find the delay of a packet. We assume the packet to remain in the transmitter until acknowledged.

Let us consider a special case of the foregoing. Suppose that the duration of a packet is a constant F bits. If the line transmission rate is R bits/sec, we have

$$\mathcal{P}(s) = e^{-(F/R)s}$$

suppose further that the ACK delay is a constant equal to the time-out, T. We have

$$B(t) = u(t - T)$$

Substituting into equation (4.32), we find that

$$\mathcal{M}(s) = \sum_{n=1}^{\infty} (1 - G)^{n-1} G e^{-nFs/R} e^{-sTn}$$

$$= \frac{G e^{-s(F/R+T)}}{1 - (1 - G) e^{-s(F/R+T)}} \tag{4.33}$$

The average and the mean square transmission times are

$$\bar{m} = (F/R + T)/G \tag{4.34a}$$

$$\overline{m^2} = (F/R + T)^2 (2 - G)/G^2 \tag{4.34b}$$

These may be substituted into equation (4.20) to find the average delay. As mentioned above, we assume that a packet remains in the transmitter until acknowledged. If, on the other hand, we assume that a packet is successfully transmitted when it is accepted by the receiver, we subtract average delay in the feedback channel to find average delay under this assumption.

These results can be further refined if we assume that the only reason a packet needs to be retransmitted is because of error in the forward channel. Suppose further that errors occur independently from bit to bit. If a packet consists of F bits then the probability of packets having at least one error is

$$1 - Q = 1 - (1 - B_E)^F \cong FB_E, \qquad B_E \ll 1 \tag{4.35}$$

where B_E is the probability of a single bit error. It is assumed that there are enough parity bits in the packet so that any likely errors can be detected.

4.3. Variation for the Initiator of a Busy Period

A variation of the foregoing imbedded Markov chain model is applicable in several communications contexts. Consider the situation where a message arriving at an empty queue receives different service from those arriving at a nonempty queue.[3] (An example is given in Exercise 4.10.) Such a message initiates what is called a busy period.† Again we imbed the Markov chain at successive departure epochs and consider the state defined by the number of messages in the system. When the queue is not empty the

---

†In Chapter 6 we shall study the probability distribution of the busy period of an $M/G/1$ queue.

equation for the successive states is that given in equation (4.3a). Recall that in this equation a_{i+1} is the average number of messages that arrive during the transmission time of a message. Now if the transmission time of a message that arrives to an empty queue is different from those that arrive to a nonempty queue, a change is necessary in equation (4.3b). We may write

$$n_{i+1} = \tilde{a}_{i+1}$$

where the tilde indicates a difference in the number of arrivals from the case of a nonempty queue. We can write this in a form analogous to equation (4.4):

$$
\begin{aligned}
n_{i+1} &= n_i - U(n_i) + a_{i+1}U(n_i) + \tilde{a}_{i+1}[1 - U(n_i)] \\
&= n_i - U(n_i) + \tilde{a}_{i+1} + (a_{i+l} - \tilde{a}_{i+1})U(n_i)
\end{aligned}
\tag{4.36}
$$

Taking expectations of both sides of equation (4.36) and assuming equilibrium we find

$$1 - P_0 = E[\tilde{a}]/(1 - E[a] + E[\tilde{a}]) \tag{4.37}$$

where P_0 is the probability of the queue being empty. The terms $E[\tilde{a}]$ and $E[a]$ are the average number of messages to arrive during the extraordinary and the ordinary message transmission times, respectively. Let $\tilde{m}$ denote the duration of a message that arrives to an empty queue. We have

$$E[\tilde{a}] = \lambda E(\tilde{m})$$

and

$$E[a] = \lambda E(m)$$

Using the same approach that led to equation (4.12), we can find the probability generating function for the number of messages in the system. For convenience we drop dependence on i. From equation (4.36) we have

$$
P(z) = E[z^n] = E[z^{n - U(n) + aU(n) + \tilde{a}[1 - U(n)]}]
$$

$$
= P_0 E[z^{\tilde{a}}] + \sum_{i=1}^{\infty} P(n = i)z^{i-1+a} \tag{4.38}
$$

$$
= P_0 \tilde{A}(z) + z^{-1}\left[\sum_{i=0}^{\infty} P(n = i)z^i - P_0\right]A(z)
$$

where $\tilde{A}(z)$ and $A(z)$ are the probability generating functions of message arrivals during the appropriate message transmission times. Solving equation (5.35) for $P(z)$ we find

$$P(z) = \frac{P_0[A(z) - z\tilde{A}(z)]}{A(z) - z}$$

(4.39)

If $\tilde{\mathcal{M}}(s)$ and $\mathcal{M}(s)$ are the Laplace transforms of message transmission time densities, then it can be shown that the Laplace transform for message delay is given by

$$\mathcal{D}(s) = \frac{P_0(\lambda\mathcal{M}(s) - (\lambda - s)\tilde{\mathcal{M}}(s))}{\lambda\mathcal{M}(s) + s - \lambda}$$

(4.40)

From these transforms moments can be found in the usual fashion. From equations (4.37) and (4.40) it can be shown that the average message delay is given by

$$\bar{d} = \frac{E[\tilde{m}]}{1 - \lambda[E(m) - E(\tilde{m})]} + \frac{\lambda E(m^2)}{2[1 - \lambda E(m)]} + \frac{\lambda[E(\tilde{m}^2) - E(m^2)]}{2[1 - \lambda E(m) + \lambda E(\tilde{m})]}$$

(4.41)

4.4. Numerical Results

It is characteristic of queueing theory at the level we have considered that results are obtained in terms of probability generating functions or Laplace transforms. Although the transforms are complete descriptions of the probability distributions we would wish to have more tangible measures such as probabilities or moments. General techniques for the inversion of transforms are well known.† We shall not consider general techniques but only those which are particular to a probabilistic context. Moreover there are situations where we have only an implicit solution for a transform.

Moments of random variables can be computed from the transforms by differentiation.‡ For a discrete random variable N with probability generating function $P(z)$, the first two moments follow from

$$E[N] = \frac{dP(z)}{dz}\bigg|_{z=1}$$

(4.42a)

---

†Among many references for Z and Laplace transforms we cite three which are most familiar to us.[4-6]
‡For an alternative approach to binding moments of delay, see Ref. 9.

$$E[N^2] = \frac{d^2 P(z)}{dz^2} + \frac{dP(z)}{dz}\bigg|_{z=1} \qquad (4.42b)$$

Higher-order moments can be found in a similar fashion. The same technique can be applied to Laplace transforms of density functions. Let $\mathscr{X}(s)$ be the Laplace transform of the density function of the random variable X:

$$E[X] = -\frac{d\mathscr{X}(s)}{ds}\bigg|_{s=0} \qquad (4.43a)$$

$$E[X^2] = \frac{d^2 \mathscr{X}(s)}{ds^2}\bigg|_{s=0} \qquad (4.43b)$$

Now given the moments of random variables, statements about probabilities of random variables can be found by application of the Chebychev inequality. A particular example is

$$P[|X - E(X)| \geq \varepsilon] \leq \frac{\text{Var } X}{\varepsilon^2} \qquad (4.44)$$

A certain amount of information may be gleaned directly from the transforms. For instance for a discrete random variable probabilities may be found by successive differentiation

$$P_j = \frac{1}{j!} \frac{d^j P(z)}{dz^j}\bigg|_{z=0} = \sum_{i=0}^{\infty} \frac{(i)(i-1)\cdots(i-j+1)}{j!} P_i z^{i-j}\bigg|_{z=0}$$

$$j = 0, 1, 2, \ldots \qquad (4.45)$$

For a continuous random variable X we have the initial value theorem

$$\lim_{t \to 0} f_x(t) = \lim_{s \to \infty} s\mathscr{X}(s) \qquad (4.46)$$

and the final value theorem

$$\lim_{t \to \infty} f_x(t) = \lim_{s \to 0} s\mathscr{X}(s) \qquad (4.47)$$

Another bound can be found by means of the Chernoff bound. Let x be a positive continuous random variable with density function $f_x(t)$ and Laplace transform $\mathscr{X}(s)$. We consider the probability $P[x > a]$, which can be written

$$P[x > a] = \int_0^\infty U(t - a) f_x(t) \, dt$$

where $U(x)$ is the unit step. Now for $\alpha \geq 0$ we have the inequality $e^{\alpha(t-a)} \geq U(t - \alpha)$ (Figure 4.4). Thus

$$P[X > a] \leq \int_0^\infty e^{\alpha(t-a)} f_x(t) \, dt = e^{-\alpha a} \mathscr{X}(-a) \tag{4.48}$$

where $\mathscr{X}(-\alpha)$ is the Laplace transform of the density function of X evaluated at $s = -\alpha$. Since this inequality holds for any value of $\alpha \geq 0$, the bound can be sharpened by choosing α such that the right-hand side of equation (4.48) is minimum. This same calculation can be made for a discrete random variable. The corresponding equation is

$$P[N > a] \leq E[e^{\alpha(N-a)}] = e^{-\alpha a} N(e^\alpha) \tag{4.49}$$

where $N(e^\alpha)$ is the probability generating function of $n(z)$ evaluated at $z = e^\alpha$, $\alpha \geq 0$. Again the right-hand side of equation (4.49) can be minimized with respect to α.

A particularly useful tool in the inversions of transforms is the Fast Fourier transform (FFT)[7] algorithm for which software is readily available. This is particularly convenient in calculations involving large systems. We begin with the observation that the following are *discrete* Fourier transform pairs:

$$g(lT) = \frac{1}{K} \sum_{k=0}^{K-1} G\left(\frac{k}{KT}\right) e^{j2\pi kl/k}, \qquad l = 0, 1, \ldots, K - 1 \tag{4.50}$$

$$G\left(\frac{k}{KT}\right) = \sum_{l=0}^{K-1} g(lT) e^{-j2\pi kl/K}, \qquad k = 0, 1, \ldots, K - 1 \tag{4.51}$$

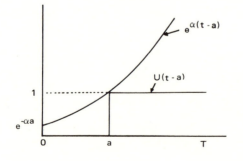

Figure 4.4. Chernoff bound.

If we have the probability generating function $N(z) = \sum_{l=0}^{K} P_l z^l$, the values P_l; $l = 0, 1, \ldots, K - 1$ can be found from equations (4.50) and (4.51). We make the identifications

$$g(lT) \leftrightarrow P_l, \qquad l = 0, 1, \ldots, K - 1$$

and

$$G\left(\frac{k}{KT}\right) \leftrightarrow N\left(\frac{2\pi k}{K}\right), \qquad k = 0, 1, \ldots, K - 1$$

The latter term is simply $N(z)$ evaluated at equally spaced points on the unit circle. In general the value of K may be unbounded. In performing the calculation one chooses K to be large enough to include all significant values of P_l.

References

1. D. G. Kendall, "Stochastic Processes Occurring in the Theory of Queues and their Analysis by the Method of the Imbedded Markov Chain," *Annals of Mathematical Statistics*, **24**, 338–354 (1953).
2. G. Fayolle, E. Gelembe, and G. Pujolle, "An Analytic Evaluation of the Performance of the 'Send and Wait' Protocol," *IEEE Transactions on Communications*, **Com-26**(3), 313–320, March (1978).
3. P. D. Welch, "On a Generalized $M/G/1$ Queueing Process in Which the First Customer in a Busy Period Receives Exceptional Service," *Operations Research*, **12**, 736–752 (1964).
4. E. J. Jury, *Theory and Application of the Z-Transform Method*, John Wiley, New York (1964).
5. W. Kaplan, *Operational Methods for Linear Systems*, Addison-Wesley, Reading, Massachusetts (1962).
6. R. V. Churchill, *Modern Operational Mathematics in Engineering*, McGraw-Hill, New York (1944).
7. E. O. Brigham, *The Fast Fourier Transform*, Prentice-Hall, Englewood Cliffs, New Jersey (1974).
8. D. R. Cox and W. L. Smith, *Queues*, Methuen, London (1961).
9. L. Kleinrock, *Queueing Systems*, Vol. 1, *Theory*, John Wiley, New York (1975).

Exercises

4.1. For the case of an $M/G/1$ queue with a FCFS discipline, show that the second moment of delay is given by

$$\overline{d^2} = \overline{m^2} + \frac{\overline{d}\lambda\overline{m^2}}{1 - \rho} + \frac{\lambda\overline{m^3}}{3(1 - \rho)}$$

4.2. Try to analyze the $M/G/1$ queue with a finite waiting room using the imbedded Markov chain approach. Why doesn't it work? Repeat for the $M/G/s$, with an infinite waiting room $s > 0$ queue.

4.3. Two Poisson streams of message traffic converge on a single queue. The average rates for the streams are given by λ_i, $i = 1$, 2. Assume that each stream has a different distribution of message lengths. Find the transform of the delay distribution for a type-1 message. (*Hint*: queueing delay is the same for both types of messages.)

4.4. For an $M/G/1$ queue find the probability generating function for the number of customers in the queue excluding the customer being served.

4.5. Consider a data communications system using the send and wait protocol. The number of bits in the messages to be transmitted by the system are uniformly distributed between 500 and 1500 bits. Acknowledgement messages are 20 bits in duration. The transmission rates in both the forward and the feedback channels are 9600 bps. Assume that the bit error rates in the forward and the feedback channel are 10^{-4}, independent from bit to bit.

(a) What is the probability that both the message and its ACK are received correctly?

   The timeout interval after transmission is $T = 20$ msec. Assume that the round trip delay has the following probability distribution function:

$$B(t) = \begin{cases} 0, & t \leq 10 \text{ msec} \\ 1 - e^{-200(t-0.01)}, & t > 10 \text{ msec} \end{cases}$$

(b) What is the total time required to transmit a message on the average?

(c) Plot the average message delay as a function of message arrival rate.

4.6. Consider a packet switching system in which messages are broken up into fixed length packets of 1000 bits. The number of packets per message is geometrically distributed with mean value five. The channel bit rate is 50 Kbps. The probability of a packet being in error is 0.01. Each packet is transmitted according to the send and wait protocol. Assume that the timeout interval is 10 msec and that the round trip delay is a constant 10 msec. Also assume that the probability of an ACK in error is negligible.

(a) What is the average time required to transmit a packet?

(b) What is the average time required to transmit a message?

(c) At what message arrival rate will the system saturate?

(d) What is the average delay of a message at half the arrival rate found in part (c)?

4.7. Messages arrive at a Poisson rate at N different buffers. A multiplexer goes from buffer to buffer in cyclic fashion removing messages for transmission over line (see Figure 4.4). Each message is preceded by an address which lasts T seconds. Empty buffers are skipped without delay. Suppose that the loading and N are such that the probability of more than one message in a buffer is negligibly small. Find the generating function for the number of messages in all buffers.

4.8. Repeat problem 4.6 under the assumption that the packets contain 5000 bits. Assume that the underlying message lengths have the same geometric distribution in both problems. Assume also that the bit error rate is the same in both problems.

4.9. Data transmission takes place over a satellite channel. The channel is in geostationary orbit and the round trip delay is approximately 0.25 sec. Assume that the messages are a constant 1000 bits long and the channel is 50 Kbps in both directions. Suppose that the probability of message error is 0.05. As in previous exercises the send and wait protocol is used and the time out interval is equal to the round trip delay.

(a) Show average message delay as a function of message arrival rate.

Suppose that more redundancy is added to messages so that errors may be corrected as well as detected. Let us assume, for the sake of illustration, that 200 more bits in a message reduces the probability of message error to 0.01.

(b) Repeat part (a).

4.10. Assume the Poisson arrival of messages at a buffer. If a message arrives to an empty buffer, a training sequence must be transmitted before the message is transmitted. This is necessary for synchronism at the receiver. If a message immediately succeeds another message, we may assume the receiver is synchronized. Let the training sequence be T seconds in duration.

(a) Find the generating function of the number of messages in the buffer. You should consider the training sequence as augmenting the duration of messages which are the first in a long string.

(b) Plot average message delay as a function of load for the case of $T = 50$ msec and 1000 bit packets transmitted over a 4800 bps channel.

5

Imbedded Markov Chain Analysis
of Time-Division Multiplexing

5.1. Introduction

In general terms, multiplexing is a means for sharing facilities among a number of users and sources. As we have seen in Section 2.4, the standard techniques for doing this in the telephone networks are frequency-division multiplexing (FDM) and time-division multiplexing (TDM). The explosive growth of digital technology has favored the development of TDM for sharing the capacity of transmission lines. Moreover, the digital basis of time-division multiplexing makes it a natural vehicle for data traffic. In this chapter we shall analyze the performance of time-division multiplexing and a variant, asynchronous time-division multiplexing. This analysis is closely related to the analysis of the $M/G/1$ queue in the previous chapter inasmuch as both use the imbedded Markov chain approach.

Time-division multiplexing operates on lines using synchronous digital transmission (see Chapter 2). The flow on the line is segmented into fixed-length frames. The frame is further segmented into slots consisting of a fixed number of bits. Each of the slots in a frame is dedicated to a data source (see Figure 5.1). The ubiquitous example of TDM in the telephone network is the T1 carrier system where each frame has a duration of 1/8000 sec and consists of twenty-four 8-bit bytes (see Figure 1.4). Time-division multiplexing may be used to multiplex transmission facilities among a number of different data sources. As we have seen in Section 2.8 the time-division technique is called *time-division multiple access* (TDMA) in satellite systems.

In many applications data sources may be characterized as bursty, meaning that there are long idle periods interspersed with periods of activity (see Section 2.2). Because of the bursty nature of such data sources,

111

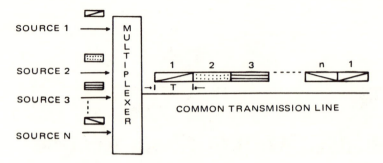

Figure 5.1. Synchronous time-division multiplexing.

dedicating transmission facilities to individual sources is not efficient. The reason for this is that it will often be the case that the channels dedicated to some sources are empty while there is congestion on others. An appropriate technique for multiplexing a number of bursty sources is called *asynchronous time-division multiplexing* (ATDM) (see Figure 5.2). Messages from each of the sources connected to the multiplexer are transmitted in order of arrival using the full capacity of the transmission line. In order to distinguish among messages from different sources sharing the line, addressing information must accompany these messages. We distinguish between the two techniques by using the term *synchronous time-division multiplexing* (STDM) to indicate the technique where capacity is dedicated to sources.

5.2. Simple and Compound Poisson Arrivals

We begin the analysis of time division multiplexing with a consideration of the message arrival process. In general it is assumed that messages are random in length. Because of this random length it is necessary to transmit

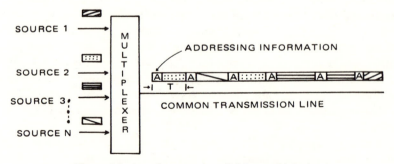

Figure 5.2. Asynchronous time-division multiplexing.

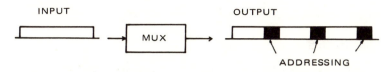

INPUT

OUTPUT

MUX

ADDRESSING

Figure 5.3. Message blocking.

some overhead information so that the beginning of one message may be distinguished from the end of another. It has been found[1] that an efficient way of doing this is to break messages into fixed-size blocks each of which are addressed (see Figure 5.3). Along with addressing information there is an indicator bit telling if a block is the last in a message. We call the block together with all addressing and overhead bits a *data unit*. In other contexts an addressed block of data is called a packet or a frame. We shall deal with these concepts in due course. Throughout our analysis we will assume that message arrival is Poisson. If messages consist of a single data unit, we have what is called *simple* Poisson arrival. *Compound* Poisson arrival designates the case of a random number of data units in a message.

Let us assume that the generating function of the number of data units in a message is expressed as $M(z)$. For example, if the number of data units in a message is geometrically distributed with parameter P, we have

$$M(z) = \sum_{k=1}^{\infty} z^k(1 - P)P^{k-1} = (1 - P)z/(1 - Pz) \qquad (5.1)$$

As we shall see when we analyze the imbedded Markov chain, the number of arrivals in a T-second interval is of importance. Since message arrival is Poisson, the number of data units that arrive in T seconds is a random sum of random variables. We calculate the probability generating function of the number of arrivals by first conditioning on the number of arrived messages, then averaging over the number of arrivals. Recall that the generating function of a sum of independent random variables is the product of generating functions:

$$A(z, T) \triangleq E[z^a] = E_j[E[z^a/j \text{ messages}]]$$
$$= E_j[M^j(z)] = \sum_{j=0}^{\infty} \frac{(\lambda T)^j}{j!} e^{-\lambda T}M^j(z) \qquad (5.2)$$
$$= e^{-\lambda T[1-M(z)]}$$

As in previous chapters, λ in equation (5.2) is the average message arrival rate.

5.3. Asynchronous Time-Division Multiplexing

5.3.1. Infinite Buffer

In systems employing asynchronous time-division multiplexing† a large number of users are multiplexed onto the same line. We assume that the aggregate arrival process to the multiplexer from all sources is λ messages per second. We also assume that the transmission rate on the synchronous line out of the buffer is $1/T$ slots per second, where a slot carries exactly one data unit. Before transmission newly arrived data units are stored in a buffer. The first question that we shall address is the size of the buffer.

We imbed a Markov chain at the points in time between slots. Let n_i be the number of data units in the buffer at the end of the ith slot. Let us assume initially that the buffer is infinite. We let a_i denote the number of data units that arrive during the ith slot, which like all slots is T seconds in duration. Since at most one data unit is transmitted we have the familiar expression

$$n_{i+1} = n_i - U(n_i) + a_{i+1} \tag{5.3}$$

where $U(\cdot)$ is the unit step. Notice that data units arriving during a slot cannot be transmitted until the beginning of the next slot. The conditions for a steady-state solution are basically the same as those for the $M/G/1$ queue (see Section 4.2). By taking the generating functions of both sides of equation (5.3) the same analysis that led to equation (4.12) yields

$$E[z^n] = P[z] = \frac{(1-\rho)(1-z)A(z, T)}{A(z, T) - z} \tag{5.4}$$

where $A(z, T)$ is the probability generating function for the number of data units arriving in a slot interval (T seconds). As in the case of the $M/G/1$ queue ρ is the system load and is given by

$$\rho = \lambda T \bar{m}$$

where $\bar{m}$ is the average number of data units in a message. As in the case of the $M/G/1$ queue, in order for a steady-state solution to exist we must have $\rho = \lambda T \bar{m} < 1$. By the same sequence of steps that led from equation (4.12) to (4.13) we have

$$\bar{n}_D = \frac{(1-\rho)A'(1, T)}{1 - A'(1, T)} + \frac{A''(1, T)}{2[1 - A'(1, T)]} \tag{5.5}$$

†The original work on ATDM is ontained in Refs. 2–4.

For the case of compound Poisson arrival where $A(z, T)$ is given by equation (5.2), we have

$$A'(z, T)|_{z=1} = \lambda TM'(z) \, e^{-\lambda T[1-M(z)]}|_{z=1} = \lambda T\bar{m} = \rho \tag{5.6a}$$

$$A''(z, T)|_{z=1} = [\lambda TM''(z) \, e^{-\lambda T[1-M(z)]} + (\lambda TM'(z))^2 \, e^{-\lambda T[1-M(z)]}]|_{z=1}$$
$$= \lambda T(\overline{m^2} - \bar{m}) + \rho^2 \tag{5.6b}$$

Substituting into equation (5.5) we have

$$\bar{n}_D = +\frac{\rho}{2} + \frac{\lambda T\overline{m^2}}{2(1 - \rho)} \tag{5.7}$$

In closing this section we point out that the arrival process in equation (5.3) need not be compound Poisson in order for the analysis to be carried through. The derivation of equation (5.4) is based only on the assumptions that the number of arrivals in a slot does not depend on the number of data units already in the system and the number of arrivals is independent from interval to interval. Suppose, for example, that random length messages arrive at a constant rate of R messages per second. The number of messages arriving in T seconds is RT and the probability-generating function of the number of data units arriving in T seconds is

$$A(z, T) = [M(z)]^{RT} \tag{5.8}$$

This may be substituted into equation (5.4) to find the probability-generating function for the number of data units in the system. The load is given by

$$\rho = RT\bar{m} \tag{5.9}$$

where $\bar{m}$ is the average number of data units per message and the necessary and sufficient condition for a steady-state solution is $\rho < 1$.

5.3.2. Finite Buffer

The analysis of the preceding paragraphs is based on the assumption of an infinite buffer. The probability distribution can be calculated from the probability-generating function by the techniques discussed in Section 4.4 of Chapter 4. In a practical application one would expect that the buffer size although finite would be large enough so that the probability of overflow would be negligible under normal operating conditions.

When the size of the buffer is such that the probability of overflow is not negligible the analysis of the preceding section leading to the probability-generating function is not applicable. The calculation of the probability-generating function in equation (5.4) assumes that the number of data units, a_i, that arrive in a slot is independent of the number already there. This assumption is violated when the buffer is full since there can be no arrivals. In the case of a finite buffer we analyze buffer occupancy by considering state transition probabilities. Again the state is the number of data units in the buffer at the beginning of a slot. At the outset of our analysis we shall assume that an equilibrium solution exists. Since we have a finite buffer, stability does not require that the average number of data units arriving in a slot be less than one. Let Q_i denote the steady-state probability that there are i data units in the buffer at the beginning of a slot. This steady-state probability is determined by the state transition probabilities.† Also let A_j denote the probability of j data units arriving in a slot. We point out that a data unit is removed from the buffer at each slot and that data units which arrive at a full buffer are lost. We may then write for the state transition probabilities

$$P_r[l \text{ data units, slot } i+1/k \text{ data units, slot } i]$$

$$\triangleq P_{kl} = \begin{cases} 0, & k-1 > l \\ A_l, & k = 0, \quad 0 \leq l < M \\ A_{l-k+1}, & 0 \leq k-1 \leq l < M \\ \sum\limits_{j=M}^{\infty} A_j, & k = 0, \quad l = M \\ \sum\limits_{j=M}^{\infty} A_{j-k+1}, & 0 \leq k-1 \leq l = M \end{cases} \tag{5.10}$$

We assume here that the data unit to be transmitted is removed at the beginning of a slot so that there is never more than M in the buffer. Summing over disjoint events, we have

$$P_r[l \text{ data units, in slot } i+1] = \sum_{k=0}^{M} P_r[k \text{ data units in slot } i]P_{kl}$$

The steady-state probabilities can then be written

$$Q_i = \sum_{j=0}^{M} P_{ji}Q_j = \begin{cases} Q_0 A_i + \sum\limits_{j=0}^{i} Q_{j+1}A_{i-j}, & 0 \leq i < M \\ Q_0 \sum\limits_{j=M}^{\infty} A_j + \sum\limits_{j=0}^{M} Q_{j+1} \sum\limits_{k=M-j}^{\infty} A_k, & i = M \end{cases} \tag{5.11}$$

†See Appendix B.

In general, problems of this sort are solved by finding an eigenvalue of the state transition probability matrix; however, in this case simple iteration yields the solution. From equation (5.11) we have

$$Q_{i+1} = \frac{Q_i - \sum_{j=1}^{i} Q_j A_{i-j+1} - Q_0 A_i}{A_0}, \qquad i = 0, 2, \ldots, M-1 \qquad (5.12a)$$

The set of $Q_1, Q_2, \ldots, Q_M$ obtained from equation (5.12a) must be such that

$$\sum_{i=0}^{M} Q_i = 1 \qquad (5.12b)$$

This suggests a simple procedure to find $Q_0, Q_1, \ldots, Q_M$. We initialize $Q_0' = 1$ and find $Q_1', \ldots, Q_M'$ from equation (5.12a). The final values are found from normalization:

$$Q_i = Q_i' \bigg/ \sum_{j=0}^{M} Q_i', \qquad i = 0, 1, 2, \ldots, M$$

An approximation based on the foregoing analysis may be used to find the steady-state probabilities for the case of an infinite buffer. This is based on the assumption for M large enough $P_j \cong 0, j \geqslant M$. One then computes the steady-state probabilities according to equations (5.12a) and (5.12b) under the assumption that the buffer size is M. The approximation may be checked by varying M.

There are several quantities that are of interest in connection with a finite buffer. For example one can calculate the average number of data units in the buffer from

$$\bar{n}_D = \sum_{i=0}^{M} i Q_i \qquad (5.13)$$

Another quantity of considerable interest in computer communications is the throughput, which is the amount of data that the transmission line carries away from the buffer. A slot will carry a data unit only if the buffer is nonempty at the beginning of the slot. Thus the fraction of slots actually carrying data is $(1 - Q_0)$. The average throughput is then $(1 - Q_0)/T$ data units per second. If the arrival rate of data units is $\lambda \bar{m}$ data units per second, the average overflow traffic is $\lambda \bar{m} - (1 - Q_0)/T$ data units per second.

Consider the following example of ATDM. Suppose that the arrival process is simple Poisson with an average rate of $\lambda < 1$ data units per slot.

The probability of j data units arriving in a slot is then

$$A_j = \lambda^j e^{-\lambda} / j!$$

This can be substituted into equations (5.12a) and (5.12b) to find Q_i, $i = 0, 1, \ldots, M$. The throughput per slot is shown as a function of buffer size with λ as a parameter in Figure 5.4. Notice that if the buffer size is large enough everything gets through. Also, as expected, as λ increases so also must M in order to attain a specified throughput.

A significant related area of research is the management of buffer resources.[5-7] For example, suppose that two or more sources share the same buffer. Suppose also that there are penalties for buffer overflow with different penalties for different sources. The question is how does one allocate the memory so as to minimize the penalty function? For two sources the optimum lies between the extremes illustrated in Figures 5.5a and 5.5b. In Figure 5.5a K units of storage are shared completely between two sources, while in Figure 5.5b storage is dedicated to each of the sources with no sharing whatever.

5.4. Synchronous Time-Division Multiplexing

In synchronous time-division multiplexing capacity in the form of recurring time slots is dedicated to each of the data sources sharing the transmission facility. Flow on the line is blocked into fixed-length frames.

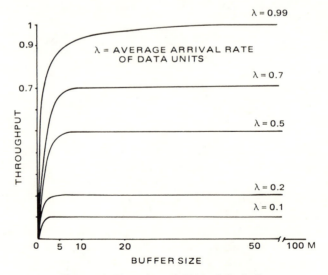

Figure 5.4. Throughput ATDM—finite buffer.

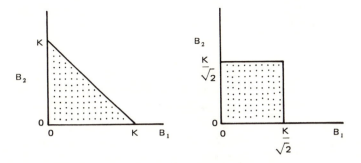

Figure 5.5. Buffer allocation strategies. (a) Complete sharing. (b) Dedication to sources.

The frame is allocated so that periodically recurring slots carry only the output of a particular source. Messages arrive at a rate of λ messages per second. These messages are stored in buffers until the portion of a frame dedicated to a source is available. For purposes of explanation it is helpful to visualize TDM as being implemented by a sort of commutator (see Figure 5.6). When it is the turn of a particular source to empty its buffer we imagine the source being visited by a server. The server stays at each buffer a fixed amount of time, removing at most a specified maximum amount of data. Since the action of the server does not depend on the traffic from the sources, the time required for the server to cycle through all sources is constant and the sources may be analyzed independently.†

Our analysis focuses on a particular source. We take the beginning of a TDM multiplexing frame to be the point where the server arrives at the source's buffer. (See Figure 5.7.) We assume that the duration of the frame is T_F seconds. The server remains at the source for bT seconds removing at most $b \geq 1$ data units from the buffer. As in previous analyses in this chapter a data unit fits exactly into a T-second slot.

†In Chapter 7, when we treat polling models, we shall see a contrasting model where the action of the server is dependent upon the traffic, with the result that there is dependence among the queues.

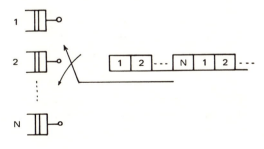

Figure 5.6. Commutator model of synchronous TDM.

Figure 5.7. Time-division multiplexing frame.

In this section we shall assume a gated or "please wait" strategy whereby data units arriving while the server is present must wait until the next frame even though the server may be idle. The alternative to "please wait" is "come right in," in which newly arrived messages may be transmitted in the same frame. We shall treat this latter strategy in a later section of this chapter.

The difference between this and previous imbedded Markov chain analyses is that the server is allowed to remove more than one data unit during a frame. If there are b or fewer data units in the buffer when the server arrives, none of these will remain when the server departs. Only new arrivals remain. We write the equation for the imbedded Markov chain for the number of data units in the buffer as

$$n_{i+1} = \max(0, n_i - b) + a_{i+1} \tag{5.14}$$

where, as previously, n_i is the number of data units in the system at the beginning of the ith frame and a_i is the number of data units arriving during the ith frame. The imbedded points are the beginnings of frames. Any messages arriving during a frame are held over to be transmitted at the beginning of the next frame. In equation (5.14) the complicating factor is whether or not $n_i - b$ is negative. In earlier analyses we had $b = 1$. [See equation (5.3).] Again we calculate the probability-generating function of the number of data units in the buffer:

$$P_{i+1}(z) \triangleq E[z^{n_{i+1}}] = E[z^{\max(n_i - b, 0) + a_{i+1}}]$$

$$= \sum_{j=0}^{\infty} P_j^i z^{\max(j - b, 0)} E[z^{a_{i+1}}] \tag{5.15}$$

$$P_{i+1}(z) = \left[\sum_{j=0}^{b-1} P_j^i + \sum_{j=b}^{\infty} P_j^i z^{j-b} \right] E[z^{a_{i+1}}]$$

In writing equation (5.15) we assume that the arrivals are independent of the number of data units already in the system. We assume that there is a steady-state solution so that $\lim_{i \to \infty} P_{i+1}(z) = P(z)$ and $\lim_{i \to \infty} P_j^i = P_j$. Continuing on we find that

$$P(z) = \left[\sum_{j=0}^{b-1} P_j + z^{-b}\left(\sum_{j=0}^{\infty} P_j z^j - \sum_{j=0}^{b-1} P_j z^j \right) \right] A(z, T_F)$$

$$= A(z, T_F) \sum_{j=0}^{b-1} P_j(1 - z^{-b+j}) + z^{-b}A(z, T_F)P(z)$$

where $A(z, T_F)$ is the probability-generating function of the number of data units arriving in a frame. Solving for $P(z)$ yields

$$P(z) = A(z, T_F) \sum_{j=0}^{b-1} P_j(z^b - z^j)/[z^b - A(z, T_F)] \qquad (5.16)$$

What is noteworthy in equation (5.16) is the presence of b unknowns P_0, $P_1, \ldots, P_{b-1}$. When $b = 1$, equation (5.16) reduces to the same form as equation (5.4). There is a single unknown P_0 which can be found from the normalizing condition $P(1) = 1$. When $b > 1$, an additional $b - 1$ equations must be obtained in order to solve for the b unknowns. These equations can be obtained by an application of Rouché's theorem.†

5.4.1. Application of Rouché's Theorem

In order to obtain $b - 1$ additional equations we consider the properties of the functions $P(z)$, z^b, and $A(z, T_F)$. We begin by noting that the function $P(z)$ is analytic within the unit disk $|z| \le 1$:

$$|P(z)| = \left| \sum_{i=0}^{\infty} z^i P_i \right| \le \sum_{i=0}^{\infty} |z|^i P_i \le \sum_{i=0}^{\infty} P_i = 1 \qquad (5.17)$$

We consider now the denominator of equation (5.16), in particular zeros of the expression $z^b - A(z, T_F)$. Recall that $A(z, T_F)$ is the generating function of the arrival process. We assume a compound Poisson arrival process for which the generating function is

$$A(z, T_F) = e^{-\lambda T_F[1 - M(z)]} \qquad (5.18)$$

where $M(z)$ is the probability-generating function of the number of data units in a message, λ is the number of message arrivals per second, and T_F

---

†The application of Rouché's theorem to bulk departures is due to Bailey.[8] For a discussion and proof of Rouché's theorem consult a text on the theory of analytic functions, e.g., Ref. 9.

is the duration of the frame. The assumption of Poisson arrivals simplifies the analysis; however, it can be shown that the same results can be obtained for any process for which arrivals are independent from frame to frame.[10]

Clearly in order that the system be stable we must have

$$b > \lambda T_F M'(1) = \lambda T_F \bar{m} \tag{5.19}$$

where $\bar{m}$ is the mean number of data units in a message. We consider now points, z_i, within the unit disk for which the denominator in equation (5.15) is equal to zero. We have

$$z_i^b = A(z, T_F) = e^{-\lambda T_F[1-M(z_i)]} \tag{5.20a}$$

For any such point z_i, such that $|z_i| \leq 1$, $i = 1, 2, \ldots$, we must have a simple root. If there were a multiple root, i.e., a factor $(z - z_i)^j$, $j > 1$, then the derivatives of both sides of equation (5.20a) would be equal and we would have

$$bz_i^{b-1} = \lambda T_F M'(z_i) e^{-\lambda T_F[1-M(z_i)]}, \qquad i = 1, 2, \ldots \tag{5.20b}$$

Substituting equation (5.20a) into (5.20b), we have

$$b = [\lambda T_F M'(z_i)]z_i$$

But

$$|M'(z_i)| = \left| \sum_{i=0}^{\infty} iz^{i-1} P(M = i) \right| \leq \sum_{i=0}^{\infty} iP(M = i) = \bar{m}$$

and equations (5.20a) and (5.20b) imply that

$$b \leq \lambda T_F \bar{m}$$

but this contradicts the stability assumption in equation (5.19). Thus all roots within the unit circle must be simple if the system is stable. The next question is how many of these simple roots are there within the unit circle? The number of zeros within the unit circle can be found by an application of Rouché's theorem.

Rouché's Theorem. Given functions $f(z)$ and $g(z)$ analytic in a region R, consider a closed contour C in R; if on C we have $f(z) \neq 0$ and $|f(z)| > |g(z)|$, then $f(z)$ and $f(z) + g(z)$ have the same number of zeros within C. (See Figures 5.8a and 5.8b for illustrations.) We emphasize that under the conditions of the theorem $f(z)$ have the same *number* of roots, not necessarily the same roots.

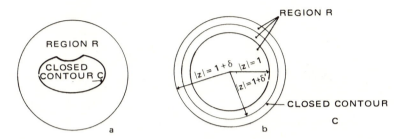

Figure 5.8. Representation of Rouché's theorem: (a) general setting; (b) specific example.

In applying this theorem we make the following identifications: $z^b = f(z)$ and $-e^{-\lambda T_F[1-M(z)]} = g(z)$. The region R consists of all z such that $|z| < 1 + \delta$, where $\delta > 0$. If δ is small enough z^b and $e^{-\lambda T_F[1-M(z)]}$ are analytic in R since they are analytic in $|z| \leq 1$. Also, for δ small enough, we can write $\delta > \delta' > 0$ and $|z| = 1 + \delta'$. From Taylor series expansions we have

$$|z|^b = (1 + \delta')^b \cong 1 + b\delta' \tag{5.21a}$$

$$\left|e^{-\lambda T_F[1-M(z)]}\right| \cong e^{-\lambda_F[1-M(1)]}[1 + \lambda T_F M'(1)\delta'] \cong 1 + \lambda T_F \bar{m}\delta' \tag{5.21b}$$

Thus, from equations (5.18), (5.20a), and (5.20b), we see that on the ring $|z| = 1 + \delta'$ we have $|z|^b > \left|e^{-\lambda T_F[1-M(z)]}\right|$, implying that z^b and $z^b - e^{-\lambda T_F[1-M(z)]}$ have the same number of roots within $|z| = 1 + \delta'$. But z^b has a root of multiplicity b at the origin, therefore $z^b - e^{-\lambda T_F[1-M(z)]}$ has b roots, which are, as we have seen, distinct. One of these roots is at $z = 1$. We designate the roots other than 1 as $z_1, z_2, \ldots, z_{b-1}$.

Since $P(z)$ is bounded on the unit disk, both the numerator and denominator in equation (5.16) must be zero for the same values of z. This condition yields the set of b simultaneous equations in b unknowns $P_0, P_1, \ldots, P_{b-1}$:

$$\sum_{j=0}^{b-1} P_j(z_i^b - z_i^j) = 0, \qquad i = 1, 2, \ldots, b - 1 \tag{5.22a}$$

A final equation comes from the normalizing condition $P(z)|_{z=1} = 1$. We apply L'Hospital's rule to equation (5.15) to obtain

$$\sum_{j=0}^{b-1} P_j(b - j) = b - A'(1, T_F) \qquad \text{for } z = 1 \tag{5.22b}$$

The remaining question is whether or not equations (5.22a) and (5.22b) have solutions $P_0, P_1, \ldots, P_b$. We examine the determinant of the matrix Δ, describing these equations:

$$\det \Delta = \begin{vmatrix} b & b-1 & b-2 & \cdots & 1 \\ z_1^b - 1 & z_1^b - z_1 & z_1^b - z_1^2 & \cdots & z_1^b - z_1^{b-1} \\ \vdots & & & & \\ z_{b-1}^b - 1 & z_{b-1}^b - z_{b-1} & z_{b-1} - z_{b-1}^2 & \cdots & z_{b-1}^b - z_{b-1}^2 \end{vmatrix}$$

By subtracting columns from one another we find

$$\det \Delta = \begin{vmatrix} 1 & 1 & 1 & \cdots & 1 \\ z_1 - 1 & z_1^2 - z_1 & z_1^3 - z_1^2 & \cdots & z_1^b - z_1^{b-1} \\ \vdots & & & & \\ z_{b-1} - 1 & z_{b-1}^2 - z_{b-1} & z_{b-1}^3 - z_{b-1}^2 & \cdots & z_{b-1}^b - z_{b-1}^{b-1} \end{vmatrix}$$

From row i one can extract the factor $(z_{i-1} - 1)$. Thus

$$\det \Delta = \begin{vmatrix} 1 & 1 & \cdots & 1 \\ 1 & z_1 & \cdots & z_1^{b-1} \\ \vdots & \vdots & & \vdots \\ 1 & z_{b-1} & & z_{b-1}^{b-1} \end{vmatrix} \prod_{j=1}^{b-1} (z_j - 1)$$

Clearly this determinant cannot vanish since all of the roots, z_i, are different and none is equal to one. Thus the matrix Δ is nonsingular and the set of linear equations (5.22a) and (5.22b) has a solution.

In summation, finding the generating function of the number of messages is accomplished in two steps:

(1) Find $b - 1$ roots of the equation

$$z^b - e^{-\lambda T_F[1-M(z)]}, \qquad z_1, z_2, \ldots, z_{b-1}$$

(2) Solve the linear equations

$$\sum_{j=0}^{b-1} P_j(b - j) = b - A'(1, T_F)$$

$$\sum_{j=0}^{b-1} P_j(z_i^b - z_i^j) = 0, \qquad i = 1, 2, \ldots, b - 1$$

In general it is necessary to resort to machine computations in order to find a solution. Software for finding roots and for solving a set of linear equations is readily available. Because of the form of $A(z, T_F)$ there is some simplification in finding the roots $z_1, \ldots, z_{b-1}$. For any integer k we have $e^{j2\pi k} = 1$; therefore for any root z_k the equation $z_k^b = e^{j2\pi k - \lambda T[1 - M(z)]}$; $k = 1, 2, \ldots, b - 1$ holds. Thus the multiple roots can be found by finding the roots of the $b - 1$ equations

$$z_k = \exp\left\{ \frac{j2\pi k}{b} - \frac{\lambda T_F}{b}[1 - M(z_k)] \right\}, \qquad k = 1, 2, \ldots, b - 1$$

It has been our experience that the simple Newton–Raphson method converges very rapidly in this case.

The mean value of n can be found by differentiating with respect to z and setting $z = 1$. We have from equation (5.16)

$$[z^b - A(z, T_F)]P(z) = A(z, T_F) \sum_{j=0}^{b-1} P_j(z^b - z^j)$$

Differentiating, we have

$$[bz^{b-1} - A'(z, T_F)]P(z) + [z^b - A(z, T_F)]P'(z)$$
$$= A(z, T_F) \sum_{j=0}^{b-1} P_j(bz^{b-1} - jz^{j-1}) + A'(z, T_F) \sum_{j=0}^{b-1} P_j(z^b - z^j)$$

After differentiating again, we have

$$[b(b - 1)z^{b-2} - A''(z, T_F)]P(z) + 2[bz^{b-1} - A'(z, T_F)]P'(z)$$
$$+ [z^b - A(z, T_F)]P''(z)$$
$$= A(z, T_F) \sum_{j=0}^{b-1} P_j[b(b - 1)z^{b-2} - j(j - 1)z^{j-2}]$$
$$+ 2A'(z, T_F) \sum_{j=0}^{b-1} P_j(bz^b - jz^{j-1}) + A''(z, T_F) \sum_{j=0}^{b-1} P_j(z^b - z^j)$$

solving for $P'(1) = \bar{n}$ we have

$$\bar{n} = \sum_{j=0}^{b-1} \frac{P_j[b(b - 1) - j(j - 1)]}{2(b - \rho)} - \frac{b(b - 1) - \lambda T_F \overline{m^2} - \rho^2 + \rho}{2(b - \rho)}$$
$$+ \rho \sum_{j=0}^{b-1} P_j(b - j)/(b - \rho) \tag{5.23}$$

where $\rho = \lambda T_F \bar{m}$. Notice that when $b = 1$ equation (5.23) reduces to equation (5.7).

5.5. Message Delay

We consider now the delay of a message as measured by the time interval between its arrival in the system and its transmission.[11] As in the $M/G/1$ queue, this delay encompasses queueing time and service time. We shall carry through an analysis of delay under the assumption that only one data unit is removed during a frame, $b = 1$. The analysis for $b > 1$ uses the same idea but is more complicated.[12] As in the previous section we assume that messages arriving after the beginning of a frame are held over until the next frame. Again we imbed a Markov chain at the beginning of the frame.

The components of message delay are depicted in Figure 5.9. In order to develop an expression for the delay encountered by a message, let us assume that a message consisting of m_{L+1} data units arrives at an empty buffer, i.e., all previous messages have been transmitted. If the message arrives τ seconds after the beginning of a frame, then a total of $T_F - \tau + T + (m_{L+1} - 1)T_F$ seconds elapse before the entire message is transmitted. T seconds are required to transmit a single data unit. If the message has more than one data unit full frames are added into the delay. If previous messages have not been transmitted, a newly arrived message suffers queueing delay as well as multiplexing delay. For the purpose of analysis, we categorize the data units of previously arrived messages into two classes: data units held over from previous cycles and data units that have arrived during the present time in the time interval τ. Let n denote the number of data units held over from previous frames. Since we imbed the Markov chain at the beginning of the frame we must take into account the fact that a data unit is removed in each frame leaving a total of $n - U(n)$ to be transmitted in future frames. The number of messages arriving in the interval $(0, \tau)$ is denoted by the random variable L. The durations of these messages are designated $m_1, m_2, \ldots, m_L$. The total delay, queueing, and multiplexing may be written

$$d = [n - U(n)]T_F + T_F \sum_{l=1}^{L} m_l + (T_F - \tau) + T + (m_{L+1} - 1)T_F$$

$$(5.24)$$

We calculate the Laplace transform of the delay by calculating the Laplace transform of independent components on the right-hand side of equation (5.24). We begin by calculating the probability generating function for the term $n - U(n)$. It is a straightforward manipulation to show that

$$\tilde{P}(z) = E[z^{n-U(n)}] = 1 - \rho + z^{-1}[P(z) - (1 - \rho)] \qquad (5.25a)$$

where $P(z)$ is the probability generating function for n given by equation

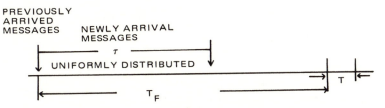

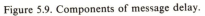

Figure 5.9. Components of message delay.

(5.16) with $b = 1$. The Laplace transform is found easily from

$$\mathscr{P}(s) = E[e^{-s[n-U(n)T_F]}] = \tilde{P}(e^{-sT_F}) \tag{5.25b}$$

Further, from basic considerations

$$E[n - U(n)]T_F = (\bar{n} - \rho)T_F \tag{5.26}$$

where $\bar{n}$ is as in equation (5.23) for $b = 1$. The Laplace transforms for the fourth and fifth terms in equation (5.24) can be found in a straightforward fashion. Let $r(t)$ denote the density function of the random variable $T_F m_i$. We have the Laplace transform

$$\mathscr{R}(s) \triangleq \mathscr{L}[r(t)] = E[e^{-sm_i T_F}] = M(e^{-sT_F}) \tag{5.27}$$

where $M(z)$ is the probability generating function of m_i.

The second and third terms are independent of the other terms but not each other. We condition on the message in question, arriving τ seconds after the start of a frame. The probability of L previous messages arriving in the interval $(0, \tau)$ is

$$P[L \text{ messages in } \tau] = (\lambda\tau)^L e^{-\lambda\tau}/L! \tag{5.28}$$

As we have seen in Chapter 3 when we discussed the properties of the Poisson process, given that there is at least one arrival in an interval, the arrival time of a particular message is uniformly distributed in the interval. This is true for all messages. Consider the random variable $f \triangleq T_F \sum_{l=1}^{L} m_l + (T_F - \tau)$ and the probability that it lies in the interval $(t, t + dt)$. There are three random variables involved here: L, which is distributed as a Poisson random variable as indicated in equation (5.28); $m_i T_F$, which has density function $r(t)$; and τ, which is uniformly distributed in the interval $(0, T_F)$. We condition first on L and τ

$$P[t < f \leq t + dt | L, \tau] = r^{(L)}(t - (T_F - \tau)) \, dt$$

where $r^{(L)}(t)$ is the L-fold convolution of $r(t)$. Averaging over L first we have

$$P(t < f \leqslant t + dt | \tau) = \sum_{L=0}^{\infty} e^{-\lambda \tau} \frac{(\lambda \tau)^L}{L!} r^{(L)}(t - (T_F - \tau)) \, dt$$

Finally, averaging over τ, which is uniformly distributed in $(0, T_F)$, gives

$$P(t < f \leqslant t + dt) = \frac{1}{T_F} \int_0^{T_F} d\tau \sum_{L=0}^{\infty} \frac{e^{-\lambda \tau} (\lambda \tau)^L}{L!} r^{(L)}(t - (T_F - \tau)) \, dt \quad (5.29a)$$

The Laplace transform of this probability density function can be shown to be

$$\mathscr{F}(s) = \frac{e^{-\lambda T_F [1 - \mathscr{R}(s)]} - e^{-s T_F}}{T_F \{ s - \lambda [1 - \mathscr{R}(s)] \}} \quad (5.29b)$$

where $\mathscr{R}(s)$ is the Laplace transform of $r(t)$ [see equation (5.27)]. Differentiating equation (5.29b) with respect to s and setting $s = 0$, we have for the mean value of f

$$\bar{f} = \frac{d\mathscr{F}(s)}{ds} \bigg|_{s=0} = \frac{T_F}{2} + \frac{\lambda T_F^2 \bar{m}}{2} \quad (5.30)$$

Recall that the random variable f is the sum of $T_F - \tau$ and the time required to transmit the messages that arrive in $(0, \tau)$. This is certainly an intuitively appealing result. Since τ is uniformly distributed in $(0, T_F)$, its mean is $T_F/2$. The average number of data units that arrive in τ seconds is $\lambda \bar{m} \tau$. T_F seconds are required to transmit each data unit.

Since the four terms $[n - U(n)] T_F, f \triangleq T_F \sum_{l=1}^{L} m_l + (T_F - \tau), (m_{L+1} - 1) T_F$, and T are independent of one another, the Laplace transform of the total delay can be found by multiplying the Laplace transforms of the density functions of individual terms. We have

$$\mathscr{D}(s) = \tilde{P}(e^{-s T_F}) \mathscr{F}(s) M(e^{-s T_F}) \, e^{s(T_F - T)} \quad (5.31)$$

See equations (5.16) ($b = 1$), (5.25a), (5.25b), (5.27), and (5.29b). By differentiating equation (5.31) with respect to s and setting $s = 0$ we find

$$\bar{d} = T_F[\bar{n} - \rho] + \bar{f} + T + (\bar{m} - 1) T_F \quad (5.32)$$

From equations (5.23) and (5.30), respectively, we find expressions for $\bar{n}$

and $\bar{f}$. We have finally

$$\bar{d} = \frac{\lambda T_F^2 \overline{m^2}}{2(1-\rho)} - \frac{T_F}{2} + \bar{m}T_F + T \qquad (5.33)$$

where $\rho = \lambda T_F \bar{m}$ and $T_F = NT$.

It is of interest to compare synchronous TDM with alternative forms of multiplexing, i.e., asynchronous TDM and frequency-division multiplexing (FDM). We assume that N users share the line equally. If each user in a frame transmits a single data unit, the duration of a frame is $T_F = NT$. We take the number of data units per message to be geometrically distributed with parameter P. From the probability-generating function given in equation (5.1) we find for the mean and the mean square values of the message length

$$\bar{m} = M'(z)\big|_{z=1} = 1/(1-P) \qquad (5.34a)$$

$$\overline{m^2} = M''(z)\big|_{z=1} + \bar{m} = (1+P)/(1-P)^2 \qquad (5.34b)$$

In Figure 5.10 we show average delay normalized to the slot time plotted as a function of λT for various values of $\bar{m}$ and N.

With minor modifications the results on synchronous TDM can be adapted to asynchronous TDM. For asynchronous TDM there is no dedication of transmission capacity so that a transmission slot is immediately available. However, all users share the same slots. If, for the moment we ignore addressing, the delay for asynchronous TDM is given by equation (5.33) with λ replaced by $N\lambda$ and T_F replaced by T. Note that $\rho = \lambda T_F \bar{m}$ is the same value for STDM and ASTDM. In order to take addressing into account one should increase the duration of a slot. In terms of bits the minimum increase should be $\log_2 N$ bits. However, in order to simplify comparisons we shall assume that addresssing introduces 10% overhead. This figure is certainly an upper bound on address overhead. If there were 1000 stations sharing the line and data units were only 100 bits long, the 10% figure would be valid. Both figures are extreme ends. The results of a computation of delay for ATDM are shown in Figure 5.11.† As we see by comparing Figures 5.10 and 5.11 for light loading, ATDM enjoys considerable advantage over synchronous TDM. As the loading increases the advantage diminishes. At very heavy loading the 10% difference in loading due to addressing causes ATDM to limit sooner. If the addressing overhead were negligible then ATDM would enjoy an advantage of a constant factor of N over the whole range of λ.

---

†Comparable results for different message length distributions are given in Ref. 11.

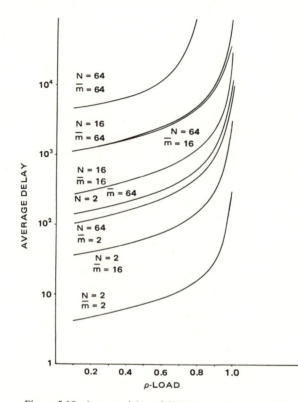

Figure 5.10. Average delay of STDM as a function of load.

In the case of frequency-division multiplexing a portion of the frequency band is dedicated to each user.[13] The line is continuously available but carries data at a slower rate. We shall assume that no guard space for filtering in the frequency band is necessary so that the time required to transmit a data unit is NT rather than T as in TDM. As in synchronous TDM we treat each source independently. Since in this case the server, i.e., the transmission line, is continuously available, the delay is given by the delay for an $M/G/1$ queue. From equation (4.20) we have

$$\bar{d}_{\text{FDM}} = \bar{m} T_F + \frac{\lambda T_F^2 \overline{m^2}}{2(1 - \lambda \bar{m} T_F)} \tag{5.35}$$

By comparing equations (5.33) and (5.35) we see that the delay for FDM is larger by $T_F/2 - T = T_F[(1/2) - (1/N)]$ sec. Over the ranges of N that are of interest, $N \gg 1$, there is a slight advantage for TDM. This advantage would increase if we were to take guard space due to filtering into account.

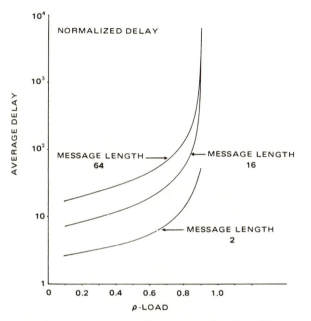

Figure 5.11. Average delay of ATDM as a function of load.

5.6. Alternate Derivation Average Delay in STDM

In Section 4.3 of Chapter 4 we considered a variation of the analysis of the $M/G/1$ queue in which the initiator of a busy period received different service than customers that had queued for service. This analysis can be applied to the derivation of message delay for synchronous time-division multiplexing.[14] Again we consider the case where a single slot per frame is dedicated to a user, i.e., $b = 1$. As in the case of the $M/G/1$ queue we imbed the Markov chain at service completion epochs. For a particular user such points occur only at the end of slots dedicated to that user. Since there may be more than one data unit in a message and since there may be idle periods, not all slot terminations are imbedded points in the chain.

In order to see how different service times arise in this context, consider the service time of a message which has queued for service. Such a message accedes to the head of the queue upon the transmission of the last data unit of the previous message. The first data unit of the message will be transmitted a full frame, T_F seconds, later. Each of the other data units of the message will be transmitted at T_F second intervals. In contrast consider the time required to transmit a message which arrives at an empty buffer. Since arrival must be in the middle of a frame, the transmission of the first data unit will occur in less than T_F seconds. The situation is illustrated in Figure 5.12. Message # 1 bearing two data units arrives at time t_1. Its first data unit completes transmission at time $t_1 + \tau + T < t_1 + T_F$. A second message bearing one data unit gains the head of the line at time t_3 and is transmitted at time $t_3 + T_F$.

The key quantity in this approach is the time elapsing between the arrival of a message and the transmission of the first data unit. This is the quantity τ in Figure 5.12. Suppose that the queue becomes empty at time zero. If a message arrives in the interval $[0, T_F - T)$, the first data unit completes transmission at time T_F. Thereafter for messages arriving in the interval $[iT_F - T, (i + 1)T_F - T]$, the first data unit completes transmission at time $(i + 1)T_F$. We define I as the duration of the idle period, i.e., the period during which the queue is empty. I is exponentially distributed with mean $1/\lambda$ seconds since it is terminated by the arrival of a message. We define Y as the interval between the end of the idle period and the beginning of the next slot ($Y = \tau$ in Figure 5.12). Clearly Y is an almost periodic function of the idle period. The relationship between Y and I is shown in Figure 5.13. We have

$$Y = \begin{cases} T_F - T - I, & 0 \leq I \leq T_F - T \\ (i + 1)T_F - T - I, & iT_F - T \leq I < (i + 1)T_F - T \end{cases} \quad (5.36)$$

The calculation of the probability distribution function of Y is an application of the law of total probability (see Appendix A):

$$P[Y \leq y] = P(Y \leq y, 0 \leq I \leq T_F - T]$$

$$+ \sum_{i=1}^{\infty} P[Y \leq y, iT_F - T \leq I < (i + 1)T_F - T]$$

$$= P[T_F - T - I \leq y, 0 \leq I \leq T_F - T] \quad (5.37)$$

$$+ \sum_{i=1}^{\infty} P[(i + 1)T_F - T - I \leq y, iT_F - T \leq I < (i + 1)T_F - T]$$

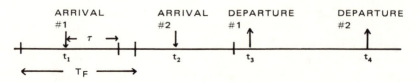

Figure 5.12. Modified Markov chain model of delay in TDM.

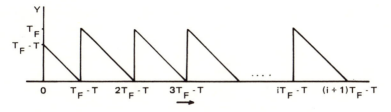

Figure 5.13. Y vs. idle time.

We deal with equation (5.37) one term at a time. For $0 \leq y \leq T_F - T$ we have

$$P[T_F - T - I \leq y, 0 \leq I \leq T_F - T] = P[T_F - T - y \leq I \leq T_F - T]$$
$$= e^{-\lambda(T_F - T)}(e^{\lambda y} - 1) \qquad (5.38a)$$

For $T_F - T \leq y \leq T_F$ we have

$$P[T_F - T - I \leq y, 0 \leq I \leq T_F - T] = P[0 \leq I \leq T_F - y]$$
$$= 1 - e^{-\lambda(T_F - T - y)} \qquad (5.38b)$$

Finally for the summation in equation (5.37) we have for $0 \leq y \leq T_F$

$$\sum_{i=1}^{\infty} P[(i+1)T_F - T - I \leq y, iT_F - T \leq I < (i+1)T_F - T]$$

$$= \sum_{i=1}^{\infty} P[(i+1)T_F - T - y \leq I < (i+1)T_F - T] \qquad (5.38c)$$

$$= \sum_{i=1}^{\infty} e^{-\lambda[(i+1)T_F - T]}(e^{\lambda y} - 1) = \frac{e^{-\lambda(2T_F - T)}}{1 - e^{-\lambda T_F}}(e^{\lambda y} - 1)$$

In calculating the quantities in equations (5.38a), (5.38b), and (5.38c) the reader is reminded that $P[t_1 \leq I \leq t_2] = \int_{t_1}^{t_2} \lambda e^{-\lambda t} \, dt$. Inserting equations (5.38a), (5.38b), and (5.38c) into equation (5.37), we obtain after some manipulation

$$F_Y(y) \triangleq P[Y \leq y]$$

$$= \begin{cases} e^{-\lambda(T_F - T)}(e^{\lambda y} - 1)/(1 - e^{-\lambda T_F}) \\ + U(y - T_F + T)(1 - e^{-\lambda(T_F - T - y)}), & 0 \leq y \leq T \\ 1, & y \geq T \end{cases} \qquad (5.39)$$

where $U(x)$ is the unit step defined previously. The probability density of Y is

$$f_Y(y) \triangleq \frac{dF_y(y)}{dy} = \frac{\lambda\, e^{-\lambda(T_F-T-y)}}{1 - e^{-\lambda T_F}} + \delta(y - T_F + T)(1 - e^{-\lambda(T_F-T-y)})$$
$$- U(y - T_F + T)\lambda\, e^{-\lambda(T_F-T-y)}, \qquad 0 \leq y \leq T_F \tag{5.40}$$

where $\delta(x)$ is the dirac delta function. It can be shown that the mean and the mean square values of Y are, respectively,

$$\bar{Y} = T_F - T - 1/\lambda + \frac{T_F\, e^{-\lambda(T_F-T)}}{1 - e^{-\lambda T_F}} \tag{5.41a}$$

$$\bar{Y}^2 = (T_F - T - 1/\lambda)^2 + 1/\lambda^2 + [(T_F^2 - 2T_F/\lambda)\, e^{-\lambda(T_F-T)}]/(1 - e^{-\lambda T_F}) \tag{5.41b}$$

We turn back now to consider the probability distribution of customers in the system when the first customer in a busy period is given extraordinary service. In Section 4.3.3 we found the probability-generating function of this number to be

$$P(z) = \frac{P_0[A(z) - z\tilde{A}(z)]}{A(z) - z} \tag{4.32}$$

where $\tilde{A}(z)$ and $A(z)$ are the probability-generating functions of the number of arrivals during extraordinary and ordinary service, respectively, and where P_0 is given by

$$P_0 = \frac{1 - \lambda A'(1)}{1 - \lambda[A'(1) - \tilde{A}'(1)]}$$

For ordinary service each data unit of a message requires a full frame. For extraordinary service the first data unit of a message requires $(Y + T)$ seconds (see Figure 5.12) while the others require T_F seconds. Differentiating equation (4.32) we find that the mean number of *messages* (not data units) in the system is given by

$$\bar{n} = P'(1) = \frac{P_0[2\tilde{A}'(1) + \tilde{A}''(1) - A''(1)] + A''(1)}{2[1 - A'(1)]} \tag{5.42}$$

If $M(z)$ is the probability-generating function of the number of data units in a message then it is a straightforward exercise to show that

$$A(z) = M(e^{-\lambda(1-z)T_F}) \tag{5.43a}$$

and

$$\tilde{A}(z) = \mathcal{Y}(\lambda(1-z))\, e^{\lambda(1-z)(T_F-T)} M(e^{-\lambda(1-z)T_F}) \qquad (5.43b)$$

where $\mathcal{Y}(s)$ is the Laplace transform of the probability density function of Y. From this point it is simply a matter of calculation and substitution to show that

$$\bar{n} = \frac{\lambda^2 T_F^2 \bar{m}^2}{2(1-\rho)} - \frac{\lambda T_F}{2} + \lambda \bar{m} T_F + \lambda T \qquad (5.44)$$

From Little's formula we see that the average delay is indeed the same as found previously [see equation (5.33)].

5.7. "Come Right In" Strategy

In the foregoing it is assumed that a "please wait" strategy is pursued. Further, it is assumed that all slots dedicated to a source are contiguous in a frame. In this section we shall sketch out an analysis which has dispensed with these assumptions.† Let us assume that the slots dedicated to a particular source are scattered throughout a frame. As in the previous cases we can consider each source acting independently. Let us assume that a frame consists of N slots, S of which are dedicated to a particular source. Let n_j denote the number of data units from the source which is in the system at the beginning of slot j. We may write the recursive relation

$$n_{j+1} = n_j - e_j U(n_j) + a_{j+1}, \qquad j = 0, 1, \ldots, N-1 \qquad (5.45)$$

where

$$e_j = \begin{cases} 1, & \text{if slot } j \text{ is dedicated to the source} \\ 0, & \text{otherwise} \end{cases}$$

In writing equation (5.45) we anticipate the existence of a steady-state solution, consequently dependence on the frame number is suppressed. In this case a_j is the number of data units that arrive during the jth slot of the frame. If all the slots are of the same duration and if the arrival of data units is compound Poisson, then the generating function for a_j is given by

$$A(z, T_F/N) = e^{-\lambda T_F[1-M(z)]/N} \qquad (5.46)$$

†See Ref. 15. For the most general treatment of the periodically available server currently available, see Ref. 16.

where $M(z)$ is the generating function of the number of data units in a message. It can be shown that if $\lambda T_F \bar{m} < SN$ then the system is stable, yielding a steady-state solution. Let $P_j(z)$ denote the generating function for n_j. It can be shown that

$$P_{j+1}(z) = \begin{cases} P_j(z)A(z, T_F/N) & \text{for } e_j = 0 \\ [z^{-1}P_j(z) + (1 - z^{-1})P_{j0}]A(z, T_F/N) & \text{for } e_j = 1 \end{cases} \qquad (5.47)$$

where P_{j0} is the probability that the buffer is empty when slot j begins. Notice that the set $\{P_{j0}\}$ constitutes a set of S unknowns. This is the same number as in the previous bulk departure case. Equation (5.47) can be written in matrix form. We define the variables ε_j and δ_j as follows:

$$\varepsilon_j = \begin{cases} z, & \text{for } e_j = 0 \\ 1, & \text{for } e_j = 1 \end{cases} \quad \text{and} \quad \delta_j = \begin{cases} 0, & \text{for } e_j = 0 \\ 1, & \text{for } e_j = 1 \end{cases}$$

We have

$$\begin{vmatrix} P_1(z) \\ P_2(z) \\ \vdots \\ P_N(z) \end{vmatrix} = \frac{A(z, T_F/N)}{z} \begin{vmatrix} 0 & 0 & \cdots & 0 & \varepsilon_N \\ \varepsilon_1 & 0 & \cdots & 0 & 0 \\ 0 & \varepsilon_2 & \cdots & 0 & 0 \\ 0 & 0 & & 0 & 0 \\ \vdots & \vdots & & \vdots & \vdots \\ 0 & 0 & \cdots & \varepsilon_{N-1} & 0 \end{vmatrix} \begin{vmatrix} P_1(z) \\ P_2(z) \\ \vdots \\ P_N(z) \end{vmatrix}$$

$$+ (1 - z^{-1})A(z, T_F/N) \begin{vmatrix} P_{N0}\delta_N \\ P_{10}\delta_1 \\ \vdots \\ P_{N-10}\delta_{N-1} \end{vmatrix} \qquad (5.48)$$

This can be written

$$\left[I - \frac{A(z, T_F/N)}{z} E(z) \right] P(z) = (1 - z^{-1})A\left(\frac{z, T_F}{N}\right) P_0 \qquad (5.49)$$

with the obvious identifications. The matrix on the left-hand side of (5.49) is invertible. Let $B(z)$ denote its inverse. The first row of this matrix, B_1, can be shown to be

$$B_1 = \frac{z^S}{z^S - A^N(z, T_F/N)}$$

$$\times \left[1, \prod_{j=2}^{N} \frac{\varepsilon_j}{z} A^{n-1}\left(\frac{z, T_F}{N}\right), \ldots, \prod_{j=n-1}^{N} \frac{\varepsilon_j}{z} A^2\left(\frac{z, T_F}{N}\right), \frac{\varepsilon_N}{z} A\left(\frac{z, T_F}{N}\right) \right]$$

(5.50)

For the remaining rows a recursive relationship can be found:

$$B_{j+1} = l_{j+1} + A\left(\frac{z, T_F}{N}\right) \frac{\varepsilon_j}{z} B_j, \qquad j = 1, 2, \ldots, N-1$$

(5.51)

where l_i is a row vector with a one in the ith place and a zero every place else. Each of the generating functions $P_j(z)$, $j = 1, 2, \ldots, s_i$ can be expressed

$$P_i(z) = (1 - z^{-1})A(z, T_F/N)B_i P_0$$

(5.52)

where P_0 is the vector of the S unknown quantities. [See equation (5.48).] Now each of the $P_i(z)$ are analytic within the unit disk, and by the same line of reasoning as the previous case $z^S - A^N(z, T_F/N)$ has S roots on the unit disk. It can be shown that evaluating the numerator of equation (5.52) at these roots gives S equations which can be solved to find the unknown probabilities. Once these quantities are known a number of quantities of interest can be determined, e.g., average number in buffer and average delay. The results of such a computation are shown in Figures 5.14, where the normalized average delay is shown as a function of the frame size with the average arrival rate as a parameter. The arrival here is simple Poisson arrival. The constraint in the equation is that half the slots in a frame are devoted to a particular user, with all of the dedicated slots contiguous. The parameter for the two curves shown is the average arrival rate in a slot.

It is often the case that the intermittently available server is approximated by a continuously available server with a lower rate. Also shown in Figure 5.14 is the average delay for an $M/D/1$ queue with the equivalent line utilization. The line is continuously available to the $M/D/1$ queue, but it goes at half the rate. The comparisons of the two sets of curves illustrate the difference between the two models. The $M/D/1$ approximation is not accurate as the frame length becomes large.

5.8. Automatic Repeat Request

The imbedded Markov chain approach can be applied to the analysis of the automatic repeat request (ARQ) technique used for error control in

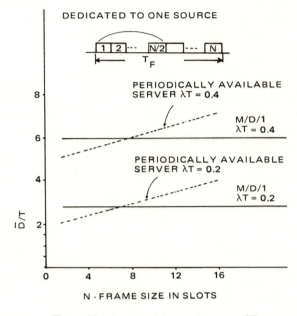

Figure 5.14. Average delay vs. frame size.[15]

ATDM systems.† As in the previous case, we assume compound Poisson arrival of data units. We assume that data units are transmitted in T second slots. (See Figure 5.2.) The new element that we shall consider is that the receiver may detect an error in the data unit. Let us assume that the probability of this event is p_E. We shall assume that errors on successive trials are independent events. As in our previous studies, a successful transmission or a failure is denoted by an ACK or a NACK, respectively. Finally we assume that there is no error in the feedback channel.

We shall analyze two different ARQ techniques. The first of these is the send-and-wait protocol considered in the previous chapter. After a data unit is transmitted, all transmission halts until an ACK or a NACK is received at the transmitter. If a transmission is not successful it is retransmitted. Since successive transmissions are assumed to be independent, the number of retransmissions is geometrically distributed. The generating function is the same as in equation (5.1) with p replaced by p_E.

As in the previous sections of this chapter we imbed a Markov chain at the points where a data unit is successfully transmitted. However, because of the possibility of error in the channel, the imbedded points are not

---

†This section is based on Ref. 17. In order to harmonize this material with the rest of the book, slight changes in the approach were made.

separated by single slot times. If $k - 1$ retransmissions of a message are required, the total number of slots required to transmit a data unit is $k(R + 1)$, where R is the round-trip delay in slots.

The analysis of the imbedded chain is the same as in this chapter and the previous chapter. The probability generating function of the number of data units in the transmit buffer is given by equation (5.4), where $A(z, T)$ is replaced by the generating function of the number of data units that have arrived between departures.

The only difference between this and the previous cases is the difference in the interdeparture interval, which is $k(R + 1)$ when there are k transmissions. This is manifested in equation (5.4) in the arrival process. If messages arrive at a Poisson rate of λ messages per second the probability of l messages arriving in this period is

$$P(l \text{ messages}/k \text{ retransmissions}) = \frac{[\lambda k(R + 1) T]^l}{l!} e^{-\lambda k(R+1) T},$$

$$l = 0, 1, \ldots \quad (5.53)$$

The probability-generating function for this number is

$$G(z) = e^{-\lambda k(R+1) T(1-z)} \quad (5.54)$$

Averaging over k we have for the generating function of the number of messages in the interdeparture interval

$$F(z) = \frac{(1 - p_E) e^{-\lambda(R+1) T(1-z)}}{1 - p_E e^{-\lambda(R+1) T(1-z)}} \quad (5.55)$$

The Markov chain is expressed in terms of data units. Under the assumption of compound Poisson arrival, the generating function of the number of data units in a message is $M(z)$. From this it follows that the probability-generating function for the number of data units which arrive during the message service interval is [compare with equation (5.2)]

$$A(z) = \frac{(1 - p_E) e^{-\lambda(R+1) T[1-M(z)]}}{1 - p_E e^{-\lambda(R+1) T[1-M(z)]}} \quad (5.56)$$

The probability-generating function of the number of data units in the buffer can be found by substituting into equation (5.4). Averages can be found in the usual way by differentiating the generating function.

The second approach to ARQ is the continuous transmission or the go-back-N technique. In this case data units are transmitted in every slot. When an error occurs, the erroneous packet as well as all succeeding data units up to the time of the reception of the NACK are retransmitted. The difference between this approach and send-and-wait lies in the service time that is seen by customers in the queue. In the absence of error the time to transmit a data unit is a single slot rather than a slot plus a round-trip delay as in the previous case. If there are k transmissions the time required to transmit a data unit is $1 + (k - 1)(R + 1)$. For simplicity we assume that a data unit leaves the system as soon as a successful transmission is completed. Actually it remains until an ACK is received.

From these considerations, the generating function of the number of newly arrived data units in an interdeparture interval is calculated in the same fashion as before. We find

$$A(z) = \frac{(1 - p_E)\, e^{-\lambda T[1 - M(z)]}}{1 - p_E\, e^{-\lambda T(R+1)[1 - M(z)]}} \tag{5.57}$$

Again this is substituted into equation (5.4) to find the probability generating function of the number of data units in the transmit buffer.

The results of computation based on equations (5.56) and (5.57) are shown in Figures 5.15 and 5.16 for send-and-wait and continuous transmission, respectively. The average queue length is shown as a function of p_E with R and λT as parameters. In computing these results it was assumed that the arrival process is simple Poisson so that each message contains a single data unit, $M(z) = z$. All of the curves show a sharp knee. Below a certain value of p_E the system is relatively insensitive to its value. For higher values the system may well be considered unstable.

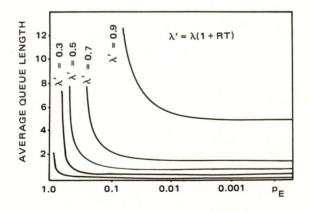

Figure 5.15. Average queue length as a function of p_E.[17]

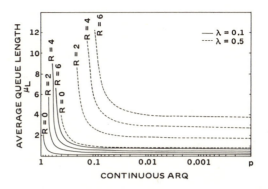

Figure 5.16. Average queue length as a function of p_E for continuous transmission.[17]

References

1. R. J. Camrass and R. G. Gallager, "Encoding Message Lengths for Data Transmission," *IEEE Transactions on Information Theory*, **IT-24**, July 1978.
2. W. W. Chu, "A Study of Asynchronous TDM for Time Sharing Computer Systems," AFIPS Conference Proceedings, Fall Joint Computer Conference (1969), Vol. 35, pp. 669–678.
3. W. W. Chu and A. G. Konheim, "On the Analysis and Modeling of a Class of Computer Communication Systems," *IEEE Transactions on Communications*, **20**(3), P. II, 645–660, June (1972).
4. H. Rudin, "Performance of Simple Multiplexer Concentrators for Data Communications," *IEEE Transactions on Communications Technology*, **Com-19**(2), 178–187, April (1971).
5. G. J. Foschini and B. Gopinath, "Sharing Memory Optimally," *IEEE Transactions on Communications*, **Com-31**(3), 352–360, March (1983).
6. F. Kamoun and L. Kleinrock, "Analysis of Shared Finite Storage in a Computer Network Environment," *IEEE Transactions on Communications*, **Com-28**(7), 992–1003, June (1980).
7. D. P. Gaver and P. A. W. Lewis, "Probability Models for Buffer Storage Allocation Problems," *Journal of the ACM*, **18**(2), 186–197, April (1977).
8. N. T. J. Bailey, "On Queueing Processes with Bulk Service," *Journal of the Royal Statistical Society* (1954).
9. K. Knopf, *Theory of Functions. Part II: Application* and *Further Development of the General Theory*. Dover, New York (1947).
10. P. E. Boudreau, J. S. Griffin, and M. Kac, "An Elementary Queueing Problem," *American Mathematical Monthly*, **69**, 713–724 (1962).
11. J. F. Hayes, "Performance Models of an Experimental Computer Communications Network," *Bell System Technical Journal*, **53**(2), 225–259, February (1974).
12. G. J. Foschini, B. Gopinath, and J. F. Hayes, "Subframe Switching for Data Communications," International Telemetry Conference, Los Angeles (1978).
13. I. Rubin, "Message Delays in FDMA and TDMA Communications Channels," *IEEE Transactions on Communications*, **Com-27**, 769–778, (1979).
14. S. S. Lam, "Delay Analysis of a Time-Division Multiple Access Channel," *IEEE Transactions on Communications*, **Com-25**(12), 1489–1494, December (1977).
15. R. R. Anderson, G. J. Foschini, and B. Gopinath, "A Queueing Model for a Hybrid Data Multiplexer", *Bell System Technical Journal*, **58**(2), 279–301, February (1979).

16. M. Kaplan, "A Single-Server Queue with Cyclostationary Arrivals and Arithmetic Service,"
    Operations Research (in press).

17. D. Towsley and J. Wolf, "On the Statistical Analysis of Queue Lengths and Waiting Times
    for Statistical Multiplexers with ARQ Retransmission," *IEEE Transactions on Communica-
    tions*, **27**(4), 693–703, April (1979).

Exercises

5.1. Suppose that for compound Poisson arrival of messages the number of data
units in a message has a binomial distribution.
   (a) Find the probability-generating function of the number of data units arriving
       in T seconds.
   (b) What is the average number of arrivals in T seconds?

5.2. Suppose that random length messages arrive at a constant rate of R messages
per second. Suppose also that the number of data units per message is geometrically distributed.
   (a) Find the generating function for the number of data units in the buffer.
   (b) What is the mean number of data units in the buffer if we have ATDM
       where a single data unit is removed at each time slot?

5.3. Consider asynchronous TDM with a slight twist. Suppose that data traffic shares
the line with higher-priority traffic. Such traffic may be, for example, voice.
Because of this other traffic the line is not always available. A crude way of
calculating the effect on data traffic is to assume that a data is transmitted in
a slot with probability $p < 1$, with independence from slot to slot. Notice that
for $p = 1$ we have the same case as before.
   (a) Set up the imbedded Markov chain for the number of data units in the buffer.
   (b) Calculate the probability-generating function for the number of data units
       in the buffer.
   (c) Find the mean number of data units in the buffer.

5.4. Suppose we have an N source model. Each of the N sources generate data
units independently. The probability that a source will generate a data unit in
T seconds is P.
   (a) Find the probability-generating function of the arrivals.
   (b) Find the steady-state probability-generating function for the number in the
       system assuming an infinite buffer.
   (c) Write down the load condition for the existence of a steady-state solution
       for the finite source model.

5.5. Suppose that we have an ATDM system in which the buffer can hold 5 bytes.
Suppose also that there are two sources each of which may generate a message
consisting of one byte independently in a slot with probability $1/4$.
   (a) What are the buffer occupancy probabilities?
   (b) What is the throughput?

5.6. Consider a synchronous TDM system in which 10 sources share the same line
equally. Compare the average delay when there are one and two dedicated slots
per user per frame (i.e., $b = 1, 2$). Assume messages are geometrically distributed
with parameter P. P should be varied over a range of values from $1/(1 - P) < 1$
to $1/(1 - P) > 2$. (You will need machine computations to do this problem.)

5.7. Consider the ARQ systems when there is an error in the feedback path. An erroneous ACK or NACK is treated as a NACK and retransmission is necessary. By suitably modifying (5.56) and (5.57), find expressions for the average number of data units in the system.

Intermittently Available Server, Priority Queues
Application to Ring Systems

6.1. Interrupted Service, Priority Queues

It is frequently the case in communications systems that transmission facilities are shared among a number of different sources. In Chapter 5, for example, time-division multiplexing is used to distribute transmission capacity among the sources sharing the same line. The allocation of resources in this case is fixed and is therefore unresponsive to the instantaneous needs of users. In this and in subsequent chapters we shall be examining techniques for sharing resources that respond to variations in instantaneous traffic levels. In this chapter sharing will be effected by granting priority to one class of users over another. As we shall see presently, this mechanism does not necessarily mean inequitable service.

A large part of our analysis is based on a model in which the transmission line is available only intermittently. Consider the situation depicted in Figure 6.1. We have two sources, where source 1 has priority over source 2. When source 1 wishes to transmit, it is given priority irrespective of the backlog from source 2. A simple example of such a priority discipline is a system in which voice and data share a line with priority given to voice. When there are no voice calls the line is used to transmit data messages. As soon as a voice call is initiated it has exclusive use of the line. Any data messages arriving during the voice call are stored until the line becomes available. From the viewpoint of the class 2 source the server appears to be subject to periodic breakdowns coinciding with the initiation of voice calls. For this particular application, it is reasonable to assume that the time intervals between interruptions and the durations

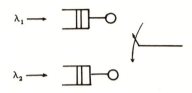

$\lambda_1 \longrightarrow$

$\lambda_2 \longrightarrow$

Figure 6.1. Two priority classes.

of voice calls are independent, exponentially distributed random variables.

Another situation where the server disappears periodically is that of two $M/G/1$ queues where one has priority over the other. In this case the line is unavailable to the class 2 source for a time interval which is equal to what is called the *busy period* of the class 1 source. As we shall see presently the busy period is the time required to serve an initiating message plus all following messages until there are no more class 1 messages in the system. Again the time between interruptions is exponentially distributed since they are caused by the arrival of class 1 messages.

In considering priorities among queues there are several priority disciplines that can be defined. To varying degrees we shall consider three types of priority disciplines: *preemptive resume, preemptive nonresume,* and *nonpreemptive.*† As we shall see these disciplines are applicable to systems with a ring topology in computer communications. All three of these disciplines may be illustrated by two classes (see Figure 6.1). Messages arrive for priority class 1 at a rate of λ_1 messages per second and for priority class 2 at a rate of λ_2 messages per second. These messages are transmitted over a transmission line which we speak of as the *server* for convenience. We may imagine that there is a message buffer for each priority class and that the server shuttles between these buffers according to the service discipline. The presence of the server at a buffer means that messages are being transmitted at a constant rate. For the *preemptive resume* discipline the server switches from the class 2 buffer immediately upon arrival of a class 1 message. The server remains at the class 1 buffer until it is empty, whereupon it returns to the class 2 buffer and continues where it left off. Notice that there is no loss of work in that no part of the message is transmitted more than once. Notice also that the time that the server is absent from buffer 2 is the duration of a busy period.

In the *preemptive nonresume* discipline there is a loss of work. As in the previous case the server interrupts work on a class 2 message immediately upon the arrival of a class 1 message. The server remains with the class 1 messages for the duration of a busy period. However, upon return to buffer 2 the buffer begins all over again at the beginning of the message that was

†For a complete treatment of priority queues, see Refs. 1. See also Refs. 2 and 3.

left behind in the class 2 buffer. In the case of exponential distributions of delay and number in the queue are the same for both the resume and the nonresume disciplines. This is not true for general message length distributions since they have memory.

Another discipline, which is appropriate in a communications context, is *nonpreemptive*. In this case the server occupied with a class 2 message switches to a newly arrived class 1 message only after the entire message has been transmitted. This is a work-preserving discipline since upon return to the class 2 buffer an entirely new message is transmitted. In the nonpreemptive discipline there is no possibility of just part of a message being transmitted.

6.2. Preemptive Resume Discipline

In some ways the preemptive resume discipline is easiest to analyze. For a class 1 message the presence of a lower class is unseen since the server is always available. The equations governing delay and buffer occupancy for class 1 messages are the same as for an $M/G/1$ queue with a message arrival rate of λ_1 messages per second. Of course the situation is different for class 2, which experiences service interruptions when a class 1 message enters the system. The time interval during which the server is available to class 2 is exponentially distributed with mean $1/\lambda_1$ since it terminates when there is an arrival for class 1. The duration of this interruption is the busy period of an $M/G/1$ queue with message arrival rate λ_1 per second. In this section we shall consider a general distribution for server absence. This makes the results more widely applicable.† The distribution for the busy period of the $M/G/1$ queue will be derived in due course.

6.2.1. Imbedded Markov Chains

An imbedded Markov chain approach can be used to find the dynamics of the class 2 queue. In this case the variation for the initiator of a busy period studied in Section 4.3 of Chapter 4 is appropriate. When a class 2 message arrives to an empty buffer the server may or may not be available and the service time is the sum of the message transmission time and the time one waits for the return of the server. This is illustrated in Figure 6.2 where the contents of a buffer holding class 2 messages is shown as a function of time. When a message arrives, there is an instantaneous jump. When the server is present, there is a steady decrease. A message that arrives

†The analysis of an $M/G/1$ queue with an intermittently available server is from Avi-Itzhak and Naor.[4]

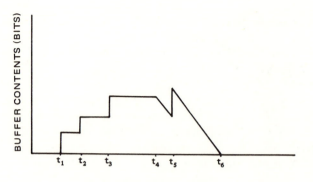

Figure 6.2. Dynamics of buffer 2.

at time t_1 to an empty buffer must wait until time t_4 when the server returns before beginning transmission. This service time is different from messages that arrive at times t_2, t_3, and t_5 to an occupied buffer. Such messages have queued for service and the server is available immediately after the previous message departs. In this case the service time is simply the time required to transmit a message. The imbedded Markov chain for the number of messages in the queue is given by

$$n_{i+1} = n_i - 1 + a_{i+1}, \qquad n_i > 0 \tag{6.1a}$$

$$n_{i+1} = \tilde{a}_{i+1}, \qquad n_i = 0 \tag{6.1b}$$

where a_{i+1} is the number of arrivals of class 2 messages during a transmission time of a class 2 message and $\tilde{a}_{i+1}$ is the number of arrivals of class 2 messages during the time of waiting for the server and the transmission time of a class 2 message.

As we have seen in Chapter 4, the probability-generating function for the number of messages in the system is given by equation (4.39), which we repeat here for convenience. Let $A(z)$ and $\tilde{A}(z)$ be the probability generating functions for a_{i+1} and $\tilde{a}_{i+1}$, respectively; then we have

$$P(z) = \frac{P_0[A(z) - z\tilde{A}(z)]}{A(z) - z} \tag{6.2}$$

where

$$P_0 = \frac{1 - A'(1)}{1 - A'(1) + \tilde{A}'(1)} = \frac{1 - \bar{a}}{1 - \bar{a} + \tilde{a}}$$

6.2.2. Message Transmission Times

The important quantities in equation (6.2) are the message arrival processes during the two types of service intervals. We begin by deriving the probability distribution for each type of service intervals. Let us begin with the service time of the message which has queued for service. The key consideration here is the service interruptions. The situation is depicted in Figure 6.3. Message transmission begins at time t_0 and is interrupted at time t_1; service resumes at time t_2, and so on. In Figure 6.3 the cross-hatched intervals are intervals in which the server is available. The sum of all of these intervals must add up to the total message length m_2. The durations of the interruptions are independent identically distributed random variables which we denote as $F_1, F_2, \ldots$. We may write the total transmission time as

$$T = m_2 + \sum_{i=1}^{n} F_i \tag{6.3}$$

where n is the number of service interruptions. The key to the calculation of the probability distribution of T is the probability distribution of n. Assume for the moment that the duration of the class 2 message is u_2 seconds. The number of service interruptions is Poisson with average $\lambda_1 u_2$. This can be seen by observing that the cross-hatched intervals in Figure 6.3 are each exponentially distributed with mean $1/\lambda_1$ and that the sum of all the intervals is u_2 seconds. Recall that for Poisson arrivals, the interarrival distribution is exponentially distributed. Taking expectations in (6.3) we have

$$\bar{T} \triangleq E[T] = \bar{m}_2 + E[n]\bar{F} = \bar{m}_2 + \lambda_1 \bar{m}_2 \bar{F} \tag{6.4}$$

where $\bar{m}_2$ is the mean message length for priority class 2 and $\bar{F}$ is the mean duration of the service interruption.

These considerations lead to an expression for the density function of the message transmission time. Suppose that the total transmission time is t seconds long and that the class 2 message is u seconds long. The sum of the n service interruptions must be $t - u$ seconds in duration. But the durations of service interruptions are independent identically distributed random variables. The probability density function of the sum is the n-fold

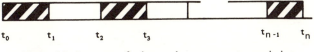

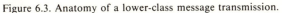

Figure 6.3. Anatomy of a lower-class message transmission.

convolution of the density function for F. We have

$$P(t < T \le t + dt/m_2 = u, \, n \text{ interruptions}) = f^{(n)}(t - u) \, dt$$

where $f(t)$ is the probability density function for F. Averaging over n, we obtain

$$P_r(t < T \le t + dt/m_2 = u) = \sum_{n=0}^{\infty} \frac{(\lambda_1 u)^n \, e^{-\lambda_1 u}}{n!} f^{(n)}(t - u) \, dt$$

Finally, averaging over the message length m_2, we have

$$T(t) \, dt = P_r(t < T \le t + dt)$$

$$= \int_0^{\infty} \sum_{n=0}^{\infty} \frac{(\lambda_1 u)^n \, e^{-\lambda_1 u}}{n!} f^{(n)}(t - u) m_2(u) \, du \, dt \qquad (6.5)$$

where $m_2(t)$ is the probability density function of the class 2 message. A more compact expression is obtained if we calculate the Laplace transform of $T(t)$

$$\mathcal{T}(s) = \int_0^{\infty} e^{-st} T(t) \, dt$$

$$= \int_0^{\infty} e^{-st} \left[\int_0^{\infty} \sum_{n=0}^{\infty} \frac{(\lambda_1 u)^n \, e^{-\lambda_1 u}}{n!} f^{(n)}(t - u) m_2(u) \, du \right] dt$$

We change the order of integration and let $v = t - u$. Let $\mathcal{F}(s)$ denote the Laplace transform of $f(t)$ and recall that n-fold convolution in time means a n-fold product of transforms

$$\mathcal{T}(s) = \int_0^{\infty} du \, m_2(u) \, e^{-\lambda_1 u} \sum_{n=0}^{\infty} \frac{(\lambda_1 u)^n}{n!} e^{-su} \mathcal{F}^n(s)$$

$$= \int_0^{\infty} du \, m_2(u) \, e^{-\lambda_1 u} \, e^{-su} \, e^{\lambda_1 u \mathcal{F}(s)}$$

Finally we obtain

$$\mathcal{T}(s) = \mathcal{M}_2(\lambda_1 + s - \lambda_1 \mathcal{F}(s)) \qquad (6.6)$$

where $\mathcal{M}_2(s)$ is the Laplace transform of $m_2(t)$, the density function of class 2 messages.

As noted earlier the difference between queued messages and messages that are first in a busy period is that the latter may find the server occupied when they arrive. We now quantify the amount of time such a message must wait until the server is available. The situation is illustrated on Figure 6.4. The class 2 buffer becomes empty at time $t = 0$. The next arrival of a class 2 message is at time $t = \tau$. As we have noted so often, τ is exponentially distributed with mean $1/\lambda_2$ since message arrival is Poisson. (The memorylessness of the exponential distribution is of considerable help here.) In the interval $[0, T]$ the server has gone through a number of cycles where it is alternately available and occupied. We denote the duration of available and occupied periods by A_i and F_i, respectively, $i = 1, 2, \dots$. Since an available period is terminated by the arrival of a class 1 message, it is exponentially distributed with mean $1/\lambda_1$. The distribution of the interval F_i where the server is unavailable has probability density function $f(t)$.

Let W denote the time between the arrival of a class 2 message and the availability of the server. In Figure 6.5 the relationship among the random variables that are involved is shown.† The random variable W is equal to zero if message arrival is during one of the intervals $A_1, A_2, \dots$. Summing over disjoint events we find that

$$P[W = 0] = \sum_{n=0}^{\infty} P\left[\sum_{i=0}^{n} (A_i + F_i) < \tau \le \sum_{i=0}^{n} (A_i + F_i) + A_{n+1} \right] \quad (6.7)$$

The memoryless property of the exponential random variable τ allows us to write for each term in the sum in equation (6.7)

$$P\left[\sum_{i=0}^{n} (A_i + F_i) < \tau \le \sum_{i=0}^{n} (A_i + F_i) + A_{n+1} \right]$$

$$= \prod_{i=0}^{n} P[A_i < \tau]P[F_i < \tau]P[\tau \le A_{n+1}] \quad (6.8)$$

†A similar relationship was used in the analysis of TDM in Section 5.6 of Chapter 5.

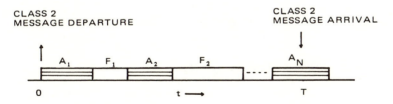

Figure 6.4. Arrival of the first message of a busy period.

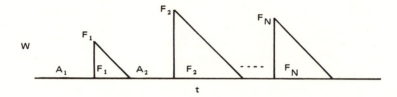

Figure 6.5. Time until server is available.

The individual terms in the product in equation (6.8) follow from the underlying distributions

$$P[A_i < \tau] = \int_0^\infty dt\, \lambda_1\, e^{-\lambda_1 t} \int_t^\infty d\tau\, \lambda_2\, e^{-\lambda_2 \tau} = \frac{\lambda_1}{\lambda_1 + \lambda_2} \tag{6.9a}$$

$$P[F_i < \tau] = \int_0^\infty dt\, f(t) \int_t^\infty d\tau\, \lambda_2\, e^{-\lambda_2 \tau} = \mathscr{F}(\lambda_2) \tag{6.9b}$$

$$P[A_{n+1} > \tau] = \int_0^\infty dt\, \lambda_2\, e^{-\lambda_2 t} \int_t^\infty d\tau\, \lambda_1\, e^{-\lambda_1 t} = \frac{\lambda_2}{\lambda_1 + \lambda_2} \tag{6.9c}$$

where $\mathscr{F}(\lambda_2)$ is the Laplace transform of $f(t)$ evaluated at λ_2. Substituting equations (6.8) and (6.9a)–(6.9c) into equation (6.7) we find after some manipulation

$$P[W = 0] = \frac{\lambda_2}{\lambda_1 + \lambda_2 - \lambda_1 \mathscr{F}(\lambda_2)} \tag{6.10}$$

The case for $W > 0$ is only slightly more complicated. Message arrival is during one of the periods of server unavailability $F_1, F_2, \ldots$. Again we sum over disjoint events. For $t > 0$

$$\begin{aligned} w(t)\, dt &= P[t < W \le t + dt] \\ &= \sum_{n=0}^\infty P\left[t < \sum_{i=0}^{n+1} (A_i + F_i) - \tau \le t + dt \right] \end{aligned} \tag{6.11}$$

From the memoryless property of τ we have

$$P\left[t < \sum_{i=0}^{n+1} (A_i + F_i) - \tau \le t + dt \right] =$$

$$= \prod_{i=0}^{n} P[A_i < \tau]P[F_i < \tau]P[A_{n+1} < \tau]$$

$$\times P[t + \tau < F_{n+1} \leqslant t + \tau + dt] \tag{6.12}$$

$$= \left(\frac{\lambda}{\lambda_1 + \lambda_2}\right)^{n+1} \mathscr{F}^n(\lambda_2) \int_0^\infty dr\, \lambda_2\, e^{-\lambda_2 r} f(r + t)\, dt$$

After substituting equation (6.12) into equation (6.11) we find

$$w(t)\, dt = \frac{\lambda_1}{\lambda_1 + \lambda_2 - \lambda_1 \mathscr{F}(\lambda_2)} \int_t^\infty dr\, \lambda_2\, e^{-\lambda_2(r-t)} f(r)\, dt \tag{6.13}$$

The foregoing gives the value of $w(t)$ for $t > 0$. The density function at $t = 0$ can be represented by a Dirac delta function with weight equal to $P(W = 0)$ given by equation (6.10). It is a straightforward exercise to find the Laplace transform of $w(t)$. From equations (6.7) and (6.13) we have

$$\mathscr{W}(s) = \frac{\lambda_2}{\lambda_1 + \lambda_2 - \lambda_1 \mathscr{F}(\lambda_2)} + \frac{\lambda_1 \lambda_2 [\mathscr{F}(s) - \mathscr{F}(\lambda_2)]}{[\lambda_1 + \lambda_2 - \lambda_1 \mathscr{F}(\lambda_2)](\lambda_2 - s)} \tag{6.14}$$

By differentiating $\mathscr{W}(s)$ and setting $s = 0$ we find

$$\bar{W} = -\mathscr{W}'(0) = (1 + \lambda_1 \bar{F})/[\lambda_1 + \lambda_2 - \lambda_1 F(\lambda_2)] - 1/\lambda_2 \tag{6.15}$$

The time spent waiting for the server to become available is independent of the time required to actually transmit the message. The Laplace transform of the time spent in the system by a class 2 message arriving at an empty buffer is given by the product

$$\tilde{\mathscr{T}}(s) = \mathscr{W}(s)\mathscr{T}(s) \tag{6.16}$$

where $\mathscr{T}(s)$ and $\mathscr{W}(s)$ are given by equations (6.6) and (6.14), respectively. During the time intervals T and W class 2 messages arrive at a Poisson rate with mean λ_2 messages per second. The probability-generating functions $A(z)$ and $\tilde{A}(z)$ may be written down directly [see equations (4.15) and (4.18) in Chapter 4]:

$$A(z) = \mathscr{T}[\lambda_2(1 - z)] \tag{6.17a}$$

$$\tilde{A}(z) = \tilde{\mathscr{T}}[\lambda_2(1 - z)] = \mathscr{W}(\lambda_2(1 - z))A(z) \tag{6.17b}$$

These can be substituted into equation (6.2) to give the probability-generating function of the number of messages in the system.

6.2.3. Message Delay

Since under the preemptive resume discipline the class 1 message is unaffected by the class 2 traffic, its delay is simply that of an $M/G/1$. If class 2 messages are served in order of arrival, then the Laplace transform of the probability density of delay is given by

$$\mathscr{D}(s) = P(1 - s/\lambda_2) \tag{6.18}$$

[Again see equations (4.15) and (4.18) in Chapter 4.]

From equations (6.2), (6.17a), (6.17b), and (6.18) we have for the Laplace transform of the probability density of message delay

$$\mathscr{D}(s) = \frac{1 - \bar{a}}{1 - \bar{a} + \tilde{a}} \frac{(\lambda_2 - s)\mathscr{W}(s)\mathscr{T}(s) - \lambda_2\mathscr{T}(s)}{\lambda_2 - s - \lambda_2\mathscr{T}(s)} \tag{6.19}$$

where $\bar{a}$ and $\tilde{a}$ are the average number of message arrivals during ordinary service, T, and first in line service, $T + W$, respectively. From equation (6.4) we have

$$\bar{a} = \lambda_2 m_2(1 + \lambda_1 \bar{F}) = \rho_2(1 + \lambda_1 \bar{F}) \tag{6.20}$$

since $\tilde{a} = \lambda_2(\bar{T} + \bar{W})$ we have $1 - \bar{a} + \tilde{a} = \lambda_2\bar{W} + 1$. From equation (6.15) it can be shown that

$$1 - \bar{a} + \tilde{a} = 1 + \lambda_2\bar{W} = \frac{\lambda_2 + \lambda_1\lambda_2\bar{F}}{\lambda_1 + \lambda_2 - \lambda_1\mathscr{F}(\lambda_2)} \tag{6.21}$$

Substituting equations (6.17) and (6.21) into equation (6.19) we find after some manipulation

$$\mathscr{D}(s) = (1 - P - \rho_2)\frac{\mathscr{T}(s)[\lambda_1\mathscr{F}(s) - \lambda_1 - s]}{\lambda_2 - s - \lambda_2\mathscr{T}(s)} \tag{6.22}$$

where $P = \lambda_1\bar{F}/(1 + \lambda_1\bar{F})$. Notice that in the derivation of equation (6.22) we have eliminated the troublesome term $\mathscr{F}(\lambda_2)$. From equation (6.22) the moments of delay can be calculated by the usual process of differentiation and setting $s = 0$. For the average delay we have

$$\bar{D} = -\mathscr{D}'(0) = \frac{\bar{m}_2}{1 - P} + \frac{\lambda_2\overline{m_2^2}}{2(1 - P - \rho_2)(1 - P)} + \frac{\lambda_1(1 - P)^2\overline{F^2}}{2(1 - P - \rho_2)} \tag{6.23}$$

Each of the individual terms in equation (6.23) can be interpreted in terms of the mechanisms of the priority queueing process. The first term is simply the time required to transmit a class 2 message. The factor $1 - P$ in the denominator is due to interruptions by the class 1 messages. Notice that $0 \leq P \leq 1$ and $P = 0$ for $\lambda_1 = 0$. The second term may be interpreted as the queueing time of a class 2 message. If λ_2 is equal to zero then this term is zero. Also if λ_1 is equal to zero then this term is equal to the queueing time of an $M/G/1$ queue with the appropriate load factors [see equation (4.27b)]. Finally the last term accounts for the fact that the server is not always available when a class 2 message arrives. If the duration of the interruption of service decreases so also does the magnitude of this term.

The foregoing results apply directly to priority queues. The transmission of a class 2 message is interrupted by the arrival of a class 1 message. (See Figure 5.2 and the attendant discussion.) The duration of the interruption is the busy period of an $M/G/1$ queue. In the next section we shall derive the probability distribution of this quantity.

6.2.4. Busy Period of the $M/G/1$ Queue

As in the foregoing, we consider the situation in which an $M/G/1$ queue models the arrival of messages at a buffer for multiplexing on a transmission line. The content of the buffer in bits as a function of time is depicted in Figure 6.6. Messages arrive at times $a_1, a_2, \ldots, a_7$. At these arrival epochs the content of the buffer increases instantaneously by a random amount which is the length of the message. In the intervals between message arrivals the buffer content declines at a steady rate according to the rate of the transmission line. In Figure 6.6 we distinguish alternating periods in which the server, i.e., the transmission line, is busy and idle. The server is busy up until epoch i_1 whereupon it is idle until the next arrival at epoch a_5. The second busy period lasts until epoch i_2 and so on.

The nature of the arrival process plays a central role in the derivation of the distribution of the busy period. Consider the second busy period

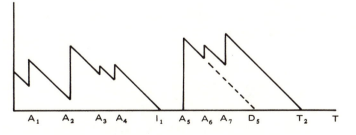

Figure 6.6. Buffer contents as a function of time.

predicted in Figure 6.6. If messages are handled in a first-come first-served fashion, the message that arrived at epoch a_5 would complete service at epoch d_5. (The depletion of the buffer of this particular message is depicted by the dotted line.) Notice, however, that in the interval (a_5, d_5) two other messages arrive at epochs a_6 and a_7. The busy period continues while these are in the buffer and while any new arrivals are transmitted. It happens that there are no arrivals shown in the interval (d_5, i_2), but since the arrival process is Poisson there could have been any number of such arrivals.

In order to illustrate the ideas involved here a derivation of the mean duration of a busy period can be carried out by dealing in message generation intervals. The first generation is simply the message that initiates the busy period. The second generation is all of the messages spawned while the first generation is being transmitted. In general the ith generation is all of the messages that arrive while the $(i - 1)$st generation messages are being transmitted. In the busy period depicted in Figure 6.6 there are only two generations. If there had been arrivals in the intervals (d_5, i_1) these would have formed the third generation. Let $\overline{N_i}$ denote the average number of messages in the ith generation. Recall that in the previous chapters we have defined a quantity ρ to be the average number of message arrivals during the transmission time of a message. If the $(i - 1)$st generation had N_{i-1} messages the average number of arrivals in that generation is $\bar{N}_{i-1}\rho$. We have

$$\bar{N}_1 = 1$$
$$\bar{N}_2 = \rho$$
$$\vdots$$
$$\bar{N}_i = \bar{N}_{i-1}\rho$$

The average number of messages in a busy period is

$$\bar{N}_{\text{BP}} = \sum_{i=1}^{\infty} \overline{N_i} = \sum_{i=1}^{\infty} \rho^{i-1} = \frac{1}{1 - \rho} \tag{6.24}$$

Since message lengths are independent of the number of messages in the queue, the average duration of a busy period is

$$\overline{\text{BP}} = \bar{m}/(1 - \rho) \tag{6.25}$$

where $\bar{m}$ is the average duration of a message.

An implicit equation for the Laplace transform of the density function of the busy period can be derived. The key to this derivation is the memory-less property of the Poisson arrival process. We begin by focusing on the number of messages that arrive during the time that the initial message is being transmitted. Two observations allow us to proceed: (1) the number of messages constitute disjoint events; (2) each message generates a busy period which has the same probability density function. We begin by decomposing the event $\{t < \text{BP} \le t + dt\}$ into a set of disjoint events according to the number of arrivals during the first generation:

$$b(t) \, dt \triangleq P[t < \text{BP} \le t + dt]$$

$$= \sum_{n=0}^{\infty} P[t < \text{BP} \le t + dt, n \text{ arrivals in service period of first generation}]$$

where BP denotes the busy period. Define m to be the time required to transmit the initial message of the busy period. For each possible value of the initial message transmission time we have a disjoint event. These events are summed through integration:

$$b(t) \, dt = \sum_{n=0}^{\infty} \int_{0}^{\infty} P[u < m \le u + du, n \text{ arrivals in } m, t < \text{BP} \le t + dt]$$

(6.26)

The integration here is over the message length distribution with variable of integration u. We now rewrite the integrand in equation (6.26) by conditioning on m and u:

$$P[u < m \le u + du, n \text{ arrivals in } m, t < \text{BP} \le t + dt]$$

$$= P(u < m \le u + du) P(n \text{ arrivals in } m/u < m \le u + du)$$

$$\times [P(t < \text{BP} \le t + dt/n \text{ arrivals in } m, m = u)] \qquad (6.27)$$

$$= [m(u) \, du] \cdot \left[\frac{e^{-\lambda u}(\lambda u)^n}{n!} \right]$$

$$\times [P(t < \text{BP} \le t + dt/n \text{ arrivals in } m, m = u)]$$

In order to find an expression for the rightmost term here we bring into play observation number (2) above: We assume that the busy period initiated by each of the n messages has probability density $b(t)$. This allows us to write

$$P[t < \text{BP} \le t + dt/n \text{ arrivals in } m, m = u] = b^{(n)}(t - u) \, dt \qquad (6.28)$$

where the superscript (n) denotes n-fold convolution. Restating equation (6.28) we have that each arrival during the first generation generates its own busy period. These busy periods have had the same distribution as each other and as the overall busy period. The sum of the newly generated busy periods and the busy period and the initial message transmission time must equal the overall busy period. From equations (6.26), (6.27), and (6.28) we have

$$b(t) = \sum_{n=0}^{\infty} \int_0^t m(u) \frac{e^{-\lambda u}(\lambda u)^n}{n!} b^{(n)}(t-u) \, du \qquad (6.29)$$

where $m(u)$ is the probability density of the time required to transmit a message. We take the transform of both sides of equation (6.29):

$$\mathscr{B}(s) = \mathscr{L}[b(t)]$$

$$= \int_0^{\infty} dt \, e^{-st} \sum_{n=0}^{\infty} \int_0^t m(u) \, e^{-\lambda u} \frac{(\lambda u)^n}{n!} b^{(n)}(t-u) \, du$$

$$= \int_0^{\infty} du \sum_{n=0}^{\infty} \frac{(\lambda u)^n}{n!} e^{-\lambda u} m(u) \int_0^{\infty} dt \, e^{-st} b^{(n)}(t-u)$$

$$= \int_0^{\infty} du \sum_{n=0}^{\infty} \frac{(\lambda u)^n}{n!} e^{-\lambda u} m(u) \mathscr{B}^n(s) \, e^{-su} \qquad (6.30)$$

$$= \int_0^{\infty} du \, m(u) \, e^{-u}[\lambda + s - \lambda \mathscr{B}(s)]$$

$$= \mathscr{M}(\lambda + s - \lambda \mathscr{B}(s))$$

where $\mathscr{B}(s)$ is the Laplace transform of the busy period and $\mathscr{M}(s)$ is the Laplace transform of the message transmission time.

In equation (6.30) we have an implicit expression for the busy period of an $M/G/1$ queue. The equation is self-consistent inasmuch as

$$\mathscr{B}(0) = \mathscr{M}(\lambda - \lambda \mathscr{B}(0)) = M_1(0) = 1$$

The mean duration of a busy period can be found by differentiation:

$$\mathscr{B}'(0) = \mathscr{M}'(0)[1 - \lambda \mathscr{B}'(0)] \qquad (6.31)$$

Therefore $\overline{BP} = \bar{m}/(1 - \rho_1)$, which checks equation (6.25). Notice that the mean value of the busy period depends upon the service time only through the mean value of the service time. Higher moments of the busy period can be found by repeated differentiation. For example, for the second moment we have

$$\mathcal{B}''(s) = [1 - \lambda \mathcal{B}'(s)]^2 \mathcal{M}''(\lambda + s - \lambda \mathcal{B}(s)) - \lambda \mathcal{B}''(s)$$
$$\times \mathcal{M}'(\lambda + s - \lambda \mathcal{B}(s)) \tag{6.32}$$

$$\overline{BP^2} = \mathcal{B}''(0) = \frac{(1 + \lambda \overline{BP})^2 \overline{m^2}}{1 - \rho} = \frac{\overline{m^2}}{(1 - \rho)^3}$$

For the case of an exponetial service time an explicit expression for the characteristic function may be found. If $\mathcal{M}(s) = \mu/(\mu + s)$, then equation (6.30) becomes

$$\mathcal{B}(s) = \frac{\mu}{\mu + \lambda + s - \lambda \mathcal{B}(s)}$$

solving for $\mathcal{B}(s)$ we obtain

$$\mathcal{B}(s) = \frac{\mu + \lambda + s - [(\mu + \lambda + s)^2 - 4\mu\lambda]^{1/2}}{2\lambda} \tag{6.33}$$

In equation (6.33) the reader will no doubt recognize the solution to the quadratic equation. The minus sign is chosen so that $\mathcal{B}(0) = 1$. This may be inverted using standard techniques to obtain

$$b(t) = \frac{1}{t(\rho)^{1/2}} e^{-(\lambda + \mu)t} I_1[2t(\lambda\mu)^{1/2}]$$

where $I_1(x)$ is the modified Bessel function of the first kind of order one. Beyond this there seems to be a dead end in the attempt to find explicit representations of the busy period by means of equation (6.30). However, using a combinatorial approach Takâcs[1,5,6] has found the following expression for the density function of the busy period

$$b(t) = \int_0^t \sum_{n=1}^\infty e^{-\lambda x} \frac{(\lambda x)^{n-1}}{n!} m^{(n)}(x)\, dx \tag{6.34}$$

In terms of the results we have obtained for the interrupted server, the busy period of the higher class queue is the amount of time that the server is unavailable. Thus $\mathcal{B}(s)$ can be substituted into equation (6.6) to find the Laplace transform of the density of the transmission time

$$\mathcal{T}(s) = \mathcal{M}_2(\lambda_1 + s - \lambda_1 \mathcal{B}(s)) \tag{6.35}$$

The transform of the delay density is found from equation (6.22) to be

$$\mathcal{D}(s) = (1 - \rho_1 - \rho_2) \frac{\mathcal{T}(s)[\lambda_1 \mathcal{B}(s) - \lambda_1 - s]}{\lambda_2 - s - \lambda_2 \mathcal{T}(s)} \tag{6.36}$$

Notice that from equation (6.31)

$$P = \frac{\lambda_1 \overline{BP}}{1 + \lambda \overline{BP}} = \rho_1 \tag{6.37}$$

Substituting equation (6.37) into (6.23) gives the average delay of a lower class message as

$$\bar{D} = \frac{\overline{m_2}}{1 - \rho_1} + \frac{\lambda_1 \overline{m_1^2} + \lambda_2 \overline{m_2^2}}{2(1 - \rho_1 - \rho_2)(1 - \rho_1)} \tag{6.38}$$

6.2.5. n Priority Classes

The analysis of the preemptive resume priority with two priority classes easily generalizes to any number of classes in which the message transmission times and the message arrival rates need not be the same for all classes. Consider the jth class of a total of n classes. Because of the preemptive discipline the classes with lower priority, $j + 1, j + 2, \ldots, n$ have no effect on the jth class. With the arrival of a message from class $1, 2, \ldots, j - 1$ the server immediately leaves off serving a class j message. The aggregate arrival rate of the higher class messages is Poisson at average rate $\lambda_h = \sum_{i=1}^{j-1} \lambda_i$, where λ_i is the arrival rate of class i messages. The distribution of message lengths can be calculated as a weighted sum. Let $\mathcal{M}_i(s)$, $i = 1, 2, \ldots, j - 1$ be the Laplace transform of the density of the message lengths in class i. The Laplace transform of the density of the messages which interrupt service to a class j message is given by

$$\mathcal{M}_h(s) = \sum_{i=1}^{j-1} \lambda_i \mathcal{M}_i(s) \Big/ \sum_{i=1}^{j-1} \lambda_i \tag{6.39}$$

As far as class j is concerned all of the messages in the higher classes act in the same fashion; consequently average delay can be found from equation (6.38) with the obvious substitutions.

When the preemptive nonresume discipline is used the class with the highest priority is unaffected. However, under the same loading condition the delay for lower priority classes is much higher than for the preemptive resume discipline. The crux of the difference lies in the time required to transmit a message. In the nonresume case the beginning of the message is retransmitted each time a higher-priority class message enters the system. Aside from this difference the analysis of message delay proceeds in very much the same fashion as the previous case. Notice that for exponentially distributed message lengths, the resume and the nonresume disciplines have the same statistical behavior.

6.3. Nonpreemptive Priorities

The nonpreemptive priority discipline is quite useful in modeling communications systems. One can conceive of situations where one type of traffic would have priority over another but without the urgency that would necessitate the interruption of a message transmission. In most practical cases of interest such an interruption would require additional protocol bits to indicate where one message left off and the other began.[†] Therefore, from the point of view of minimizing overhead, it would be advantageous to complete transmission of a message once begun.

A complicating factor in the analysis of nonpreemptive priority queues is that there is interaction between all priority levels. For example, suppose that a message from the highest-priority class arrives in the system to find a lower-priority class message being transmitted. Even if no class 1 messages are in the system, there is a delay until the lower class message has completed transmission. This delay is affected by the length of the lower-class message. The probability of a lower-class message being in service is also affected by the relative arrival rates of all classes. This stands in contrast to the preemptive priority discipline where higher-class messages are oblivious to lower-class traffic. Because of this interaction it is necessary to consider no less than three priority classes. The middle class is affected by both lower- and higher-priority classes.

As in most of our work on $M/G/1$ queues we shall rely on the imbedded Markov chain to carry out the analysis.[‡] We assume that messages from all three classes arrive independently at a Poisson rate with average λ_k, $k = 1, 2, 3$, respectively. Again the Markov chain is imbedded at service completion epoch. However, since there are three distinct classes of messages we find it necessary to distinguish among the imbedded points as to which class completed service. This is indicated by the term k *class epoch*, where $k = 1, 2$, or 3. Let n_{ik} be the number of class k messages in the system at the ith departure epoch. As in the previous cases we can express n_{ik} in

---

[†]In Section 6.4 we shall consider an example of such overhead as part of a protocol for ring networks.
[‡]The analysis of the nonpreemptive discipline presented here is from Cox and Smith.[3]

terms of the number in the system at the previous epoch and the number of new arrivals. Suppose that the $(i + 1)$st departure epoch is class 1. The impact of this is that a class 1 message has departed and that new messages of all three types have arrived while this message was being transmitted. We may write for $n_{i1} > 0$

$$n_{i+1,1} = n_{i1} - 1 + a_{11} \qquad (6.40a)$$

$$n_{i+1,2} = n_{i2} + a_{21} \qquad (6.40b)$$

$$n_{i+1,3} = n_{i3} + a_{31} \qquad (6.40c)$$

where a_{jk}, j, $k = 1, 2, 3$ is the number of class j messages to arrive during the transmission of a class k message. For the sake of simplicity of notation we have dispensed with any reference to the departure time in a_{jk}. If the $(i + 1)$st departure is class 2 we have for $n_{i2} > 0$

$$n_{i+1,1} = a_{12} \qquad (6.41a)$$

$$n_{i+1,2} = n_{i2} - 1 + a_{22} \qquad (6.41b)$$

$$n_{i+1,3} = n_{i3} + a_{32} \qquad (6.41c)$$

Because of the priority discipline, there could not have been any class 1 messages in the system at the ith departure. In considering a class 3 epoch we recognize that the ith departure must have left the system devoid of class 1 and 2 messages. We have for $n_{i3} > 0$

$$n_{i+1,1} = a_{13} \qquad (6.42a)$$

$$n_{i+1,2} = a_{23} \qquad (6.42b)$$

$$n_{i+1,3} = n_{i3} - 1 + a_{33} \qquad (6.42c)$$

The final equation is obtained by considering the situation when the ith departure leaves the system completely empty. The total message arrival rate is $\lambda \triangleq \lambda_1 + \lambda_2 + \lambda_3$. The probability that the next message to arrive is of class 1, 2, or 3 is λ_1/λ, λ_2/λ, or λ_3/λ, respectively. At the $(i + 1)$st departure all messages in the system arrive during the transmission time of this message. Thus with probability λ_k/λ we have

$$n_{i+1,l} = a_{lk}, \qquad k, l = 1, 2, 3 \qquad (6.43)$$

for $n_{i1} = n_{i2} = n_{i3} = 0$. We recognize that equations (6.40a)–(6.40c) to (6.43) are generalizations of the imbedded Markov chain analysis for a single class of customers.

As in the earlier analysis we compute the probability generating function. In the foregoing we recognized that there are four disjoint events in the queue dynamics: $\{n_{i1} > 0\}$, $\{n_{i1} = 0, n_{i2} > 0\}$, $\{n_{i1} = n_{i2} = 0, n_{i3} > 0\}$, and $\{n_{i1} = n_{i2} = n_{i3} = 0\}$. Consider the probability of the last event, an empty system. The priority system has the same probability of being empty as a queue with the same loading but without priorities. This follows from the fact that in either case the server is never idle. We have then that

$$\Pi_0 \triangleq P[n_{i1} = n_{i2} = n_{i3} = 0] = 1 - \lambda_1 \bar{m}_1 - \lambda_2 \bar{m}_2 - \lambda_3 \bar{m}_3 \qquad (6.44a)$$

where $\bar{m}_k$, $k = 1, 2, 3$, is the average length of a class k message. As in earlier work we define the traffic intensity as

$$\rho \triangleq \lambda_1 \bar{m}_1 + \lambda_2 \bar{m}_2 + \lambda_3 \bar{m}_3 \qquad (6.44b)$$

Now considering the dynamics of the process over a long time interval, the probability of a k epoch is equal to the probability of a class k message arriving to a nonempty buffer. We find

$$\Pi_1 \triangleq P[n_{i1} > 0] = \lambda_1 \rho / \lambda \qquad (6.44c)$$

$$\Pi_2 \triangleq P[n_{i1} = 0, n_{i2} > 0] = \lambda_2 \rho / \lambda \qquad (6.44d)$$

$$\Pi_3 \triangleq P[n_{i1} = n_{i2} = 0, n_{i3} > 0] = \lambda_3 \rho / \lambda \qquad (6.44e)$$

We calculate the two-dimensional probability-generating functions of $n_{i+1,1}$ and $n_{i+1,2}$ by conditioning on these four events. From equations (6.40a)–(6.40c) to (6.43) we have

$$\begin{aligned}
E[z_1^{n_{i+1,1}} z_2^{n_{i+1,2}}] \\
&= \Pi_1 E[z_1^{n_{i1}-1+a_{11}} z_2^{n_{i2}+a_{21}} / n_{i1} > 0] \\
&\quad + \Pi_2 E[z_1^{a_{12}} z_2^{n_{i2}-1+a_{22}} / n_{i1} = 0, n_{i2} > 0] \qquad (6.45) \\
&\quad + \Pi_3 E[z_1^{a_{13}} z_2^{a_{23}} / n_{i1} = n_{i2} = 0, n_{i3} > 0] \\
&\quad + \Pi_0 \sum_{k=1}^{3} (\lambda_k / \lambda) E[z_1^{a_{1k}} z_2^{a_{2k}} / n_{i1} = n_{i2} = n_{i3} = 0]
\end{aligned}$$

We follow the same steps as in the one-dimensional case to solve for the probability generating function. The number of message arrivals is independent of the number of messages in the system. The fact that message arrivals are Poisson over a random interval leads to a familiar relationship. We have

$$
E[z_1^{a_{11}} z_2^{a_{21}}] = \int_0^\infty \sum_{m=0}^\infty z_1^m \frac{(\lambda_1 t)^m}{m!} e^{-\lambda_1 t} \sum_{n=0}^\infty z_2^n \frac{(\lambda_2 t)^n}{n!} e^{-\lambda_2 t} m_1(t)\, dt
$$

$$
= \mathcal{M}_1(\lambda_1(1 - z_1) + \lambda_2(1 - z_2))
$$

(6.46a)

where $m_1(t)$ and $\mathcal{M}_1(s)$ are, respectively, the probability density function and the Laplace transform of the density function for a class 1 message. Similar relationships can be found for the other message classes:

$$
E[z_1^{a_{12}} z_2^{a_{22}}] = \mathcal{M}_2(\lambda_1(1 - z_1) + \lambda_2(1 - z_2))
$$

(6.46b)

$$
E[z_1^{a_{13}} z_2^{a_{23}}] = \mathcal{M}_3(\lambda_1(1 - z_1) + \lambda_2(1 - z_2))
$$

(6.46c)

Again by conditioning on events we may write

$$
E[z_1^{n_{i+1,1}} z_2^{n_{i+1,2}}] = \Pi_1 E[z_1^{n_{i+1,1}} z_2^{n_{i+1,2}}/ n_{i+1,1} > 0]
$$

$$
+ \Pi_2 E[z_2^{n_{i+1,2}}/ n_{i+1,1} = 0, n_{i+1,2} > 0]
$$

(6.47)

$$
+ 1 - \Pi_1 - \Pi_2
$$

By assuming equilibrium has been attained we may write

$$
G_1[z_1, z_2] \triangleq E[z_1^{n_{i1}} z_2^{n_{i2}}/ n_{i1} > 0]
$$

$$
= E[z_1^{n_{i+1,1}} z_2^{n_{i+1,2}}/ n_{i+1,1} > 0]
$$

(6.48a)

and

$$
G_2(z_2) \triangleq E[z_2^{n_{i2}}/ n_{i1} = 0, n_{i2} > 0]
$$

$$
= E[z_2^{n_{i+1,2}}/ n_{i+1,1} = 0, n_{i+1,2} > 0]
$$

(6.48b)

Substituting equations (6.46a)–(6.46c), (6.47), and (6.48a) and (6.48b) into equation (6.45), we obtain

$$
\Pi_1 G_1(z_1, z_2) + \Pi_2 G_2(z_2) + 1 - \Pi_1 - \Pi_2
$$

$$
= \Pi_1 z_1^{-1} G_1(z_1, z_2) \mathcal{M}_1(\lambda_1(1 - z_1) + \lambda_2(1 - z_2))
$$

$$
+ \Pi_2 z_2^{-1} G_2(z_2) \mathcal{M}_2(\lambda_1(1 - z_1) + \lambda_2(1 - z_2))
$$

$$
+ \Pi_3 \mathcal{M}_3(\lambda_1(1 - z_1) + \lambda_2(1 - z_2))
$$

$$
+ \Pi_0 \sum_{k=1}^3 \frac{\lambda_k}{\lambda} \mathcal{M}_k(\lambda_1(1 - z_1) + \lambda_2(1 - z_2))
$$

Rearranging terms gives

$$
\begin{aligned}
&\Pi_1 G_1(z_1, z_2)[1 - z_1^{-1} \mathcal{M}_1(\lambda_1(1 - z_1) + \lambda_2(1 - z_2))] \\
&+ \Pi_2 G_2(z_2)[1 - z_2^{-1} \mathcal{M}_2(\lambda_1(1 - z_1) + \lambda_2(1 - z_2))] \\
&+ \Pi_3(1 - \mathcal{M}_3(\lambda_1(1 - z_1) + \lambda_2(1 - z_2))) \\
&+ \Pi_0\left[1 - \sum_{k=1}^{3} \frac{\lambda_k}{\lambda} \mathcal{M}_k(\lambda_1(1 - z_1) + \lambda_2(1 - z_2))\right] = 0
\end{aligned}
\tag{6.49}
$$

By differentiating with respect to z_1 and z_2 and setting $z_1 = z_2 = 1$, we corroborate the relation $\Pi_j = \lambda_j \rho / \lambda, j = 1, 2, 3$. (This corresponds to demonstrating that $P_0 = 1 - \rho$ in the one-dimensional case.) By differentiating a second time with respect to z_1 and with respect to z_2 we obtain three partial derivatives corresponding to all pairs of z_1 and z_2. Setting $z_1 = z_2 = 1$ in these equations yields three simultaneous equations

$$
\bar{n}_{11} = 1 + \frac{\lambda_1 \sum_{k=1}^{3} \lambda_k \overline{m_k^2}}{2\rho(1 - \lambda_1 \overline{m_1})}
\tag{6.50a}
$$

$$
\overline{n_{21}} = \frac{\rho\lambda_2 \overline{m_1}(\overline{n_{11}} - 1) + \rho\lambda_2 \overline{m_2}(\overline{n_{22}} - 1) + \lambda_2 \sum_{k=1}^{3} \lambda_k \overline{m_k^2}}{\rho(1 - \lambda_1 \overline{m_1})}
\tag{6.50b}
$$

$$
\overline{n_{22}} = \frac{2\rho + 2\rho\lambda_1 \overline{m_1}\, \overline{n_{21}} + \lambda_2 \sum_{k=1}^{3} \lambda_k \overline{m_k^2}}{2\rho(1 - \lambda_2 \overline{m_2})}
\tag{6.50c}
$$

where

$$
\overline{n_{11}} = \left. \frac{\partial G_1(z_1, z_2)}{\partial z_1} \right|_{z_1=z_2=1} = E[n_1/n_1 > 0]
$$

$$
\overline{n_{21}} = \left. \frac{\partial G_1(z_1, z_2)}{\partial z_2} \right|_{z_1=z_2=1} = E[n_2/n_1 > 0]
$$

and

$$
\overline{n_{22}} = \left. \frac{\partial G_2(z_2)}{\partial z_2} \right|_{z_2=1} = E[n_2/n_1 = 0, n_2 > 0]
$$

Solving equations (6.50b) and (6.50c) for $\overline{n_{22}}$ we find that

$$
\overline{n_{22}} = 1 + \frac{\lambda_2 \sum_{k=1}^{3} \lambda_k \overline{m_k^2}}{2\rho(1 - \lambda_1 \overline{m_1} - \lambda_2 \overline{m_2})(1 - \lambda_1 \overline{m_1})}
\tag{6.51}
$$

Both $\overline{n_{11}}$ and $\overline{n_{22}}$ represent similar quantities, the expected number of messages given that one is beginning transmission. The average number of messages which have arrived during the queueing time of the message to be transmitted are $\overline{n_{11}} - 1$ and $\overline{n_{22}}$ for class 1 and class 2, respectively. All of these late arriving messages arrive to a nonempty system with probability ρ. Since messages that arrive to an empty system suffer no queueing delay, we have for the average queueing delay for each class message

$$\overline{Q_1} = \rho(\overline{n_{11}} - 1) = \frac{\sum_{k=1}^{3} \lambda_k \overline{m_k^2}}{2(1 - \lambda_1 \overline{m_1})} \tag{6.52a}$$

$$\overline{Q_2} = \rho(\overline{n_{22}} - 1) = \frac{\sum_{k=1}^{3} \lambda_k \overline{m_k^2}}{2(1 - \lambda_1 \overline{m_1})(1 - \lambda_1 \overline{m_1} - \lambda_2 \overline{m_2})} \tag{6.52b}$$

These equations admit easy generalizations to a larger set of classes. Consider class j of L classes where $j > 2$ and $L > 3$. All of the classes 1, 2, ..., $j - 1$ can be lumped together, and we have

$$\overline{Q_j} = \frac{\sum_{k=1}^{L} \lambda_k \overline{m_k^2}}{2(1 - \sum_{k=1}^{j-1} \lambda_k \overline{m_k})(1 - \sum_{k=1}^{j} \lambda_k \overline{m_k})} \qquad j = 1, 2, \ldots, L \tag{6.53a}$$

The average delay of a class j message including transmission time is

$$\overline{D_j} = \overline{m_j} + \overline{Q_j}, \qquad j = 1, 2, \ldots, L \tag{6.53b}$$

There is an interesting relationship between the analysis of the non-preemptive discipline and the $M/G/1$ queue treated in Chapter 4 when messages of all classes have the same distribution. One can view the nonpreemptive discipline as merely changing the order in which messages are transmitted. If we disregard class, the total number of messages in the system is governed by equation (4.4) in Chapter 4. As a consequence the average number of messages in the system is the same as that of an $M/G/1$ queue and is given by equation (4.17), where $\lambda = \lambda_1 + \lambda_2 + \cdots + \lambda_L$. From Little's formula the average delay of a message, averaged over all classes, is given by equation (4.20). This may be verified by showing that

$$\frac{\sum_{i=1}^{L} \lambda_i \overline{D_i}}{\sum_{i=1}^{L} \lambda_i} = \bar{m} + \frac{\lambda \overline{m^2}}{2(1 - \rho)}$$

where $\overline{D_i}$ is as in equation (6.53b).

6.4. Application to Local Area Networks with the Ring Topology

In Section 2.7 of Chapter 2 we considered the role of the ring topology in local area networks. In particular in Section 2.7.4.2 the different protocols for sharing the transmission medium were discussed. In this section we shall apply our results on priority queue to two of these protocols: demand multiplexing and buffer insertion.

6.4.1. Demand Multiplexing

In Figure 6.7 the ring topology is depicted in some detail. Flow around the ring is synchronous with the direction of flow being counterclockwise. The first technique we shall study is called demand multiplexing. In this case, flow on the line is segmented into slots. These slots circulate around the ring conveying data in a manner analogous to a train of boxcars. In this case the size of a slot is in the order of hundreds, even thousands, of bits. We call the data unit fitting into a slot a *packet*. At the beginning of a slot there is a bit indicating whether or not the slot is available. A station having data to transmit senses this bit and seizes an available slot. A station seizing a slot in order to transmit data changes the occupancy bit. The station must also transmit source destination addresses in each seized slot. Stations also monitor destination addresses for incoming packets. The addressed station removes the packet from the line, thus freeing the slot. The indicator bit is changed accordingly. A line monitor prevents endlessly circulating packets caused by the failure of a station. When a packet passes the monitor, a specific bit in the header field is changed. At the second attempted passage through the monitor this bit is detected and the packet is removed.

A salient feature of this technique is that the availability of the line as seen by a station may be interrupted by an "upstream" station. In some cases this is very much like a preemptive priority queueing system. To illustrate this, suppose that Figure 6.7 represents a data collection system

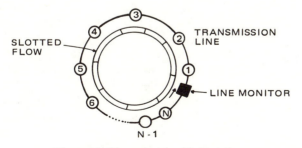

Figure 6.7. Ring network with N stations.

in which all of the traffic on the ring travels from stations $1, 2, \ldots, N - 1$ to station N. Station 1 corresponds to the highest priority class since the line is always available. Station 2 corresponds to the second priority class since the line can be preempted by traffic from station 1. So it goes with station j corresponding to priority class j. It is obvious that this multiplexing technique leads to inequitable service in the case of the data collection ring. However, when traffic is symmetric with each station transmitting and receiving data in equal amounts each station preempts as often as it is preempted and fair service is attained.

We shall apply the analysis of preemptive priority queues to the ring multiplexing technique described in the preceding paragraphs.[7] In order to do this certain approximations are necessary. Because of the slotted nature of message flow on the line, periods of server availability and unavailability are discrete rather than continuous random variables. Secondly, because of the way messages are multiplexed on and off and line, obtaining exact distributions for these busy and idle periods is difficult in general. For the data collection system the analysis is relatively straightforward. The line is available to station j if stations $1, 2, \ldots, j - 1$ have no messages to transmit. Under the assumption of Poisson message arrival, the sequence of idle slots follows a geometric distribution. This follows from the fact that a quantized version of an exponentially distributed random variable follows a geometric distribution. The difficulty arises when traffic is symmetric. Slots formerly occupied by traffic from station 1 to $j - 1$, for example, will cause gaps in the flow seen by station j. The durations of such gaps are in general not geometrically distributed. Analogous conclusions may be reached on the nature of periods of server unavailability. For the data collection system the line busy period as seen by station j is the busy period of the aggregate of traffic from stations $1, 2, \ldots, j - 1$. Again, when the traffic is symmetric the situation is more complicated.

In order to carry out the analysis with the tools that are available to us we make several approximations. The validity of these approximations has been certified by means of simulation.[10] First of all we ignore the discrete† nature of the idle periods on the line.† If an idle period is terminated by the arrival of a message, then the duration of the idle period is taken to be exponentially distributed. This approximation will be best when other factors such as queueing time and message length are long compared to a slot time. We also assume that all idle periods are due to message arrival and are therefore exponentially distributed. Finally, we assume that the periods where the line is not available take the form of a busy period. Let λ_{ij}, $i, j = 1, 2, \ldots, N$ denote the average arrival rate of messages at station i which are destined for station j. Notation is simplified, with no loss of

---

†The discrete case is treated for a data collection system by Spragins.[9]

generality, if we focus on the performance at terminal N. The average rate of message flow through terminal N is

$$\Lambda_N = \sum_{i=2}^{N-1} \sum_{j=1}^{i-1} \lambda_{ij} \tag{6.54}$$

If we assume that slots carrying packets addressed to terminal N are available for use by terminal N, the durations of line idle periods as seen by terminal N have mean $1/\Lambda_N$. If traffic is symmetric, i.e.,

$$\lambda_{ij} = \frac{\lambda}{N-1}, \qquad i,j = 1, 2, \ldots, N, \qquad i \neq j, \qquad \lambda_{ii} = 0, \qquad i = 1, 2, \ldots, N$$

then

$$\Lambda_1 = \Lambda_2 = \cdots = \Lambda_N = \frac{\lambda N}{2} - \lambda$$

Let us assume that the probability distribution of the number of bits in a message is given by $b(k)$, $k = 1, 2, \ldots$. If each line slot which has duration T holds P information bits, the probability distribution of the time required to transmit a message is

$$P[m = (l+1)T] = \sum_{k=lP+1}^{(l+1)P} b(k), \qquad l = 0, 1, 2, \ldots \tag{6.55}$$

Given $b(k)$, P, and T the moments of the message transmission time are easily calculated from equation (6.55). These quantities can be related to the line speed. The accessing technique requires that each packet be accompanied by address bits and bits indicating occupancy and history. The minimum packet size is then $P + 2[\log_2 N]^+ + 2$, where $[x]^+$ is the smallest integer greater than x. If R is the bit rate, the time required to transmit a single packet is then

$$T = \frac{P + 2([\log_2 N]^+ + 1)}{R} \text{ sec} \tag{6.56}$$

It is necessary to consider overhead in this level of detail in order to make fair comparisons. Alternative techniques do not require this amount of overhead.

The calculation of average delay is a straightforward application of the results we have derived. In equation (6.38) we have average delay in accessing the line as a function of the parameters of higher-priority traffic, m_1^2, ρ_1, and λ_1, and lower-priority traffic, $\overline{m_2}$, m_2^2, ρ_2, and λ_2. In the present application the message arrival rate for the higher-priority traffic is given by equation (6.54) and the message statistics can be found from equations (6.55) and (6.56). Recall that the multiplexing technique requires delay sufficient to examine a packet address. In the symmetric case a packet travels halfway around the loop on the average, and this factor would add an average delay of $(N/2)(2 + [\log_2 N]^+)/R$ seconds to the delay. Summing these factors we find the average delay of a message in the symmetric case to be

$$\bar{D} = \frac{\bar{m}}{1 - \rho_1} + \frac{(\lambda N/2)\overline{m^2}}{2(1 - \rho_1 - \rho_2)(1 - \rho_1)} + \frac{N}{2}\frac{(2 + [\log_2 N]^+)}{R}$$

where λ is the average arrival rate of messages and $\bar{m}$ is the average duration of a message, $\rho_1 = (\lambda N/2 - \lambda)\bar{m}$, and $\rho_2 = \bar{m}\lambda$. In applying the results of the preemptive priority analysis we recognize a particular point that may lead to serious inaccuracy: The transmission of a final packet of a message cannot be interrupted by the arrival of a higher class message. We take this into account by replacing $\bar{m}/1 - \rho_1$ by $(\bar{m} - T)/(1 - \rho_1) + T$. The final result is

$$\bar{D} = \frac{\bar{m} - T}{1 - \rho_1} + T + \frac{(\lambda N/2)(\overline{m^2})}{2(1 - \rho_1 - \rho_2)(1 - \rho_1)} + \frac{N}{2}\frac{(2 + [\log_2 N]^+)}{R} \quad (6.57)$$

We consider an example where a number of stations share a T1 transmission line. Recall from Chapter 1 that the transmission rate for this line is 1.544 Mbps. Suppose that the lengths of messages in bits given by the probability distribution $b(k) = (1 - \beta)\beta^{k-1}$, $k = 1, 2, \ldots$. The mean here is $1/(1 - \beta)$. The average delay of a message in going from source to destination in the symmetric case is shown as a function of λ in Figure 6.8. The parameters are the average number of bits in a message, P, the average number of information bits in a slot, and N, the number of terminals. Notice that from equation (6.55) the probability distribution of m is

$$P[m = (l + 1)T] = (1 - \beta^P)\beta^{lP}$$

6.4.2. Buffer Insertion Rings

There is an obvious difficulty with the multiplexing technique examined in the immediately preceding section. Since messages consisting of several packets can be interrupted in the middle of a transmission, it is necessary

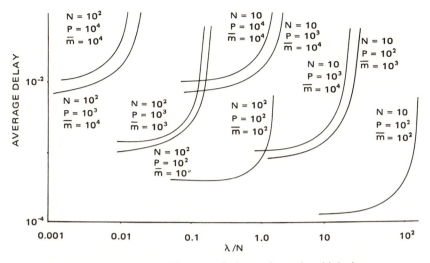

Figure 6.8. Average delay vs. arrival rate, demand multiplexing.

to transmit addressing information with each packet. Also there is a random reassembly time of a message at the destination. Adequate storage must be provided at destinations only so that incomplete messages can be buffered during assembly. An alternative technique which avoids these problems is a form of nonpreemptive priority in which messages cannot be interrupted once transmission has begun. The technique is called *buffer insertion.*[10] The flow into a station consists of two streams, locally generated traffic and through-line traffic from other stations. Depending upon implementation, one or the other of these is given nonpreemptive priority. While a message from one of these streams is being transmitted, messages from the other are buffered. After the transmission of a message, any messages of higher priority stored in the station are transmitted. When all higher-priority messages are transmitted then any lower priority messages present are transmitted. This alternation is indicated by the switch shown in Figure 6.9. In the case of symmetric traffic it is reasonable to assume that the traffic already on the line has priority. However, for the data collection ring more equitable service may be obtained if locally generated traffic has priority.

The average delay of a message in a buffer insertion system can be found by the application of the results of the nonpreemptive queue analysis and Little's formula. We assume that the message arrival rate at each station follows an independent Poisson distribution. The average arrival rate for station i is λ_i messages per second. A final crucial assumption is that the message lengths for each station are independent identically distributed random variables with mean and mean square values $\bar{m}$ and $\overline{m^2}$, respectively. The basic principle of the analysis can be explained by

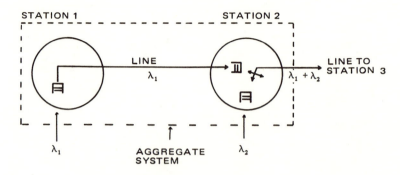

Figure 6.9. Stations 1 and 2 of buffer insertion ring.

considering stations 1 and 2 of a data collection ring in which stations transmit all their messages to the nth station (see Figure 6.9). We are interested in the average delay of a message which starts at station 1. At station 1 it suffers the average delay of an $M/G/1$ queue with message arrival rate λ_1. We indicate this delay by $F(\lambda_1)$. The difficulty is in calculating the delay in passing through station 2. If station 2 is empty it goes on without delay to the rest of the system. However, even if line traffic has priority over locally generated traffic, the presence of messages at station 2 will cause delay to station 1 messages. The trick is to find the average of this second component of delay. Consider the aggregate system formed by stations 1 and 2 where, for the moment we assume no delay between stations 1 and 2. We may analyze this system by imbedding a Markov chain at the points when messages depart over the output line between stations 2 and 3. Once transmission of a message from station 1 or 2 has begun it continues unhindered. Messages arrive at the system at a Poisson rate with average $\lambda_1 + \lambda_2$ messages per second. When a transmission is completed a new message is chosen for transmission according to established priorities. When a message arrives at an empty system, it is immediately transmitted over the output line. Considering all of these elements it is clear that the total number of messages at stations 1 and 2 is governed by the equation same as that governing the $M/G/1$ queue [see equation (4.4)]. We conclude that the average number of messages at terminals 1 and 2 is given by equation (4.17) with $\lambda = \lambda_1 + \lambda_2$. From Little's formula the average delay of a message entering the aggregate system is given by equation (4.20) with $\lambda_1 + \lambda_2$. We indicate this overall average delay by $\bar{F}(\lambda_1 + \lambda_2)$. The average delays in stations 1 and 2 are denoted $\bar{F}(\lambda_1)$ and D_2, respectively. From these quantities the average number of messages in the system may be calculated two ways. From the application of Little's formula we have

$$(\lambda_1 + \lambda_2)\bar{F}(\lambda_1 + \lambda_2) = \lambda_1 \bar{F}(\lambda_1) + (\lambda_1 + \lambda_2)\bar{D}_2 \tag{6.58}$$

We emphasize that $\overline{D_2}$ is the average delay for all messages passing through station 2. This delay may be decomposed into two components according to the origin of messages. The average delay of messages generated at station 2 can be calculated from known results since message generation is Poisson. If line traffic has priority, the average delay of such messages is, from equations (6.53a) and (6.53b),

$$\overline{D_{22}} = \bar{m} + \frac{(\lambda_1 + \lambda_2)\overline{m^2}}{2(1 - \rho_1)(1 - \rho_1 - \rho_2)} \tag{6.59a}$$

where $\rho_1 = \lambda_1 \bar{m}$ and $\rho_2 = \lambda_2 \bar{m}$. If locally generated traffic has priority the average delay is

$$\overline{D_{22}} = \bar{m} + \frac{\lambda_2 \overline{m^2}}{2(1 - \rho_1)(1 - \rho_1 - \rho_2)} \tag{6.59b}$$

Once again we proceed by using Little's formula. We calculate the average number of messages in station 2 from two approaches. The result is

$$(\lambda_1 + \lambda_2)\overline{D_2} = \lambda_1 \overline{D_{21}} + \lambda_2 \overline{D_{22}} \tag{6.60}$$

The average delay of a message in transit through station 2 is given by equations (6.58), (6.59a), (6.59b), and (6.60). We find

$$
\begin{aligned}
\overline{D_{21}} &= \frac{(\lambda_1 + \lambda_2)}{\lambda_1}\,\overline{D_2} - \frac{\lambda_2}{\lambda_1}\,\overline{D_{22}} \\
&= \frac{\lambda_1 + \lambda_2}{\lambda_1}\left[\bar{F}(\lambda_1 + \lambda_2) - \frac{\lambda_1}{\lambda_1 + \lambda_2}\bar{F}(\lambda_1)\right] - \frac{\lambda_2}{\lambda_1}\overline{D_{22}}
\end{aligned}
\tag{6.61}
$$

where $\bar{F}(\lambda)$ is the average delay of a message in an $M/G/1$ queue with message arrival rate λ, and $\bar{D}_{22}$ is given by equation (6.59a) or (6.59b)

$$\overline{D_1} = \bar{F}(\lambda_1) + \overline{D_{21}} = \frac{\lambda_1 + \lambda_2}{\lambda_1}\bar{F}(\lambda_1 + \lambda_2) - \frac{\lambda_2}{\lambda_1}\overline{D_{22}} \tag{6.62}$$

The delay suffered by a message generated at station 2 is given by equation (6.59a) or (6.59b) depending upon the priority.

The result generalizes easily for the case of a data collection ring of N stations where all messages have the same destination, station N. Consider the transient delay for a message passing through the ith station. For all intents and purposes, the first $i - 1$ stations act like a single $M/G/1$ queue.

The transit delay through station i is given by equations (6.59a) or (6.59b) and (6.61) with λ_1 replaced by $\sum_{j=1}^{i-1} \lambda_j$ and λ_2 by λ_i, where λ_i is the arrival rate of messages to the ith station. A message starting at station i suffers transit delay at stations $i+1, i+2, \ldots, N-1$. In addition to the transit delay there is a delay at the station where the message is generated. Depending upon the priority, this initial delay is given by equation (6.59a) or (6.59b). For the first station in the data collection ring the initial delay formula degenerates to that of the $M/G/1$ queue.

In the case of more symmetric traffic the foregoing analysis cannot be used to yield exact results; approximations must be employed. Again we used equations (6.59)–(6.61) with λ_1 replaced by the number of messages per second passing through the terminal under consideration and λ_2 by the generation rate of local messages. The average rate of messages passing through the Nth station is given by equation (6.54). For the case of symmetric traffic the rate of messages flowing through a station is given by $N\lambda/2 - \lambda$. The rate of locally generated traffic is λ. These quantities are used in equations (6.59a), (6.59b), and (6.61) to find queueing and transit delay. We point out that a message suffers a transit delay for each station it passes through. In the symmetric case, for example, messages pass through $N/2$ stations on the average. In each of the stations on the route of a packet it is necessary to examine the header. This factor is similar to that encountered in the analysis of the previous section, i.e., $(N/2)([\log_2 N]^+ + 2)/R$ seconds on the average.

In order to implement the buffer insertion technique a certain amount of overhead is necessary. A practical way to implement the buffer insertion technique involves segmenting the flow on the line into slots. User messages are segmented into fixed length packets which fit into these slots. As in the case of the other multiplexing technique considered in this chapter, we mark the beginning of the slot to indicate occupancy. Also, there is a bit to indicate whether or not a slot contains the last packet of a message. As in the previously considered technique, the time required to transmit the data in a message is given by equation (6.56). In this case it is not necessary to transmit addresses along with each packet, and the duration of a slot is given by

$$T = (P + 2)/R \text{ sec}$$

where R is the bit rate on the line. We may assume that address information which must accompany each message may be packaged in a special packet consisting of $2[\log_2 N]^+$ bits. The mean and mean square values of the time required to transmit a message can be calculated from these considerations in a straightforward fashion. This calculation is left as an exercise for the reader.

References

1. N. K. Jaiswal, *Priority Queues*, Academic Press, New York (1968).
2. J. W. Cohen, *The Single-Server Queue*, North-Holland, Amsterdam (1969).
3. D. R. Cox and W. L. Smith, *Queues*, Methuen, New York (1961).
4. B. Avi-Itzhak and P. Naor, "Some Queueing Problems with the Service Station Subject to Breakdown," *Operations Research*, **11**(3), 303–320 (1963).
5. L. Takâcs, *Combinatorial Methods in the Theory of Stochastic Processes*, John Wiley, New York (1967).
6. L. Kleinrock, *Queueing Systems*, Vol. 1: *Theory*, John Wiley, New York (1975).
7. J. F. Hayes and D. N. Sherman, "Traffic Analysis of a Ring-Switched Data Transmission System," *Bell System Technical Journal*, **50**(9), 2947–2978, November (1971).
8. R. R. Anderson, J. F. Hayes, and D. N. Sherman, "Simulated Performance of a Ring-Switched Data Network," *IEEE Transactions on Communications*, **Com-20**(3), 516–591, June (1972).
9. J. D. Spragins, "Simple Derivation of Queueing Formulas for Loop Systems," *IEEE Transactions on Communications*, **Com-23**, 446–448, April (1977).
10. E. R. Hafner, Z. Nenadal, and M. Tschanz, "A Digital Loop Communication System," *IEEE Transactions on Communications*, **Com-22**(6), 877–881, June (1974).
11. W. Bux and M. Schlatter, "An Approximate Method for the Performance Analysis of Buffer Insertion Rings," *IEEE Transactions on Communications*, **Com-31**(1), 50–55, January (1983).

Exercises

6.1. We wish to find the delay of a data message in a system where voice and data share the same line. The arrival of messages and the initiation of calls are independent, but both occur at a Poisson rate. The duration of the voice call is exponentially distributed and data messages have an arbitrary distribution. Voice calls have preemptive priority over data traffic. As soon as a voice call is initiated data messages are stored in an infinite buffer. While a call is in progress new calls are lost.

(a) Write down an expression for the Laplace transform of the probability density of message delay.

(b) What is the average delay of a message?

6.2. Consider the preemptive resume priority in which the message durations for both class 1 and class 2 messages are exponentially distributed. This can be analyzed by means of a two-dimensional birth–death process where, as in Chapter 3, message arrival is represented by a birth and message transmission by a death. The priority structure is represented by the fact that there can be no class 2 departures while there are class 1 messages in the system.

(a) Sketch the state transition flow diagram.

(b) Write down the equilibrium equations for $P_{ij} \triangleq P_r[i \text{ class 1 messages}, j \text{ class 2 messages}]$.

(c) Find the expected number of class 2 messages

$$\overline{n_2} = \sum_{i=0}^{\infty} \sum_{j=0}^{\infty} j P_{ij}$$

(d) Calculate the joint probability generating function

$$P(z_1, z_2) \triangleq \sum_{i=0}^{\infty} \sum_{j=0}^{\infty} z_1^i z_2^j P_{ij}$$

6.3. Messages having a constant length arrive at a Poisson rate to a multiplexer with an infinite buffer.

(a) Write down an expression for the busy period.

Suppose that transmission is interrupted by higher priority messages arriving at a Poisson rate. These messages also have a constant length but are so long that only one of them can be stored at a time.

(b) Write down an expression for the average delay of the lower priority messages.

6.4. Consider the frustrating situation where the server breaks down only when it is in the middle of transmitting a message. This means that it is always available to begin transmission.

(a) Assuming a general breakdown distribution, find the Laplace transform of message delay. Assume the usual Poisson arrival of messages with general distributions.

(b) Find the average delay of a message.

6.5. Now assume that the server never breaks down once transmission has begun, although it may not be available to a message that arrives to an empty terminal.

(a) Under the usual assumptions on message lengths and arrivals, find the Laplace transform of the delay density.

(b) Calculate the average delay.

6.6. Derive an expression for the duration of a busy period which begins with j messages rather than one message as in the foregoing. This is called the j busy period.

6.7. Suppose we have a server, which upon completing service to the last message in a busy period, goes on holidays. Suppose that the vacation period is random with density $V(t)$.

(a) Find the generating function for the number of messages awaiting the server when it returns.

(b) Find the Laplace transform of the probability density of the resulting busy period assuming that if the server finds no messages he goes on another vacation. (*Hint*: There is a concentration at zero.)

(c) Calculate the mean of this busy period.

6.8. Consider the preemptive nonresume discipline. Again assume Poisson arrivals and general service distributions for messages. What is the probability distribution of the time required to transmit a message?

6.9. Consider the case where 64 stations share the same ring network using demand multiplexing (see Section 6.4.1). The line rate is 1.544 Mbps. Information packets are 512 bits in duration. Assume that the numbers of bits in a message are distributed according to $(1 - \beta)\beta^{k-1}$, $k = 1, 2, \ldots$, where $k = 0.999$. Calculate the average delay for the 1st station, the 32nd station, and the 63rd station in a data collection context.

6.10. Repeat Exercise 6.9 for the case of buffer insertion when local traffic has priority.

6.11. Suppose that the initiator of a busy period has a different length distribution from noninitiators. Find an expression for the Laplace transform of the probability density of the duration of a busy period.

6.12. For the same sets of parameters as in Figure 6.8, calculate average delay for the buffer insertion ring.

Polling

7.1. Basic Model: Applications

In Section 2.7.4 of Chapter 2 the role of polling in access protocols for local area networks was discussed. In the model of polling systems a number of independent sources share a common facility, usually a transmission line; however, unlike priority queues, the sharing is equal. Again we use the commutator analogy where a server cycles among source buffers. The model is depicted in Figure 7.1. Messages arrive at N queues, with queue i receiving an average rate of λ_i messages/sec. In most cases of interest we take the arrival process to be Poisson. The server goes from queue to queue in some prescribed order, pausing to remove messages from each of the queues. A salient feature of the model is that the amount of time spent by the server at a queue depends upon the number of messages in the queue when the server arrives. As we shall see, this leads to complex dependencies between the queues. A second important factor is walk-time or overhead. After a server leaves a queue and before it begins work on the next queue there is a period during which there is a walk-time and the server remains idle. In most cases of interest this walk-time between queues is a constant. However, analyses can be carried out under more general assumptions. In carrying out the analyses of polling systems there are two basic quantities of interest: the time required by the server to complete a cycle through all queues, and the delay of a message in obtaining and completing service.

7.1.1. Roll-Call Polling

A prime application of the polling† model is in local distribution. Figure 7.2 depicts the situation in which a number of geographically

†For more details on polling systems for local distribution, see Refs. 1–3.

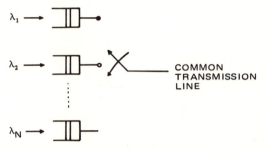

Figure 7.1. Polling model.

dispersed customers are bridged across a common transmission line which is connected to a central processor. The topology here is the tree. The function of this local distribution system is to convey messages arriving at the remote stations to the central processor over the common line. The mechanism used to achieve this is what is called *roll-call polling*. Each station is assigned a unique address, each of which is broadcast over the common line by the central processor. After each broadcast the processor pauses and waits for a response from the station address. If the station has a message, the polling cycle is interrupted while the message is transmitted. When the station has been served the polling cycle resumes where it left off.

This local distribution system contains all of the features of the polling model from a mathematical point of view. Messages arrive at random. The time required to serve a particular station depends upon the number of messages in a station buffer and their duration. The overhead or walktime consists of the amount of time required to broadcast an address and to wait for a reply. Since the central processor is receiving from a number of different stations over different lines with different transfer characteristics, part of this listening time may be used in adjusting equalizers and acquiring phase and timing where necessary. (See Chapter 2 for background material here.)

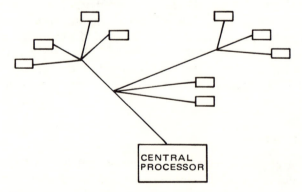

Figure 7.2. Local distribution: tree topology, roll-call polling.

The time required for equalizer adjustment is correlated with the speed of transmission over the line.

There are several ways that messages may be returned to the stations from the central processor. If the line connecting the central processor to the stations is two wire (see Chapter 2), then transmission must be half duplex, i.e., in only one direction at a time. In this case the return traffic may be transmitted at the end of the polling cycle. In the case of four-wire systems transmission is full duplex and return traffic may be handled during interruptions in the polling cycle while messages are being transmitted by the stations. To varying degrees of approximation both of these techniques can be modeled by techniques considered in the sequel.

Hub Polling

As we shall see presently a big influence on performance in roll-call polling is the overhead expended in the dialogue between the central processor and the individual stations. In systems where stations can communicate with one another this overload may be reduced by means of a technique called *hub polling*. Suppose that the topology is that of the bus shown in Figure 7.3 where stations are strung out along a transmission line. The important feature of the configuration is that stations may communicate with one another directly without intervention of the central processor. The central processor begins a polling cycle by polling the most distant station. After this station has completed its transaction, the opportunity to transmit messages is passed on to the next most distant station. The process continues for each of the stations on the bus until control is returned to the central processor. The overhead here is the time required to pass control from one station to another.

7.1.2. Token Passing

The reader may have noticed that in going from roll-call polling to hub polling there is a reduction of the role of the central processor. This decentralization of control continues to the third local distribution technique we consider: *token passing*[4] This technique is usually associated with local

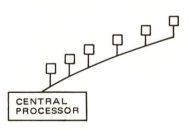

Figure 7.3. Local distribution: bus topology, hub polling.

area networks with a ring topology. This model is depicted in Figure 7.4. A number of stations are connected to a transmission line which assumes[4,5] the ring topology. Transmission around the ring is in one direction (indicated as clockwise in Figure 7.4). Randomly arriving messages are multiplexed on the line when a station is granted access to the line. The discipline used to share access is that only one station at a time is allowed to put messages on the line. These messages are presumably addressed to one or more stations on the line. The messages are removed from the line by the addressed station. When a station has sent all that it is going to send, an "end of message" character is appended to the transmission. This character indicates that another station having a message can seize control of the line. First priority is granted to the station immediately downstream. If this station has no message it appends a "no message" character to the transmission from the upstream station. From the point of view of mathematical modeling this system has the same characteristics as the previous polling model. The time that a station has access to the line is random depending upon the message arrival process. The time required to transmit end of message and no message characters is overhead.

The token passing technique is also applicable to the bus topology (see Figure 7.3). In this case the token is passed from station to station in some preassigned order without intervention of a central processor. Again the same models apply.

7.1.3. Statistical Multiplexing

A final application of the polling model that we shall consider lies in statistical multiplexing as depicted in Figure 7.5. A number of low-speed terminals share a common high-speed line through the good offices of a statistical multplexer. Messages generated by a terminal are held in a buffer until access to the high-speed line is obtained. This access is granted to

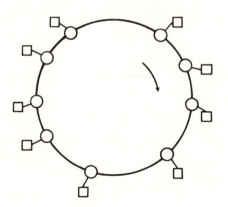

Figure 7.4. Local distribution: ring topology, token passing.

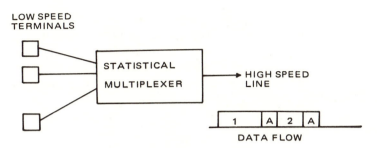

Figure 7.5. Statistical multiplexing.

terminals by the multiplexer in a cyclic fashion. Between messages from the terminals are interspersed terminal addresses allowing a demultiplexer to distinguish messages from different terminals. These addresses play the role of overhead or walk-time in the model. This last model stands in contrast to asynchronous time-division multiplexing considered in Chapter 5. In the present case several messages from the same terminal can have a single address, whereas for ATDM each message is accompanied by an address.

7.2. Average Cycle Time: Infinite Buffer

As stated earlier the quantities of interest are the cycle time—i.e., the time required by the server to offer access to all stations—and message delay. The difficulty in computing these quantities lies in the complex dependencies among the queues. Let T_c denote the cycle time. The server goes from source buffer to source buffer. At buffer i it pauses for T_i seconds to remove messages. Between buffers $i - 1$ and i the server is inactive for W_i seconds. Because of an analogy with early work in machine repair problems W_i is traditionally called the walk-time.† The duration of a cycle may be written in terms of these quantities. We have

$$T_c = \sum_{i=1}^{N} W_i + \sum_{i=1}^{N} T_i \tag{7.1}$$

If message arrival is Poisson, the number of messages in a queue depends on the cycle time, which as we see from equation (7.1) depends upon the time spent at each of the queues $T_1, T_2, \ldots, T_N$. This circularity gives rise

---

†A review of the literature of polling is contained in Section 7.5.

to the dependencies among the random variables $T_1, T_2, \ldots, T_N$. Dealing with these dependencies is the key challenge in the analysis of polling systems.

In spite of these dependencies an expression for the mean polling time can be derived quite easily. From the linearity of the expectation operator we find from equation (7.1) that†

$$\bar{T}_c = \sum_{i=1}^{N} \bar{W}_i + \sum_{i=1}^{N} \bar{T}_i \tag{7.2}$$

The average time spent at a queue is the average time required to transmit all of the messages that arrive in a cycle. Assuming Poisson arrivals and infinite storage capacities for queues we have

$$\bar{T}_i = \lambda_i \bar{T}_c \bar{m}_i = \rho_i \bar{T}_c \tag{7.3}$$

where $\bar{m}_i$ is the average time to transmit a message from queue i and ρ_i is the loading in erlangs due to source i. Substituting equation (7.3) into (7.2) we find

$$\bar{T}_c = \sum_{i=1}^{N} \bar{W}_i \bigg/ \left(1 - \sum_{i=1}^{N} \rho_i\right) \tag{7.4a}$$

In the symmetric case where $\bar{W}_i = \bar{W}$ and $\rho_i = \rho$, $i = 1, 2, \ldots, N$ equation (7.4a) becomes

$$\bar{T}_c = N\bar{W}/(1 - N\rho) \tag{7.4b}$$

In equations (7.4a) and (7.4b) we have a characteristic queueing theory form. The numerator represents overhead, the average amount of time during a cycle that a server is not serving a customer. This quantity is independent of traffic. All of the traffic information is embodied in the denominator. As in the previous queueing models there is a point of instability when the total load equals one. In the sequel we shall assume that the total load is less than one. There is a model in which $\bar{W} = 0$, giving an average cycle time of zero.[6,7] This is not inconsistent since whenever all queues are empty we can imagine that the server makes an infinite number of cycles of zero duration.

---

†Recall that the expectation of a sum of random variables is equal to the sum of the expectations irrespective of the dependencies involved.

7.3. Single-Message Buffers

An analysis by Kaye[9], based on work by Mack et al.[8], gives the distribution of message delay. We consider the following model for polling systems. A processor cycles in a fixed order through N stations, polling each in turn. Each station has a buffer which can hold a single fixed-length message. The station interrupts the polling cycle to transmit a message if it is present; otherwise the next station is polled immediately. Let us assume that in polling a station a fixed amount of time, W seconds, is required. (We shall see presently that there is some flexibility in this assumption.) Fixed-length messages arrive at the queue at a Poisson rate. We assume that the message arrival rate is the same for all buffers. Since station buffers can hold only one message, a message arriving at an occupied station is lost. Another way of looking at this is that the arrival time of a message to an empty buffer is exponentially distributed and there are no arrivals to full buffers.

7.3.1. Probability Distribution of Cycle Time

Under these rather restrictive assumptions we shall derive the probability distribution of the time required to complete a polling cycle, i.e., the time required to poll all stations once and to transmit all messages in station buffers. The first step in this derivation is to define a particular Markov chain describing the system. We consider the chain as starting at a particular station. Because of the symmetry of the system it does not matter which station is chosen as the starting point. The states of the chain are the sets of stations having messages as seen by the processor as it cycles through all stations. Let it be emphasized that the state is *not* the set of stations having messages at a particular point in time. As far as the definition of the state is concerned, the message occupancy of a station is only relevant when the station is polled. If there are N stations in the system, there are 2^N possible states. From this definition of state the duration of a cycle follows directly. If any set of R stations has messages then the time required to complete a polling cycle is $NW + Rm$, where W is the walk-time and m is the time required to transmit a message.

The assumptions allow a considerable simplification of the analysis. As we shall see, the probability of a state depends only on the number of stations having messages and not on the order of stations having messages in the polling cycle. Thus in a ten-station system, the probability that stations 1, 3, and 5 have messages when polled is the same as 2, 6, and 9. There is a great simplification since there are $N + 1$ rather than 2^N unknowns. We note that this result would follow if station occupancy were independent from station to station. In this latter case we would have a sequence of

Bernouli trials in which the order is irrelevant. We shall return to Bernouli trials in connection with polling the sequel.

Given the previous state in the Markov chain, one could, in principle, calculate the probability distribution of the next state. The key to this calculation is the Poisson arrival process. If the server has been absent from a station for T seconds the probability that it has a message upon return of the server is $1 - e^{-\lambda T}$, where λ is the arrival rate of message at the station. Conditioned on the previous state one could calculate the probabilities of the next state simply by calculating the duration of server absences. This calculation is tedious but possible. Fortunately there is an easier way to find the answer, but the consideration of the brute force approach brings out the general properties of the polling process. First of all it should be clear that we do indeed have a Markov chain. All that is required to calculate the probability of any succeeding state is the previous state. It is not difficult to show that the transition of any state to any other state occurs with nonzero probability. We conclude then that the Markov chain is irreducible and aperiodic, hence there is a unique set of state probabilities in the steady state. We require this assurance since the technique for finding the steady-state probabilities differs from the conventional approaches.

Let us consider a cycle which begins with the server leaving a particular station (call it L). Now suppose the server finds that a particular set of R stations has messages; the probability of this event is indicated as $p(i, j, \ldots, s)$, with $s < N$. (Here $i, j, \ldots, s$ indicates the ith, the jth, $\ldots$, the sth station counting from L and not counting L itself.) The server leaves station L empty and it requires $NW + Rm$ seconds to return. The probability that a message has arrived at station L in the interim is $1 - \exp[-\lambda(NW + Rm)]$ where λ is the arrival rate of messages at each station in messages per second. Due to the symmetry of the system we assume that, once the system is in equilibrium, all of these probabilities will be the same for all starting points of a cycle.

Now consider two possible cycles with station L as a starting point. The occurrences of the two cycles are disjoint events which partition the space of cycles in which station L is found empty on return. In the first of these the next station after L, $L + 1$ mod N, is found empty. In the second it has a message. In both cycles there are R remaining stations with messages $i, j, \ldots, s$. Suppose also in both cycles that upon return to station L, it is found to be empty. We can write an equation for the probability of the cycle starting at the $(L + 1)$st buffer. Since everything is now referenced to the $(L + 1)$st station we speak of the $(i - 1)$st, $(j - 1)$st, and $(s - 1)$st station as having messages with probability $p(i - 1, j - 1, \ldots, s - 1)$. We have then

$$p(i - 1, j - 1, \ldots, s - 1) = p(i, j, \ldots, s) \exp[-\lambda(NW + Rm)]$$

$$+ p(1, i, j, \ldots, s) \exp[-\lambda(NW + (R + 1)m)] \tag{7.5}$$

In equation (7.5) we reiterate that the probability $p(...)$ is the same for any starting station. On the left-hand side the starting station is $L + 1$ and on the right-hand side it is L. Now look at the same two cycles with the difference that station L has a message on return of the multiplexer. Starting from station $L + 1$ the $(N - 1)$st station is seen as having a message. We may write

$$p(i - 1, j - 1, \ldots, s - 1, N - 1)$$
$$= p(i, j, \ldots, s)\{1 - \exp[-\lambda(NW + Rm)]\} \tag{7.6}$$
$$+ p(1, i, j, \ldots, s)\{1 - \exp[-\lambda((NW + (R + 1)m))]\}$$

Adding equations (7.5) and (7.6) give

$$p(i - 1, j - 1, \ldots, s - 1) + p(i - 1, j - 1, \ldots, s - 1, N - 1)$$
$$= p(i, j, \ldots, s) + p(1, i, j, \ldots, s) \tag{7.7}$$

Notice that the states on both sides of equation (7.7) represent the same number of stations in a cycle having messages. We can, in theory, solve equations (7.5) and (7.6) for $p(\cdot)$ for all combinations of values $i, j, \ldots, s$ for all values of R. We shall see, however, that a unique solution is found for $p(i, j, \ldots, s)$ depending only on R, the number of buffers having messages, and not on particular buffers $i, j, \ldots, s$. Let us assume for the moment that this is true. Let $p(R)$ denote the probability that a particular set of R buffers all have messages and all other buffers are empty. Equation (7.5) becomes

$$p(R) = p(R) \exp[-\lambda(NW + Rm)]$$
$$+ p(R + 1) \exp[-\lambda(NW + (R + 1)m)]$$

which has the recursive solution given by

$$p(R + 1) = \exp[\lambda(NW + (R + 1)m)]$$
$$\times \{1 - \exp[-\lambda(NW + Rm)]\}p(R) \tag{7.8}$$

Notice that the argument for $p(\cdot)$ has the values 0, 1, $\ldots$, $N - 1$, since $p(\cdot)$ refers to $N - 1$ stations excluding the one just departed.

Now we show the probability that of *all* N buffers the probability that R have messages is independent of the particular set of R. This is done by showing that for two different cycles, each leaving the same number of messages, the probabilities are the same. Consider a cycle beginning with a departure from buffer L. We consider two possible cycles according to the Lth buffer being empty or full upon return. The probability of R messages and L empty is equal to the probability of R messages in the remaining buffers times the probability of L empty:

$$P(R) = p(R) \exp[-\lambda(N\dot{W} + Rm)] \tag{7.9}$$

In equation (7.9) we have R buffers out of N with messages but not including the Lth upon return. This represents one of the 2^N possible states. Now suppose we have a cycle which includes the Lth and $R-1$ others. This is another state with R messages. The probability is

$$P'(R) = p(R-1)\{1 - \exp[-\lambda(NW + (R-1)m)\} \tag{7.10}$$

Now if we substitute equation (7.8) into equation (7.10) we see that equations (7.9) and (7.10) are the same. Using the symmetry property we could obtain this same result for any pair of cycles each having the same number of messages. We may write the probability that a specified set of R out of N stations have messages as

$$P(R) = p(R) \exp[-\lambda(Rm + NW)], \qquad R = 0, 1, 2, \ldots, N-1 \tag{7.11a}$$

$$P(N) = p(N-1)\{1 - \exp[-\lambda(Rm + NW)]\} \tag{7.11b}$$

where $p(R)$ is given in the recursive relationship of equation (7.8). Notice that there are $\binom{N}{R}$ ways that N stations can have R messages. The probability of R stations, in any order, having messages is

$$Q(R) \overset{\Delta}{=} \binom{N}{R} P(R) \tag{7.12}$$

From equations (7.9), (7.10), and (7.12) we can find the following recursive relation for $Q(R)$:

$$Q(k) = Q(k-1)\left(\frac{N-k+1}{k}\right)\{\exp[\lambda(NW + (k-1)m)] - 1\} \tag{7.13}$$

The normalizing condition is

$$\sum_{k=0}^{N} Q(k) = 1 \tag{7.14}$$

There is a final point in connection with this solution having to do with overhead. Throughout the derivation the time that the multiplexer spends in going between buffers in a complete cycle is lumped into the term NW. Now suppose that the time between queues $i - 1$ and i were W_i, which could be different for different i but the same constant value from cycle to cycle. The derivation would go through in the same manner as before with NW replaced by $\sum_{i=1}^{N} W_i$. In the sequel we shall denote all of the overhead by $\Omega \overset{\Delta}{=} \sum_{i=1}^{N} W_i$. This, alas, is the only generalization that the model permits. Any change in the assumptions leads to great complexity. For example, in a companion paper Mack[10] analyzed the case of random message sizes. The result is far more complicated.

By carrying out the iteration of equation (7.13) we may express the probability of k stations having messages as

$$Q(k) = C\binom{N}{k} \prod_{j=0}^{k-1} \{\exp[\lambda(\Omega + jm)] - 1\} \tag{7.15}$$

where C is a normalization constant which may be found from equation (7.14). The dependencies among the queues at the stations is reflected in the term jm in the exponent in equation (7.15). Suppose that NW is large compared to jm, a situation that is a result of high overhead and light loading. Equation (7.15) may be expressed as

$$Q(k) = C\binom{N}{k}[\exp(\lambda\Omega) - 1]^k \tag{7.16a}$$

Now suppose that station occupancies are independent from station to station. Let the probability of a station having a message be P. The probability of k stations having messages is the binomial distribution

$$Q'(k) = \binom{N}{k} P^k(1 - P)^{N-k} = (1 - P)^N \binom{N}{k}\left(\frac{P}{1 - P}\right)^k \tag{7.16b}$$

We see that equations (7.16a) and (7.16b) have exactly the same form. Equating like terms we find that $P = 1 - e^{-\lambda\Omega}$, which is the probability of message arrival in a cycle Ω seconds in duration. The results of calculation of cycle times from the exact formula [equation (7.15)] and the approximate formula (7.16a) are shown in Figure 7.6. Indeed, the results indicate that for higher overhead and lighter loading the queues tend toward independence.

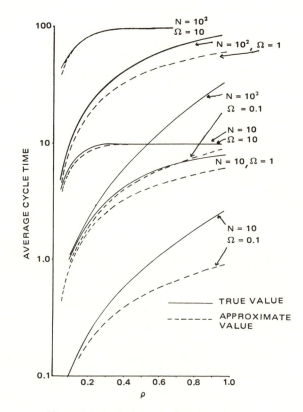

Figure 7.6. Cycle time as a function of load.

7.3.2. Probability Distribution of Delay

Cycle time gives some measure of the performance of the system; however, a quantity of more direct interest is the access delay, which we define as the time elapsing between the arrival of a message and the beginning of its transmission to the central facility. This corresponds to queueing delay in an $M/G/1$ queue. In order to find message delay, the message transmission time is added to access delay. For the case of buffers containing only single fixed-length messages which arrive at a Poisson rate, the distribution of access delay has been found exactly.[9] A server cycle in which a message is transmitted is depicted in Figure 7.7. The server departs from a particular queue at time t_1 and returns at time t_2 and departs again at time t_3. Since we stipulate that a message is transmitted, $t_3 - t_2 = m$. A message arrives to the empty queue at time $t_2 - D_A$. A server cycle in this case is the time interval $t_3 - t_1$. Notice that unlike the case of TDM studied in Chapter 6 the cycle is random. Since messages are more likely to arrive

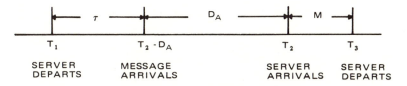

Figure 7.7. Illustration of message delay.

in long cycles than short, message arrival and the duration of a cycle are correlated. Let A denote the event of a message arriving during a cycle. We consider first the joint event of A occurring and $T_c = \Omega + km$, i.e., k messages in a cycle:

$$P[T_c = \Omega + km, A] = P[T_c = \Omega + km]P[A/T_c = \Omega + km] \quad (7.17)$$

The probability $P[T_c = \Omega + km]$ is given by equation (7.15). The term $P[A/T_c = \Omega + km]$ can be found by straight counting as follows. From symmetry there are $\binom{N}{k}$ equiprobable ways for a cycle to have duration $T_c = \Omega + km$. If a particular station is constrained to have a message, there are $\binom{N-1}{k-1}$ ways for this cycle duration to occur. Substituting into equation (7.17) we have

$$P[T_c = \Omega + km, A] = \frac{\binom{N-1}{k-1}}{\binom{N}{k}} Q(k) = \frac{k}{N} Q(k) \quad (7.18)$$

The cycle duration conditioned on message arrival can be found quite simply

$$P[T_c = \Omega + km/A] = \frac{P[T_c = \Omega + km, A]}{\sum_{k=1}^{N} P[T_c = \Omega + km, A]}$$

$$= \frac{(k/N)Q(k)}{\sum_{k=1}^{N} (k/N)Q(k)} = \frac{kQ(k)}{\bar{k}}, \qquad k = 1, 2, \ldots, n \quad (7.19)$$

where $\bar{k}$ is the mean number of stations having messages in a cycle.

As indicated on Figure 7.7 the access delay of a message is the quantity D_A. We now proceed to find the probability distribution of D_A. Since the station holds only a single message this arrival is the first and last of the cycle. We begin by conditioning upon event A, message arrival, and the duration of a cycle, $\Omega + km$. Define the quantity $\tau = t_2 - t_1 - D_A = \Omega + (k-1)m - D_A$, indicating the time elapsing from the beginning of the cycle until the message arrives. We have

$$P[D_A \le d/T_c = \Omega + km, A] = P[\tau \ge \Omega + (k-1)m - d/T_c = \Omega + km, A]$$

$$= 1 - P[\tau \le \Omega + (k-1)m - d/T_c = \Omega + km, A] \quad (7.20)$$

The joint event $\{T_c = \Omega + km, A\}$ implies that message arrival is in the interval $0, \tau \le \Omega + (k-1)m$, i.e.,

$$\{T_c = \Omega + km, A\} = \{T_c = \Omega + km, \tau \le \Omega + (k-1)m\}$$

Further,

$$\{\tau \le \Omega + (k-1)m - d, T_c = \Omega + km, A\}$$
$$= \{\tau \le \Omega + (k-1)m - d, T_c = \Omega + km\}$$

Substituting into equation (7.20) we find

$$P[D \le d / T_c = \Omega + km, A]$$
$$= 1 - \frac{P[\tau \le \Omega + (k-1)m - d / T_c = \Omega + km]}{P[\tau \le \Omega + (k-1)m / T_c = \Omega + km]} \quad (7.21)$$

The time interval until the first arrival is exponentially distributed and we have, for example,

$$P[\tau \le \Omega + (k-1)m / T_c = \Omega + km] = 1 - \exp\{-\lambda[\Omega + (k-1)m]\}$$

Substituting into equation (7.21) we find

$$P[D \le d / T_c = \Omega + km, A] = \frac{e^{\lambda d} - 1}{e^{\lambda[\Omega + (k-1)m]} - 1} \quad (7.22)$$

The unconditioned distribution of D is found by averaging over k, employing the distribution given in equations (7.15) and (7.19). In carrying out the computation care must be taken to average over the proper values of k since, for $d \ge \Omega + (k-1)m$, $P[D \le d / T_c = \Omega + km, A] = 1$. We have then

$$D(d) \triangleq P[D \le d / A]$$
$$= \sum_{k=1}^{n(d)} \frac{kQ(k)}{\bar{k}} + \frac{e^{\lambda d} - 1}{\bar{k}} \sum_{n(d)+1}^{N} Q(k)/\{e^{\lambda[\Omega + (k-1)m]} - 1\} \quad (7.23)$$

where $Q(k)$ is as given in equation (7.15) and where $n(d)$ is the maximum value of n for which $n < d/m - (\Omega/m + 1)$.

In principle moments of delay can be found from equation (7.23); however, it is easier to find moments another way. From equation (7.22) mean delay conditioned on the cycle duration is given by

$$E[D_A/T_c = (\Omega + km), A] = \int_0^{\Omega+(k-1)m} \frac{\tau\lambda \, e^{\lambda\tau}}{e^{\lambda[\Omega+(k-1)m]} - 1} \, d\tau$$

$$= \frac{[\Omega + (k-1)m] \, e^{\lambda[\Omega+(k-1)m]}}{e^{\lambda[\Omega+(k-1)m]} - 1} - \frac{1}{\lambda}$$

(7.24)

Averaging with respect to the cycle duration given by equation (7.15) we find the following expression for the average access delay:

$$\bar{D}_A = \frac{1}{\bar{k}} \sum_{k=0}^{N-1} (\Omega + km) \, e^{\lambda(\Omega+km)}(N - k)Q(k) - \frac{1}{\lambda} \qquad (7.25a)$$

as $\lambda \to 0$ it can be shown that $\bar{D}_A = \Omega/2$, which is what we would expect. It has been shown that a reasonable approximation for access delay is

$$\bar{D}_A = \frac{\Omega}{2}(1 + N\lambda m) \qquad (7.25b)$$

An approximate formula such as given in equation (7.25b) can be useful in ordinary design.

The results for average delay calculations are plotted in Figure 7.8 where access delay normalized to message length is shown as a function of $\rho = \lambda m N$ with the number of stations, N, and the total overhead Ω as parameters. The salient result of this plot is that the delay is strongly a function of overhead. It is only at the lighter loading that traffic has the predominant influence. Also shown in Figure 7.8 are delay calculations when stations are assumed independent. Again we see the effect of overhead and loading.

This same technique can be used to find higher moments of delay. For example, it can be shown that the mean square value of delay is given by

$$\bar{D}_A^2 = \frac{1}{\bar{k}} \sum_{k=0}^{N-1} (\Omega + km)^2 \, e^{\lambda(\Omega+km)}(N - k)Q(k) - \frac{2}{\lambda}\bar{D}_A + \frac{2}{\lambda^2} \qquad (7.26)$$

Recall that a basic assumption was that stations held only one message. If messages arrive at a Poisson rate, all messages arriving to a full buffer are lost. From the foregoing the portion of messages that are lost can be determined. During the time that a message is waiting for the server and being transmitted an average of $\bar{l} = N\lambda(\bar{D}_A + m)$ are lost. Since for every message that is transmitted $\bar{l}$ messages are lost, the portion of messages

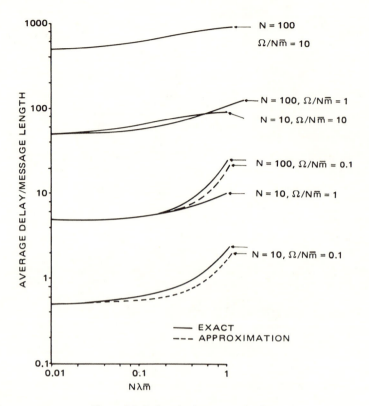

Figure 7.8. Delay single-message buffer.

that are lost is

$$P_l = \frac{N\lambda(\bar{D}_A + m)}{1 + N\lambda(\bar{D}_A + m)} \tag{7.27}$$

where $\bar{D}_A$ is given in equation (7.25).

7.4. Analysis: Infinite Buffer

We consider now the case where the buffer can hold an unlimited number of messages with a Poisson arrival of messages. The procedure employed in calculating delay is similar to the foregoing. First we find an expression for the cycle time. Based on the cycle time an expression for delay is found. The problem is that an analysis of cycle time in this case is not easy. In order to simplify matters, we follow an approach first suggested by Liebowitz[11] and assume that the contents of different queues are independent. As we have seen for single message buffers, independence among queues tends to hold for high overhead and light loading. We shall assume that a "please wait" or gating discipline is employed. If a message arrives at a queue while a server is present, it is held over until the next cycle. An exact solution to this problem and the "come right in" version have been obtained by Hashida.[12] The approach used in this solution is the derivation of N-dimensional probability generating functions. We shall not present this solution simply because it is too complicated for this level of text. Furthermore the approximate technique illustrates several results which are widely applicable. We shall compare the approximate with the exact results in due course.

7.4.1. Probability Distribution of Cycle Time

We begin the analysis by focusing upon the amount of time spent by a server at a queue. Let us denote the density function of this time as $r(t)$ and the Laplace transform of the density function as $\mathcal{R}(s)$. Under the "please wait" discipline, the time spent at a queue is simply the time required to transmit the number of messages present when the server arrived. Let Q_j be the probability of j such messages. We have

$$r(t) = \sum_{j=0}^{\infty} Q_j m^{(j)}(t) \tag{7.28}$$

where $m^{(j)}(t)$ is the j-fold convolution of the probability density function of the time required to transmit a message. For consistency we define $m^{(0)}(t)$ to be zero. Taking transforms of both sides of equation (7.28) we find

$$\mathcal{R}(s) = \sum_{j=0}^{\infty} Q_j \mathcal{M}^j(s) = G(\mathcal{M}(s)) \tag{7.29}$$

where $\mathcal{M}(s)$ is the Laplace transform of $m(t)$ and where $G(z)$ is the generating function of the number of messages in the buffer when the server arrives.

The next step in the analysis is to consider the duration of a cycle which is the time interval between successive arrivals of a server. In order to proceed it is necessary to make the key independence assumption. We assume that the times that a server resides at different queues are independent of one another. Under this assumption we write the density function of the cycle time as

$$t_c(t) = w^{(N)}(t) * r^{(N)}(t) \tag{7.30}$$

where $w(t)$ is the probability density function of the walk-time. Convolution is denoted by superscripts and by $*$. Taking the transform of both sides of equation (8.30) we find

$$\mathscr{T}_c(s) = \mathscr{W}^N(s)\mathscr{R}^N(s) \tag{7.31}$$

where $\mathscr{W}(s)$ is the transform of $w(t)$. All of the messages that greet the server have arrived during a cycle. We have the familiar theme of Poisson arrivals during a random time interval. We find that

$$Q_j = P_r(j \text{ arrivals}) = \int_0^\infty \frac{(\lambda t)^j}{j!} e^{-\lambda t} t_c(t) \, dt$$

The generating function of the number of arrivals is

$$G(z) = \mathscr{T}_c(\lambda(1-z)) \tag{7.32}$$

From equations (7.28)–(7.32) we have finally that the Laplace transform of the density function of the cycle time is

$$\mathscr{T}_c(s) = [\mathscr{W}(s)\mathscr{T}_c(\lambda - \lambda\mathscr{M}(s))]^N \tag{7.33}$$

By successive differentiation of equation (7.33) it can be shown that the mean and the mean square values of the cycle time are given, respectively, by

$$\bar{T}_c = \frac{N\bar{w}}{1 - \lambda\bar{m}N} \tag{7.34a}$$

$$\overline{T_c^2} = \frac{N(N-1)[\bar{w} + \lambda\bar{T}_c\bar{m}]^2 + N[\overline{w^2} + 2\bar{w}\bar{T}_c\lambda\bar{m} + \lambda\overline{m^2}\bar{T}_c]}{1 - N(\lambda\bar{m})^2} \tag{7.34b}$$

where $\bar{w}$ and $\bar{m}$ are the mean values of the walk-time and the message length, respectively, and $\overline{w^2}$ and $\overline{m^2}$ are the mean square values. Again we point out that the mean in equation (7.34a) is not affected by the independence assumption and consequently is the same as that obtained previously [see equations (7.4a) and (7.4b)]. The distribution and the mean square cycle time have been compared to results obtained for an exact analysis when $n = 2$. The results[11] show agreement to terms of the order of λ^3. Thus for heavy loading the approximate analysis breaks down. We would expect, from the heuristic arguments put forward when we examined single message queues, that the approximate technique would be even better for larger N since the overhead increases.

7.4.2. Probability Distribution of Delay

We now consider message delay based[13] on these results for cycle time. The analysis is similar to that carried out in Chapter 6 in connection with TDM. In Figure 7.9 is shown a server cycle. The successive arrival times of the server at a queue are t_1 and t_2. Under the please wait discipline messages arriving in the (t_1, t_2) interval are transmitted after time t_2. We are interested in the delay of a message arriving at time $t_2 - Y$. This delay consists of three components, the time until the return of the server, the time required to transmit previously arrived messages in the cycle, and the time to transmit the message in question. This all can be expressed as

$$D = Y + \sum_{i=1}^{K} m_i + m_{K+1} \tag{7.35}$$

where K is the number of previously arrived messages and m_i is the time required to transmit the ith message. The derivation of the distribution function for D is complicated by the fact that the first and second terms in equation (7.35) are not independent. For a given cycle duration, the larger Y is the smaller K is.

We begin the analysis assuming that the distribution of the cycle time is given. A well-known attribute of point processes is that the distribution of cycles in which messages arrive and the general distribution of cycles is not the same.† An arriving message selects longer cycles. The following heuristic derivation illustrates the selection process. Suppose for the moment that cycles may assume only L discrete values, $x_1, x_2, \ldots, x_L$. Now consider K successive random cycles. Let K_i be the number of cycles of duration x_i. $K_i x_i$ is duration of all ith intervals and $\sum_{i=1}^{L} K_i x_i$ is duration of the interval of all message arrivals. The relative frequency of message arrival in an interval of duration x_i is

$$r_i = \frac{x_i K_i}{\sum_{i=1}^{L} x_i K_i} = \frac{x_i (K_i / K)}{\sum_{i=1}^{L} x_i (K_i / K)}$$

†For a discussion of this topic see Ref. 14.

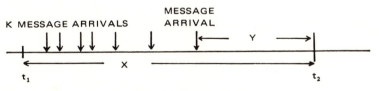

Figure 7.9. Server cycle.

Letting $K \to \infty$ we have $(K_i/K) \to P_i$ and

$$r_i = \frac{x_i P_i}{\sum_{i=1}^{L} x_i P_i} = \frac{x_i P_i}{\bar{X}} \tag{7.36}$$

where P_i is the probability of an interval of duration x_i and $\bar{X}$ is the mean duration of an interval. We carry this result over to the continuous case. Now if the density function of the cycle time is $t_c(x)$, the density function of the cycle time in which a message arrives is

$$f(x) = \frac{x t_c(x)}{\bar{T}_c} \tag{7.37}$$

Recall that for single message buffers a similar result was obtained using quite different methods [see equation (7.18)].

Referring to Figure 7.9, let K denote the number of messages arriving in the interval $X - Y$. We condition on the duration of the cycle, X, and the interval between message arrival and server arrival

$$P[K = k/x < X \leqslant x + dx, \tau < Y \leqslant \tau + d\tau] = \frac{(\lambda(x - \tau))^k}{k!} e^{-\lambda(x-\tau)} \tag{7.38}$$

Given that a message has arrived in the interval X, its arrival time is uniformly distributed in the interval $(0, x)$ with density function $1/x$:

$$f(K, \tau) \overset{\Delta}{=} P[K = k, \tau < Y \leqslant \tau + d\tau]$$

$$= \int_{\tau}^{\infty} dx \, P[x < X \leqslant x + dx] P[\tau < Y \leqslant \tau + d\tau / x < X \leqslant x + dx]$$

$$\times P[K = k/x < X \leqslant x + dx, \tau < Y \leqslant \tau + d\tau] \tag{7.39}$$

$$= \int_{\tau}^{\infty} dx \left[\frac{x t_c(x)}{\bar{T}_c} \right] \left(\frac{1}{x} \right) \frac{(\lambda(x - \tau))^k e^{-\lambda(x-\tau)}}{k!} \, d\tau$$

Finding the density function for the term $Y + \sum_{i=1}^{K} m_i$ in equation (7.35) is a two-step process. We first condition on Y and K. The only variable involved is the sum of K message transmission times

$$P\left[t < Y + \sum_{i=1}^{K} m_i \leqslant t + dt / \tau < Y \leqslant \tau + d\tau, K = k \right]$$

$$= m^{(k)}(t - \tau) \, dt$$

where the superscript indicates k-fold convolution. Averaging over W and K gives

$$
P\left[t < Y + \sum_{i=1}^{K} m_i \leq t + dt \right]
$$

$$
= \int_0^\infty d\tau \sum_{k=0}^{\infty} m^{(k)}(t - \tau) \int_\tau^\infty dx \frac{t_c(x)}{\bar{T}_c} \frac{(\lambda(x - \tau))^k}{k!} e^{-\lambda(x-\tau)} dt
$$

(7.40)

Equation (7.40) gives the density function of the time elapsing between message arrival and the beginning of transmission. This corresponds to queueing delay in single queue systems. In order to find total delay one convolves a message length distribution with the foregoing density. This follows from the fact that message length is independent of the other quantities.

Finding the characteristic function of the delay is a straightforward application of previously seen techniques. We take the Laplace transform of equation (7.40) and multiply by the Laplace transform of the message length distribution. We find that

$$
\mathcal{D}(s) = E(e^{-Ds}) = \mathcal{M}(s) \frac{\mathcal{T}_c(\lambda - \lambda\mathcal{M}(s)) - \mathcal{T}_c(s)}{\bar{T}_c(s - \lambda + \lambda\mathcal{M}(s))}
$$

(7.41)

where $\mathcal{T}_c(s)$ is given in equation (7.33). Successive differentiation of equation (7.41) gives moments of delay. It can be shown that the average delay is given by

$$
\bar{D} = \frac{\overline{T_c^2}}{2\bar{T}_c} (1 + \lambda\bar{m}) + \bar{m}
$$

(7.42)

where $\bar{T}_c$ and $\overline{T_c^2}$ are given in equations (7.34a) and (7.34b), respectively. The total average message delay is plotted in Figure 7.10.

As we mentioned earlier, Hashida[12] has done an exact analysis of this model. The average access delay can be shown to be

$$
\bar{D} = \frac{N\lambda\overline{m^2}}{2(1 - N\lambda\bar{m})} + \frac{N(1 + \lambda\bar{m})W}{2(1 - N\lambda\bar{m})}
$$

(7.43)

where $\rho = \lambda\bar{m}$. The walk-time is assumed to be constant and the same for all stations. (Hashida has found more general results.) The results of calculation using the exact formula are shown in Figure 7.10.

A second queueing discipline that is of interest is the exhaustive service or the "come right in" discipline, in which messages arriving while a server

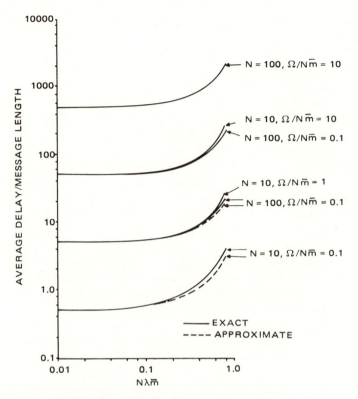

Figure 7.10. Delay infinite-buffer, gated strategy as a function of load.

is at a queue are transmitted in the same cycle. Thus when a server departs from a queue, it is empty. As in the case of the please wait discipline, the characteristic function of the cycle time can be found by invoking as assumption of independence between queues. The salient difference between the analyses of the "please wait" and the "come right in" disciplines lies in the time spent at a queue. In the latter case the time spent by a server greeted by j messages is the j busy period of these messages. Thus the density function of the time spent at a queue is

$$r(t) = \sum_{j=0}^{\infty} Q_j b^{(j)}(t) \tag{7.44a}$$

where, as in equation (7.28), Q_j is the probability of j messages at a queue when the server arrives and $b^{(j)}(t)$ is the j-fold convolution of the busy period density function. Taking transforms we have

$$\mathscr{R}(s) = G(\mathscr{B}(s)) \tag{7.44b}$$

where $G(z)$ is the generating function of the number of messages in the queue and $\mathscr{B}(s)$ is the Laplace transform of $b(t)$ and is given by equation (6.30) in Chapter 6. The messages that are present in the queue have arrived in the time interval between the departure of the server and its return to the queue. This represents a slight difference from the previous case since it is not a complete cycle. In the same manner as equation (7.32) in the foregoing we have

$$G(z) = \mathscr{R}^{N-1}(\lambda(1-z))\mathscr{W}^{N}(\lambda(1-z)) \tag{7.45}$$

The characteristic function of the cycle time is given by

$$T_c(s) = \mathscr{R}^{N}(s)\mathscr{W}^{N}(s) \tag{7.46}$$

Clearly the independence assumption is necessary in the derivations of equations (7.45) and (7.46). By successive differentiation moments of the cycle time can be found.

The derivation of the delay from the cycle time in the case of "come right in" is not as simple as the "please wait discipline." The difficulty is mainly a matter of the bookkeeping required to account for messages arriving while a server is at a queue. In view of the approximations required to calculate the cycle time it does not seem appropriate to be too precise in calculating delay based on cycle time. We therefore calculate delay using equation (7.42) which was derived for the "please wait" discipline. The expressions for $\bar{T}_c$ and $\overline{T_c^2}$ are those derived from equations (7.44)–(7.46). The effect of this approximation is less manifest as the walk-time increases, the load decreases, and the number of queues increases since the message will be less likely to arrive while the server is present. The average delay calculated by this technique is plotted in Figure 7.11. An exact calculation of delay for the "come right in" discipline has been carried out by Hashida.[12] The average access delay can be shown to be

$$\overline{D_A} = \frac{W}{2} + \frac{(N-1)W}{2(1-N\lambda\bar{m})} + \frac{N\lambda\overline{m^2}}{2(1-N\lambda\bar{m})} \tag{7.47}$$

The result of this analysis are also shown in Figure 7.11. Again we take the walk-times to be constant and the same for all stations. The comparison of the results of the two sets of computations bears out the same lessons we have seen in previous models. The approximation is most effective for larger walk-time, lighter load, and more queues.

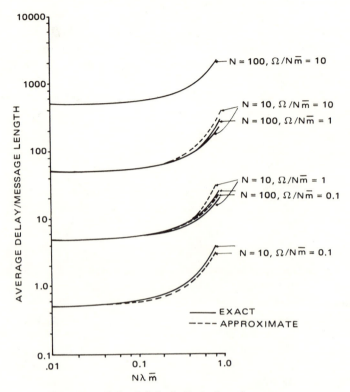

Figure 7.11. Delay infinite-buffer, exhaustive strategy.

7.5. Review of Literature

The analysis of polling systems has a long and interesting history. For example, there is an analogy between polling systems and machine patrolling in which a repairman examines N machines in a fixed sequence. If a machine is broken he pauses to make repairs. This is the analog in polling systems to message transmission. The overhead that is incurred is the time required to walk between machines. This walk-time corresponds to the time required to poll a terminal. In Section 7.3 of the text we have treated the work of Mack et al.[18] on this problem. As we have pointed out in the text, Kaye[9] applied this work to communications. For a treatment of work on related problems, see Cox and Smith.[16]

A great deal of work has been devoted to the case of the infinite buffer. The earliest work in this area involved just two queues with zero overhead.[17,18] Later, this was generalized to two queues with nonzero overhead.[19,20] In terms of the models that we are concerned with, the first papers of interest are those of Cooper and Murray[6] and Cooper.[7] The number of buffers is arbitrary and both the gated and exhaustive services models are considered. The drawback is that the analysis assumes zero overhead. The characteristic functions of the waiting times are found. Also found is a set of $n(n + 1)$ linear equations whose solution yields the mean waiting time at each buffer when the message arrival time is different for each. The assumption of zero overhead here may yield useful lower bounds on performance.

For a long time, the only work on an arbitrary number of queues with nonzero overhead was by Liebowitz,[11] who suggested the independence approximation. In 1972, both Hashida[12] and Eisenberg[21] separately published results on multiple queues with nonzero overhead. Both used imbedded Markov chain aproaches. Computer communications stimulated the next significant step in polling models. Konheim and Meister[22] studied a discrete time version of model. Transmission time over the channel is divided into fixed size discrete units called slots. Messages are described in terms of data units which fit into these slots. (An 8-bit byte is a good example of a data unit.) The analysis is carried out by imbedding a Markov chain at points separated by slots. In most of this work, the emphasis was upon symmetric traffic. Konheim and Meister's work has been extended to the case of asymmetric traffic.[23] Interestingly, it was found that in the case of asymmetric traffic, the order in which terminals are polled affects performance.

A significant remaining problem involves nonexhaustive service where, at most, a fixed number of messages are transmitted from a particular buffer. If there are more than the fixed number of messages at the buffer they are held over until the next cycle. If there are less than this fixed number the next terminal is polled immediately after the buffer is emptied. At the present writing no exact analysis is available. There have been several analyses of systems of this kind based upon approximations.[24-26] The latest of these is by Kuehn, who obtains results when at most one message is removed at a time. Kuehn evaluates his results by comparing them to earlier results by Hashida and Ohara and to simulation.

References

1. M. Schwartz, *Computer Communication Network Design and Analysis*, Prentice-Hall, Englewood Cliffs, New Jersey (1977).
2. A. S. Tanenbaum, *Computer Networks*, Prentice-Hall, Englewood Cliffs, New Jersey (1981).
3. W. R. Franta and J. Chamatac, *Local Networks*, Lexington Books, Lexington, Massachusetts (1981).
4. W. D. Farmer and E. E. Newhall, "An Experimental Distributed Switching System to Handle Bursty Computer Traffic," *Proceedings of the ACM Symposium, Problems in Optimization Data Communication Systems*, pp. 1–34, Pine Mountain, Georgia (1969).

5. W. Bux, T. Closs, P. Janson, K. Kümmerle, and H. S. Müller, "A Reliable Token System for Local-Area Communication," National Telecommunication Conference, pp. A2.2.1–A2.2.6, New Orleans, December (1981).

6. R. B. Cooper and G. Murray, "Queues Served in Cyclic Order," *Bell System Technical Journal*, **48**(3), 675–689, March (1969).

7. R. B. Cooper, "Queues Served in Cyclic Order: Waiting Times," *Bell System Technical Journal*, **49**(3), 399–413, March (1970).

8. C. Mack, T. Murphy, and N. L. Webb, "The Efficiency of N Machines Undirectionally Patrolled by One Operative when Walking and Repair Times are Constant," *Journal of the Royal Statistical Society, Series B*, **19**, 166–172 (1957).

9. A. R. Kaye, "Analysis of Distributed Control Loop for Data Transmission," *Proceedings of the Symposium on Computer Communications Network Teletraffic*, Polytechnic Institute of Brooklyn, New York (1972).

10. C. Mack, "The Efficiency of N Machines Unidirectionally Patrolled by One Operative when Walking Time is Constant and Repair Times are Variable," *Journal of Royal Statistical Society, Series B*, **19**, 173–178 (1957).

11. M. A. Liebowitz, "An Approximate Method for Treating a Class of Multiqueue Problems," *IBM Syst. J.*, **5**, 204–209, July (1961).

12. O. Hashida, "Analysis of Multiqueue," *Review of the Electrical Communication Laboratories* NTT **20**,(3, 4), 189–199, March (1972).

13. J. F. Hayes and D. N. Sherman, "A Study of Data Multiplexing Techniques and Delay Performance," *Bell System Technical Journal*, **51**, 1985–2011, November (1972).

14. L. Kleinrock, *Queueing Systems*: Vol. 1, *Theory*, John Willey, New York (1975).

15. J. F. Hayes, "Local Distribution in Computer Communications," *IEEE Communications Magazine*, **19**,(2), March (1981).

16. D. R. Cox and W. L. Smith, *Queues*, Methuen London (1961).

17. B. Avi-Itzhak, W. L. Maxwell, and L. W. Miller, "Queues with Alternating Priorities," *Journal of the Operations Research Society of America*, **13**(2), 306–318 (1965).

18. L. Takacs, "Two Queues Attended by a Single Server," *Operations Research*, **16**, 639–650 (1968).

19. J. S. Sykes, "Simplified Analysis of an Algernating Priority Queueing Model with Setup Time," *Operations Research*, **18**, 399–413 (1970).

20. M. Eisenberg, "Two Queues with Changeover Times," *Operations Research*, **19**, 386–401 (1971).

21. M. Eisenberg, "Queues with Periodic Service and Changeover Times," *Operations Research* **20**, 440–451 (1972).

22. A. G. Konheim and B. Meister, "Waiting Lines and Times in a System with Polling," *Journal of the ACM*, **21**, 470–490, July (1974).

23. G. B. Swarz, "Polling in a Loop System," *Journal of the ACM*, **27**(1), 42–59, January (1980).

24. O. Hashida and K. Ohara, "Line Accommodation Capacity of a Communication Control Unit," *Review of the Electrical Communications Laboratories*, NTT, **20**, 231–239 (1972).

25. S. Halfin, "An Approximate Method for Calculating Delays for a Family of Cyclic Type Queues," *Bell System Technical Journal*, **54**(10), 1733–1754, December (1975).

26. P. J. Kuehn, "Multiqueue Systems with Nonexhaustive Cyclic Service," *Bell System Technical Journal*, **58**(3), 671–699, March (1979).

27. L. Kleinrock, *Queueing Systems, Vol. 1: Theory*, Wiley-Interscience, New York (1975).

Exercises

7.1. A multipoint private line, such as that illustrated in Figure 7.2, serves 20 stations. Modems at these stations transmit at a rate of 2400 bps. For these modems the startup time in which phase and timing are recovered is 20 msec in duration. Access to the line for the stations is controlled by a central processor by means of roll-call polling. The walktime required to access each station is 30 msec. This includes the 20-msec modem startup time. Assume that the messages to be transmitted are 240 bits in duration and arrive at the stations at a Poisson rate which is the same for all stations. Finally, assume that each station can hold only one message at a time. These assumptions would fit a credit checking system. The arrival of messages would correspond to the insertion of a credit card into a reader. There are no new insertions until a response to a previous inquiry has been obtained.

(a) Find the average delay as a function of the message arrival rate.

(b) If the message arrival rate at each station is 0.5 messages per second, find the maximum number of stations that may share the line under the requirement that the maximum message delay is 1 sec.

In doing this problem a computer is required for an exact solution. In the absence of such equipment the approximate solution may be used.

7.2. An alternative to the 2400-bps modem considered in Exercise 7.1 is a 4800-bps modem. In order to operate at this higher speed, a longer startup time is required because of equalizer training. Assume that the walk time is 60 msec for each station. Repeat Exercise 7.1 for this modem and compare the results. How would the answer to part (b) change if the messages were 480 bits long?

7.3. Suppose that the polling cycle for the system described in Exercise 7.1 is interrupted for 1 sec in order to return messages to the stations. Repeat Exercise 7.1.

7.4. Assume that interval between buses at rush hour is exponentially distributed, with an average value of 3 min. Show that the interval in which a randomly arriving customer arrives has a mean value of 6 min and has a two-stage Erlangian distribution. (See Section 3.10.)

7.5. Show that for a message arriving at random during a server cycle, the probability density for the interval until the arrival of the server is given by

$$g(t) = [1 - T_c(t)]/\bar{T}_c$$

where $T_c(t)$ is the distribution of the cycle time and $\bar{T}_c$ is the average duration of a cycle. The random variable here is called the residual life. [*Hint*: Given that the duration of an arrival interval is x, the time until the arrival of the server is uniform in $(0, x)$.] Notice that if the cycle time is exponentially distributed, so is the residual life. (See Ref. 27, Section 5.2.)

7.6. Suppose that ten independent data sources share a line by means of statistical multiplexing. Assume that the messages are a constant 100 bits in duration and that the line speed is 9.6 Kbps. Assume also that 10 overhead bits are associated with transmission from each of the buffers associated with the data sources.

(a) Find average delay as a function of message arrival rate under the assumption of infinite buffers.

(b) Suppose that the ATDM technique studied in Chapter 5 is used to multiplex the sources. Assume that each slot holds 110 bits. Compare this to the method considered in part (a).

7.7. Consider a ring system using the token passing technique to provide access. Suppose that there are 200 stations sharing a coaxial carrying cable data at a rate of 5 Mbps. Further, suppose that 5-bit intervals are required to transfer the token from one station to another. The lengths of the messages to be transmitted are uniformly distributed between 500 and 1500 bits. The traffic is symmetric.

(a) What is the maximum allowable message arrival rate if the average cycle time is to be less than 1 msec?

(b) Calculate the mean delay for the message arrival rate found in part (a).

7.8. Based on the analysis given in Section 7.4 of the text, find an expression for the mean square message delay in the case of infinite buffers.

7.9. Suppose that a polling system contains two classes of stations, each with different message length distributions. Making the same assumptions as in Section 7.4, find an expression for the Laplace transform of the probability of the cycle time.

8

Random Access Systems

8.1. ALOHA and Slotted ALOHA

8.1.1. ALOHA

The salient result that emerges from the analyses of polling systems in the previous chapter is the large impact of overhead—particularly at light loading. Because of overhead, performance deteriorates with the number of stations irrespective of the total traffic in the system. On the other hand, as the total traffic in the system increases, the impact of overhead diminishes. All of this may be attributed to the overhead inherent in the action of a central controller. In terms of the effect of overhead on performance similar results apply to TDMA. These properties motivate the consideration of random access techniques in which control is distributed. As we shall see, random access systems are relatively insensitive to the number of active stations in the systems so that performance is best when there are a large number of lightly loaded sources. The difficulty is that these systems are very vulnerable to increases in the level of aggregate traffic.

The genesis of the random access technique was in the ALOHA system at the University of Hawaii.[1,2] The ALOHA system was a packet switched network in which a radio channel was shared among a number of users. In its pure form the ALOHA technique is totally distributed. When a station generates a message, it is transmitted immediately regardless of the activity at the other stations in the system. Of course there is the obvious difficulty that messages from two or more stations transmitting simultaneously collide and are thereby rendered unintelligible. By various mechanisms the station can be apprised of a collision. For example, in systems where every station can hear every other, collisions will be detected simply by monitoring the line. Another possibility is for the receiving station to return positive acknowledgments when a message is received correctly. If a transmitting station has not received a positive acknowledgment after an appropriate interval, it is presumed that a collision has taken place. When a station discovers, by whatever means, that a collision has occurred, the message is retransmitted. In order to avoid repeated collisions involving the same message, each station should have a different time-out interval. A simple and fair way to do this is for the time-out interval for each station to be a random variable.† If the variance of this random variable is large enough the probability of repeated collisions is small. However, as we shall see, choosing a variance that is too large increases the delay of a message.

A significant feature of the ALOHA system is instability—a property which we shall illustrate by means of a simple analysis.‡ In view of the rapid pace of work in this area, the results of this analysis may be termed classical. Nevertheless, in broad terms, the results point out the root cause of instability in the ALOHA system. To varying degrees this characterization holds for the more sophisticated random access systems which succeeded ALOHA. Assume that all of the stations sharing the same channel generate fixed-length messages at a Poisson rate. Assume also that there are many lightly loaded stations so that each holds no more than a single message at a time. Let the time in seconds required to transmit a message over the channel be denoted as m and let λ denote the average rate at which messages are generated in messages per second. The dimensionless quantity $\rho = m\lambda$ is the by now familiar load offered to the communications channel. In order for the system to be stable we must have $m\lambda < 1$ in the absence of overhead traffic. The flow on the line will consist of retransmitted as well as newly generated messages. Let the total average rate of flow of new and retransmitted messages be denoted as Λ messages per second. In order to carry the analysis forward it is assumed that the total traffic on the line has a Poisson distribution. In making the Poisson assumption the reliance is upon the mixing of traffic from a large number of lightly loaded stations. A message will be involved in a collision if another station transmits in a window $2m$ seconds in duration about the message (see Figure 8.1). From the Poisson assumption we have

$$P_r[\text{collision}] = 1 - e^{-2\Lambda m} \tag{8.1}$$

The average rate at which messages are retransmitted is $\Lambda(1 - e^{-2\Lambda m})$. Adding the newly generated and the retransmitted message traffic, we have

$$\Lambda = \lambda + \Lambda(1 - e^{-2\Lambda m}) \tag{8.2}$$

---

†In the next chapter we shall consider a nonrandom method of conflict resolution–tree search.
‡For a rigorous, comprehensive treatment of instability in random access systems the reader is referred to the work in Meditch and Lea.[19]

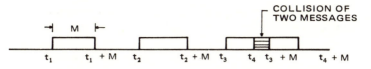

Figure 8.1. Line flow on the pure ALOHA channel.

The quantities $\rho \triangleq \lambda m$ and $R = \Lambda m$ are, respectively, the newly generated load and the total carried load on the channel. From equation (8.2) we have

$$\rho = R e^{-2R} \qquad (8.3)$$

We point out in connection with equation (8.3) that ρ is the independent variable and R the dependent. Equation (8.3) is plotted in Figure 8.2. We see that for ρ small enough the relation is linear; however, as ρ increases the proportion of retransmission increases and there is a point of saturation. By solving the equation $d\rho/dR = 0$ the point of saturation can be shown to be $R = 1/2$ and $\rho = 1/2e \cong 0.18$. Thus, although the delay at very light loading is minimal, less than one fifth of the channel capacity is available to carry newly generated traffic. It is true that the analysis here is based on a Poisson assumption; however, simulation studies show that equation (8.3) holds for more realistic traffic flow distributions. We point out that there is potential instability in that for a wide range of newly offered traffic there are two possible loads on the line, values of R. The larger of the two implies

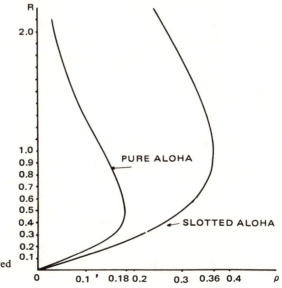

Figure 8.2. Carried load vs. offered load.

a larger volume of retransmitted messages, a phenomenon that implies larger message delay.

8.1.2. Slotted ALOHA

The throughput performance of the ALOHA system can be improved dramatically by adding a small amount of structure in the form of timing pulses broadcast to all stations[3] (see Figure 8.3). Again we assume that the messages require a constant m seconds to be transmitted. The interval between timing pulses is set equal to m seconds. Messages are transmitted at times coinciding with these timing pulses. For very light loading this leads to a delay between message generation and message transmission averaging $m/2$ seconds. However, since only messages generated in the same slot between adjacent timing pulses can interfere with one another, the probability of a message being involved in a collision is considerably reduced. Again we assume that the total traffic flow newly generated and retransmitted is Poisson with average rate Λ messages/second. The probability of a message being involved in a collision is

$$P(\text{collision}) = 1 - e^{-\Lambda m} \tag{8.4}$$

Following the same line of reasoning that led to equation (8.3) in the case of pure ALOHA gives in the case of slotted ALOHA

$$\rho = R\, e^{-R} \tag{8.5}$$

From the plot of equation (8.5) in Figure 8.2 we see that the point of saturation is doubled, residing at $\rho = 1/e \cong 0.36$. Thus with a small amount of overhead, which causes a minimal deterioration of performance, the channel throughput has doubled. We notice once again that there is potential instability since there are two possible loads on the line for the same offered load.

8.1.3. Analysis of Stability

For both pure and slotted ALOHA we have seen evidence for unstable operation in that there are two operating points for the same input rate to

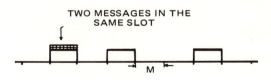

TWO MESSAGES IN THE SAME SLOT

Figure 8.3. Line flow on the slotted ALOHA channel.

the system. In this section we shall explore this phenomenon in some detail following an analysis by Kleinrock and Lam[4,5] for slotted ALOHA.† The results of this analysis apply in broad terms to other forms of random access systems.

We shall assume that messages arrive at a Poisson rate, λ, and that each message has a constant transmission time equal to the duration of a slot. Further, we shall assume that there are N stations, each of which can hold at most one message. If a message arrives at a station whose buffer is full, it is assumed to be lost. The probability of a message arriving in a slot interval is equal to

$$\sigma \triangleq 1 - e^{-\lambda m} \tag{8.6}$$

It is assumed that a message arriving during a slot is transmitted at the beginning of the next slot.

In order to carry out an analysis of slotted ALOHA it is necessary to assume a certain memorylessness in connection with the random retransmission interval after a collision. We assume that after an initial transmission which suffers a collision, the message is retransmitted in every succeeding interval with probability α until a successful transmission has taken place. This does not accurately model a realistic system if a constant interval of time is required to detect a collision. However, simulation studies have shown that performance is not sensitive to the form of the probability distribution of the retransmission interval as long as the mean value is the same. For example, suppose that instead of a geometrically distributed retransmission interval, the interval is uniformly distributed in slots $D + 1$, $D + 2, \ldots, D + K$, where D is a detection interval after initial transmission. For the geometric case the probability of retransmission in the ith slot is $(1 - \alpha)^{i-1}\alpha$ and in the uniform case, $1/K$ for $D + 1 \le i \le D + K$ and zero otherwise. Equating mean retransmission times for the two cases, we find that the performances of the two techniques will be the same as long as

$$\alpha = \frac{1}{D + (K + 1)/2} \tag{8.7}$$

Based on the memoryless arrival and retransmission distributions we can analyze the input–output characteristics of the system. Let us assume that at the beginning of a slot, k of the N stations are backlogged, i.e., holding messages which have undergone collision. The probability that each of these backlogged stations will transmit is α. Let σ denote the probability that each of the remaining $N - k$ stations transmits a message in a slot.

†An alternate treatment of instability is given in Ref. 6.

This probability is simply the probability of message arrival in the previous slot. [See equation (8.6).] There will be a successful transmission if only one message, new or old, is transmitted. The probability that only one of the n backlogged stations transmits and all others remain silent is $k\alpha(1-\alpha)^{k-1}(1-\sigma)^{N-k}$. Similarly the probability that only a newly generated message is transmitted is $(N-k)\sigma(1-\alpha)^k(1-\sigma)^{N-k-1}$. The probability of a successful transmission is then

$$T_k = k\alpha(1-\alpha)^{k-1}(1-\sigma)^{N-k} + (N-k)\sigma(1-\sigma)^{N-k-1}(1-\alpha)^k$$
$$k = 0, 1, 2, \ldots, N \tag{8.7}$$

Notice that T_k is the rate at which messages depart the system conditioned on k stations backlogged. Under the same conditioning, the rate at which messages enter the system is $S = (N-k)\sigma$. For N large enough and σ small enough we may approximate (8.7) by

$$T_k = k\alpha(1-\alpha)^{k-1}e^{-S} + Se^{-S}(1-\alpha)^k \tag{8.8}$$

[The limiting process that leads to equation (8.8) from equation (8.7) is similar to that which lead to the Poisson distribution from the binomial distribution in Chapter 3.]

For given values of k and α this system may be said to be in *equilibrium* when $T_k = S$, implying that the output rate, T_k, is equal to the input rate. In Figure 8.4 we show a plot of an equilibrium contour obtained by setting $S = T_k$, holding α fixed, and varying k, the number of backlogged stations. In the shaded region $S < T$ and the tendency is for the number of backlogged stations to decrease in the next slot. The opposite tendency prevails in the region above the contour. Although the model we considered in the preceding section is simpler, it is nevertheless of interest to compare Figures 8.2 and 8.4. The variables in the abscissa, ρ and S, are quite similar in both cases, both corresponding to a rate of generating messages. When the message generation rate is small they are equal. The ordinate values in Figures 8.2 and 8.4 represent, respectively, total average transmission rate and average number of backlogged stations. These quantities are related inasmuch as αk, where α is as defined above, indicates the rate of retransmitting messages. At high rates of total transmission a substantial portion of the traffic consists of retransmitted messages. Notice that on both curves there is a saturation when the input traffic is at approximately 0.36 of full capacity.

In the foregoing the probability of retransmission is held constant. The effect of varying the retransmission probability, α, is illustrated in Figure 8.5. As α decreases the average retransmission interval is longer and the

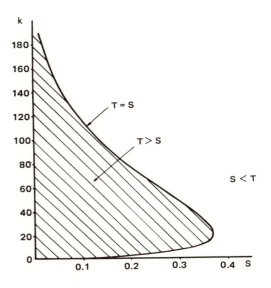

Figure 8.4. Equilibrium contour.

number of backlogged stations at saturation is larger. The operating point of the system must lie on the load line $S = (N - k)\sigma$, where S is the rate at which messages are generated in a slot. In Figures 8.6a and 8.6b the load lines for two different values of α are shown. As we remarked earlier in

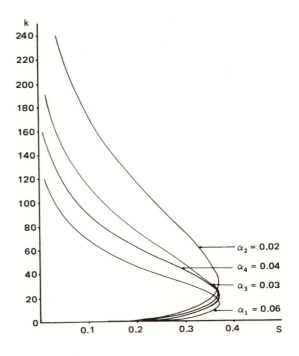

Figure 8.5. Effect of varying α.

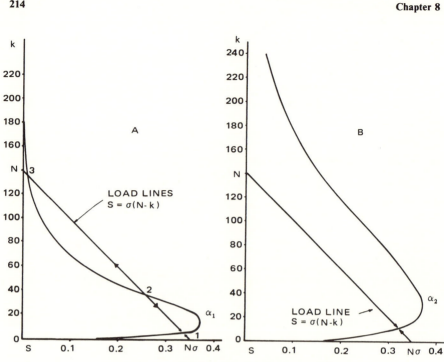

Figure 8.6.(a) Unstable system. (b) Stable system.

connection with Figure 8.4, the region within the equilibirum contour tends toward a decreasing backlog. This is indicated by the arrows shown on the load line. Similarly arrows on the load line in the opposite direction indicate the tendency for the backlog to increase in the region outside the curve. We observe that point 1 in Figure 8.6a is a stable point inasmuch as minor perturbations do not lead to wide excursions—the tendency is back to the point. The opposite is true of point 2, which is inherently unstable. Notice that point 2 corresponds to higher backlog and lower throughput than point 1. The final point where the load line crosses the equilibrium contour is point 3. This is a point of saturation where all of the stations are backlogged and throughput is negligible. The system will jump between these states with the usual fluctuations in the traffic levels. However, when there are N backlogged stations the probability of a successful transmission is small, $T_N = Np(1 - P)^{N-1}$, and the system tends to remain in this state for a long time.

An unstable system can be made stable by decreasing α as indicated in Figure 8.6b. In this case there is a single stable point where the load line and the equilibrium contour cross. Now the system can be destabilized again by increasing N, the number of stations, while keeping everything else constant. In the limit for an infinite number of stations no increase in the transmission time will be enough (see Figure 8.7a). Finally, if N and σ (the arrival rate) are large enough, there will be a single operating point—saturation (see Figure 8.7b). The fact that decreasing α reduces the probability of conflict leads to an adaptive strategy for conflict resolution. A station that has been thwarted through conflict automatically reduces α in each subsequent transmission.[7,8]

8.1.4. Analysis of Delay

The technique used in the first analysis of delay for slotted ALOHA has provided a basic methodology which has been used in a number of subsequent analyses of more sophisticated random access systems. A Markov chain whose state is the number of messages in the system is embedded at the appropriate points. The solution to the steady-state equilibrium distribution of the chain allows one to find the average number of messages in the system. The application of Little's formula yields average delay.

For the slotted ALOHA system the natural embedding point is the beginning of a slot. The state of the system is the number of backlogged stations or equivalently the number of messages in the system (recall that

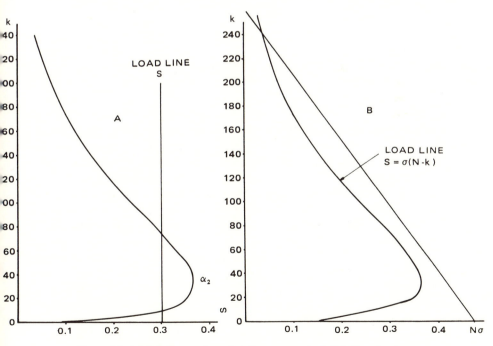

Figure 8.7. (a) Infinite number of stations, s constant. (b) N and σ large.

a station may hold no more than one message). Again we assume that the probability of a message arriving in a slot is σ and that the probability of retransmitting a message in a slot is α. It is asumed that the messages have a constant transmission time equal to the slot duration. Based on these assumptions a state transition matrix can be derived. Let t_{ij} denote the probability that there are j messages in the system at slot $k+1$ given that there were i messages in the system at slot k. Since there can be no more than one successful transmission in a slot $t_{ij} = 0$ for $j < i - 1$. If there are no new messages arriving and if only one of the i stations having messages transmits, then $j = i - 1$. We have the event $i = j$ in two ways: no new arrivals and none or two or more of the backlogged stations transmit messages, or one new arrival and no transmission from the backlogged stations. Recall that a newly arrived message is transmitted in the very next time slot. The event $j = i + 1$ occurs only if there is an arrival and one or more of the backlogged terminals transmits. Finally, for $j \geq i + 2$ there are $j - i$ messages arriving at $N - i$ empty stations. The probability of occurrence of all of these events can be expressed as

$$
t_{ij} = \begin{cases}
0, & j \leq i - 2 \\
i\alpha(1-\alpha)^{i-1}(1-\sigma)^{N-i}, & j = i - 1 \\
(1-\alpha)^i(N-i)\sigma(1-\sigma)^{N-i-1} & \\
\quad + [1 - i\alpha(1-\alpha)^{i-1}](1-\sigma)^{N-i}, & i = j \\
(N-i)\sigma(1-\sigma)^{N-i-1}[1-(1-\alpha)^i], & j = i + 1 \\
\binom{N-i}{j-i}\sigma^{j-i}(1-\sigma)^{N-j}, & j > i + 1
\end{cases} \tag{8.9}
$$

In verifying equation (8.9) the reader should bear in mind that the probability of only one backlogged packet being transmitted is $i\alpha(1-\alpha)^{i-1}$ and the probability of none or of two or more transmitted is $1 - i\alpha(1-\alpha)^{i-1}$. From the same considerations as in the previous cases, the existence of a steady-state probability distribution for the Markov chain is assured.

If we let $N \to \infty$ and $\sigma \to 0$ in such a way that $N\sigma = S$ equation (8.9) becomes

$$
t_{ij} = \begin{cases}
0, & j \leq i - 2 \\
i\alpha(1-\alpha)^{i-1}\exp(-S), & j = i - 1 \\
(1-\alpha)^i S \exp(-S) + [1 - i\alpha(1-\alpha)^{i-1}]\exp(-S), & j = i \\
S \exp(-S)[1 - (1-\alpha)^i], & j = i + 1 \\
\dfrac{S^{j-i}}{i!(j-i)!}\exp(-S), & j \geq i + 2
\end{cases} \tag{8.10}
$$

Equation (8.10) gives the state transition probability for the Markov chain for the number of backlogged stations at the imbedded points. Let P_i, $i = 0, 1, 2, \ldots, N$ denote the steady-state probability of there being i backlogged stations in the system. In the steady state these probabilities must satisfy the equation

$$P_j = \sum_{i=0}^{N} t_{ij}P_i, \qquad j = 0, 1, \ldots, N \tag{8.11a}$$

where t_{ij} is given by equation (8.10). Of course the steady-state probabilities must also satisfy the normalizing condition

$$\sum_{i=0}^{N} P_i = 1 \tag{8.11b}$$

Any one of a number of standard software packages can be used to solve equations (8.11a) and (8.11b).

The mean number of messages in the system can be calculated from

$$\bar{k} = \sum_{i=0}^{N} iP_i \tag{8.12}$$

The average delay can be found by an invocation of Little's theorem in the following manner. Conditioned on there being n backlogged stations the average rate at which messages enter the system is $\sigma(N - n)$ messages/slot. (Here it is natural to use the slot as the unit of time.) Removing the conditioning we find that the overall average rate of message arrival is

$$S_{\text{IN}} = \sigma(N - \bar{k})$$

The average delay in terms of slots is then

$$\bar{D} = \frac{\bar{k}}{\sigma(N - \bar{k})} \tag{8.13}$$

The average delay here is the interval between message arrival and its final transmission when it departs the system. In a realistic system allowance must be made for time to determine whether a collision has taken place. Thus, to the average delay determined in (8.13) must be added this detection time if one wishes to compute the average time a message must be held at the transmitter until it can be said to have been received correctly. The average delay, $\bar{D}$, of the system as a function of σ, the message arrival rate, with α as a parameter is shown in Figure 8.8. As we see, there is an abrupt

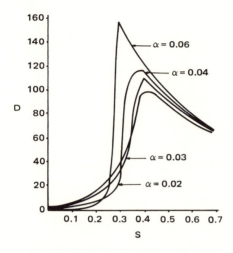

Figure 8.8. Average delay versus input rate.

increase in the average delay which is due to the onset of instability. At each value of σ there seems to be an optimum value of α, the retransmission probability. As the system become more heavily loaded, a longer retransmission interval is required. As a rough rule of thumb[4] it appears that the optimum value of α is $N\sigma$. In fact, performance is improved if the retransmission interval is varied according to the state of the channel as perceived by the stations.[8]

8.1.5. Analysis of Pure ALOHA

The simplicity and elegance of the preceding Markov chain model of slotted ALOHA is due in part to the fact that the pulse times are convenient embedding points. In unslotted pure ALOHA there is no similar point; as a consequence the analysis is more difficult. There have been several analyses which bear resemblance to the analysis of the $M/G/1$ queue. The key parameter in this work is the probability of collision when either a new or old message is transmitted. Clearly from the foregoing analysis of the slotted system it is clear that this probability is a function of the number of backlogged stations. However, in order to carry the analysis forward for unslotted systems it is assumed that the probability is a constant whose value depends on the traffic levels and the retransmission period. If the retransmission period is spread over a wide enough interval there will be a kind of mixing which will tend to validate this assumption. A second feature of these analyses is the tacit assumption that the system is stable. As in the slotted system this will be determined in part by the retransmission period. Perhaps the simplest (also the oldest and least accurate) analysis of this sort is due to Hayes and Sherman.[9] It is assumed that the time-out interval is exponentially distributed with mean value $1/\gamma$. It is assumed that constant length messages arrive at a Poisson rate with average value λ messages per second. The total traffic on the line, Λ messages/second, is the solution of equation (8.3), where R is the total load given by $R = \Lambda m$. Since the system is modeled as an $M/G/1$ queue, the key question is the calculation of the service time, which is, in this case, the time required for successful transmission. It is assumed that the probability of collision for a newly arrived message is $1 - e^{-2R}$. In order to take into account the effect of the retransmission interval it is assumed that the probability of conflict on subsequent retransmissions is given by $1 - e^{-2(R+\gamma)}$. The use of this equation is justified by the behavior of the system at extreme points. If $\gamma = 0$, infinite retransmission delay, there is no effect. In contrast, for $\gamma = \infty$, immediate retransmission, the probability of collision is 1. The remainder of the analysis is straightforward. The service time consists of the time required to transmit a message plus a geometrically distributed number of intervals. These intervals consist of an exponentially distributed retransmission time and an interval, usually taken to be a constant, which indicates the time required to determine that a collision has taken place. The details of this analysis are left to the reader as an exercise (see Exercise 8.3). The results of such an exercise are shown in Figure 8.9, where we show average message delay as a function of message arrival rate for several values of γ. It seems that the rule of thumb for the best value of γ, the retransmission parameter, is $\gamma = \lambda m$.

More complex and more accurate models which have been verified by simulation have been analyzed by Ferguson.[10,11] In all of these analyses

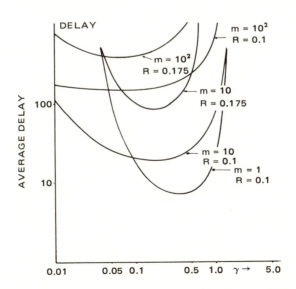

Figure 8.9. Average delay as a function of load; pure ALOHA.

based on the $M/G/1$ queue only results in terms of average delay emerge. It is not possible to compute higher moments of delay directly from the distribution of buffer occupancy since messages are not served in their order of arrival. The service is more like random selection. Because to space limitations we shall not consider this work; however, some of the analysis in the next section on carrier sense systems is appropriate to ALOHA in its pure form.

8.2. Carrier Sense Multiple Access

The current successor to ALOHA is carrier sense multiple access (CSMA) and its many variations. Because of the distributed nature of these protocols, they are well suited to local area networks where flexibility and simplicity of operation are most important.† Furthermore, since wide bandwidth is available, the system can be operated at relatively low loadings and unstable conditions can be avoided. Finally, as we shall see presently, the performance of CSMA is inversely proportional to the end-to-end propagation delay in the system; hence local area networks as discussed in Chapter 7 are most appropriate to CSMA. The topology appropriate to CSMA is the bus structure (see Figure 2.20b).

As the name implies, a basic assumption in carrier sense multiple access systems is that the stations can sense signals on the common channel. This capability reduces the number of conflicts since terminals will transmit only if there is no signal on the line. Now conflict is possible if two stations separated by a propagation time of Δ seconds both begin transmission in an interval Δ seconds in duration. Clearly the larger the end-to-end propagation delay in the system, the larger will be the probability of collision.

As we have indicated previously, the behavior of CSMA has the same general characteristics as more primitive random access systems. We begin with the consideration of throughput characteristics. We shall obtain curves similar to those shown in Figures 8.2 illustrating the characteristic saturation effect. However, owing to the sensing capability, the maximum throughput is higher in CSMA systems.

Variations within the CSMA technique center about the action of a station when the line is sensed busy or idle. In the case of nonpersistent CSMA, upon detecting a signal on the line the station acts as though a collision had taken place. Retransmission is scheduled after a random time interval, whereupon the line is sensed once again. The nonpersistent protocol is illustrated in Figure 8.10a. A station senses the line to be busy at times

---

†Indeed the Ethernet,[12] which is, at this writing, the leading local area network, employs a form of random access technique.

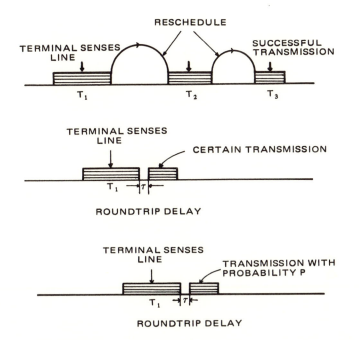

Figure 8.10. (a) Nonpersistent CSMA. (b) 1-persistent CSMA. (c) P-persistent CSMA.

t_1 and t_2 and to be clear at time t_3. The difficulty with the nonpersistent strategy is that after the present transmission, there is a good chance the line may be idle. The obvious alternative is the so-called "1-persistent" strategy, where the station continuously senses the line and transmits as soon as the line is sensed to be free (see Figure 8.10b). Even within the persistent technique there are variations. If while the line was busy, two or more stations receive messages, then conflict is certain under the 1-persistent strategy. An alternative is to randomize transmission whereby stations having messages transmit with probability P when the line becomes free. (See Figure 8.10c.) If a station does not transmit its message, it waits for an interval equal to the round-trip propagation time of the system and senses the line. If the line is sensed idle after this interval, the message is transmitted. If the line is busy, the station repeats the foregoing procedure. This strategy is called P-persistent, and the 1-persistent strategy is clearly a special case.

The nonpersistent and the P-persistent strategies can be implemented irrespective of whether or not timing pulses which create slots are available. However, analysis is considerably simplified if it is assumed that transmission on the line is slotted. In the previous case the duration of a slot was the time required to transmit a fixed-length message; but in slotted

CSMA systems it is convenient to set the duration of a slot equal to the maximum propagation delay between any two stations n in the system—a parameter which we shall designate as τ. As we have seen, two stations separated by propagation delay Δ seconds come into conflict if they transmit messages within Δ seconds of one another. The significance of the parameter τ is that it is the maximum interval of potential conflict.

Throughput Analysis—Unslotted CSMA

As in the analyses of more primitive random access systems the analysis of the throughput of CSMA systems begins with the assumption that there are a large number of sources (an infinite number for all intents and purposes) with an aggregate message arrival rate of λ per second. Further we assume that the lengths of the messages are constant with a transmission time of m seconds. Finally, as in the previous analyses, it is assumed that each station may hold no more than one message at a time. As in pure and slotted ALOHA simulation, results seem to indicate that performance is sensitive to the retransmission interval only with respect to its mean value. We designate the average retransmission interval as $1/\alpha$. (Obviously we have in mind here geometrically or exponentially distributed retransmission intervals.) We shall assume that $1/\alpha \gg m$ thus ensuring a kind of mixing of the message arrival process. The result of this mixing is that the interval between message transmission can be assumed to be exponentially distributed.

The calculation of throughput for all of the techniques discussed above follows the same basic pattern.[13] Flow on the line consists of alternating busy and idle periods. A busy period is initiated by the arrival of a message to the system when the common channel is sensed idle. The busy period may assume either of two forms. If there are no interfering messages from other stations it is simply the time required to transmit a message. When there are conflicting messages the busy period is followed by an interval in which the line is sensed idle by all stations. We point out that, for all the techniques under consideration, there is a random retransmission interval. Now during the busy–idle cycle there is at most one message transmitted successfully. From these considerations, renewal theory yields the following equation for the average throughput:

$$\rho = \frac{\bar{T}}{\bar{B} + \bar{I}} \tag{8.14}$$

where $\bar{T}$ is the average duration of a busy period in which a message was transmitted successfully, $\bar{B}$ is the average duration of a busy period including successful and unsuccessful transmissions, and $\bar{I}$ is the average duration of an idle period.

In Figure 8.11 a cycle consisting of a busy and idle period is depicted. The computation of the average duration of busy and idle periods for all of the various forms of random access systems is based on the assumption that the message flow on the line is Poisson with average rate Λ messages per second. The mean duration of an idle period is then $1/\Lambda$ seconds. The duration of a busy period must be at least $m + \tau$ whether or not there are collisions. When there is a collision the busy period is longer. The situation is illustrated in Figure 8.11 under the assumption that $\tau \leq m$. A busy period commences at time t. Because of the Poisson assumption there may be any number of messages colliding with this initial message. We denote the time of arrival of the last of these as $t + d$; since stations are sensing the line, it must be that $d < \tau$. As indicated in Figure 8.11 the busy period lasts until $t + d + m + \tau$ since this is the first time that all of the stations sense that the line is idle. Thus collisions augment the busy period by d seconds. The computation of the probability distribution of the random variable d again relies on the Poisson assumption. Under the assumption that $\tau \leq m$ we have for the distribution function of d

$$P[d \leq x] = P[\text{no message arrivals in } \tau - x]$$
$$= \exp[-\Lambda(\tau - x)] \qquad 0 \leq x \leq \tau \tag{8.15}$$

The mean value of d is then

$$\bar{d} = \tau - \frac{1}{\Lambda}(1 - e^{-\Lambda\tau}) \tag{8.16}$$

We have then that the sum of the idle and busy periods is

$$\bar{I} + \bar{B} = \frac{1}{\Lambda} + m + 2\tau - \frac{1}{\Lambda}(1 - e^{-\Lambda\tau}) \tag{8.17}$$

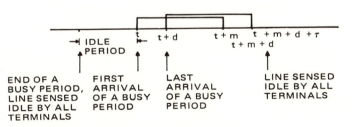

Figure 8.11. Busy and idle periods.

Finally, we consider the quantity $\bar{T}$ which is the average amount of time in a cycle which is required to transmit a message successfully. Given that there are no collisions the average is simply m. Again calling the Poisson assumption into play, we find that the probability of no collision is the probability of no message arrivals in τ seconds and

$$\bar{T} = m\,e^{-\Lambda\tau} \qquad (8.18)$$

From equations (8.14), (8.17), and (8.18) we have

$$\rho = \frac{\Lambda m\,e^{-\Lambda\tau}}{\Lambda m + 2\Lambda\tau + e^{-\Lambda\tau}} \qquad (8.19a)$$

As in the case of the ALOHA random access system we define $R \triangleq m\Lambda$. Also let $a \triangleq \tau/m$. We have then

$$\rho = \frac{R\,e^{-Ra}}{R(1 + 2a) + e^{-Ra}} \qquad (8.19b)$$

In Figure 8.12, ρ is shown as a function of R for various values of a. The strong dependence on the round-trip delay through the parameter a is clearly evident. As we see the smaller the round-trip delay relative to the message duration, the larger is the potential throughput. The advantage is that the carrier sense mechanism eliminates a certain number of collisions.

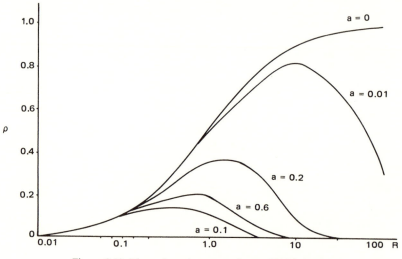

Figure 8.12. Throughput in nonpersistent CSMA (Ref. 13).

Although the curves in Figure 8.12 exhibit the same double valued characteristic as those shown in Figures 8.2 and 8.4, the significance is somewhat different. In the present analysis the total traffic, R, carried is the independent variable. From various values of R the potential throughput is evaluated. This different perspective is indicated by the way in which the curves are drawn with the abscissa representing the independent variable. Now if the rate of newly generated traffic is less than the maximum through-put for the appropriate value of a, presumably the total offered traffic will be at one of the two values indicated by the curve. The same analysis of throughput can be carried out for slotted nonpersistent CSMA and for slotted and unslotted P-persistent CSMA. In Figures 8.13a and 8.13b throughput is plotted as function of total traffic for $a = 0.01$ and for $a = 0.1$, respectively, for different values of P. As is indicated there is an optimum value of P for each value of a. In Figure 8.14 we have a kind of summary of throughput as a function of total traffic. The indication here is that for systems with round-trip delay that is small relative to the message, the carrier sense technique can lead to considerable improvement in throughput.

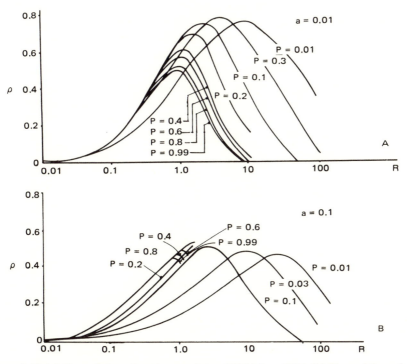

Figure 8.13. (a) Channel throughput in p-persistent CSMA ($a = 0.01$). (b) Channel throughput in p-persistent CSMA ($a = 0.1$) (Ref. 13).

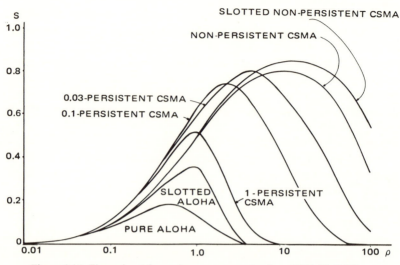

Figure 8.14. Throughput for various access modes ($a = 0.01$) (Ref. 13).

For example for $a = 0.01$ P-persistent and nonpersistent CSMA achieve approximately 0.8 throughput. This is to be compared to 0.36 throughput for slotted ALOHA. The results show an advantage for slotted systems over unslotted even in the case of CSMA. However, the improvement due to slotting is nowhere near as large as it was in the ALOHA system.

Further improvement can be obtained by means of collision detection whereby once a collision has been detected, transmission is aborted. This would reduce the duration of the busy period $\bar{B}$, since in the foregoing calculation it is assumed that once message transmission has begun, it will continue until completion. This technique is called CSMA/CD.

8.3. Delay Calculations CSMA/CD

In a number of calculations of delay in random access systems the same basic technique is used. A Markov chain model is developed in which the state is the number of messages in the system. By whatever technique is appropriate to the model, the average numbers of messages in the system are found. In this section we shall consider an analysis which is similar to the embedded Markov chain[14] approach in the analysis of the $M/G/1$ queue. An alternative technique involves the derivation of the state transition matrix and the calculation of the eigenvectors[15,16] to give the steady-state probabilities.

In order to apply the embedded Markov chain approach to carrier sense multiple access with collision detection (CSMA/CD) by making certain randomizing assumptions are required. During idle and contention periods we take the flow on the line to be slotted. The duration of the slot is $T = 2\tau$, where τ is the maximum delay between any two stations in the system. This slot interval allows a collision to be detected and transmission to be aborted. The randomizing assumption is that the probability of successful transmission in a slot is independent of the number of messages in the system. Simulation studies have shown that this assumption is justified for systems in which the retransmission strategy adapts to the number of messages.[5,8,12,17,18] Such a strategy might be implemented by the variation of the probability of transmission after each unsuccessful attempt. We recognize that the probability of failure is a function of the number of messages in the system. It can be demonstrated that the adaptive strategy in a slotted ALOHA system yields a probability of successful transmission equal to $1/e \cong 0.368$.

As in the study of throughput it is assumed that each station may hold at most one message. We assume that the system operates under the P-persistent protocol in which stations with messages transmit with probability P in the slot following a collision. After the successful transmission of a message, the channel is sensed idle by all users and stations transmit with probability 1 in the succeeding slot. It is assumed that terminals can sense successful transmission as well as collisions. The line traffic under this protocol is depicted in Figure 8.15. Let I_{i+1} be the idle period in seconds following the ith transmission. Owing to the protocol described above, the idle period is nonzero only if the system is empty after message departure. An idle period terminates with the arrival of a message. Since a Poisson message arrival model is assumed the duration of the idle period is geometrically distributed:

$$P[I_{i+1} = lT/\text{system empty}] = (1 - P_0)P_0^{l-1}, \qquad l = 1,2,\ldots \qquad (8.20)$$

where $P_0 = e^{-\lambda T}$ and λ is the average arrival rate of messages from all sources.

A contention period begins either immediately after a successful transmission when there is more than one message in the system or after an idle

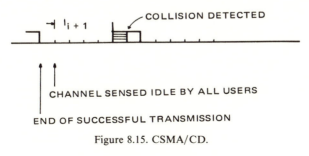

Figure 8.15. CSMA/CD.

period when two or more messages arrive in the same slot. The contention period ends at the commencement of successful transmission. Under the basic assumption that the probability of successful transmission is independent of the number of messages in the system, the duration of a contention period is geometrically distributed and we have

$$P[C_{i+1} = kT/\text{collision}] = (1 - \nu)^{k-1}\nu, \qquad k = 1, 2, \ldots \qquad (8.21)$$

where C_{i+1} denotes the duration of the $(i + 1)$th contention interval and ν is the probability of successful transmission.

A message transmission is assumed to last for an arbitrarily distributed amount of time. Each of the message-bearing stations can sense successful transmission and accordingly it remains silent. After a message has been completed there is a period of silence on the line lasting for τ seconds. This time gives all of the stations time to transmit. If there had been only one message in the system and if there were no arrivals during either message transmission or during the τ second listening interval, a new idle period begins.

A key element of the embedded Markov chain analysis is the message arrival process. Let a_{i+1} denote the number of messages that arrive in the interval $I_{i+1} + C_{i+1}$. The number of messages that arrive during the transmission of the $(i + 1)$st message and in the succeeding slot is denoted as b_{i+1}. We remind the reader that the distribution of message lengths is arbitary.

We are now in a position to write down the state equations at the embedded points. Let n_i denote the number of messages in the system after the departure of the ith message. As in the analysis of the $M/G/1$ queue in Chapter 4 we have

$$n_{i+1} = n_i + a_{i+1} + b_{i+1} - 1 \qquad (8.22)$$

The essential difference between this and the earlier analysis is that the arrivals, a_n, depend upon the state of the system. As we have seen when $n_i = 0$ there is an idle period which terminates upon the arrival of one or more messages. If there is only one arrival there is no contention period. The probability of j arrivals in a slot is

$$P_j = e^{-\lambda T}(\lambda T)^j/j!, \qquad j = 0, 1, 2, \ldots \qquad (8.23a)$$

Conditioned on there being an arrival in a slot the probability of j arrivals is

$$P_j' = P_j/(1 - P_0) \qquad (8.23b)$$

Also let R_k indicate the probability of k arrivals during a contention period.

We condition on the value of n_i in computing the probability distribution of a_{i+1}. First for $n_i = 0$ we have

$$P[a_{i+1} = 1/n_i = 0] = P_1' \tag{8.24a}$$

$$P[a_{i+1} = j + k/n_i = 0] = P_j' R_k, \qquad j > 1, \qquad k = 0, 1, \ldots \tag{8.24b}$$

If $n_i = 1$ successful transmission begins immediately and there is neither an idle nor a contention period. We have

$$P[a_{i+1} = 0/n_i = 1] = 1 \tag{8.24c}$$

Finally, if $n_i > 1$, there is no idle period, only a contention period, and

$$P[a_{i+1} = k/n_i > 1] = R_k \tag{8.24d}$$

The duration of a contention period is geometrically distributed, given by equation (8.21). Since message arrivals are Poisson, it is not difficult to show that the probability-generating function of the number of arrivals is

$$R(z) = \nu [e^{\lambda T(1-z)} - (1 - \nu)]^{-1} \tag{8.25}$$

The generating function for b_{i+1} in equation (8.22) is simply the generating function for the number of messages arriving during the message transmission period and a slot time and is given by

$$B(z) = \mathcal{M}(\lambda(1 - z)) e^{-\lambda T(1-z)} \tag{8.26}$$

where $\mathcal{M}(s)$ is the Laplace transform of the density of the time required to transmit a message.

An expression for the probability-generating function of the number of messages in the system can be derived from equation (8.22) in the usual fashion. Let

$$q_{ij} \triangleq p(n_i = j)$$

and

$$Q_i(z) \triangleq \sum_{j=0}^{\infty} q_{ij} z^j$$

$$Q_{i+1}(z) = E[z^{n_i + a_{i+1} + b_{i+1} - 1})$$

$$= \left\{ q_{i0}[zP_1' + R(z) \sum_{j=2}^{\infty} P_j' z^j] + zq_{i1} \right.$$

$$\left. + R(z)Q_i(z) - R(z)(q_{i0} + q_{i1}z) \right\} B(z) z^{-1} \tag{8.27}$$

If the average message arrival rate to the system is less than the average departure rate, i.e., $\lambda(\bar{m} + \tau + T/\nu) < 1$, then there is a steady-state solution and we have $Q_{i+1}(z) = Q_i(z) = Q(z)$. Solving equation (8.27) for $(Q)(z)$ we find

$$Q(z) = \frac{\{q_0[P_1'z + R(z)\sum_{j=2}^{\infty} P_j'z^j] + zq_1 - R(z)(q_0 + q_1z)\}B(z)}{z - R(z)B(z)} \quad (8.28)$$

As seen in equation (8.28), the probability generating function for the number of messages in the system is expressed in terms of two unknowns, q_0 and q_1, the probability of none and one messages in the system, respectively. However, the structure of the problem allows us to solve for these parameters. The event that the system is empty is the union of two disjoint events:

1. System empty at the last imbedded point and only one arrival in the slot that ended the idle period.
2. One message in the system at the last point and no new arrivals during message transmission.

These considerations lead to the equation

$$q_0(1 - e^{-\lambda T}) = q_0\lambda T e^{-\lambda T}B(0) + q_1 B(0)(1 - e^{-\lambda T})$$

or

$$q_1 B(0) = q_0\left[1 - \frac{\lambda T e^{-\lambda T}}{1 - e^{-\lambda T}} B(0)\right] \quad (8.29a)$$

Notice that $B(0)$ is the probability of no arrivals during message transmission. Equation (8.29a) combined with the normalizing condition $Q(1) = 1$ yields the equation

$$q_0 = \frac{1 - \lambda(T/\nu + \bar{m} + \tau)}{[\lambda T/(1 - e^{-\lambda T})] - [\lambda T/\nu B(0)]} \quad (8.29b)$$

where $\bar{m}$ is the number of slots required to transmit a message. From (8.28), (8.29a), and (8.29b) the average number of messages in the system can be derived, $Q'(1)$. The application of Little's theorem yields average delay. It can be shown that the average delay is

$$\bar{D} = \bar{m} + \tau + T(\tfrac{1}{2} + 1/\nu)$$

$$- \left\{\frac{1 - e^{-\lambda T}}{2[B(0)\nu - (1 - e^{-\lambda T})]}\right\}[2/\lambda - 2T] \quad (8.30)$$

$$+ \frac{\lambda[\overline{m^2} + 2\bar{m}\tau + \tau^2 + 2(\bar{m} + T)(T/\nu) + T^2(2 - \nu)/\nu^2]}{1 - \lambda(\bar{m} + \tau - T/\nu)}$$

8.4. Performance Comparisons

Equation (8.30) allows us to assess the delay performance of CSMA/CD. As in previous results on carrier sense multiple access, performance is sensitive to the quantity τ, which is the maximum delay between any pair of stations. This is shown in Figure 8.16, where average delay normalized to average message length is shown as a function of offered load $\rho = \bar{m}\lambda$. The parameter a is τ normalized to average message duration, $a = \tau/\bar{m}$. In computing the curves in Figure 8.16 it is assumed that retransmission is optimized so that the probability of success is $\nu = 1/e$.

The curves for CSMA/CD exhibit the form for delay as a function of load which is characteristic of many queueing theory results. The strong dependence on a is most interesting. As indicated for $a = 0.001$ saturation is quite close to unity and the system behaves like an $M/G/1$ queue. For comparison with CSMA/CD we also show in Figure 8.16 average delay as a function of load for polling systems for systems with 10 and 100 stations. The parameter a now becomes the walk-time (see Chapter 7). The results are clear illustration of the effect of overhead on performance. At light loading the polling system suffers a deterioration in proportion to this overhead. However, as the load increases this explicit overhead becomes less important. The polling systems saturate at unity load. The CSMA system is far more sensitive to increase of load. The implicit overhead in propagation determines the point at which saturation takes place.

The token passing protocol, discussed in the previous chapter in connection with the ring topology, is an alternative access technique to CSMA/CD in the bus configuration. Again a single station at a time has

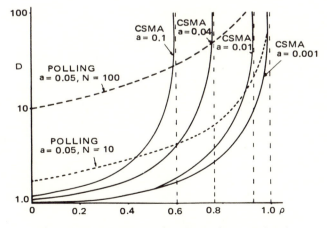

Figure 8.16. Delay versus throughput. (From Ref. 20.)

control of the transmission medium. Control is relinquished by broadcasting a token. There is a preassigned order in which stations may seize the token. As in the ring system the protocol may be modeled as a polling system in which the walk-time is the time required to pass the token from one station to another.

In order to make valid comparisons between the two techniques analytical models based on the same sets of assumptions must be used. Fortunately we have developed models which conform to this requirement. In Section 7.3 of Chapter 7 a polling model in which a station could hold only one fixed length message was analyzed. It was assumed that message arrival was Poisson and the same for each station. This same set of assumptions hold for the analysis of the CSMA/CD protocol considered in the immediately preceding section of this chapter.

Typical results of calculations are shown in Figure 8.17. Messages 10,240 bits in duration are transmitted over 10-Mbps lines. It is assumed that there are 50 stations sharing the line. Average delay is shown as a function of load, λm, where m is the message arrival rate. For the token passing system average delay is given by equation (7.25a). The average delay for CSMA/CD is found from equation (8.30).

The results of computation show an advantage for CSMA/CD only at light loading. As soon as the loading moves beyond the lightest loading the token passing shows better performance. This delay reflects the low overhead for token passing which was assumed to be 47μsec. This trend has been seen in other studies of local area networks.[26] For related work in this area see Refs. 23 and 25.

8.5. Reservation Techniques

The techniques we have considered up to this point are well suited to bursty traffic where there are many users, each generating short messages. However, in many applications there is a significant amount of traffic which consists of long messages. There may be a large number of sources so that the dedication of facilities through TDMA or FDMA is not economical. In order to handle this amount of traffic a number of reservation techniques incorporating random access techniques have been proposed.†

Among the earlier reservation techniques is reservation ALOHA.[21] As in slotted ALOHA, line flow is organized into fixed length slots. A fixed number of slots makes up a frame much as in TDMA. Initially all stations having messages contend for slots in the usual ALOHA fashion. When a

---

†In preparing this section we have benefited from the survey by Tobagi.[20] This survey deals with the whole spectrum of the accessing techniques.

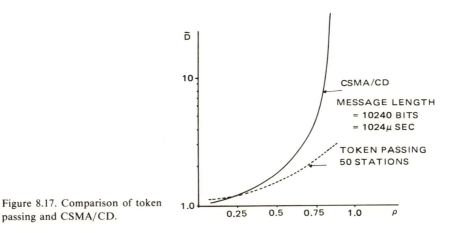

Figure 8.17. Comparison of token passing and CSMA/CD.

station gains a slot, it is assigned this slot on a recurring basis. If a station leaves its assigned slot bank for one frame the reservation is lost and the slot joins the unreserved pool. Stations having messages to transmit contend for the slots in this pool. Since there is at least one slot wasted per message, this technique is suited for applications where there are messages consisting of a number of slots.

A second technique is more efficient in terms of line utilization at the expense of delay.[22] Again line flow is slotted. A sequence of M slots is reserved by particular stations. The $(M + 1)$st slot is segmented into a number of minislots. Reservation messages, from stations having data messages, contend for these minislots in the usual way. A station may reserve up to eight slots. These reservations are broadcast so that each station can keep track of how many messages are waiting at all of the stations. Therefore a station knows when is the next free slot.

Another technique employs elements of the CSMA technique.[24] We assume that there are a limited number of stations, N, sharing the line. Again flow is segmented into frames consisting of M slots. Each user is assigned M/N slots. Before transmitting, however, the station senses the times of the slots it has been assigned. If the slots are occupied, transmission is postponed in the same manner as CSMA. If $M/N = 1$ the scheme looks like what is called minislot alternating priorities (MSAP), which is a form of polling. For $M/L = M$ we have pure CSMA.

References

1. N. Abramson, "The ALOHA System—Another Alternative for Computer Communications," 1970 Fall Joint Computer Conference, *AFIPS Conference Proceedings*, **37**, 281–285 (1970).

2. N. Abramson, "The ALOHA System," *Computer Communications Networks*, N. Abramson and F. Kuo, eds., Prentice-Hall, Englewood Cliffs, New Jersey (1973).

3. L. G. Roberts, "ALOHA Packet System with and without Slots and Capture," *Computer Communications Review* 5, 28–42, April (1975).

4. L. Kleinrock and S. S. Lam, "Packet Switching in a Multiaccess Broadcast Channel: Performance Evaluation," *IEEE Transactions on Communications*, **COM**-23(4), 410–422, April (1975).

5. S. S. Lam, "Packet Switching in a Multiaccess Broadcast Channel with Application to Satellite Communication in a Computer Network," UCLA Technical report, UCLA-ENG-429, April (1974).

6. A. B. Carleial and M. E. Helman, "Bistable Behavior of ALOHA-Type Systems," *IEEE Transactions on Communications* **COM**-23(4), 401–410, April (1975).

7. G. Fayolle *et al.*, "Stability and Optical Control of the Packet Switching Broadcast Channels," *Journal of the Association for Computing Machinery* 24, 375–380, July (1977).

8. S. S. Lam and L. Kleinrock, "Packet Switching in a Multiaccess Broadcast Channel: Dynamic Control Procedures," *IEEE Transactions on Communications* **COM**-23(9), 891–904, September (1975).

9. J. F. Hayes and D. N. Sherman, "A Study of Data Multiplexing Techniques and Delay Performance," *Bell System Technical Journal* 51, 1985–2011, November (1972).

10. M. J. Ferguson, "Approximate Analysis of Delay for Fixed and Variable Length Packets in an Unslotted ALOHA Channel," *IEEE Transactions on Communications* **COM**-25(7), 644–654, July (1977).

11. M. J. Ferguson, "A Bound and Approximation of Delay Distribution for Fixed-Length Packets in an Unslotted ALOHA Channel and a Comparison with Time-Division Multiplexing (TRDM)," *IEEE Transactions on Communications* **COM**-25(1), January (1977).

12. R. M. Metcalfe and D. R. Boggs, "Ethernet: Distributed Packet Switching for Local Computer Networks," *Communications of the ACM*, 19, 395–404, July (1976).

13. L. Kleinrock and F. A. Tobagi, "Packet Switching in Radio Channels: Part 1—Carrier Sense Multiple-Access Modes and their Throughput–Delay Characteristics," *IEEE Transactions on Communications*, **COM**-23(12), 1400–1416, December (1975).

14. S. S. Lam, "A Carrier Sense Multiple Access Protocol for Local Networks," *Computer Networks*, 4(1), 21–32, January (1980).

15. F. A. Tobagi and V. B. Hunt, "Performance Analysis of Carrier Sense Multiple Access with Collision Detection," *Computer Networks*, 4(5), 245–259, November (1980).

16. T. N. Saadawi and A. Ephremedes, "Analysis, Stability and Optimization of Slotted ALOHA with a Finite Number of Buffered Users," *IEEE Transactions on Automatic Control*, **AC**-26(3), 680–689, June (1981).

17. S. S. Lam and L. Kleinrock, "Dynamic Control Schemes for a Packet-Switched Multiaccess Broadcast Channel," *AFIPS Conference Proceedings*, Vol. 44, AFIPS Press, Montvale, New Jersey (1975).

18. M. Gerla and L. Kleinrock, "Closed-Loop Stability Controls for S-ALOHA Satellite Communications," *Proceedings of the Fifth Data Communications Symposium*, Snowbird, Utah, September (1977).

19. J. S. Meditch and C.-T. A. Lee, "Stability and Optimization of the CSMA and CSMA/CD Channels," *IEEE Transactions on Communications*, **COM**-31(6), 763–774, June (1983).

20. F. Tobagi, "Multiaccess Link Control," *Computer Network Architectures and Protocols*. P. E. Green, Jr., ed., Plenum Press, New York (1982); reprinted from Special Issue of *IEEE Transactions on Communications*, **COM**-28, April (1980).

21. W. R. Crowther, R. Rettberg, D. Walden, S. Ornstein, and F. Heart, "A System for Broadcast Communication: Reservation ALOHA," *Proceedings 6th Hawaii International Systems Science Conference*, January (1973).

22. L. Roberts, "Dynamic Allocation of Satellite Capacity through Packet Reservations," *AFIPS Conference Proceedings*, **42**, June (1973).
23. I. Chlamtac, W. R. Tranta, and K. D. Levin, "BRAM: The Broadcast-Recognizing Access Method," *IEEE Transactions on Communications*, **COM-27**(8), 1183–1190, August (1979).
24. L. W. Hansen and M. Schwartz, "An Assigned-Slot Listen-Before-Transmission Protocol for a Multiaccess Data Channel," *IEEE Transactions on Communications*, **COM-27**(6), 846–857, June (1979).
25. L. Kleinrock and M. Scholl, "Packet Switching in Radio Channels: New Conflict Free Multiple Access Schemes for a Small Number of Data Users," International Conference on Communications, Chicago, Illinois (1977).
26. W. Bux, "Local Area Subnetworks: A Performance Comparison," *IEEE Transactions on Communications*, **COM-29**(10), October (1981).

Exercises

8.1. Suppose that stations with messages in a slotted ALOHA system have a good estimate for the number of messages. It is reasonable then to decrease the collision probability by choosing the retransmission probability to be inversely proportional to this number. Find an equilibrium contour similar to that shown in Figure 8.4 for this strategy.

8.2. Suppose that n stations in a slotted ALOHA system have messages. Assume that newly arrived messages are not transmitted until all n messages have been transmitted.

(a) Show that the average number of slots until one of these messages is transmitted is $1/[1 - nP(1 - P)^{n-1}]$, where P is the probability of transmitting in a slot.

(b) What is the average number of slots required to transmit all n messages.

(c) Repeat (a) and (b) under the retransmission assumption of Exercise 8.1.

8.3. Find an expression for the average message delay in the pure ALOHA system using the $M/G/1$ queueing analysis mentioned on page 219. You should be able to reproduce the curves in Figure 8.9.

8.4. Show that the throughput for slotted nonpersistent CSMA is given by

$$\rho = m\tau\Lambda\, e^{-\tau\Lambda}/[m(1 - e^{-\tau\Lambda}) + \tau]$$

The quantities τ, m, and Λ are the same as those defined in the text.

8.5. In connection with the derivation of throughput for CSMA which led to equation (8.19) it was stated that collision detection would increase throughput. Carry through an analysis of throughput assuming collision detection.

8.6. Repeat the comparison of token passing and CSMA/CD contained in Section 8.2.3 under the assumption that 2000 stations share the line. Find the average delay as a function of load.

Probing and Tree Search Techniques

9.1. Overhead and Information Theory

In the two preceding chapters we have studied two contrasting techniques for sharing a common channel among a number of geographically dispersed stations. As we have seen, the two have complementary characteristics. Due to large overhead, polling is inefficient at light loading, but as loading increases the effect of overhead diminishes. In contrast, random access techniques have minimal overhead and, as a consequence, are best at light loading. However, for the random access techniques we considered the instability appears as the loading increases. A direct comparison between polling in the form of token passing and CSMA (see Figure 8.17) shows that the advantage that CSMA holds at light loading dissipates as the load increases.

The deleterious effect of overhead in local distribution has led to the development of adaptive algorithms. These algorithms are based on tree search techniques whose origins may be traced to certain information theoretic concepts. We turn now to the consideration of these concepts. Since our objective is only to point out the connection between local distribution and information theory, we shall cover only the barest essentials from information theory.†

Consider an information source producing symbols, S_i, $i = 1, 2, \ldots, M$ at a rate of $1/\text{sec}$, where the probability of symbol S_i is Q_i. We measure the amount of information produced by the source by means of a quantity called entropy. If successive symbols are independent, the entropy of symbol S_i is $-\log_2 Q_i$ bits and the average entropy of the source is

$$H = - \sum_{i=1}^{M} Q_i \log_2 Q_i \tag{9.1}$$

---

†More complete treatments may be found in any one of a number of texts on the subject of information theory. At the end of the chapter we cite two with which we are most familiar.[1,2]

Loosely speaking the entropy of a source is the minimum average number of yes/no questions that are necessary to determine a particular source output. The optimum sequence of questions is a tree search procedure prescribed by Huffman coding. The entropy for the case $M = 2$ is shown in Figure 9.1. Notice that the entropy in this case is unimodal attaining a maximum of one bit at $Q_i = 1/2$; $i = 1, 2, \ldots, M$. As one moves away from this in either direction the average amount of information decreases. It is not hard to show that the entropy is maximum for equiprobable outputs, $Q_i = 1/M$, $i = 1, 2, \ldots, M$.

These basic concepts of information theory furnish guidance on techniques for granting access to stations in a local area network.† As we shall see, the key is a tree search of a different form than the Huffman coding technique alluded to above. A polling system may be considered to be a sequence of questions directed to each station, "Do you have a message?" For lightly loaded systems the answer is almost always "no," and in terms of entropy, little information is gained. For example, suppose that the probability of a negative reply is 0.9; from Figure 9.1 we see that the amount of information gained is only 0.2 out of a maximum of 1 bit. Moreover, we have not taken account of any dependencies between successive stations which would reduce the information further. The idea of entropy in polling systems can be more fully illustrated by means of one of the models considered in Chapter 7. Fixed-length messages arrive at a Poisson rate to a station whose buffer can hold only one message at a time. In each polling cycle a constant amount of overhead is expended. The probability that in a cycle i stations will have messages is given by $Q(i)$ in equation (7.15). The probability that a particular set of i stations have messages is given by

†The idea of applying rudimentary information theoretic concepts to local distribution is from Hayes.[3]

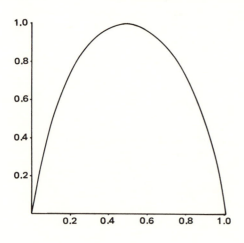

Figure 9.1. Entropy of a binary source.

$Q(i)/\binom{N}{i}$, since all such sets are equally probable. In a certain sense the object of polling is to determine which of the possible 2^N sets of stations have messages. Imagine that we have a source with 2^N possible outputs having probabilities given by $Q(i)/\binom{N}{i}$, $i = 0, 1, \ldots, N$. The entropy of such a source is

$$H = - \sum_{i=0}^{N} Q(i) \log_2\left[Q(i)\Big/\binom{N}{i}\right] \text{ bits} \qquad (9.2)$$

The quantity H in (9.2) is an indication of the amount of information that is obtained in a polling cycle. In Figure 9.2, H is plotted as a function of message arrival rate for the case of 32 stations. Also shown is the average number of messages contained in a cycle obtained from equation (7.15). As we see, at light loading when only one or two messages are transmitted in a cycle, the entropy is five or fewer bits. The entropy is at the maximum value of 32 bits when all 2^N sets are equally probable. This occurs when each station independently has a message with probability $1/2$. Notice that as the loading increases beyond the maximum point the entropy decreases. This is due to the fact that as loading increases beyond a certain point, it is more certain that a station has a message and less information is gained from a poll. Although these information theoretic considerations give insight, they do not, at this writing, furnish source coding techniques akin to Huffman coding. In this respect a more relevant mathematical foundation may be group testing.† The relevance of earlier work on group testing to local distribution was discovered after initial work on tree search.[6]

---

†As its name implies, group testing concerns the search for defectives in a pool of samples.[4] It began with tests on blood samples.[5] A review of the pertinent work is contained in Ref. 6.

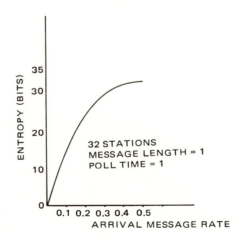

Figure 9.2. Entropy versus load (Ref. 3).

9.2. Probing

The viewpoint of information theory has motivated a tree search technique for finding stations with messages. In this approach groups of stations rather than individuals are polled. In order for this approach to be implementable it is necessary that a central controller, or its equivalent, have the ability to broadcast to all stations simultaneously. By broadcasting an address common to a group of stations the controller asks, in effect, "Do any of the stations have a message?" A station responds affirmatively by putting a noise signal on the line. If an affirmative answer is received the group is split in two and the question is repeated to each of the subgroups. The process is repeated until all stations having messages are isolated. To this technique of polling groups and subdividing according to the response we give the name *probing*. The probing technique is illustrated in Figure 9.3 for eight stations where the sequence of probing inquiries when only station 6 has a message is shown. In response to an affirmative answer, the group of eight is split in two branches. The upper branch is found to be empty and probing continues on the lower branch only.

Probing can also be applied in what might be called a *random access context*. In this case a station with a message responds to a probe by transmitting the message. Messages are assumed to be accompanied by addresses so that a single responding station gets through immediately. A conflict among two or more stations responding to a probe simultaneously is resolved by splitting the group in two and probing each of the subgroups in turn. The process continues until stations with messages are isolated in their own subgroup. At this point probes of groups with a single message elicit message transmission without conflict. The probing process in the random access context can also be illustrated by a system involving eight nodes. In Figure 9.4a the sequence of inquiries are shown when stations 5, 7, and 8 have messages. Once again, because of a positive answer in response

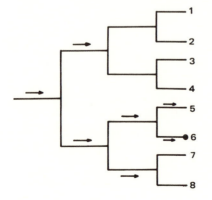

Figure 9.3. Probing technique in polling model.

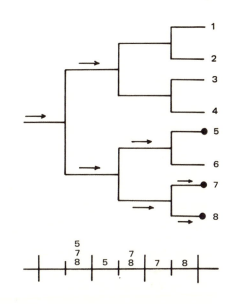

Figure 9.4. (a) Probing technique in random access model. (b) Binary tree algorithm.

to an inquiry directed at the whole group, two branches are formed. Probes of each branch result in further splitting when there is conflict. The probing of a subgroup ends when it has no more than one message.

Control of the adaptive process need not be as centralized as the foregoing implies.[7,8] Suppose that, as in slotted ALOHA, synchronizing pulses are broadcast to all stations. Suppose further that the slots between synch pulses are subdivided into two equal subslots. The messages in the system are assumed to be of constant length with each message fitting into a subslot. In the tree search protocol the first subslot is devoted to an upper branch and the second to a lower. In Figure 9.4b the sequence of slots for the case where stations numbers 5, 7, and 8 in a group of eight stations have messages is shown. The first subslot is empty since it is dedicated to stations 1–4. In the second subslot stations 5, 7, and 8 conflict. The conflict is resolved in subsequent slots.

In the foregoing we have had messages arriving at stations having fixed addresses. There is a random addressing alternative which is equivalent to fixed addressing when the number of stations is very large. Consider a station having a message which is a member of a group being probed. The station responds to a probe with a probability 1/2. (One can imagine a station flipping a fair coin.) Stations in conflict form a subgroup, each member of which responds to the next probe with probability 1/2. The process continues until only one station with messages responds. On subsequent trials stations which did not respond to previous probes are given another opportunity. The mechanism here is mathematically identical to an infinite tree in which branches are chosen randomly. The key difference between this access technique and the P-persistent, with $P = 1/2$, CSMA technique studied in the previous chapter is that a subgroup is formed from stations directly in conflict—memory is introduced into the search procedure in a particular way.

It seems likely that the probing technique results in considerable savings under light loading when only one or two stations have messages in a large group. For example if a group of 2^n stations contains a single message, only $2n + 1$ probing messages are required in a polling system. This contrasts with an overhead proportional to 2^n by conventional polling. The problem is that under heavy loading, when many stations have messages, probing of a group will result in more overhead than polling of individual stations. For example if each of 2^n stations has a message, $2^{n+1} - 1$ inquiries are necessary to read out all messages. As in the case of light loading rudimentary information theory furnishes insight. Under heavy loading the answer to the question "Does anyone have a message?" is nearly always "yes" and little information is obtained. The obvious remedy is to reduce the size of the groups that are probed. Thus, in the examples in Figures 9.3 and 9.4, one may probe two groups of four stations rather than a single group of eight stations. As we shall see presently, the introduction of adaptive tree search into the random access context eliminates the problems of instability that were discussed in Chapter 8.

9.3. Cycle Time in Probing

We may view the probing or tree search algorithm as consisting of a sequence of cycles. The cycle begins by subdividing the entire group of stations into subgroups; each subgroup is probed in turn until all messages in the system at the beginning of the cycle have been transmitted. We impose the rule that messages arriving after a cycle has begun are held over until the succeeding cycle. A Markov chain model of the cycle then applies. Messages are assumed to arrive at each station independently at a Poisson rate with an average of λ messages per second. The probability that a messsage arrives at a cycle of duration T seconds is

$$P = 1 - e^{-\lambda T} \tag{9.3}$$

If the basis for choosing the sizes of the subgroups at the beginning of a cycle is P, then the cycle durations form a Markov chain in as much as the probability distribution of the duration of a cycle can be calculated from the duration of the previous cycle.

Although any number of performance criteria are possible, the easiest to handle mathematically is the average duration of a cycle. Accordingly, given P, a quantity whose value depends upon the duration of the previous cycle, the group of stations are segmented so that the average duration of the next cycle is minimized. The first step in the derivation of this optimum strategy is finding the probability-generating function of the duration of a cycle. The average duration of a cycle follows immediately from standard techniques. Further, as we shall see, the probability-generating function gives the means to evaluate the performance of the system with respect to message delay.

The derivation of the probability-generating function of the duration of a cycle is based on the assumptions that messages in the system have a constant duration and that each station can hold at most one message. While these last assumptions are not necessary, they considerably simplify the analysis without obliterating the basic features of the model. We begin by considering a group of 2^i stations with the probability of each station having a message being P given in equation (9.3). It is convenient to measure all quantities, cycle duration, and message length in terms of the time required to make a single inquiry. We define $Q(l, i)$ as the probability that l inquiries are required to probe 2^i stations, i.e., to isolate stations having messages and to read out all of the messages that arrived during the previous cycle. The generating function of a cycle is defined to be

$$Q_i(z) = \sum_{k=1}^{\infty} Q(k, i)z^k, \qquad i = 1, 2, \ldots, n \qquad (9.4)$$

A recursive relationship for the probability-generating function can be derived in both the polling and the random access contexts using the same technique. We begin with the polling context. The 2^i stations are segmented into upper and lower branches each consisting of 2^{i-1} stations. We may distinguish four mutually exclusive events: (1) both branches empty; (2) only the upper branch empty; (3) only the lower branch empty; (4) neither the upper nor the lower branch empty. If event (1) occurs, only a single inquiry is needed. For the remaining events the group is split and each subgroup probed in turn. For events (2) and (3) only single inquiries are needed for the empty branches. The probability that a nonempty branch requires $k > 1$ inquiries is given by $Q(k, i - 1)$ when $i > 1$. When $i = 1$ a branch contains a single station and the time required to poll and read out a message is described by the probability generating function $M(z)$. Summing over disjoint events, we find the probability generating function of the duration of a cycle to be

$$Q_j(z) = Q^2(1, i - 1)z + 2Q(1, j - 1) \sum_{k>1} Q(k, i - 1)z^{k+2}$$

$$+ \sum_{k>1} \sum_{l>1} Q(k, i - 1)Q(l, i - 1)z^{k+l+1}$$

which becomes, after some manipulation,

$$Q_j(z) = (z - z^3)Q^2(1, j - 1) + zQ_{j-1}^2(z), \qquad j > 1 \tag{9.5a}$$

For the case $j = 1$ we have simply

$$Q_1(z) = (1 - P)^2 z + 2P(1 - P)z^2 M(z) + P^2 z M^2(z) \tag{9.5b}$$

In equations (9.5a) and (9.5b) the probability for a single inquiry, i.e., all stations empty, are given by

$$Q(1, i) = (1 - P)^{2^i}, \qquad i = 0, 1, \dots$$

where P is as in equation (9.3).

The generating function for the length of a probing cycle may be used in several ways. The moments of the cycle duration is found by differentiating and setting $z = 1$. For example the mean duration of a cycle of probing 2^i stations is given by

$$Q_i'(1) = 2Q_{i-1}'(1) + 1 - 2Q^2(1, i - 1) \tag{9.6a}$$

$$Q_1'(1) = 1 + 2P[M'(1) + Q(1, 0)] \tag{9.6b}$$

The mean cycle time is shown as a function of P in Figure 9.5 for the case $M(z) = 1$. $M(z) = 1$ corresponds to the situation where the time

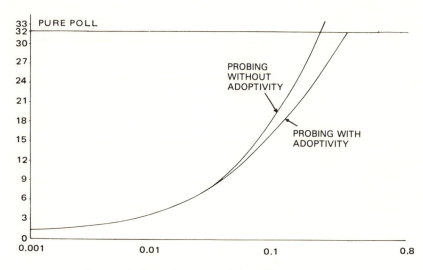

Figure 9.5. Cycle time versus P for polling context.

required to respond to a poll by transmitting a message is negligibly different from the time required to respond with a noise signal. This may be the situation when probing is used to make reservations. In any case the assumption emphasizes the virtues of the probing technique since only overhead is evident. In the sequel we shall use this result on average cycle time in the derivation of the optimum probing strategy. The probabilities of the durations of cycles can also be found; from equation (9.5) we have

$$Q(k, i) = \frac{1}{k!} \frac{d^k Q_i(z)}{dz^k} \bigg|_{z=0} \tag{9.7}$$

Equations (9.3), (9.5), and (9.7) give the state transition matrix for the duration of the probing cycle. For each assumed duration of a cycle the probability of a station having a message can be found. The probability distribution of the following cycle can be found. Once the state transition matrix is known the probability distribution for the cycle duration can be found by means of standard techniques. (The total computation may be long but is easily handled in machine computation.)

The probing technique as explained in the foregoing contains a certain redundancy. Suppose that only the upper branch is empty and that the upper branch is probed first. Since the probe of the entire group prior to splitting would indicate a message present, it may be deduced that the lower branch contains at least one message-bearing station. In this event probing the entire branch is not necessary and the branch should be split into two subbranches immediately.† For obvious reasons we call this technique level skipping. (See Exercises 9.4 and 9.5 for results when level skipping is used.)

In the application of the probing technique in a random access context, the basic difference is that only one probe is required if a group contains at most one message. In deriving the probability-generating function of the cycle time we distinguish nine disjoint events according to whether the upper and lower branch contain zero, one, or more than one message. (In the polling context we were interested in a branch being empty or not.) If both branches are empty or if only one of the two branches contains a single message, only one inquiry for the whole group is necessary. The probability of this event is

$$Q(1, i) = (1 - P)^{2^i} + 2^i P(1 - P)^{2^i - 1} \tag{9.8}$$

As in the polling context we shall assume that the time required to probe and read out a single message has probability-generating function $M(z)$. If each branch has a single message, then a total of three inquiries are necessary to resolve the conflict between the upper and lower branches.

---

†The modification to eliminate redundancy in tree search is from J. L. Massey, cited in Ref. 7.

The probability of this event is $[2^{i-1}P(1-P)^{2^{i-1}-1}]^2$. As in the polling context the probability that a branch requires k inquiries is given by $Q(k, i-1)$: $k > 1$. By summing over the various disjoint events the probability generating function can be found. For simplicity of expression it is assumed that $M(z) = z$, i.e., the time required to transmit a message is so short compared to the time of an inquiry that it may be neglected. In the distributed random access algorithm the flow is slotted with messages fitting exactly in slots. In this instance the inquiry time is the time required to transmit a message

$$Q_i(z) = Q(1, i)z + [2^{i-1}P(1-P)^{2^{i-1}-1}]^2 z^3 + 2Q(1, i-1) \sum_{k>1} Q(k, i-1)z^{k+2}$$

$$+ \sum_{k>1} \sum_{l>1} Q(k, i-1)Q(l, i-1)z^{k+l+1} \qquad (9.9)$$

The third term in equation (9.9) is a composite of the four events that occur when the upper or the lower branches but not both have at most one message.

For the case $i = 1$ the probability-generating function for the cycle time is

$$Q_1(z) = Q(1, 1)z + z^3 P^2 \qquad (9.10)$$

The following recursive expression for the probability-generating function for the duration of a cycle in the random access context can be found from equation (9.9):

$$Q_i(z) = zQ(1, i) + [2^{i-1}P(1-P)^{2^{i-1}-1}]^2 z^3 + zQ_{i-1}^2(z) - z^3 Q^2(1, i-1) \qquad (9.11)$$

The probability-generating function for the cycle duration can be used in the same way as it was in the polling context. The derivatives with respect to z give the moments of the cycle time when $z = 1$. From equations (9.10) and (9.11) the following expressions for the first moment of the cycle time may be found:

$$Q_1'(1) = Q(1, 1) + 3P^2 \qquad (9.12a)$$

$$Q_i'(1) = Q(1, i) + 3[2^{i-1}P(1-P)^{2^{i-1}-1}]^2 - 3Q^2(1, i-1) + 1 + 2Q_{i-1}'(1) \qquad (9.12b)$$

The average cycle time is shown in Figure 9.6 as a function of P. The probabilities of the various durations of cycle time may be found by differentiating the probability-generating function and setting $z = 0$. The state transition matrix can be calculated. From the state transition matrix the probability distribution of the cycle time can be found.

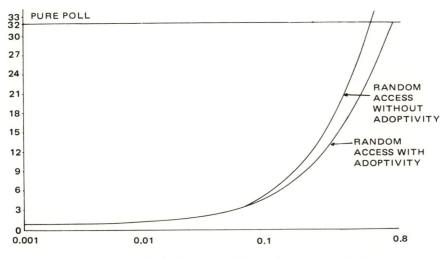

Figure 9.6. Cycle time versus P for random access context.

In Figures 9.5 and 9.6 the average cycle time as a function of P is shown for probing in the polling and the random access contexts, respectively. For comparison the average cycle time for ordinary polling is shown. Since we have assumed that the time required to transmit a message does not affect the duration of an inquiry, the cycle time in the polling case is independent of P. As we see from Figure 9.5 there is considerable reduction in cycle time when P is small corresponding to light loading. As P increases the advantage decreases until for large P convential polling has a shorter cycle time. Once again the reason may be expressed using basic information theoretic concepts. As the probability of single station having a message increases, the answer to the question "Does any station have a message?" is more and more likely to be "yes" and less and less information is gained. Accordingly, for large P, probing large groups is of little value. It is more efficient to break a large group into smaller groups initially and to probe each of these in turn. As mentioned above we shall choose the size of a group so as to minimize the average duration of a cycle, which we define to be the time required to probe all subgroups.

We begin the derivation of the optimum group size by considering probing in the polling context. We shall assume that there are 2^n stations in the system each of which independently have the same probability of having a message [see equation (9.3)]. The symmetries are such that it seems we should consider equal size groups each consisting of 2^i stations. The time required to probe all 2^n stations with this initial segmentation is

$$R_i = 2^{n-i}Q_i'(1), \qquad i = 0, 1, 2, \ldots, n$$

where $Q'_i(1)$ is given in equation (9.6). The question of the value of 2^i can be resolved quite simply by considering adjacent levels, i.e., we decide between groups of size 2^i and 2^{i-1} for all possible values of i. An initial grouping of size 2^i will give a small cycle time duration if

$$2Q'_{i-1}(1) > Q'_i(1) \tag{9.13}$$

From equations (9.6) and (9.13) we find that the optimum criterion is to choose groups of size 2^i over groups of size 2^{i-1} if

$$Q^2(1, i-1) = (1-P)^{2^i} > 1/2 \tag{9.14}$$

where P is as given in equation (9.3). The optimum group size is the largest value of i for which equation (9.14) holds. Notice that $Q(1, j)$ is the probability that all of the 2^i stations are empty and as a consequence only a single inquiry is necessary. The optimum group is the largest value of i for which the inequality in (9.14) holds. Now suppose that the duration of the previous cycle is T_c seconds and that the average message arrival rate is λ. From equations (9.3) and (9.14) the optimum value of i is the minimum of n and

$$j = [-\ln (\lambda T_c/\ln 2)/\ln 2]^- \tag{9.15}$$

where $[X]^-$ is the largest integer smaller than X. If λT_c is very large then j turns out to be negative, which we take to mean that all stations should be polled. The average duration of a cycle when initial groups are optimized is shown in Figure 9.5. As seen the adaptivitity preserves the good performance at light loading without a penalty for heavy loading.

Successive cycles of the adaptive probing process form a Markov chain since the probability distribution of the duration of a cycle depends only on the duration of the previous cycle. The probability generating function of the cycle duration is given by $[Q_i^*(z)]^{n-i^*}$ where i^* indicates the optimum value of i given by equation (9.15). The probability distribution of the cycle time duration can once again be found by differentiation and setting $z = 0$ [see equation (9.7)]. Given the state transition matrix the steady-state distribution of the duration of a cycle can be found. All of this is within the realm of relatively straightforward machine computation.

The foregoing applies to probing in a random access context without much difficulty. As seen in Figure 9.6 the random access technique without adaptivity suffers poor performance when P is large. Again we seek to minimize the average duration of a cycle by segmenting the 2^n stations in the system into equal size groups each consisting of 2^i stations. Again the criterion for choosing groups of size 2^i over groups of size 2^{i-1} is given by the inequality in (9.13). The optimum segmentation of groups is given by the largest value of i for which (9.13) holds. By combining equations (9.12) and (9.13) the following optimum grouping can be found: choose i^* to be the maximum value of j for which

$$Q(1, i) + 3[2^{i-1}P(1 - P)^{2^{i-1}-1}]^2 - 3Q^2(1, i - 1) + 1 \leqslant 0 \qquad (9.16)$$

Again in the random access system the successive probing cycles form a Markov chain. The optimum group size given by equation (9.16) is purely a function of P, which is in turn a function of the duration of the previous cycle [see equation (9.3)]. If 2^{i^*} is the optimum group size the probability-generating function for the duration of a cycle if there are 2^n stations is

$$R_n(z) = [Q_{i^*}(z)]^{n-i^*} \qquad (9.17)$$

where $Q_i(z)$ is as in equations (9.11) and (9.12).

The average cycle time is shown in Figure 9.6. As we see once again the adaptive feature improves performance at light loading with no penalty for heavy loading.

The cycle times shown in Figures 9.5 and 9.6 are shown in terms of inquiry times. Between the random access and the probing techniques there may be a difference in the actual amount of time required to make an inquiry.[9] For example, suppose that we are dealing with a network of voice band modems dispersed over a limited geographical area. Suppose that a tree topography connects the modems to a central processor. In the random access context a station replies to an inquiry from the central processor by transmitting a message. In order for this message to be received correctly phase and timing must be acquired and it may be necessary to train an equalizer. This start-up process may take tens of milliseconds. In contrast, for the polling approach the central processor need only detect the presence of a signal, a process which one may assume is very much shorter. In Figure 9.7 the cycle time is shown as a function of P for random

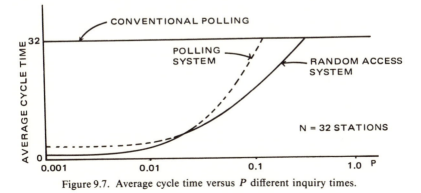

Figure 9.7. Average cycle time versus P different inquiry times.

access and polling systems when the ratio of the inquiry time for random access to inquiry time for polling is 3.901. This is the smallest value of the ratio for which the cycle time for random access is larger than that for polling for all values of P. In the region where this ratio is greater than 3.901 the performance of the polling approach is clearly superior to that of the random access approach.

9.4. Message Delay

At this point we have in hand the transition matrix for the transition probabilities for the duration of a probing cycle. It may be complicated but, in principle at least, one can calculate the steady-state probabilities of the duration of a cycle. While the duration of a cycle gives some measure of the performance of a system, it certainly is not as tangible to the user as the delay of a message. The problem is that in this case calculation of message delay is complicated. Rather than going into details we shall content ourselves with outlining approaches to the calculation and with presenting the salient results.

Under the assumption that messages arriving during the ith probing cycle are held over until the $(i + 1)$st cycle, we may decompose message delay into two components (see Figure 9.8). The first of these is the interval between the arrival of the message and the end of the ith cycle and the second is the interval between the beginning of the $(i + 1)$st cycle and message departure. The calculation of the first component, D_1 is relatively straightforward. The distribution of D_1 is the same as that encountered in the approximate analysis of polling systems in Chapter 7. The probability density is given by equation (7.37) with $t_c(x)$ and $\bar{T}_c$ denoting, respectively, the probability density function of the probing cycle and the mean duration of the probing cycle. The average value of this component of message delay is given by

$$\bar{D}_1 = \frac{\overline{T_c^2}}{2\bar{T}_c} \tag{9.18}$$

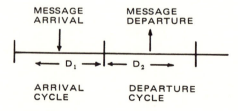

MESSAGE   MESSAGE
ARRIVAL   DEPARTURE

ARRIVAL   DEPARTURE
CYCLE   CYCLE

Figure 9.8. Components of delay.

where $\overline{T_c^2}$ is the mean square probing cycle. We point out that if the steady-state probabilities of a probing cycle are known, $\bar{T}_c$ and $\overline{T_c^2}$ can be calculated easily.

It is the second component of message delay which presents problems. The basic difficulty is that the duration of this part of the probing cycle depends upon the pattern of the stations having messages as well as on the number of stations with messages. This is illustrated by the examples shown in Figures 9.9a and 9.9b where we have two different patterns of two stations of eight with messages. We assume the random access context where stations respond to an inquiry by transmitting a message. As indicated in the figures, seven inquiries are needed for the pattern in Figure 9.8a while only three are needed for the pattern in Figure 9.8b. The reader should have no difficulty devising other examples where there is dependence upon patterns as well as upon the number of stations. Now consider the delay of a message arriviing at the ith station. Before it can be transmitted messages in stations $0, 1, \ldots, i - 1$ must also be transmitted. While the probability distribution of the number of such messages is a simple binomial distribution, the time required to transmit them is pattern dependent.

There have been two approaches to analyzing the average delay. A fairly complicated iterative technique gives an exact solution.[9] An alternative approach, bounding, gives more tangible results, thereby yielding significant insight into adaptive systems. In order to give some feeling for the latter approach we shall present elements of a calculation of delay in a random access system, due to Massey,[10] which was a refinement of earlier work of Capetanakis.[4] In all of this work it is assumed the time required to transmit a message is negligible compared to the inquiry time. Consider that in the first half of the departure cycle conflicts are resolved and actual

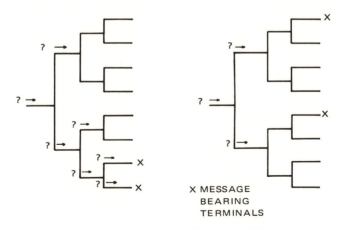

Figure 9.9. Pattern sensitivity in probing.

transmission takes place. From this we have the bounds on the waiting time

$$\tfrac{1}{2}E[T_d - 1] \le \overline{D_2} \le E[T_d - 1] \tag{9.19}$$

where T_d denotes the duration of the departure cycle in terms of inquiries and $E[\ ]$ denotes expectation.

As we said in connection with equation (9.18), if the steady-state probabilities of the duration of a cycle have been found it would be possible to compute the bounds in equation (9.19) immediately. However, it is possible to obtain approximations to these bounds which give reasonably tight bounds on average delay. The first step is to obtain bounds for the duration of a departure cycle. We begin with the observation that if k messages are distributed uniformly among 2^n stations the probability of the upper branch containing i messages is given by

$$C_i(k, n) = \binom{2^{n-1}}{i}\binom{2^{n-1}}{k - i} \Big/ \binom{2^n}{k} \tag{9.20a}$$

For $k \ll 2^{n-1}$ it can be shown that

$$C_i(k, n) \cong \binom{k}{i} 2^{-k} \tag{9.20b}$$

Notice that in equation (9.20b) there is no dependence on the total number of terminals. Let $T_c(k, n)$ indicate the average duration of a probing cycle measured in inquiry times for 2^n terminals conditioned on k of them having messages. Clearly for $k = 0$ or $k = 1$ only a single inquiry is required, and we have

$$T_c(0, n) = T_c(1, n) = 1 \tag{9.21}$$

An iterative relationship can be derived for $k > 1$. The number of inquiries needed for all of the stations is one more than the sum of the number required for the upper and lower branches. If we do not assume level skipping, the numbers for both branches are the same. We have then

$$T_c(k, n) = 1 + 2 \sum_{i=0}^{k} \binom{k}{i} 2^{-i} T_c(i, n - 1) \tag{9.22}$$

Assuming $n \gg 1$ we make the approximation $T_c(i, n - 1) \cong T_c(i, n)$ and equation (9.22) gives

$$T_c(k) = \frac{1 + 2 \sum_{i=0}^{k-1} \binom{k}{i} 2^{-i} T_c(i)}{1 - 2^{-k+1}} \tag{9.23}$$

For convenience we have dropped the dependence on n in equation (9.23). Equation (9.23) is shown as a function of k in Figure 9.10. From the plot in Figure 9.10 it can be shown that the conditional duration of a probing cycle can be bounded by linear functions of k for large enough k. We have

$$2.8810k - 1 + 2\delta_{0k} - 0.8810\delta_{1k} \leq T_d(k) \leq 2.8867k + \delta_{0k} - 1.8867\delta_{1k}$$
$$(9.24)$$

where δ_{ik} is the Kronecker delta. Now assuming that messages arrival is Poisson with an average rate of λ messages per inquiry time, the average value of k, the number of messages present at the beginning of a probing cycle, is $\lambda \bar{T}_a$, where $\bar{T}_a$ is the average duration of an arrival cycle. Averaging over k in (9.24) we have

$$2.8810\lambda \bar{T}_a - 1 + 2P[k = 0] - 0.881P[k = 1] \leq \bar{T}_d$$
$$\leq 2.8867\lambda \bar{T}_a + P[k = 0] - 1.8867P[k = 1]$$
$$(9.25)$$

$P[k = 0]$ and $P[k = 1]$ are, respectively, the probability of zero and one message arrivals in an arrival interval. These probabilities can be under- and overbounded. First of all, $P[k = 1] \geq \lambda P[k = 0]$ and $P[k = 0] = e^{-\lambda T_a} \leq e^{-\lambda}$ since a probing cycle must be at least as large as a single inquiry. Further $P[k = 1] \leq 1$ and $P[k = 0] \geq e^{-\lambda \bar{T}_a}$ from Jensen's inequality.†

†If $f(X)$ is a convex function of the random variable X, then $E(f(X)) \geq f(E(X))$.

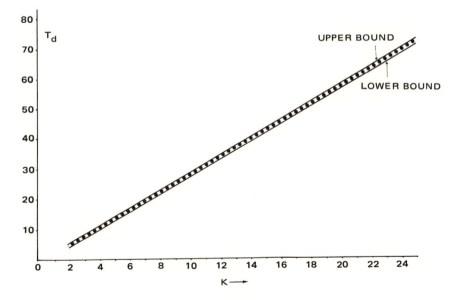

Figure 9.10. Upper and lower bounds versus arrival rate for delay.

From these considerations equation (9.25) becomes

$$2.8810\lambda \bar{T}_a - 1.881 + 2\,e^{-\lambda \bar{T}_a} \leqslant \bar{T}_d$$
$$\leqslant 2.8867\lambda \bar{T}_a + (1 - 1.8867\lambda)\,e^{-\lambda} \tag{9.26}$$

Thus we have expressed the mean departure cycle in terms of the mean arrival cycle. Equation (9.26) combined with equation (9.19) gives a bound on message delay in terms of the duration of the arrival cycle, $\bar{T}_a$. By means of an even more involved analysis $\bar{T}_a$ can be bounded. It can be shown that

$$\bar{T}_a \leqslant \begin{cases} \dfrac{\dfrac{5.964\lambda + 1 - 5.964\lambda(1-\lambda)(1-2.8867\lambda)}{[1-2.8867\lambda(1-\lambda)]}}{1 - 8.333\lambda^2}, & \lambda \leqslant 0.22 \\[4mm] \dfrac{5.964\lambda + 1}{1 - 8.333\lambda^2}, & 0.22 < \lambda < 0.3464 \end{cases} \tag{9.27a}$$

$$\bar{T}_a \geqslant \begin{cases} \dfrac{\dfrac{5.897\lambda + (1 - 5.897\lambda)(1-2.8867\lambda)}{[1-2.8867\lambda(1-\lambda)]}}{1 - 8.300\lambda^2}, & \lambda \leqslant 0.1696 \\[4mm] \dfrac{1}{1 - 8.300\lambda^2}, & 0.1696 < \lambda < 0.3464 \end{cases} \tag{9.27b}$$

Equations (9.27a) and (9.27b) show that there is saturation at $\lambda = 0.3464$. Recall that this is somewhat less than the point of saturation encountered in the slotted ALOHA system [see equation (8.5)], so that the tree search offers no obvious improvement. The difficulty is that there is no adaptivity in the foregoing in that we probe a large group even though the message arrival rate and the probability of conflict are high. This was the point of breaking the group into subgroups each of which are probed individually. In an analysis of delay which is of the same flavor as that presented above, Capetanakis has shown that average message delay is dominated by a term $(1 - (2.325\lambda)^2)^{-1}$ indicating saturation at $\lambda = 0.43$. The lower and upper bounds for average delay for the adaptive algorithm are shown as a function of λ on Figure 9.11. We compare this with the throughput for slotted ALOHA, which is $\lambda = 0.36$. Moreover for a large but finite number of stations the system is always stable. This is a direct result of adaptivity, for when the previous cycle is long giving large P the tendency is to probe small groups. In the limit we have conventional TDMA.

There has been considerable effort in the direction of increasing maximum throughput. In each of these studies the same basic model is

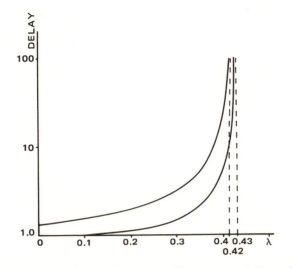

Figure 9.11. Lower and upper bounds for average delay versus arrival rate for the adaptive algorithm.

considered: fixed length messages arrive at a Poisson rate. Flow on the common line is slotted with a message fitting precisely into a slot. If two stations attempt to transmit in the same slot the ensuing collision is made known to all stations before the beginning of the next slot. The first advance after the work of Capetanakis and Massey was made by Gallager.[11] The time axis is segmented so that groups are formed according to when messages arrived. This approach improves the maximum throughput to 0.4872. A bonus in this technique is that messages are served in order of arrival. Clearly uniform timing throughout the system is necessary for this system to be practical. This value of throughput was subsequently improved to 0.48775.[12] Another aspect of the work in this area is an attempt to find upper bounds on the throughput. A number of workers have successively reduced the upper bound on throughput to the point where it is 0.5254 at the present writing.[13] For related work see Refs. 14–16.

9.5. More Complete State Information

In the polling model the information that is fed back in response to a probe consists of no messages or at least one message in a group. In the random access model the information that is fed back consists of no messages, one message, or more than one message. A third possibility is that each station in the system is able to estimate the number of stations that are involved in a collision. This information can then be used in conjunction with a tree search. Again at the beginning of the search the stations are segmented into groups according to some criterion of optimality. For example in the first work[17] under this assumption, groups were chosen so as to maximize the probability of the group containing a single message. Under the assumption that there are N stations, k of which have messages, it can be shown that the optimum group size is given by

$$\gamma_{opt} = \left[\frac{N+1}{k}\right]^{+} \tag{9.28}$$

where $[X]^{+}$ is the smallest integer greater than x.

We hasten to add in connection with equation (9.28) that choosing this size group does not necessarily minimize a more tangible performance criterion such as time required to grant access to all stations having messages or message delay.

In another line of investigation[18,19] is is assumed that the criterion of performance is the time required to grant access to all stations.† Since it is assumed that the number of stations involved in each of the conflicts is known, strategy is based on this information. The reader may recall that in Section 9.2 we pointed out that an equivalent way of conducting a tree search is for stations having a message to respond to a probe with probability $1/2$. Now given that there are n stations in conflict, we assume that a station responds to a probe with probability σ_n. The objective is to choose σ_n so as to minimize the duration of a probing cycle.

Let $L_n(\sigma_n)$ indicate the average number of probes required to resolve conflicts among n message bearing stations when each station responds to a probe with probability σ_n. Now given n we wish to find σ_n such that $L_n(\sigma_n)$ is minimized. The optimization problem can be formulated in such a manner that the application of the principles of dynamic programming yields a solution. Assume that for $i < n$ the optimum values of σ_i are known. We indicate the minimum number of probes required for the optimal σ_i by L_i^*, $i < n$. Now in response to a probe the group of n stations is split into k which respond and $n - k$ which do not. The probability of this event is given by the binomial distribution

$$b(k; \sigma_n, n) = \binom{n}{k}\sigma_n^k(1 - \sigma_n)^{n-k} \tag{9.29}$$

since it is assumed that the optimimum value for σ_k is known for $k < n$ we may write the following relation for $L_n(\sigma_n, k)$, which we designate as the

†See also Ref. 20.

average number of probes given that k stations respond to the first probe:

$$L_n(\sigma_n, k) = \begin{cases} 1 + L_n(\sigma_n), & k = 0 \quad \text{or} \quad k = n \\ 1 + L^*_{n-1}, & k = 1 \\ 1 + L^*_k + L^*_{n-k}, & 1 < k < n - 1 \\ 2 + L^*_{n-1}, & k = n - 1 \end{cases} \tag{9.30}$$

The derivation of this relation is fairly obvious and is therefore left as an exercise for the reader; however, we point out that when $k = n - 1$, the nonresponding station forms a group of one which may be read out with a single probe. Now averaging over k and substituting in equation (9.30), we obtain

$$\begin{aligned} L_n(\sigma_n) &= \sum_{k=0}^{n} L_n(\sigma_n, k) b(k; \sigma_n, n) \\ &= \sum_{k=0}^{n-1} \binom{n}{k} \frac{\sigma_n^k (1 - \sigma_n)^{n-k} + (1 - \sigma_n)^k \sigma_n^{n-k}}{1 - \sigma_n^n - (1 - \sigma_n)^n} L^*_k \\ &\quad + \frac{1 + n\sigma_n^{n-1}(1 - \sigma_n)}{1 - \sigma_n^n - (1 - \sigma_n)^n} \end{aligned} \tag{9.31}$$

In equation (9.31) we employ the convention $L^*_0 = L^*_1 = 0$. When the number of collisions is 2 we have from equation (9.31) that $\sigma^*_2 = 0.5$ and $L^*_2 = 3$. The form of equation (9.31) leads to a dynamic programming solution, in which assuming L^*_k known for $k < n$, L^*_n can be found. In each case this optimum can be found by means of a search procedure over σ_n. In Table 9.1 the optimal values of σ_i and L_i are tabulated as a function of i. An interesting feature of the solution is that for the range of values studied $\sigma_i i > 1$, indicating that choosing groups which isolate single message-bearing stations is not the best choice in minimizing the duration of the conflict interval. Further it can be shown that when i is large enough performance is not sensitive to σ_i and we may just as well set $\sigma_i = 1/2$ as previous studies.

Finally, we conclude this section by mentioning the results of a simulation study on the accuracy to which the number of conflicting stations need be known. In Table 9.2 message delay as a function of message arrival rate with the resolution of the number of conflicting stations as a parameter is tabulated. For example, $k = 3$ indicates that the conflicts that may be discerned are 0, 1, 2, and 3 or more. When the number of conflicts is greater than k the previous algorithm is modified by cutting the resolution interval Δ in half. This continues until the number of conflicting messages in an

Table 9.1[a]

N	L_N^*	σ_N^*
3	$0.478795D + 01$	$0.411972D + 00$
4	$0.663253D + 01$	$0.342936D + 00$
5	$0.848559D + 01$	$0.288214D + 00$
6	$0.103427D + 02$	$0.249289D + 00$
7	$0.122038D + 02$	$0.219964D + 00$
8	$0.140677D + 02$	$0.196794D + 00$
9	$0.159338D + 02$	$0.178050D + 00$
10	$0.178015D + 02$	$0.162585D + 00$
11	$0.196705D + 02$	$0.149603D + 00$
12	$0.215406D + 02$	$0.138548D + 00$
13	$0.234117D + 02$	$0.129020D + 00$
14	$0.252835D + 02$	$0.120722D + 00$
15	$0.271560D + 02$	$0.113429D + 00$
16	$0.290290D + 02$	$0.106970D + 00$
17	$0.309026D + 02$	$0.101208D + 00$
18	$0.327766D + 02$	$0.960365D - 01$
19	$0.346510D + 02$	$0.913688D - 01$
20	$0.365258D + 02$	$0.871345D - 01$
21	$0.384008D + 02$	$0.832760D - 01$
22	$0.402762D + 02$	$0.797452D - 01$
23	$0.421518D + 02$	$0.765020D - 01$
24	$0.440277D + 02$	$0.735127D - 01$
25	$0.459038D + 02$	$0.707485D - 01$
26	$0.477801D + 02$	$0.681849D - 01$
27	$0.496566D + 02$	$0.658008D - 01$
28	$0.515332D + 02$	$0.635779D - 01$
29	$0.534100D + 02$	$0.615005D - 01$
30	$0.552870D + 02$	$0.595546D - 01$

$$L_0^* = L_1^* = 0, \qquad L_2^* = 3, \qquad \sigma_2^* = 0.5$$

[a] Reference 19.

Table 9.2[a]

	Expected delay						
λ	$K = 1$	$K = 2$	$K = 3$	$K = 4$	$K = 5$	$K = 6$	$K = 7$
0.100	0.925	0.815	0.806	0.809	0.806	0.808	0.807
0.200	1.738	1.275	1.221	1.221	1.220	1.219	1.217
0.350	10.017	3.556	3.184	3.086	3.054	3.024	2.955
0.400	27.535	6.199	4.762	4.528	4.322	4.566	4.460
0.500	—	—	35.410	27.857	22.717	22.637	21.717
0.520	—	—	—	66.032	55.231	49.070	35.790

[a] Reference 19.

interval is found. At this point the previous algorithm is employed. The salient result here is the rapid diminution of return with increasing sensitivity. Increasing from 1 to 2 yields an improvement of 14.6% whereas only 4.7% improvement is realized in going from 2 to 3.

References

1. N. Abramson, *Information Theory and Coding*, McGraw-Hill, New York (1963).
2. R. G. Gallager, *Information Theory and Reliable Communications*, John Wiley, New York (1968).
3. J. F. Hayes, "An Adaptive Technique for Local Distribution," *IEEE Transactions on Communications*, COM-26(8), 1178–1186, August (1978).
4. M. Sobel and P. A. Groll, "Group Testing to Eliminate Efficiently All Defectives in a Binomial Sample," *Bell System Technical Journal*, 38, 1179–1253, September (1959).
5. R. Dorfman, "Detection of Defective Members of Large Populations," *Annals of Mathematical Statistics*, 28, 1033–1036 (1953).
6. T. Berger, N. Mehravari, D. Towsley, and J. K. Wolf, "Random Multiple Access Communication and Group Testing," *IEEE Transactions on Communications*, Com-32(7), July (1984).
7. J. Capetanakis, "Tree Algorithms for Packet Broadcast Channels," *IEEE Transactions on Information Theory*, IT-25, 505–515, September (1979).
8. B. Tsybakov and V. A. Mikhailov, "Free Synchronous Packet Access in a Broadcast Channel with Feedback," *Problems of Information Transmission*, 14, 259–280, April (1979).
9. A. Grami, J. F. Hayes, and K. Sohraby, "Further Results on Probing," *Proceedings of the International Conference on Communications, Philadelphia, 1982.* pp. IC3.1–IC.3.5 (1982).
10. J. L. Massey, "Collision Resolution Algorithms and Random-Access Communications," Technical report, UCLA-ENG-8016, April (1980).
11. R. C. Gallager, "Conflict Resolution in Random Access Broadcast Networks," *Proceedings of the AFSOR Workshop in Communication Theory and Applications, September 17–20, Provincetown, Massachusetts* (1978), pp. 74–76.
12. J. Mosley, "An Efficient Contention Resoution Algorithm for Multiple Access Channels," Report LIDS-TH-918, Laboratory for Information and Decision Systems, Massachusetts Institute of Technology, June (1979).
13. T. Berger, N. Mehravari, and G. Munson, "On Genie-Aided Upper Bounds to Multiple Access Contention Resolution Efficiency," *Proceedings of the 1981 Annual Conference on Information Sciences and Systems*, The Johns Hopkins University, Baltimore, Maryland.
14. J. I. Capetanakis, "Generalized TDMA: The Multi-Accessing Tree Protocol," *IEEE Transactions on Communications*, COM-27, 1476–1484, October (1979).
15. M. L. Molle, "On the Capacity of Infinite Population Multiple Access Protocols," Computer Science Department, UCLA (1980).
16. N. Pippenger, "Bounds on the Performance of Protocols for a Multiple Access Broadcast Channel," *IEEE Transactions on Information Theory*, IT-27(2), 145–152, March (1981).
17. Y. Yemini and L. Kleinrock, "An Optimal Adaptive Scheme for Multiple Access Broadcast Communications," *Proceedings, 1978 International Communications Conference*, pp. 7.2.1–7.2.5.
18. B. Tsybakov and V. A. Mikhailov, "Free Synchronous Packet Access in a Broadcast Channel with Feedback," *Problems of Information Transmission*, 14, 259–280, April (1979).
19. L. Georgiadis and T. Papantoni-Kazakos, "A Collision Resolution Protocol for Random Access Channels with Energy Detectors," *IEEE Transactions on Communications*, COM-30(11), 2413–2420, November (1982).

20. B. S. Tsybakov, "Resolution of a Conflict of Known Multiplicity," *Problems of Information Transmission,* **16**(2), 134–144 [Translated from *Problemy Peredachi Informatsii,* **16**(2), 69–82, April–June (1980)].

Exercises

9.1. In the classic penny weighing problem there are 2^n pennies, one of which is heavier than the others. A balance scale is to be used to find the odd penny.
(a) What is the minimum number of weighings that are required?
(b) What is the information theoretic implication of the solution in part (a)?

9.2. Consider the probing technique to be used in a system with 2^n stations. We assume the polling context where stations with messages respond to a probing message by putting a noise signal on the line. Suppose that there are exactly two stations with messages with all possible pairs being equally probable.
(a) Find the minimum number of transmissions in a probing cycle.
(b) Find the maximum number of transmissions in a probing cycle when there are two stations with messages.
(c) What is the average number of transmissions in a cycle?

9.3. Repeat Exercise 9.2 for the random access context where stations with messages respond to a probe by transmitting a message.

9.4. Find the average number of inquiries in a probing cycle for the polling context when the number of stations is 16 with a probability of each station having a message being 0.05. Repeat if two groups of eight stations are probed initially.

9.5. Repeat Exercise 9.4 for the random access context.

9.6. Derive equation (9.20b) from (9.20a) under the assumption $k \ll 2^{n-1}$.

9.7. For the polling context with level skipping, find the probability generating function for a cycle probing 2^j stations. Recall that when it is known that a group of stations has at least one message and the upper of two branches is empty, an inquiry can be saved on the lower branch.

9.8. Find the probability-generating function for 2^j stations for the random access context for probing under the assumption of level skipping.

9.9. From Table 9.1 it can be seen that the optimal values of L_n^* are approximately linear with n, $L_n^* \cong \alpha n + C$.
(a) Find linear functions which give upper and lower bounds on L_n^*.
As stated in the text, conflicts are resolved for arrivals in Δ second intervals. In order for the system to be stable Δ must be larger than the average time required to resolve the conflicts.
(b) Find regions of system stability and instability in terms of Δ and message arrival rate.

10

Networks of Queues

10.1. Introduction—Jackson Networks

An appropriate model for a number of systems is a network of queues in which the output of one queue is fed into another. Under a wide range of assumptions, these networks may be modeled and analyzed by means of multidimensional birth–death processes. The salient result of this work is the *product form* solution in which the joint distribution of queue occupancies is the product of functions of the number in the individual queues. Networks satisfying the proper set of assumptions are called Jackson networks after J. R. Jackson, who discovered the product form solution.[1] In this chapter the model is applied to store-and-forward message-switched networks. Using the theory of Jackson networks we shall find queue occupancy and delay in message-switched networks. These results enable us to allocate transmission capacity in an optimum fashion. In the next chapter these same ideas are extended in order to model flow control in a store-and-forward network.

The first example of a network of queues to be treated in the literature was the machine shop. (The modern equivalent is probably the automated office.) The machine shop is equipped with a number of specialized machines—lathes, drill presses, etc. (See Figure 10.1.) A number of different types of jobs are handled by the shop. Depending on its type, each job is treated by a different sequence of these machines. The time that each machine works on a job may be modeled as a random variable. At each of the machines we allow a queue of jobs to form. Certainly a quantity of interest is the joint distribution of the lengths of these queues. A related quantity that is of interest is the time elapsing between the entrance of a job into the shop and its completion. As we shall see, after certain groundwork has been laid, this same basic model may be applied to store-and-forward communications networks. Variable length messages and network nodes correspond to jobs and machines, respectively.

261

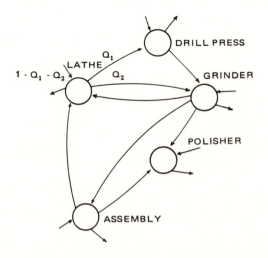

Figure 10.1. Model of machine shop.

Store-and-forward message-switched systems† may be modeled as *open* systems in that all messages arrive to the network from external sources and eventually depart from the system. If a network is operating normally we would also expect it to be *acyclic,* meaning that each message visits a node at most once. A contrasting model is that of the digital computer, which may be represented over a short time interval by means of the *closed* network of queues depicted in Figure 10.2. Over a short time interval of interest it is assumed that there are neither arrivals or departures and a constant K jobs are being processed. After a job has received service from the central processor it is passed to one of $N - 1$ peripherals. The job returns to the central processor after having been serviced by the peripherals. At both the peripherals and the central processor there are buffers where jobs queue for service. We have then a closed set of queues among which jobs circulate continuously. The service times of the jobs at the peripherals

†Store-and-forward networks were discussed in Chapter 2; see Section 2.6 and Figure 2.19.

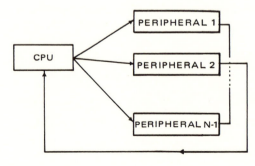

Figure 10.2. Digital computer model.

at the control processor are modeled as random variables.[†] As we shall see in Chapter 11, with a certain type of flow control, store-and-forward message-switched systems may also be modeled as closed systems.

10.2. Multidimensional Birth–Death Processes; Queues in Tandem

The theory of Jackson networks is based on multidimensional birth–death processes, which is a straightforward extension of the one-dimensional process studied in Chapter 3. The state of the system is described by a vector.[‡] In networks of queues, for example, each component of the state vector is the number in each of the queues. As in the one-dimensional case at most one event can occur in an incremental interval. Thus a vector component can change by at most one. Further, the number of components that can change in an incremental interval is limited to at most two, corresponding to a transfer from one queue to another.

Perhaps the simplest example of the multidimensional birth–death process is the network formed by two queues in tandem. (See Figure 10.3.) Customers arrive at the first queue at a Poisson rate of λ per second. The service time is exponentially distributed with mean value $1/\mu_1$. After completion of service, the customer goes to a second queue where the service is also exponentially distributed but is independent of the first and has mean $1/\mu_2$.

Using the same approach as in Chapter 3, we can find the joint distribution of the queue lengths in each of the queues. We shall do this under the assumption that each queue has only one server. The multiple-server case is a straightforward extension. Let $Q_1(t)$ and $Q_2(t)$ denote the number of customers in queues one and two, respectively, at time t. We define the joint probability

$$P(k_1, k_2, t) = P[Q_1(t) = k_1 \text{ and } Q_2(t) = k_2]$$

Since the arrival process is Poisson and the service time distributions are exponential, only a limited change of state can occur in an incremental time interval. There can be an arrival at queue 1, a departure from queue 1, or a departure from queue 2. The joint probability at time $t + \delta$ may be

---

[†]For a detailed discussion of the application of Jackson network theory to closed-network modeling computers, see Chapter 3 of Ref. 3.

[‡]In the method of stages (see Section 3.10) the idea of a state vector was introduced.

Figure 10.3. Two queues in tandem.

written in terms of the probability at time t. We have

$$P(0, 0; t + \delta) = P(0, 1; t)\mu_2\delta + (1 - \lambda\delta)P(0, 0; t) \tag{10.1a}$$

$$\begin{aligned} P(0, k_2; t + \delta) &= P(1, k_2 - 1; t)\mu_1\delta + P(0, k_2 + 1; t)\mu_2\delta \\ &\quad + [1 - (\lambda + \mu_2)\delta]P(0, k_2; t), \qquad k_2 > 0 \end{aligned} \tag{10.1b}$$

$$\begin{aligned} P(k_1, 0, t + \delta) &= P(k_1 - 1, 0; t)\lambda_1\delta + P(k_1, 1; t)\mu_2\delta \\ &\quad + [1 - (\lambda + \mu_1)\delta]P(k_1, 0; t), \qquad k_1 > 0 \end{aligned} \tag{10.1c}$$

$$\begin{aligned} P(k_1, k_2; t + \delta) &= P(k_1 + 1, k_2 - 1; t)\mu_1\delta \\ &\quad + P(k_1 - 1, k_2; t)\lambda\delta + P(k_1, k_2 + 1; t)\mu_2\delta \\ &\quad + [1 - (\lambda + \mu_1 + \mu_2)\delta]P(k_1, k_2; t) \end{aligned} \tag{10.1d}$$

As in the one-dimensional case we let $\delta \to 0$, obtaining a set of differential equations for the joint probability. We find

$$\frac{dP(0, 0; t)}{dt} = P(0, 1; t)\mu_2 - P(0, 0; t)\lambda \tag{10.2a}$$

$$\begin{aligned} \frac{dP(0, k_2; t)}{dt} &= P(1, k_2 - 1; t)\mu_1 + P(0, k_2 + 1; t)\mu_2 \\ &\quad - P(0, k_2; t)(\lambda + \mu_2) \end{aligned} \tag{10.2b}$$

$$\begin{aligned} \frac{dP(k_1, 0; t)}{dt} &= P(k_1 - 1, 0; t)\lambda + P(k_1, 1; t)\mu_2 \\ &\quad - P(k_1, 0; t)(\lambda + \mu_1) \end{aligned} \tag{10.2c}$$

$$\begin{aligned} \frac{dP(k_1, k_2; t)}{dt} &= P(k_1 + 1, k_2 - 1; t)\mu_1 + P(k_1 - 1, k_2; t)\lambda \\ &\quad + P(k_1, k_2 + 1; t)\mu_2 - P(k_1, k_2; t)(\lambda + \mu_1 + \mu_2) \end{aligned} \tag{10.2d}$$

If $\lambda < \mu_1$ and $\lambda < \mu_2$, a steady-state solution $P(k_1, k_2)$ exists. Letting $dP(k_1, k_2; t)/dt = 0$, we have from equations (10.2a)–(10.2d) the set of equilibrium equations.

$$P(0, 0)\lambda = P(0, 1)\mu_2 \tag{10.3a}$$

$$P(0, k_2)(\lambda + \mu_2) = P(1, k_2 - 1)\mu_1 + P(0, k_2 + 1)\mu_2 \tag{10.3b}$$

$$P(k_1, 0)(\lambda + \mu_1) = P(k_1 - 1, 0)\lambda + P(k_1, 1)\mu_2 \qquad (10.3c)$$

$$P(k_1, k_2)(\lambda + \mu_1 + \mu_2) = P(k_1 + 1, k_2 - 1)\mu_1 + P(k_1 - 1, k_2)\lambda$$
$$+ P(k_1, k_2 + 1)\mu_2 \qquad (10.3d)$$

The normalizing condition is

$$\sum_{k_1=0}^{\infty} \sum_{k_2=0}^{\infty} P(k_1, k_2) = 1$$

These are the same sort of equilibrium equations that were derived in Chapter 3. The expression on the left-hand side represents flow out of a state and on the right-hand side flow into a state. The state transition flow diagram is shown in Figure 10.4. We assume that the solution to these equilibrium equations has the form

$$P(k_1, k_2) = P_1(k_1)P_2(k_2) \qquad (10.4)$$

where

$$P_1(k_1) = (1 - \rho_1)\rho_1^k, \qquad k = 0, 1, \ldots$$

substituting (10.4) into (10.3) and canceling terms we find

$$P(0)\lambda = P(1)\mu_2 \qquad (10.5a)$$

$$P(k_2)(\lambda + \mu_1) = P(k_2 - 1)\lambda + P(k_2 + 1)\mu_2 \qquad (10.5b)$$

As we have seen in Chapter 3, the solution to equation (10.5) is

$$P(k_2) = (1 - \rho_2)\rho_2^{k_2}, \qquad k_2 = 0, 1, \ldots \qquad (10.6)$$

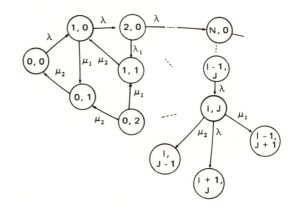

Figure 10.4. State transition diagram, two queues in tandem.

It is not difficult to show that these results carry over to more than two single-server queues in tandem. The joint distribution is the product of geometric distributions. We have

$$P(k_1, k_2, \ldots, k_N) = \prod_{i=1}^{N} (1 - \rho_i)\rho_i^{k_i} \qquad (10.7)$$

where $\rho_i = \lambda/\mu_i$ and $1/\mu_i$ is the average service time in the ith service center. It can also be shown that these same results hold when there is more than one server at a facility.

Equation (10.7) indicates that the marginal probability distribution of each of the queues is that of the $M/M/1$ queue. In view of Burke's theorem (Section 3.9) this is no surprise. The departure process from the first $M/M/1$ queue is Poisson, hence the second queue is $M/M/1$ and the process replicates.

However, these considerations would not show that the queues are independent of one another as does equation (10.4). Although the proof in the general case is not obvious, it is also not surprising that the delays of a message, queueing time plus service time, in each of the queues is independent.[4,5] A seemingly paradoxical fact is that the queueing times in tandem queues are not independent.[6]

10.3. Networks of Queues—Product Form Distribution

From the characteristics of the Poisson process developed in Chapter 3, we would expect the product form to hold in networks even more complicated than tandem queues.† Consider, for example, the network shown in Figure 10.5. Messages arrive at each of the four nodes shown at independent Poisson rates. At each of the nodes the service time is independent and

†For surveys of results on networks of queues see Refs. 9 and 10.

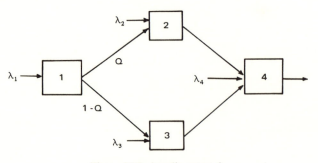

Figure 10.5. Acyclic network.

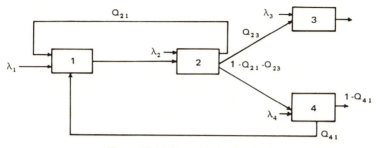

Figure 10.6. Network with feedback.

exponentially distributed. A customer leaving queue 1 goes to queue 2 with probability Q and to queue 3 with probability $1 - Q$. At queues 2 and 3 traffic from queue 1 merges with external arrivals. The flow into queue 4 is the sum of flows from queues 2 and 3 and external flow. As we have seen, the sums of Poisson processes are Poisson and the random bifurcation of Poisson processes yields Poisson processes. Furthermore, from Burke's theorem the output of an $M/M/S$ queue is Poisson. From all of these considerations the flows within the network are Poisson. Therefore one would expect the product form to hold with individual queues behaving as $M/M/S$ queues.

The situation is not so straightforward when there is a feedback path. (See Figure 10.6, for example.) The presence of a feedback path destroys the Poisson character of the flow within the network. This may be illustrated by the network of two tandem queues shown in Figure 10.7a. The arrivals are Poisson with an assumed average rate of 1 per hour. The output of the second queue is fed back to the first with probability $P = 0.999$. The service times in each of the queues are assumed to be independent and exponentially distributed with mean 1 nsec! With this extreme set of parameters, the outputs of the first queue tend to be in bursts. A typical output sequence is shown in Figure 10.7b. This illustrates the general result, in that it can

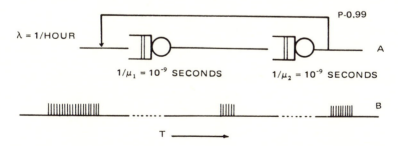

Figure 10.7. (a) Tandem queues with feedback. (b) Typical sequence out of queue 1.

be shown that flow on links between queues within a feedback loop is not Poisson.[7,8] Nevertheless, as we shall see, the product form still holds.

10.3.1. Equilibrium Equations

The product form of the joint distribution of queue lengths holds for a network of queues under a certain set of conditions. First of all external arrivals to the network must be Poisson. A second requirement is that the routing between queues must be what we shall call probabilistic. This means that queue outputs are routed to other queues with probabilities that yield desired flows to these queues. A particular pattern of flows may be required to minimize average delay, for example. (See Chapter 12.) The set of flows can be attained by probabilistic routing among the paths between queues which may consist of one or more links. In real networks it is unlikely that routing will be done on a probabilistic basis. However, the same effect is achieved if there is sufficient mixing of queue outputs.

With respect to the nodes of the networks, it is required that waiting rooms be infinite. In Jackson networks the service times at each of the queues are independent of one another. Beyond these basic requirements there are a number of different conditions which give the product form solution. The simplest of these is exponentially distributed service with different mean values at each of the queues. Fortunately this is the case of greatest interest in a communications context. In the sequel we shall derive the product form for this case with a single server at each queue and an infinite waiting room. The multiple-server case is a straightforward extension. In the next chapter, Chapter 11, we shall consider other sets of conditions for which the product form solution holds.

Following an analysis by Jackson for open networks, the product form can be shown to be the solution to a multidimensional birth–death equation describing the evolution of the system. Let us assume that there are N nodes in the network, each with a single exponential server whose average service time is $1/\mu_i$, $i = 1, 2, \ldots, n$. We assume that customers arrive at these queues from sources external to the network at a Poisson rate with an average of λ_i per second. As in the models depicted in Figures 10.5a and 10.5b, the routing of customers within the network is assumed to be probabilistic. Let q_{ij}, $i, j = 1, 2, \ldots, N$ be the probability that a customer goes directly from queue i to queue j. We denote q_{iN+1} as the probability that a customer departs the system when it leaves queue i. Clearly $\sum_{i=1}^{N+1} q_{ij} = 1$, $i = 1, 2, \ldots, N$. If Λ_i is the total average flow into queue i, internal and external, we have the traffic equation

$$\Lambda_i = \lambda_i + \sum_{j=1}^{N} \Lambda_j q_{ji}, \qquad i = 1, 2, \ldots, N \qquad (10.8a)$$

Equation (10.8a) simply states that the flow into node i is the sum of the newly arriving traffic and the traffic from other nodes. Equation (10.8a) can be put into a matrix form

$$(I - \mathbf{Q}^T)\Lambda = \lambda \tag{10.8b}$$

where

$$\Lambda^T = [\Lambda_1, \ldots, \Lambda_N] \quad \text{and} \quad \lambda^T = [\lambda_1, \ldots, \lambda_N]$$

$\mathbf{Q}$ is an $N \times N$ matrix with elements q_{ij} and I is the identity matrix. A necessary condition for a solution to equation (10.8) is that $\sum_{j=1}^{N} q_i < 1$ for at least one i. Otherwise, the matrix $I - Q^T$ would be singular. The set of network flows, $\Lambda_1, \Lambda_2, \ldots, \Lambda_N$, can be found by solving (10.8). Now if node i has S_i exponential servers each with mean $1/\mu_i$, then a condition for stability in the network is $\Lambda_i/S_i\mu_i < 1$, $i = 1, 2, \ldots, N$. In the sequel we shall assume that this condition applies.

The state of the system at a given time instant is the number of customers in each of the N queues denoted by the N-dimensional random variable, $Q_1(t), Q_2(t), \ldots, Q_N(t)$. We denote the state probability at time t by

$$P(k_1, k_2, \ldots, k_N; t) \triangleq P(Q_1(t) = k_1, Q_2(t) = k_2, \ldots, Q_N(t) = k_N)$$

We consider the possible changes of the state in an incremental interval. As in lower dimensions, the intervals between arrivals and departures are exponentially distributed. Over the incremental interval the probability of more than one arrival or departure is negligibly small. We have four possible events in the state over an incremental interval: (1) an external arrival, (2) a departure from the system, (3) a customer going from one queue to another, (4) no change. We write the state probability at time $t + \delta$ as

$$P(k_1, k_2, \ldots, k_N; t + \delta)$$

$$= \sum_{i=1}^{N} P(k_1, k_2, \ldots, k_i - 1, \ldots, k_N; t)\lambda_i\delta$$

$$+ \sum_{i=1}^{N} P(k_1, k_2, \ldots, k_i + 1, \ldots, k_N; t)\mu_i q_{iN+1}\delta \tag{10.9}$$

$$+ \sum_{i,j=1}^{N} P(k_1, \ldots, k_i + 1, \ldots, k_j - 1, \ldots, k_N; t)\mu_i q_{ij}\delta$$

$$+ \left(1 - \delta \sum_{i=1}^{N} \lambda_i - \delta \sum_{i=1}^{N} \mu_i\right) P(k_1, k_2, \ldots, k_N; t)$$

In writing equation (10.9) we have not taken special notice of the case $k_i = 0$. It is obvious that the probability of a system with a negative queue should be zero. Furthermore there can be no departures from an empty queue. Letting $\delta \to 0$ we find

$$\frac{dP(k_1, k_2, \ldots, k_N; t)}{dt}$$

$$= \sum_{i=1}^{N} P(k_1, k_2, \ldots, k_i - 1, \ldots, k_N; t)\lambda_i$$

$$+ \sum_{i=1}^{N} P(k_1, k_2, \ldots, k_i + 1, \ldots, k_N; t)\mu_i q_{iN+1} \qquad (10.10)$$

$$+ \sum_{i,j=1}^{N} P(k_1, \ldots, k_i + 1, \ldots, k_j - 1, \ldots, k_N; t)\mu_i q_{ij}$$

$$- \left(\sum_{i=1}^{N} \lambda_i + \sum_{i=1}^{N} \mu_i \right) P(k_1, k_2, \ldots, k_N; t)$$

Now if $\Lambda_i < \mu_i$; $i = 1, 2, \ldots, N$ a steady-state solution to the birth–death equation exists:

$$\frac{dP(k_1, k_2, \ldots, k_N; t)}{dt} = 0$$

We have for the steady-state probability, the following equilibrium equation:

$$P(k_1, k_2, \ldots, k_N) \left[\sum_{i=1}^{N} \lambda_i + \sum_{i=1}^{N} \mu_i \right]$$

$$= \sum_{i=1}^{N} P(k_1, k_2, \ldots, k_i - 1, \ldots, k_N)\lambda_i$$

$$+ \sum_{i=1}^{N} P(k_1, k_2, \ldots, k_i + 1, \ldots, k_N)\mu_i q_{iN+1} \qquad (10.11)$$

$$+ \sum_{i,j=1}^{N} P(k_1, \ldots, k_i + 1, \ldots, k_j - 1, \ldots, k_N)\mu_i q_{ij}$$

As in the lower-dimensional cases, the left-hand side represents flow out of a state and the right-hand side flow into a state. Now let us assume a solution of the form

$$P(k_1, \ldots, k_N) = \prod_{i=1}^{N} (1 - R_i) R_i^{k_i} \qquad (10.12)$$

where $R_i = \Lambda_i/\mu_i$ with Λ_i being the average total flow in messages per second into node i [see equation (10.8)]. The form of equation (10.12), a product of geometric distributions, facilitates computation since

$$P(k_1, k_2, \ldots, k_i \pm 1, \ldots, k_N) = R_i^{\pm 1} P(k_1, k_2, \ldots, k_i, \ldots, k_N) \tag{10.13}$$

After canceling common terms, we have from equations (10.11) and (10.13)

$$\sum_{i=1}^{N} \lambda_i + \sum_{i=1}^{N} \mu_i = \sum_{i=1}^{N} \frac{\lambda_i}{R_i} + \sum_{i=1}^{N} \mu_i R_i q_{iN+1} + \sum_{i=1}^{N} \sum_{j=1}^{N} \frac{R_i}{R_j} \mu_i q_{ij} \tag{10.14}$$

This equation is verified by means of equation (10.8) and the definition of q_{ij}. We deal with individual terms

$$\sum_{i=1}^{N} \frac{\lambda_i}{R_i} = \sum_{i=1}^{N} \frac{\mu_i \lambda_i}{\Lambda_i} \tag{10.15a}$$

$$\sum_{i=1}^{N} \mu_i R_i q_{iN+1} = \sum_{i=1}^{N} \Lambda_i \left(1 - \sum_{j=1}^{N} q_{ij}\right) = \sum_{i=1}^{N} \Lambda_i - \sum_{j=1}^{N} \sum_{i=1}^{N} \Lambda_i q_{ij}$$

$$= \sum_{j=1}^{N} \lambda_j \tag{10.15b}$$

$$\sum_{i=1}^{N} \sum_{j=1}^{N} \frac{R_i}{R_j} \mu_i q_{ij} = \sum_{j=1}^{N} \frac{\mu_j}{\Lambda_j} \sum_{i=1}^{N} \Lambda_i q_{ij}$$

$$= \sum_{j=1}^{N} \mu_j - \sum_{j=1}^{N} \frac{\mu_j \lambda_j}{\Lambda_j} \tag{10.15c}$$

Substitution of equations (10.15a)–(10.15c) into equation (10.14) shows the equality. Thus, in order for the product form for the probability distribution to hold, equation (10.8) must hold.

10.3.2. Local Balance Equations

The solution given by equation (10.12) suggests a simpler approach to the analysis of Jackson networks. The local or independent balance equations

$$\mu_i P(k_1, \ldots, k_N) = \Lambda_i P(k_1, \ldots, k_i - 1, \ldots, k_N), \qquad i = 1, 2, \ldots, N \tag{10.16}$$

have equation (10.12) as a solution and are as well a sufficient condition for equation (10.11) to hold. Notice that equation (10.16) is the multi-dimensional analog of the balance equation encountered in the one-dimensional birth–death process. [See equation (3.25).] In order to show the sufficiency, we substitute equation (10.8a) into equation (10.16) to obtain

$$\mu_i P(k_1, \ldots, k_N) = \lambda_i P(k_1, \ldots, k_i - 1, \ldots, k_N)$$

$$+ \sum_{j=1}^{N} \Lambda_j q_{ji} P(k_1, \ldots, k_i - 1, \ldots, k_N) \tag{10.17a}$$

and

$$\lambda_i P(k_1, \ldots, k_N) = \mu_i P(k_1, \ldots, k_i + 1, \ldots, k_N)$$

$$- \sum_{j=1}^{N} \Lambda_j q_{ji} P(k_1, \ldots, k_N) \tag{10.17b}$$

By summing both sides of equations (10.17a) and (10.17b) and rearranging terms using the relation $\sum_{j=1}^{N+1} q_{ij} = 1$, we find

$$P(k_1, \ldots, k_N) \left(\sum_{i=1}^{N} \mu_i + \sum_{i=1}^{N} \lambda_i \right)$$

$$= \sum_{i=1}^{N} P(k_1, \ldots, k_i - 1, \ldots, k_N) \lambda_i$$

$$+ \sum_{i=1}^{N} \mu_i P(k_1, \ldots, k_i + 1, \ldots, k_N) q_{iN+1} \tag{10.18}$$

$$+ \sum_{i=1}^{N} \sum_{j=1}^{N} q_{ij} [\mu_i P(k_1, \ldots, k_i + 1, \ldots, k_N)$$

$$- \Lambda_i P(k_1, \ldots, k_N) + \Lambda_j P(k_1, \ldots, k_j - 1, \ldots, k_N)]$$

Repeated application of equation (10.16) shows that equation (10.18) is the same as equation (10.11).

10.4. The Departure Process—Time Reversal

If, as in the foregoing, the external arrival processes are Poisson and the service times at each of the nodes are exponentially distributed then it can be shown that the departure processes from the network are Poisson.

In order to show this we employ an argument based on time reversal.†
Consider a continuous time Markov chain X_t defined on $(-\infty, \infty)$. The
first step is to show that the Markov property is time reversible, i.e., for
$t_1 \le t_2 \le \cdots \le t_n$, the Markov property

$$P[X_{t_n} = k_n / X_{t_1} = k_1, \ldots, X_{t_{n-1}} = k_{n-1}] = P[X_{t_n} = k_n / X_{t_{n-1}} = k_{n-1}]$$

(10.19a)

implies that

$$P[X_{t_1} = k_1 / X_{t_2} = k_2, \ldots, X_{t_n} = k_n] = P[X_{t_1} = k_1 / X_{t_2} = k_2] \qquad (10.19b)$$

This is easily seen from

$$P[X_{t_1} = k_1 / X_{t_2} = k_2, \ldots, X_{t_n} = k_n]$$

$$= \frac{P[X_{t_1} = k_1, X_{t_2} = k_2, \ldots, X_{t_n} = k_n]}{P[X_{t_2} = k_2, \ldots, X_{t_n} = k_n]}$$

$$= \frac{\begin{aligned}P[X_{t_1} = k_1]P[X_{t_2} = k_2 / X_{t_1} = k_1]\\ \times P[X_{t_3} = k_3 / X_{t_2} = k_2] \cdots P[X_{t_n} = k_n / X_{t_{n-1}} = k_{n-1}]\end{aligned}}{P[X_{t_2} = k_2]P[X_{t_3} = k_3 / X_{t_2} = k_2] \cdots P[X_{t_n} = k_n / X_{t_{n-1}} = k_{n-1}]}$$

$$= \frac{P[X_{t_1} = k_1]P[X_{t_2} = k_2 / X_{t_1} = k_1]}{P[X_{t_2} = k_2]} = P[X_{t_1} = k_1 / X_{t_2} = k_2]$$

When a process is in equilibrium there is a balance in the flow between
states and we have

$$P[X_{t_1} = k_1, X_{t_2} = k_2] = P[X_{t_1} = k_2, X_{t_2} = k_1], \qquad t_1 < t_2 \quad (10.20)$$

Since in equilibrium $P[X_{t_1} = k_1] = P[X_{t_2} = k_1]$ this balance can be stated
in terms of conditional probabilities:

$$P[X_{t_2} = k_2 / X_{t_1} = k_1] = P[X_{t_1} = k_2 / X_{t_2} = k_1] \qquad (10.21)$$

From the fact that the Markov process is defined on the interval $(-\infty, \infty)$
and from equations (10.19a) and (10.19b) and (10.21) we see that indeed
the Markov process in equilibrium is symmetric with respect to the direction
of time.

---

†For a complete discussion of time reversibility see Ref. 11, Chapters 4 and 5.

Consider now the process X_t' which we construct as the time reverse of the process X_t, i.e., if $x(t)$ are realizations of X_t, the realizations of X_t' are the functions $x(-t)$. If X_t is a Markov process in equilibrium it is time reversible and X_t and X_t' are mirror images of one another following the same dynamics as given in equations (10.19)–(10.21). An arrival at the process X_t occurs at the same time as a departure from X_t' and vice versa. Now suppose that X_t is the N-dimensional vector describing the number of customers at each of the queues in an N node network. The arrivals to the network cause increases in the components of the vector. Since arrivals at X_t are Poisson, the departure from X_t' are Poisson as well. Now from the complete symmetry of the two processes, as demonstrated in the foregoing, the arrival and the departure processes are the same for both systems. Thus the departure processes from the network are Poisson. Notice for the case $N = 1$, the time reversal argument furnishes an alternate proof to the theorem that the departure process from an $M/M/S$ queue is Poisson.

10.5. Store-and-Forward Communication Networks

As we said at the beginning of this chapter, our interest in Jackson networks is motivated by their application to store-and-forward communication networks. However, in order to apply the results we have obtained, certain additional assumptions are necessary. In order to put these assumptions into the proper perspective, we need to consider a model of the network node† (see Figure 10.8). Messages entering the node on an incoming link are fed directly to a central processor. The processor examines each message, checking for errors and determining the next node in the itinerary of a packet. Messages are routed from the central processor to one of the output links. At both the central processor and the output links messages are buffered. If there are N nodes and L links in the system, it is modeled by a network of $N + L$ queues. Now in a realistic system the speed of the

†In Section 11.4 we shall consider a somewhat more detailed model of the node in a store-and-forward network.

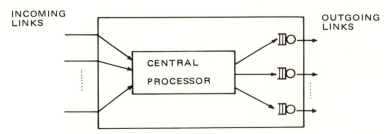

Figure 10.8. Model store-and-forward network node.

central processor will be much faster than the transmission rates over the links. Thus the N processor queues can be ignored and the system can be modeled as consisting of L queues, one for each link in the network. This is illustrated in Figure 10.9, where a three-node network is depicted. There are links in both directions between the nodes.

The service time of a message at each node is the time required to transmit it over an outgoing link. We shall assume that this is an exponentially distributed random variable. If messages are of durations in the order of hundreds of bits or more, the effect of representing a discrete quantity by a continuous random variable should be negligible. If the average duration of a message is in bits and the capacity of the outgoing link is C_l bits per second, the average service time is $\bar{m}/C_l$.

Messages are assembled and routed by central processors. Since the processor's operation is rapid, the arrival of messages to an output buffer is almost instantaneous and may be modeled as Poisson arrival. We point out that the arrival of messages to a node is over a nonzero interval of time and the arrival of several messages in a short time interval is impossible. By mixing together and assembling messages from several input lines the Poisson arrival model is emulated. The processor also routes messages in a fashion that may be modeled as being probabilistic. As we have seen this preserves the Poisson character of the message flow.

The final assumption that we require is an *independence* assumption which was made by Kleinrock in his classic work on store-and-forward networks.[22] In the queueing networks we have dealt with up to this point, it was stated that the service times were associated with the server and that

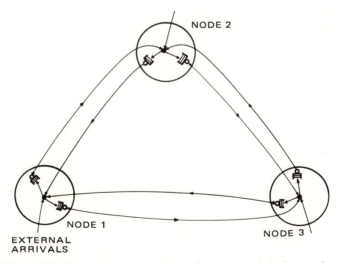

Figure 10.9. Three-node store-and-forward message-switched network.

servers were independent. For example, in the machine shop it was assumed that the time required by a job at the drill press is independent of the time required at the grinder. In communications networks this is not possible since the service time depends upon the length of the message which is carried from queue to queue. This introduces dependencies between the arrival process and the length of message or the service time. Under the independence assumption it is assumed that the service time of a message is chosen independently at each node. The justification for this assumption is in networks where many different sources are feeding into the same node resulting in a mixing of message lengths. Kleinrock[22] has verified this assumption by means of Monte Carlo simulation on a digital computer.

10.5.1. Message Delay

A quantity which is a widely used measure of performance in computer communications networks is message delay, which we define as the time interval between the arrival of a message to the network from an external source and its final departure from the network. In this section we shall consider the calculation of the statistics of message delay for the special case of acyclic networks with a single server at each node. As pointed out earlier, this model is particularly appropriate for store-and-forward communications networks. We would not expect that messages would be fed back to previously visited nodes.

As in the previous work in this chapter, we assume that the external arrivals of messages are Poisson and that the message lengths are exponentially distributed, implying exponentially distributed service times. In carrying out the analysis of message delay we assume that messages are transmitted first come first served regardless of origin. Thus messages newly arrived to the network from an external source are treated in the same fashion as messages from other nodes within the network.

The first step in calculating moments of delay is to find a recursive relation for the Laplace transform of the probability density of delay conditioned on the node at which a message enters the network. Let T_i be a random variable indicating the delay of a message from its entry to node i to its final departure. Under our basic assumption this same delay applies to new and old messages. Having completed service at node i, with probability q_{ij} a message goes from node i to node j where it incurs a delay of T_j seconds. A customer may also leave the system after service at node i, an event that occurs with probability q_{iL+1}. The delay through the system from node i can be written

$$T_i = \begin{cases} D_i & \text{with probability } q_{iL+1} \\ D_i + T_j & \text{with probability } q_{ij} \end{cases} \qquad (10.22)$$

where D_i is the delay through node i and consists of queueing time plus service time. Let $\mathcal{D}_i(s)$ and $\mathcal{T}_i(s)$ denote the Laplace transforms of the probability density functions for D_i and T_i, respectively. Since the delay in node i is independent of the delays in the other nodes of the system, we have

$$\mathcal{T}_i(s) = E[e^{-s(D_i+T_j)}]$$

$$= \mathcal{D}_i(s)\left[q_{iL+1} + \sum_{j=1}^{L} q_{ij}\mathcal{T}_j(s)\right] \tag{10.23}$$

As we have seen the queues at each of the nodes are $M/M/1$. The total traffic into node i is Λ_i messages per second and the average duration of a message is $1/\mu_i$. From equation (10.7) the number of messages in each node is geometrically distributed. By the same line of reasoning that led to equation (3.44) in Chapter 3, we have

$$f_{D_i}(t) = (\mu_i - \Lambda_i)\, e^{-(\mu_i-\Lambda_i)t} \tag{10.24}$$

The Laplace transform is then

$$\mathcal{D}_i(s) = \frac{\mu_i - \Lambda_i}{s + \mu_i - \Lambda_i}$$

where, under an assumption of stability, $\mu_i > \Lambda_i$. As usual μ_i and Λ_i are, respectively, service rates and arrival rates.

Consider now the delay of a message from any source entering the network. The Laplace transforms of the probability density of this delay may be written

$$\mathcal{T}(s) = \frac{1}{\alpha} \sum_{i=1}^{L} \lambda_i \mathcal{T}_i(s) \tag{10.25}$$

where

$$\alpha \triangleq \sum_{i=1}^{L} \lambda_i$$

This transform can be expressed in terms of known quantities. We begin by computing $\sum_{i=1}^{L} \Lambda_i \mathcal{T}_i(s)$. From equation (10.23) we have

$$\sum_{i=1}^{L} \Lambda_i \mathcal{T}_i(s) = \sum_{i=1}^{L} \Lambda_i\left[\mathcal{D}_i(s) + \sum_{j=1}^{L} q_{ij}\mathcal{T}_j(s)\right]$$

Substituting equation (10.8) yields

$$\sum_{i=1}^{L} \Lambda_i \mathcal{T}_i(s) = \sum_{i=1}^{L} \Lambda_i \mathcal{D}_i(s) + \sum_{i=1}^{L} \Lambda_i \mathcal{T}_i(s) - \sum_{i=1}^{L} \lambda_i \mathcal{T}_i(s)$$

From this it follows that

$$\mathcal{T}(s) = \frac{1}{\alpha} \sum_{i=1}^{L} \Lambda_i \mathcal{D}_i(s) \tag{10.26}$$

Thus the transform of message delay can be found by solving equation (10.8) and substituting equation (10.24) into equation (10.26). From the Laplace transform of the density function of message delay, moments of delay can be found.

A widely used measure of performance is the average delay of a message entering the network at any node. This can be calculated directly from equations (10.25) and (10.26):

$$\bar{T} = \frac{1}{\alpha} \sum_{i=1}^{L} \lambda_i \bar{T}_i = \frac{1}{\alpha} \sum_{i=1}^{L} \Lambda_i \bar{D}_i \tag{10.27}$$

where T_i is the average delay of messages entering at node i and $\bar{D}_i$ is the average delay suffered at node i alone.

Equation (10.27) could have been obtained directly from Little's formula. The average number of messages in the network is given by $\bar{T} \sum_{i=1}^{L} \lambda_i$. The average number of messages in the network which have entered the network at node i is $\lambda_i \bar{T}_i$. Summing over i gives the total average number. Finally the term $\sum_{i=1}^{L} \Lambda_i \bar{D}_i$ gives the average number by adding up all the averages in each of the link buffers.

Under the assumption that an exponentially distributed amount of time is required to transmit a message, we have from equations (10.24) and (10.27) that

$$\bar{T} = \frac{1}{\alpha} \sum_{i=1}^{L} \Lambda_i / (\mu_i - \Lambda_i) \tag{10.28}$$

where $1/\mu_i$ is the average time required to transmit a message. If the average duration of a message is $\bar{b}$ bits and if the transmission rate is C_i then $1/\mu_i = \bar{b}/C_i$. The average delay is

$$\bar{T} = \frac{1}{\alpha} \sum_{l=1}^{L} \frac{\Lambda_l}{C_l/\bar{b} - \Lambda_l} = \frac{1}{\alpha} \sum_{l=1}^{L} \frac{I_l}{C_l - I_l} \tag{10.29}$$

where $I_l = \bar{b}\Lambda_l$ is the traffic load in link i in bits per second. Notice that the units for Λ_l is message per second.

As we said at the beginning of this section the work presented is for Poisson arrivals and exponentially distributed service times. Classical work has been done on delay for tandem queues with service times having an arbitrary distribution.[13,14] The salient result is that the queueing delay is independent of the order of the queues and is given by the queueing delay of the queue with the longest service time. To find the overall path delay, the service times of each of the queues is added to this queueing delay.

10.6. Capacity Allocation

10.6.1. Linear Costs, Continuously Available Capacity

The expression for average message delay given in equation (10.29) has been extensively employed in network optimization problems. These problems fall into two basic classes: capacity allocation and routing. We shall consider the first of these in this chapter. The question of routing will be taken up in Chapter 12. In considering optimum capacity allocation, we shall assume that the routing as embodied in the terms q_{ij} [see equation (10.8)] is fixed. We wish to allocate the capacities of the links, $C_1, C_2, \ldots, C_L$, so as to minimize average message delay with a constraint on the total capacity. The simplest form of the optimization problem results when line capacity may assume any value which is specified by the optimization procedure. The usual form of the optimization problem is to minimize the average delay subject to a constraint on the cost of transmission facilities. The cost of a transmission link in the network is a function of the bandwidth of the link. For many networks, in particular networks using telecommunication network facilities, the cost per unit bandwidth is a function of length of a link. We then express the total cost as

$$W = \sum_{l=1}^{L} w_l C_l \tag{10.30}$$

where, as in equation (10.29), C_i is the capacity of link i usually expressed in bits per second. The effect of link length on cost is embodied in the quantity w_i which gives cost per unit bandwidth in link i. The cost per unit capacity may differ from link to link because link distances are different.

From the expression for delay and cost we form the Lagrangian

$$\frac{1}{\alpha} \sum_{l=1}^{L} \frac{I_l}{C_l - I_l} + \gamma \sum_{l=1}^{L} w_l C_l \tag{10.31}$$

where γ is a Lagrange multiplier. The property of equation (10.31) that facilitates optimization problems is that they are separable, i.e., sums of functions each of which are functions of a single variable. We differentiate with respect to C_l, set the result equal to zero, and solve for the set C_l, $l = 1, 2, \ldots, L$. This gives the so-called square root capacity assignment:

$$C_l = I_l + \left(\frac{I_l}{\gamma w_l} \right)^{1/2} \tag{10.32}$$

The Lagrange multiplier, γ, is determined by the constraint total cost expressed by equation (10.30). We find

$$C_l = I_l + \frac{(W - \sum_{l=1}^{L} w_l I_l)(I_l w_l)^{1/2}}{w_l \sum_{l=1}^{L} (w_l I_l)^{1/2}}, \qquad l = 1, 2, \ldots, L \tag{10.33}$$

The solution presented by equation (10.33) says to allocate to the link its requirement, I_l, plus an excess in proportion to $W - \sum_{l=1}^{L} w_l I_l$, which is the money remaining after the basic requirements are met in each link. Substituting into equation (10.29) we have for the average delay the expression

$$\bar{T} = \frac{1}{\alpha} \left[\sum_{l=1}^{L} (w_l I_l)^{1/2} \right]^2 \Big/ \left(W - \sum_{l=1}^{L} w_l I_l \right) \tag{10.34}$$

As one would expect the delay is inversely proportional to the cost margin.

A number of variations in the basic problem are possible. The most straightforward of these is to consider a fixed element of delay for each node visited by a message. This would account for processing at the nodes and for propagation delay between nodes. The average delay in this case can be written

$$\bar{T} = \frac{1}{\alpha} \sum_{l=1}^{L} \left(\frac{I_l}{C_l - I_l} + \Lambda_l P_l \right) \tag{10.35}$$

where P_l is the propagation and processing delay on link l. There are instances where the cost of a link does not depend upon its length. As we saw this is true of satellite links. The same is true to a degree in local area networks where link lengths are short and differences in distance between different links are negligible compared to other costs. With each link regardless of length there may be a fixed cost. We express these considerations by means of the cost function

$$W = w \sum_{i=1}^{L} C_i + K \tag{10.36}$$

(In the exercises at the end of the chapter, results for these cost functions may be worked out.)

Another variation in the basic problem is obtained by considering generalizations of the random component of the delay.[17] We define the performance measure

$$T^k \triangleq \left[\frac{1}{\alpha} \sum_{l=1}^{L} \Lambda_l \left(\frac{\bar{b}}{C_l - I_l} \right)^k \right]^{1/k} \tag{10.37}$$

This criterion reduces to average delay for $k = 1$. For $k = 2$ we have the standard deviation of flow in the network. This follows from the fact that the delay in an $M/M/1$ queue is exponentially distributed [see equation (10.24)]. For exponentially distributed random variables the variance is the square of the mean. Since the delays are assumed to be independent, from node to node, the variance of the sum is the sum of the variances. A final case of interest is for $k \to \infty$. In this case we have

$$T^\infty = \lim_{k \to \infty} \left[\frac{1}{\alpha} \sum_{l=1}^{L} \Lambda_i \left(\frac{\bar{b}}{C_l - I_l} \right)^k \right]^{1/k}$$

$$= \frac{I_{k*}}{\alpha(C_{k*} - I_k^*)} \tag{10.38}$$

where k^* is the value of l for which $m_l/(C_l - I_l)$ is maximum over $l = 1, 2, \ldots, L$. The idea then is to allocate capacity so as to minimize the maximum link delay. (In an exercise at the end of the chapter this criterion is used in a capacity assignment problem.)

10.6.2. General Capacity Allocation—Dynamic Programming

From a practical point of view the greatest difficulty with this optimization procedure is that it is predicted on continuously available transmission capacity. This is generally not the case in realistic systems. For example, in the telephone system the data rates that are available over voice-grade lines are 300, 600, 1200, 2400, 4800, and 9600 bits per second. A second less serious problem with the optimization technique is that costs are usually not linear with increasing bit rate. The higher rates tend to be more economical in terms of cost per unit of transmission capacity.

The capacity allocation problem with a finite number of available capacities and nonlinear costs can be solved by means of dynamic programming,[18,19] an optimization technique which is widely used in operations research and control theory. Dynamic programming is best explained as a computational technique which finds a shortest path through a maze. It is based on the so-called "principle of optimality," which simply states that every portion of an optimum path is optimum in the sense of being minimum distance. Were this not true one could replace the nonoptimum portion, thereby obtaining a better overall optimum—a contradiction. Consider the example shown in Figure 10.10. We have a network consisting of six nodes with the distances between nodes as indicated.† The problem is to find the minimum of the possible paths between nodes A and F. We recognize that the optimum path must pass through either node D or node E. Now by the principle of optimality part of the optimum path from node A to node F must consist of the optimum path to node D or to node E. We therefore compute the optimum paths to these intermediate nodes. Both are via node B in this example. The overall optimum is then found by conditioning on each of the possible subpaths to compute two contending total paths. The minimum of these two is chosen as the optimum. Computations are saved on this last step since there is no need to consider alternate paths to nodes D and E. In this example the application of the principle of optimality is obvious. In general the trick is to structure an optimization so that the principle applies.

Let us restate the capacity allocation problem. Given a set of network flows $I_1, I_2, \ldots, I_L$ in the L links of a network and a set of available capacities $C_1, C_2, \ldots, C_M$, find the allocation of capacities to each link such that the average delay

$$\bar{T} = \frac{1}{\alpha} \sum_{l=1}^{L} \frac{I_l}{C_l - I_l} \tag{10.39a}$$

is minimized subject to the constraint

$$\sum_{l=1}^{L} w_l(C_l) \leq W_{\max} \tag{10.39b}$$

where $w_i(C_i)$ is the cost of capacity C_i on link i. Now there are $L \times M$ possible capacity allocations, which is a large enough number in a practical

†A more descriptive form of this example is given in Ref. 20.

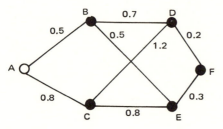

Figure 10.10. Dynamic programming example.

system to obviate simple enumeration. Many of these potential solutions can be dismissed quite easily by means of the idea of *dominated pairs*. With each of the $L \times M$ possible capacity allocations, we associate a pair of numbers $(\bar{T}_j, W_j), j = 1, 2, \ldots, L \times K$ indicating the average delay and the total cost. We say that the pair (T_m, W_m) is dominated by (T_n, W_n) if $T_m > T_n$ and $W_m > W_n$. Clearly we can eliminate a dominated pair from consideration since it has greater cost and higher delay than an alternative. Thus we need only consider capacity allocations which are characterized by nondominated pairs. If we have the list of nondominated pairs for an L node network we choose the one with the least delay from those satisfying the cost constraint. With different cost constraints each of these nondominated pairs could correspond to an optimum solution.

The key to compiling the list of nondominated pairs for L links is that it grows out of a nondominated list for any subset of $L - 1$ links. To see this consider the allocations among links $l = 1, 2, \ldots, L - 1$. For each allocation we can calculate a pair from equations (10.39a) and (10.39b) summing only to $L - 1$. The list of pairs characterizing these allocations must be nondominated since a dominated pair in the subnetwork would lead to a dominated pair in the whole network. A nondominated pair for a subnetwork here corresponds to the shortest path to an intermediate node in Figure 10.10. The principle of optimality says that in order for a network to have optimal allocation each subnetwork must also have optimum allocation.

Since the optimum allocation for a network grows from subnetworks, the steps of the algorithms are straightforward. We form a list of nondominated pairs for two links. To this network of two nodes we append a third link and form a new list of nondominated pairs. This is a simple process of adding and eliminating dominated pairs. The process continues in this fashion until all links in the network are included. The property of the cost functions which allows the dynamic solution is separability. Each of the cost functions is separable in that they are sums of functions of one variable. Thus, given the values of the delay and the cost of i links, finding these values for $i + 1$ links is a simple addition without change to the previous sum.

An example of a capacity assignment is illustrated by means of the three link networks shown in Figure 10.11. The traffic entering the system is $J_1 = 2.5$ kbps, $J_2 = 4$ kbps, and $J_3 = 1.5$ kbps. The routing matrix, $\gamma_{ij} \triangleq$ flow in bits per second from i to j, is as shown below:

r_{ij}	1	2	3
1	—	1.5	1.0
2	0.5	—	3.5
3	1.0	0.5	—

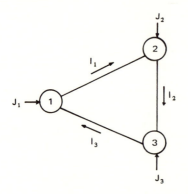

Figure 10.11. Three-node network illustrating capacity allocation.

The resulting link flows are $I_1 = 3$, $I_2 = 5$, and $I_3 = 2$. Now suppose that the capacities that are available are as shown below:

Capacity (kbps)	Cost ($K/km)
4	10
8	15
16	20

Finally, suppose that the lengths of each of the links in the network are $l_1 = 5$ km, $l_2 = 3$ km, and $l_3 = 6$ km. We begin the optimization by listing in terms of increasing delay the pairs for each link; in calculating delay, we drop the common factor $1/\alpha$:

Link 1		Link 2		Link 3	
Delay	Cost	Delay	Cost	Delay	Cost
3	50	∞	30	0.5	60
0.6	75	1.66	45	0.33	90
0.23	100	0.45	60	0.14	120

We combine links 1 and 2, eliminating dominated pairs:

Links 1 and 2	
4.66	95
3.45	110
2.26	120
1.05	135
0.68	160

In compiling this list we have ruled out a 16-kbps link 1 and a 8-kbps link 2 since it gives a dominated pair. The next step is to combine with the list for link 3. The final list of nondominated pairs is

5.16	155
3.95	170
2.76	180
1.55	195
1.18	220
1.01	250
0.82	280

Now suppose that we wish to minimize the delay under the condition that the system cost less than $200 K. The optimum solution corresponds to the fourth pair on the list. The optimum allocation is $C_1 = 8$ kbps, $C_2 = 16$ kbps, and $C_3 = 4$ kbps.

Although the dynamic programming technique reduces the number of computations from what would be required in a brute force enumeration, the required computations are large for reasonable size L. In fact it can be shown that the capacity assignment problem is $N - P$ complete. Asymptotically the growth of the number of calculations is exponential with the number of links. An alternative which is suboptimum but which requires fewer computations is given by Cantor and Gerla.[21]

References

1. J. R. Jackson, "Networks of Waiting Lines," *Operations Research*, **5**, 518–521 (1957).
2. J. R. Jackson, "Jobshop-like Queueing Systems," *Management Science*, **10**, 131–142 (1963).
3. H. Kobayashi, *Modeling and Analysis—An Introduction to System Performance Methodology*. Addison-Wesley, Reading, Massachusetts (1978).
4. E. Reich, "Waiting Time when Queues are in Tandem," *Annals of Mathematical Statistics*, **28**, 768–773 (1957).
5. P. J. Burke, "The Output Process of a Stationary $M/M/S$ Queueing System," *Annals of Mathematical Statistics*, **37**(4), 1144–1152 (1968).
6. P. J. Burke, "The Dependence of Delays in Tandem Queues," *Annals of Mathematical Statistics*, **35**, 874–875 (1964).
7. B. Melamed, "On Poisson Traffic Processes in Discrete State Markovian Systems with Applications to Queueing Theory," Technical Report 77-7, Department of Industrial and Operations Engineering, University of Michigan (1977).
8. F. J. Beutler and B. Melamed, "Decomposition and Customer Streams of Feedback Networks of Queues in Equilibrium," *Operations Research*, **26**(6), 1059–1072, November–December (1978).
9. A. J. Lemoine, "Networks of Queues—A Survey of Equilibrium Analysis," *Management Science*, **24**(4), 464–481, December (1977).
10. F. Baskette *et al.*, "Open, Closed and Mixed Networks of Queues with Different Classes of Customers," *Journal of the Association for Compting Machinery*, **22**, 248–260 (1975).
11. S. M. Ross, *Stochastic Processes*, John Wiley, New York (1983).
12. L. Kleinrock, *Communication Nets: Stochastic Message Flow and Delay*. McGraw-Hill, New York (1964), out of print; reprinted Dover, New York (1972).

13. B. Avi-Itzhak, "A Sequence of Service Stations with Arbitrary Input and Regular Service Times," *Management Science*, **11**(5), 565–571, March (1965).
14. H. D. Friedman, "Reduction Methods for Tandem Queueing Systems," *Operations Research*, **13**, 121–133 (1965).
15. I. Rubin, "Message Path Delays in Packet Switching Communication Networks," *IEEE Transactions on Communications*, **COM-23**(2), 186–192, February (1975).
16. M. Kaplan, "A Two-fold Tandem Net with Deterministic Link and Source Interfaces," *Operations Research*, **28**, 512–526, May–June (1980).
17. B. Meister, H. R. Mueller, and H. Rudin, "New Optimization Criteria for Message-Switched Networks," *IEEE Transactions on Communications Technology*, **COM-19**(3), 256–260, June (1971).
18. R. E. Bellman, *Dynamic Programming*, Princeton University Press, Princeton, New Jersey (1957).
19. S. E. Dreyfus, *Dynamic Programming and the Calculus of Variations*, Academic Press, New York (1965).
20. J. F. Hayes, "The Viterbi Algorithm Applied to Digital Data Transmission," *IEEE Communication Society*, **13**(2), 15–20, March (1975).
21. D. G. Cantor and M. Gerla, "Capacity Allocation in Distributed Computer Networks," Proceedings of 7th Hawaii International Conference on System Science (1974), pp. 115–117.
22. L. Kleinrock, *Communication Nets: Stochastic Message Flow and Delay*, McGraw-Hill, New York (1964), out of print; reprinted by Dover, New York (1972).

Exercises

10.1. In the text it was shown that the joint equilibrium distribution of tandem $M/M/1$ queues is the product of the marginals. Repeat this tandem for $M/M/S$ queues when $S > 1$.

10.2. Consider the simple network of two queues in tandem shown in Figure 10.7a. Customers arrive at the first queue at a Poisson rate. The service times in each of the queues are independent and exponentially distributed with different mean values. Assume that the output of the second queue is fed back to the input of the first queue with probability P. With probability $1 - P$ a customer leaves the system after queue 2. Assume infinite waiting rooms in each queue.

(a) Sketch the state transition flow diagram for this system.

(b) Write down the equilibrium equations.

(c) Solve the equations derived in (b) for the joint density.

10.3. Suppose that two classes of jobs arrive at a service facility each at an independent Poisson rate. The facility is equipped with K servers. The class 1 jobs require a single server for an exponentially distributed time interval. In contrast, the class 2 jobs require all K servers for an exponentially distributed time period. Assume that there is no room to store jobs so that a job that cannot be served immediately departs.

(a) Sketch the state flow transition flow diagram for the number of jobs of both types at the facility.

(b) Write down the equilibrium equations.

(c) Find the joint probability distribution for the number of jobs of each class in the facility.

10.4. An astrologer and a stock broker share the same waiting room in an office building. Clients for each of these arrive at a Poisson rate and require an exponentially distributed period of consultation. Assume that the waiting room can hold no more than two clients of either type. Potential clients arriving at a full waiting room take their business elsewhere.

(a) Sketch the state transition flow diagram for the number of clients of either type in consultation or in the waiting room.

(b) Write down the equilibrium equations.

(c) Find steady-state joint probability distribution for the number of clients of either type.

Now suppose that the stock broker's client can just as well consult with the astrologer with the same distribution of consulting time as the astrologer's regular clients. People seeking financial advice immediately enter the astrologer's office if he is free and the stock broker is busy.

(d) Repeat (a), (b), and (c) above.

10.5. (a) Under what conditions does the network of tandem queues with feedback, such as in Figure 10.7a, form a Jackson network, i.e., the joint distribution of the queue lengths is in the product form.

(b) For the conditions given in (a), write down the joint distribution of queue lengths in terms of the external arrival rate, the average service times, and the feedback probability.

10.6. Suppose that in Figure 10.6 we have the following values for the various quantities depicted:

(1) $\lambda_1 = 10$, $\lambda_2 = 5$, $\lambda_3 = 20$, and $\lambda_4 = 10$, all messages per second;

(2) the average service times in seconds in each of the nodes are $1/\mu_1 = 40$, $1/\mu_2 = 50$, $1/\mu_3 = 50$, $1/\mu_4 = 50$;

(3) $Q_{21} = 1/4$, $Q_{23} = 1/4$, $Q_{41} = 1/2$;

(4) each node has a single server.

Write down the steady-state distribution of the joint queue distributions.

10.7. Suppose that the network shown in Figure 10.6 is a store-and-forward message switched network. Assume that the messages' arrival rates are as given in Exercise 10.6 as are the routing probabilities. But the service times are determined in message lengths and transmission capacities. We assume that all of the message lengths have the same average 1000 bits. Assume that the capacities of the various transmission lines are as follows:

(i)   between nodes 1 and 2, 50 kbps

(ii) between nodes 2 and 3, 25 kbps

(iii) between nodes 2 and 1, 25 kbps

(iv) between nodes 2 and 4, 50 kbps

(v)   out of node 3, 50 kbps

(vi) out of node 4, 50 kbps

Find the joint distributions of the number of messages in each of the buffers serving output lines.

10.8. Again assume the same topology as in Figure 10.6 and the same parameters as in Exercise 10.7, except for link capacities. Assume that the total capacity in each of the links must be such that $\sum_{i=1}^{L} C_i \leq 250$ kbps per second. Find the capacity allocation which minimizes the average delay.

10.9. Suppose that in Exercise 10.8 each message suffers a constant propagation delay of 20 msec in each link it traverses. [See equation (10.36).] Find the optimum allocation of capacity.

10.10. Find the capacity allocation for arbitrary k in equation (10.37). What is the general solution when $k \to \infty$?

10.11. We redo the capacity allocation problem of Figure 10.11 considered in the text. Suppose that the only quantities that are changed are the flows from external sources. Let $J_1 = 3$, $J_2 = 2$, and $J_3 = 4$. Calculate the optimum allocation of capacities.

Congestion and Flow Control

11.1. Introduction

In terms of the open systems interconnection protocol discussed in Section 2.3, the models that we have considered to this point are part of the link level. In this and in the next chapter we develop models for higher-level protocols, primarily at the network level. In this chapter we study congestion and flow control, in the next, routing.

The role of flow control as well as routing in computer communications networks is to provide for the orderly transition of information of data through a network which may consist of a number of links.† Consider the simple packet switched network shown in Figure 11.1. In Chapter 10 we developed measures of performance for such a network—average delay, for example. These measures assume a particular pattern of flow into and within the network. The pattern is a function of the control of flow, of routing, and of the demand made by the users. But in any realistic situation user demands are not static. The volume of traffic and its origins and destination can change with time. Now it may well happen that changing traffic patterns cause a concentration of flow at a few nodes thereby creating bottlenecks and a precipitous deterioration of performance.

The effect of congestion within a network is portrayed by the graph in Figure 11.2, where throughput is shown as a function of input traffic. In an ideal case where traffic is perfectly scheduled, the throughput rises linearly as a function of the input until the capacity of the network is reached. In the case of uncontrolled flow, the rise is linear for very light loading but the system saturates well before full capacity. Beyond the saturation point, the throughput may actually decline. This decline may be due to deadlocks

---

†For a more detailed discussion of particular techniques of congestion and flow control, the reader is referred to the survey paper by Gerla and Kleinrock.[1] For a survey of performance models in flow control and related areas, see Ref. 2.

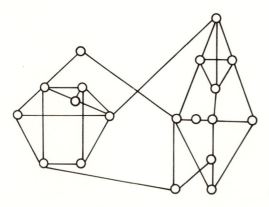

Figure 11.1. Packet-switched network.

within the network. The everyday example of this is automobile traffic jams. On the link level of communication networks, a good example of congestion caused by uncontrolled flow is the ALOHA system studied in Chapter 8.

We may contrast the foregoing to the situation where the traffic is controlled. The throughput may be less at light loading due to the overhead incurred by control. However, as the load increases, the throughput can also increase to a figure close to full capacity. There is an illustration of this concept at the link level. In the token passing technique studied in Chapter 7, the overhead required to pass the token allows an orderly flow of traffic at moderate to heavy loading.

As we have indicated, the avoidance of congestion within a network is accomplished by both flow control and routing. Flow control restricts the entry of traffic to facilities. It may be practiced at several levels: the whole network, paths within the network, or at the link level within the network.†Although we concentrate on flow control in this chapter and

---

†As pointed out by Gerla and Kleinrock,[1] the term "congestion control" is applied by some authors to the lower protocol levels, while the term "flow control" is reserved for the session level. We shall not persevere in this distinction.

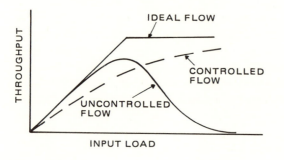

Figure 11.2. Illustration of the effect of flow control.

thereby divide the two approaches, we shall see in the next chapter that certain forms of flow control and routing can be modeled under the same mathematical framework.

Two generic problems necessitate the control of flows within networks: (1) sinks whose speed are not matched to source speeds, and (2) bottlenecks caused by the convergence of traffic at nodes within the network. The idea of flow control is to shift congestion from the interior of the network to its periphery where the traffic enters. The role of routing is to allocate flow within the network once it has been admitted. By means of this policy, transit delay is minimized at the expense of entry delay. Three general techniques have been suggested to accomplish this task. The window flow control technique operates on paths between source–destination pairs. Only the maximum number of unacknowledged packets or messages may be in this path. The so-called "isarithmic" technique limits the number of packets or messages in the entire network. Slots that may carry packets or messages circulate throughput the network. A user must obtain one of these slots in order to transmit data. A final technique is to limit the traffic entering the network by limiting the storage for newly entering traffic. Priority for storage is given to traffic already in the network. We shall be presenting models for the first and the third of these techniques.

11.2. Link Level Flow Control—HDLC

11.2.1. Higher-Level Data Link Control

We begin the modeling of congestion and flow control with a link level protocol, designated *higher-level link control* (HDLC) by ISO. HDLC is derived from the *synchronous data link control* (SDLC) protocol developed by IBM as part of its system level architecture (SLA). We focus on this particular link level protocol because it is an international standard and because it has been the subject of far more analytical studies than alternative techniques.†

We view HDLC as a kind of bridge between lower- and higher-level protocols since it contains features of both. As we shall see, HDLC provides for error control in the same way as the error control protocols exemplified in Chapters 4 and 5. Similarly to higher-level protocols, HDLC implements flow control by means of a window mechanism. Messages are transmitted without acknowledgment until some maximum number of unacknowledged messages is reached. The difference between this maximum and the number of unacknowledged messages is called the window. When the number of

---

†For a comparison of these alternatives the reader is directed to Ref. 3.

unacknowledged message reaches the maximum, the window is closed and no new messages may be transmitted.

We shall now sketch out the general operation of HDLC.† The flow of information in this protocol is carried out by means of entities called *frames*, of which there are three types: *information, supervisory*, and the *unnumbered* frames. The format of the information frame is shown in Figure 11.3. The frame begins with an eight-bit sequence, 01111110, called the *flag*. This is followed by an 8-bit *address field* indicating destination in the case of multipoint lines. (Multipoint lines are illustrated in Figure 7.2.) Next is the *control field*, also consisting of eight bits. The role of this field is particular to the type of frame under consideration. In information frames the control field contains information on sequencing. We shall see in a moment that sequencing is important to flow and error control. The control field is followed by the information to be transmitted. The duration of the information field is arbitrary. Sixteen parity check bits which range over the whole frame follow the information bits. The end of the frame is indicated by the same flag that initiated the frame.

There is no restriction on the length or on the content of the information in a frame. The flag terminating the frame prematurely could be replicated in the data sequence, unless preventative measures are taken. The preventative measure is stuff bits. Consider the case where the flag is 01111110. Suppose that the data sequence produces 0111111, a string of six ones. A seventh one is stuffed into the sequence. At the receiver it is understood that in a sequence of seven ones the seventh is a stuff bit and should be discarded.

The supervisory and the unnumbered frames differ from the information frame in that there are no data fields. There is also a difference in the control fields. The supervisory frame is used directly with the information frame in conjunction with the flow of data. The function of the unnumbered frame is network control and system maintenance and tests.

There are three modes of operation for HDLC. The *normal response mode* (NRM) is used in multipoint operations where a central station is communicating with a number of outlying stations. In the *asynchronous response mode* (ARM), a single primary station communicates with a single secondary station. Finally, the flow of information between two logically equal stations is governed by the *asynchronous balanced mode* (ABM).

†For more details, see Ref. 4.

Figure 11.3. Information frame.

As we stated above, control fields are used in regulating the flow of information. The fields contain a 3-bit subfield giving the sequence number of the frame. The sequence number identifies a frame in acknowledgments. There is a window flow control mechanism in which transmission of frames is halted when there are seven unacknowledged frames. The control field also contains a three-bit subfield which may be used to acknowledge received frames. Received frames may also be acknowledged in the control field of the supervisory packet.

Supervisory frames are used in the event of erroneous or lost frames. Depending on the implementation of the systems, various actions are possible. A simple negative acknowledgement, called a *reject*, can be transmitted. The frame rejected as well as all subsequent frames are then retransmitted. One may also implement a selective reject strategy whereby only the frame in error is transmitted. (Recall that these strategies were studied in Chapters 4 and 5.) The supervisory frame may also indicate that the receiver is simply not ready for an Information frame; the receiving buffer may be full, for example.

Several facets of the HDLC protocol pose obstacles to analysis. As we have seen in Chapters 4 and 5, in order to analyze the send and wait and the go back N protocols, certain approximations are required. Secondly, transmissions of acknowledgments are carried out in the frame formats. These are "piggybacked" onto information frames or carried in supervisory frames and depend on the availability of either type frame. Perhaps the most interesting feature of the protocol for modeling is the flow control window limiting the number of frames that may be transmitted without acknowledgment.

There have been a number of analyses of the HDLC protocols, each focusing on different aspects. For example, Easton[5] finds the maximum throughput under different error recovery methods with no consideration given to windowing. In Ref. 6 the effect of windowing on throughput and delay is studied. The most complete model may be found in Ref. 7.

11.2.2. A Throughput Model

In consonance with the objectives of this chapter, we shall consider a study of the HDLC protocol which deals with flow control.[6] A basic assumption in this model is that the duration of a frame is exponentially distributed. When one considers the overhead that goes along with the data, the crudeness of this approximation is evident. As in the case of similar approximations in previous chapters, the justification lies in simulation results which say that the results are sensitive to mean values and not to the exact distribution. A second assumption is that there is a constant propagation delay between transmitting and receiving stations. The maximum window size is represented by the variable W. This is the maximum number of messages that may be transmitted without acknowledgment.

The model for the system is shown in Figure 11.4. The transmitter is represented as a queue in which the service time is exponentially distributed with mean duration $1/\mu_1$. The output of this queue is fed into one of W branches. No more than one message may be in one of these branches at a time. When all of the branches are full, messages are blocked from leaving the transmit queue. The branches are composed of three stages, each representing part of the acknowledgment process. These stages are reminiscent of the stages studied in Section 3.10 in that only one message may reside at a time. The first stage is a constant delay representing the round-trip propagation and processing delay. When a message arrives at the receiver, an acknowledgment is transmitted after any ongoing transmission. We make the pessimistic assumption that there is always such transmission in progress. This is represented by the second stage, which is exponentially distributed with mean duration $1/\mu_2$. This is the mean duration of messages returning from the receiver. If there is a second message waiting to be transmitted over the return channel, the acknowledgment is piggybacked onto it. Again we make the pessimistic assumption that this delay is incurred. This third delay is represented by the third stage, which is exponentially distributed with mean duration $1/\mu_2$.

The model represented in Figure 11.4 may be used to do a calculation of the maximum throughput. We assume that the transmit queue is always full. Under this assumption, the interval between message departures is exponentially distributed with a mean time between departures equal to $1/\mu_1$ seconds. The set of W parallel branches may be viewed as a system of W servers with no queueing for service. Therefore the appropriate model is an $M/G/W/W$ queue in which the mean service time is $(T + 2/\mu_2)$ and the mean arrival rate of messages is μ_1 per second. In Section 3.6.4 it was

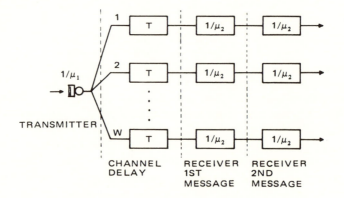

Figure 11.4. Model of window control.[6]

shown that for the $M/M/W/W$ queue the probability of n servers being occupied is

$$P_n = P_0 \rho^n / n!, \qquad n = 1, 2, \ldots \tag{11.1}$$

where ρ is the traffic load and is equal to $\rho = \mu_1 \bar{m}$. $\bar{m}$ is the mean value of the service time. As remarked earlier, it can be shown that this result depends on the mean value of the service time and not on its distribution. Therefore equation (11.1) applies to the model of Figure 11.4 with $\bar{m} = (T + 2/\mu_2)$. The maximum throughput for this system is then

$$S = \mu_1(1 - P_n) \tag{11.2}$$

In Figure 11.5 the activity which is defined to be S/μ_1 is plotted as a function of the window size W for several different values of $T + 2/\mu_2$. These values were computed for line speeds of 4.8, 19.2, and 50 kbps and message lengths of 300 and 1000 bits as indicated. Also shown are the results of a simulation of the model shown in Figure 11.4. From the comparison with simulation, it appears that the approximation yields accurate results. These results also indicate that a window size of $W = 8$ is adequate for symmetric traffic and the lower line speeds. At 48 kbps with asymmetric traffic, a larger window is necessary.

11.3. Flow Control and Jackson Networks

11.3.1. Extended Class of Jackson Networks

As we have seen in Chapter 10, networks are composed of a number of links as well as buffers and processors. All of these elements must come into play in the flow control strategy which operates at the network level.

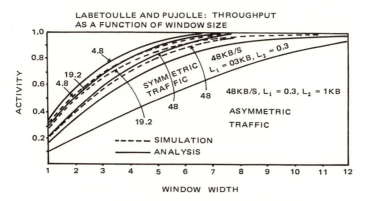

Figure 11.5. Throughput and simulation.[6]

A broadened form of the Jackson network model studied in Chapter 10 can be used to model flow control in the context of an entire network. In the previous chapter we considered open networks in which message lengths, hence service times, are exponentially distributed. In this and succeeding sections of the chapter, we show that the product form solution obtains for other message length distributions. We shall focus on forms of the results that are directly applicable to flow control. The proofs use flow control models. However, these results are applicable to other network models, computer systems for example. In order to see the breadth of the theory of Jackson networks, see Refs. 8 and 9.

The extension of Jackson network theory is carried out in the context of the study of flow control.[10] The first extension that we shall consider is networks which have more than one class of message. The different message classes share the same transmission line and processors. As in the previous chapter, routing among the nodes of the network is probabilistic. Although it is not relevant to our particular models, messages may also change class probabilistically, i.e., in an incremental interval a message may go from one class to another with a given probability. Networks may be mixed with respect to class in that they may be closed for one class, no external arrivals and no departures, and open for another.

In addition to the first-come first-served (FCFS) exponentially distributed service studied in the previous chapter, there are three other kinds of service for which the product form of the joint distribution obtains. The first of these is processor sharing in which each message in the queue receives equal simultaneous service. Thus, if there are n messages, they are all transmitted at a rate $1/n$. The second service type is the infinite server model considered in Section 3.6.4. In this case there is never queueing of messages. As we shall see, this type is useful is modeling store-and-forward systems. The final service type for which the product form holds is last-come-first-served, in which newly arrived messages are served with a preemptive resume discipline. In all three of these the Laplace transform of the probability density may be a rational function.† Furthermore, for each of these three service disciplines, different classes of messages may have different service time distributions. When service time is exponential FCFS, all classes must have the same service time distribution.

Finally, arrivals may be Poisson and may be dependent on the state of the network. A good example of such dependence models is limited storage. Message arrival is inhibited when buffers are full. This is the same sort of thing we saw in Section 3.6.2 in our study of the one-dimensional case.

---

†Recall that this form of service distribution was introduced in Section 3.10 in the discussion of the method of stages.

11.3.2. Window Flow Control: A Closed-Network Model

We consider an end-to-end window flow control scheme which limits the number of messages flowing between a particular source destination pair which may be in the network at any given point in time. The path between source and destination is depicted in Figure 11.6. There are N nodes which we shall model as having independent exponentially distributed service with mean value $1/\mu_i$, $i = 1, 2, \ldots, N$. Several messages are in transit at any given point in time. The maximum number of such messages is W. At this limit no new messages from the originating station may enter the path until one of these messages has been acknowledged. We model the forward direction and the return path as a chain as shown. The possible difference between message and acknowledgment lengths may be taken into account by the different average service times in each of the nodes.

It is difficult to model the process of holding the messages until there is room in the chain and we seek a simplifying approximation. We assume that messages arrive at the source node at an average rate of λ_0 messages per second and that message arriving to a full chain are lost. This will allow us to calculate the throughput of the path between the source and the destination. This last model can be represented as shown in Figure 11.7. The original N nodes are augmented by phantom node. The service rate of this node is λ_0 messages per second. Messages from the source–destination pair that we are interested in circulate in this closed chain. If W internal messages are outstanding, the phantom node is empty and there can be no new arrivals to node 1. When there are less than W messages in nodes 1 to N, there is at least one message in the phantom node. In this case messages arrive to node 1 at a rate of λ_0 messages per second.

The flow between any source–destination pair in the network can be modeled by means of a closed chain. Clearly the same node may be part

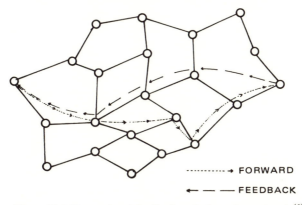

Figure 11.6. Forward and feedback path through a network.[6]

of more than one chain. Traffic flowing in chains other than the one we are interested in is modeled as entering and departing as shown in Figure 11.7. The effect of this external traffic is to impede the flow within the chain. For simplicity we shall assume that the same volume of traffic, λ_i in messages per second, enters the chain at the input to node i and departs the loop at the output of node $i, i = 1, 2, \ldots, N$. As we shall see, there is no loss of generality in this assumption. In keeping with its function in the model, there can be no external traffic in the phantom node. In this model the internal and the external traffic form separate classes of messages. Because of the mixing of traffic within the network we assume that the independence assumption discussed in the previous chapter holds. The service times are independent from node to node.

With the internal and the external traffic, we have a mixed network of queues. The state of this network is given by the number of messages of each class in each of the queues. We distinguish between externally arriving messages and messages that are circulating internally. The phantom node is designated as node 0. We define the state as $(k_1, k_2, \ldots, k_N; l_1, l_2, \ldots, l_N)$, where $k_i, i = 0, 1, \ldots, N$ and $l_j, 1, 2, \ldots, N$ are, respectively, the number of internal and external messages in node i. As in the case of an open network, there can be only a limited number of changes in the state in an incremental interval. An internal message may go from one queue to another within the chain. External message arrive or depart. The equilibrium equation is then

$$\left(\sum_{i=0}^{N} \lambda_i + \sum_{i=1}^{N} \mu_i \right) P(k_0, k_1, k_2, \ldots, k_N; l_1, l_2, \ldots, l_N)$$

$$= \lambda_0 P(k_0 + 1, k_1 - 1, \ldots, k_N; l_1, l_2, \ldots, l_N)$$

$$+ \sum_{i=1}^{N} \lambda_i P(k_0, \ldots, k_N; l_1, \ldots, l_1, \ldots l_i - 1, \ldots, l_N)$$

$$+ \sum_{i=1}^{N-1} \mu_i[(k_i + 1)/(k_i + l_i + 1)]$$

$$\times P(k_0, \ldots, k_i + 1, k_{i+1} - 1, \ldots, k_N; l_1, \ldots, l_N) \qquad (11.3)$$

$$+ \mu_N[(k_N + 1)/(k_N + l_N + 1)]$$

$$\times P(k_0 - 1, k_1, \ldots, k_N + 1; l_1, l_2, \ldots, l_N)$$

$$+ \sum_{i=1}^{N} \mu_i[(l_i + 1)/(k_i + l_i + 1)]P(k_0, \ldots, k_N; l_1, \ldots, l_i + 1, \ldots, l_N)$$

In equation (11.3) terms such as $[(k_i + 1)/(k_i + l_i + 1)]$ reflect the portion of the contents of node i which is internal traffic. Clearly equation

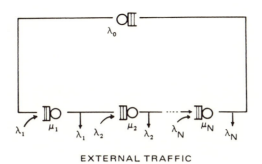

EXTERNAL TRAFFIC

Figure 11.7. Logical network chain.

(11.3) cannot be true for all values of k_i and l_i. First of all, there can be no departures from an empty queue. If, for example, $k_i = 0$, then the term μ_i is omitted on the left-hand side. Furthermore, equation (11.3) holds only for states such that $\sum_{i=0}^{N} k_i = W$.

The flows of internal and external traffic into node i are λ_0 and λ_i messages per second, respectively. A sufficient condition for equation (11.3) to hold are the local balance equations which involve a single node at a time:

$$\mu_i[k_i/(k_i + l_i)]P(k_0, k_1, \ldots, k_N; l_1, l_2, \ldots, l_N)$$

$$= \lambda_0 P(k_0, k_1, \ldots, k_i - 1, \ldots, k_N; l_1, \ldots, l_N), \qquad i = 1, 2, \ldots, N$$

(11.4a)

$$\mu_i[l_i/(k_i + l_i)]P(k_0, k_1, \ldots, k_N; l_1, \ldots, l_N)$$

$$= \lambda_i P(k_0, k_1, \ldots, k_N; l_1, \ldots, l_i - 1, \ldots, l_N), \qquad i = 1, 2, \ldots, N$$

(11.4b)

Simple substitution shows that the solution to equations (11.4a) and (11.4b) is of the product form given by

$$P(k_0, \ldots, k_N; l_1, \ldots, l_N) = P(0) \prod_{i=1}^{N} \left(\frac{\lambda_0}{\mu_i}\right)^{k_i} \rho_i^{l_i}(k_i + l_i)!/(k_i!l_i!)$$

(11.5)

where $P(0)$ is a normalizing constant such that the probabilities sum to one over the allowable states and where $\rho_i = \lambda_i/\mu_i$, $i = 1, 2, \ldots, N$. The value of $P(0)$ is determined by summing equation (11.5) over all allowable values of k_i and l_i, $i = 1, 2, \ldots, N$. For the latter variable this is simple. Since there is no restriction on storage in the node and since external traffic flows in an open chain, there is no constraint on the numbers of external messages in the nodes 1 through N. We sum over l_i to obtain after a rearrangement of terms

$$P(k_0, \ldots, k_N)$$

$$= \sum_{l_1=0}^{\infty} \sum_{l_2=0}^{\infty} \cdots \sum_{l_N=0}^{\infty} P(k_0, \ldots, k_N; l_1, \ldots, l_N) \tag{11.6}$$

$$= P(0) \sum_{l_1=0}^{\infty} \sum_{l_2=0}^{\infty} \cdots \sum_{l_N=0}^{\infty} \prod_{i=1}^{N} (\lambda_0/\mu_i)^{k_i} \rho_i^{l_i} (k_i + l_i)!/(k_i! l_i!)$$

Consider one of the summations in equation (11.6) as a separate entity for the moment. As a further temporary simplification we suppress the dependence on i:

$$(1/k!) \sum_{l=0}^{\infty} \rho^k (k + l)!/(k!) = (1/k!) \sum_{l=0}^{\infty} \frac{d^k(\rho^{k+l})}{d\rho^k}$$

$$= (1/k!) \frac{d^k[\rho^k/(1-\rho)]}{d\rho^k} = 1/(1-\rho)^{k+1} \tag{11.7}$$

where $d^k/d\rho^k$ is the kth derivative with respect to ρ. Substituting equation (11.7) into (11.6) in the same fashion, we find

$$P(k_0, \ldots, k_N)$$

$$= P(0) \prod_{i=1}^{N} (\lambda_0/\mu_i)^{k_i} [1/(1-\rho_i)^{k_i+1}] \tag{11.8}$$

$$= \frac{P(0)}{\prod_{i=1}^{N} (1-\rho_i)} \prod_{i=1}^{N} [\lambda_0/(\mu_i - \lambda_i)]^{k_i}$$

In equation (11.8) the term $\prod_{i=1}^{N} (1 - \rho_i)$ can be absorbed into the constant since it does not depend upon k_i. The resulting equation shows that the only effect of the external traffic on the internal is to reduce the rate at which internal messages are served from μ_i to $\mu_i - \lambda_i$. Clearly stability requires that $\lambda_i < \mu_i$. The form of the probability distribution for internal messages is independent of the external traffic.

11.4. Computational Techniques—Closed Networks

11.4.1. Convolutional Algorithm for Closed Networks

In order to find $P(0)$ in equation (11.8), we sum over all possible combinations of k_i—a formidable task. The fundamental difficulty is numerical, having to do with the number of possible combinations that are possible. There are only W internal messages in circulation an there are $\binom{N+W}{N}$ ways for these messages to be arranged in the $N + 1$ nodes. This is an enormous number even for modest values of W and N. For example, if $N + 1 = 20$ and $W = 10$, there are 10^7 possible states. This difficulty is endemic to closed networks of queues. Fortunately techniques which considerably reduce the computational effort have been found. A number of these techniques are based on a convolutional algorithm derived simultaneously by Buzen[11] and by Reiser and Kobayashi.[12] We shall consider this algorithm in its simplest form. The idea is to provide an introduction to the technique in the context of flow control. An alternative approach to computation in a closed network of queues is the mean value analysis pioneered by Reiser and Lavenberg.[13] We shall consider this approach in due course.

We begin by defining the set of n, $n = 1, 2, \ldots, N$ nonnegative integers which sum to w, $w = 1, 2, \ldots, W$.

$$S(w, n) = \left\{ k_0, k_1, \ldots, k_n \middle/ \sum_{i=0}^{n} k_i = w \right\},$$

$$w = 0, 1, \ldots W; n = 0, 1, \ldots, N \tag{11.9}$$

By summing over this set we define the quantity

$$g(w, n) = \sum_{S(w,n)} \prod_{i=0}^{n} \gamma_i^{k_i} \tag{11.10}$$

where $\gamma_i = \lambda_0/(\mu_i - \lambda_i)$ and where we define $\gamma_0 = 1$. We split the summation on the basis of the value of k_n to obtain

$$g(w, n) = \sum_{\substack{S(w,n) \\ k_n=0}} \prod_{i=0}^{n} \gamma_i^{k_i} + \sum_{\substack{S(w,n) \\ k_n>0}} \prod_{i=0}^{n} \gamma_i^{k_i} \tag{11.11}$$

From equation (11.11) the following recursive relationship is apparent:

$$g(w, n) = g(w, n - 1) + \gamma_n g(w - 1, n) \tag{11.12a}$$

We note also that

$$g(w, 0) = 1, \qquad w = 0, 1, \ldots, W \tag{11.12b}$$

and

$$g(0, n) = 1, \qquad n = 0, 1, \ldots, N \tag{11.12c}$$

From equations (11.12a)–(11.12c) we can compute the quantity $g(W, N) = 1/P(0)$ in a recursive fashion. This calculation is illustrated in Table 11.1. The calculation begins in the upper left-hand corner and proceeds to the lower right. It is never necessary to store more than N values.

It is serendipitous that intermediate values of $g(w, N)$, obtained in the course of calculating $g(W, N)$, are also useful. Consider first the probability that there are more than k messages in a particular node:

$$
\begin{aligned}
P(k_i \geqslant k) &= \sum_{\substack{S(W,N) \\ k_i \geqslant k}} \prod_{i=0}^{N} \gamma_i^{k_i} / g(W, N) \\
&= [\gamma_i^k / g(W, N)] \sum_{S(w-k,N)} \prod_{i=0}^{N} \gamma_i^{k_i} \qquad (11.13) \\
&= \gamma_i^k g(W - k, N) / g(W, N)
\end{aligned}
$$

From this we have

$$
\begin{aligned}
P(k_i = k) = [\gamma_i^k / g(W, N)][g(W - k, N) \\
- \gamma_i g(W - k - 1, N)], \qquad i = 0, 1, 2, \ldots, N
\end{aligned} \qquad (11.14)
$$

Finally we have that the mean number of internal messages in a node is

$$
E(k_i) = \left[\sum_{k=1}^{W} \gamma_i^k g(W - k, N) \right] / g(W, N), \qquad i = 0, 1, 2, \ldots, N \qquad (11.15)
$$

The mean number of external messages in a queue, $E(l_i), i = 1, 2, \ldots, N$, has a particularly simple form. Were there no internal traffic, it follows from the theory of the $M/M/1$ queue that this mean would be $\rho_i/(1 - \rho_i)$. It is not difficult to show that the presence of internal traffic simply adds the term $E(k_i)$, $i = 1, 2, \ldots, N$ to this. We have then

$$
E(l_i) = E(k_i) + \rho_i/(1 - \rho_i), \qquad i = 1, 2, \ldots, N \qquad (11.16)
$$

Table 11.1. Calculation of $g(W, N)$

	0	1	i	n		N
0	1	1 $\cdots$	1 $\cdots$	1	$\cdots$	1
1	1					$g(1, N)$
2	1					$g(2, N)$
.				$g(w - 1, n)$		.
.				$\downarrow$		.
.			$g(w, n - 1) \rightarrow g(w, n)$			.
W	1					$g(W, N)$

11.4.2. Numerical Results—Window Flow Control

These results can be used to give insight to the window flow control technique. We focus on two measures of performance. As stated earlier, new internal messages are blocked when the phantom node is empty. The blocking probability is found from equation (11.14) as

$$P_B = P(k_0 = 0) = 1 - g(W - 1, N)/g(W, N) \qquad (11.17)$$

The second measure of performance that we use is the increase of the delay of external messages due to internal traffic. This can be written

$$L = \sum_{i=1}^{N} [(D_i - D_{i0})/D_{i0}] \bigg/ \sum_{i=1}^{N} \lambda_i$$

where D_i and D_{i0} are the average delays with and without internal traffic, respectively. From Little's formula and equation (11.16), this reduces to

$$L = \sum_{i=1}^{N} \lambda_i E(k_i) \bigg/ \sum_{i=1}^{N} \lambda_i \qquad (11.18)$$

where $E(k_i)$ is given by equation (11.15).

These results have been applied to the case of a chain consisting of three nodes.[10] It is assumed that service rates and the rate of external arrivals are the same for all three nodes, i.e., $\mu_1 = \mu$ and $\lambda_i = \lambda$, $i = 1, 2, \ldots, N$. The effect of the window size on the external traffic is shown in Figure 11.8, where L is shown as a function of λ_0/μ for a particular load and for several window sizes including no limitation whatever. We see a window does indeed reduce the interference. Of course, this is not without

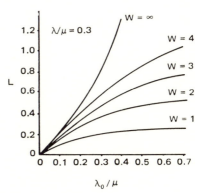

Figure 11.8. L as a function of load.[10]

cost since the window flow control induces blocking of the internal traffic. This is shown in Figure 11.9, where L is shown as a function of P_B with window size as a parameter for a particular load. The effect of changing load is shown in Table 11.2. The values of L and P_B are shown for two different loadings and window sizes. The results seem to show that the window flow control mechanism moderates the effect of the increasing load.

11.4.3. Mean Value Analysis of Closed Chains

Although it is not apparent from the foregoing, there are numerical problems associated with the convolutional approach. These difficulties may surface in the computation of large networks.† An alternative approach to the convolutional is the mean value analysis.[13,14] As its name implies, the mean value analysis yields means rather than distributions as does the convolutional approach. However, in many applications this is sufficient, particularly if computation is simpler.

The mean value approach is appropriate for any closed chain in which the product form solution obtains. In this section we simplify the presentation by assuming that messages are exponentially distributed and service is FCFS. The results also hold for the three service disciplines discussed above. Messages circulating in the same closed chain constitute the same class. The technique is based on a theorem which states that, within a closed chain, the distribution of the number of messages of its own class seen by a message arriving at a node is the steady-state distribution for the case of one less message in the chain, $W - 1$. In contrast for Poisson arrivals in an open network, the steady-state distribution and the distribution seen by arriving messages are the same. We first apply this result to a single chain

†For a discussion of the numerical problems encountered in connection with closed networks of queues, see Refs. 15 and 16.

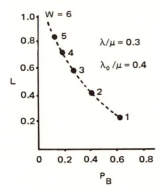

Figure 11.9. L as a function of blocking probability.[10]

Table 11.2. Variation of P_B and L

W	P_B $\lambda_0/\mu = 0.2$	L $\lambda_0/\mu = 0.3$	P_B $\lambda_0/\mu = 0.6$	L $\lambda_0/\mu = 0.3$
3	0.1	0.32	0.47	0.7
4	0.03	0.36	0.36	0.93

such as that shown on Figure 11.7. Assume for the moment that there is no external traffic. Again we assume that the number of circulating messages is W. Let m_i denote the service times of messages in node i, $i = 0, 1, 2, \ldots, N$. The delay of a message at a node is the sum of its own transmission time plus the transmission time of messages encountered upon arrival. Therefore from the theorem we just quoted, the mean delay of an internal message in node i is given by

$$d_i(W) = \bar{m}_i[1 + n_i(W - 1)], \qquad i = 0, 1, \ldots, N \qquad (11.19a)$$

where $n_i(W - 1)$ is the mean number of messages in queue i when there are $W - 1$ messages in circulation. From Little's formula we have

$$\lambda(W) = W \Big/ \sum_{i=0}^{N} d_i(W) \qquad (11.19b)$$

where $\sum_{i=0}^{N} d_i(W)$ is the total delay around the chain and $\lambda(W)$ is the throughput. We also have from Little's formula for each node

$$n_i(W) = \lambda(W)d_i(W), \qquad i = 0, 1, \ldots, N \qquad (11.19c)$$

From equations (11.19a)–(11.19c) a recursive solution can be found starting with the initial values:

$$n_i(0) = 0, \qquad i = 0, 1, \ldots, N \qquad (11.19d)$$

11.4.4. Application to Flow Control

As stated in the previous section, for the purpose of modeling flow control,[16] a network can be viewed as consisting of a number of closed chains, one for each source destination pair. Let us represent the number of such chains as R. If in an N-node network there is a single class of traffic between each pair of nodes, then $R = N(N - 1)$. Each chain may contain a different number of messages, which we denote as $W^r, r = 1, 2, \ldots, R$. Let $R(i)$, $i = 1, 2, \ldots, N$ denote the set of chains having queue i in common and let $Q(r)$, $r = 0, 1, \ldots, R$ denote the set of queues in chain R. Since we are confining ourselves to exponential FCFS service, we are constrained to the same service distribution for all chains. The average number of messages of each class in a node is a function of the total number of messages circulating in the network, in all R chains. We denote this average as

$$n_i^r(W^1, W^2, \ldots, W^R), \qquad i = 0, 1, \ldots, N, \qquad r = 1, 2, \ldots, R$$

From the basic theorem we have that the average number encountered at node i by a message in chain r is

$$n_i^r(W^1, W^2, \ldots, W^r - 1, \ldots, W^R), \qquad i = 0, 1, \ldots, N, \qquad r = 1, 2, \ldots, R$$

Again the delay experienced by a message at a node is its own transmission time plus the transmission times of the messages already there. These latter would include messages from other chains. The total delay may then be expressed as

$$d_i^r = m_i^r[1 + n_i^r(W^1, W^2, \ldots, W^r - 1, \ldots, W^R)], \qquad r = 1, 2, \ldots, R$$
$$(11.20a)$$

Again we have from Little's formula the two equations

$$\lambda(W^r) = W^r \Big/ \sum_{Q(r)} d_i^r, \qquad r = 1, 2, \ldots, R \qquad (11.20b)$$

and

$$n_i^r = \lambda(W^r)d_i^r, \qquad r = 1, 2, \ldots, R \qquad (11.20c)$$

For simplicity in equations (11.20b) and (11.20c) we have surpressed the dependencies on W^r, $r = 1, 2, \ldots, R$. As in the one-dimensional case, a recursive solution can be found. We begin with the initial values

$$n_i^r(0) = 0, \qquad i = 1, 2, \ldots, M^r, \qquad r = 1, 2, \ldots, R$$

11.5. Networks with Blocking

11.5.1. Network of Queues Model

In the preceding network models there is no provision for blocking within the network caused by a limitation on storage intrinsic to store-and-forward networks. In fact, such limitations may serve to control the flow of traffic into and within the network.

From an analytical point of view the difficulty with networks with blocking is that they do not allow the product form solution. An approximate model, in which a node is modeled as a network of queues, gives satisfactory results.[17,18]

The model for a node in a store-and-forward network is shown in Figure 11.10. Messages enter node i, $i = 1, 2, \ldots, N$ from a number of input lines. The messages are first treated by the node's central processor. The processor checks for errors and determines whether or not there is space for the message in the node. Depending on the outcome of these tests an ACK or a NACK is sent to the transmitting node. The processor then determines the destination of an accepted message and places it on the appropriate output channel buffer. Messages are then transmitted over the appropriate output line. We denote the set of lines out of node i as $O(i)$. One of these lines may be an exit from the network. At the receiving node the process is repeated. The transmission–retransmission process is modeled by the time-out and the ACK boxes shown in Figure 11.10. It is assumed that with probability $Q_{ij}, j = 1, 2, \ldots, O(i)$ the attempted transmission over output channel j fails either through blocking or through channel error. We model this event as having the message enter the time-out box where it resides for a random interval of time. The probability of successful transmission is modeled as having the message enter the ACK box for a random

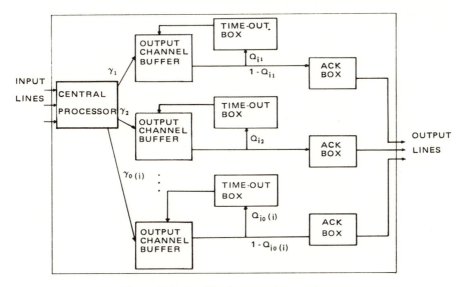

Figure 11.10. Model of store-and-forward node.

time interval. The residence times in both the time-out and the ACK boxes represent such quantities as propagation and processing times at the receiver.

We assume that messages arrive at a Poisson rate. However, an assumption that is new is that the arrival process depends upon the number of messages already in the node. This will allow us to model blocking within the network.

The messages are assumed to have exponential length. The central processor is modeled as having an exponentially distributed service time. This assumption may be difficult to justify, since even exponential length messages would require a constant processing time. However, the operating speed of the central processor is so much faster than any other processor that its service distribution has little effect on the operation of the node. At the output channel buffer the service time is the time required to transmit a message and is therefore exponentially distributed. We also invoke the independence assumption between the service times in the central processor and the output channel buffer.

Both the time-out and the ACK boxes are modeled as infinite server queues. The service times represent the duration of the protocol. It is assumed that the residence times are independent random variables. Each may have different distributions. In both cases it is assumed that the Laplace transforms of the probability densities of the residence times are rational functions. We assume that these residence times are independent of the service times in the central processor and the output channel buffer. These models for the time-out and the ACK boxes fit in with a selective reject policy where messages are held in the transmitter until a positive acknowledgment is received.

11.5.2. Product Form Solution

We shall now show that the foregoing assumptions allow us to represent the node as a Jackson network for which the product form solution holds. The full network has a total of $3N + 1$ queues. However, the basic principles can be demonstrated by means of a much simpler network. We consider only an isolated branch of the network beginning with a channel output buffer. As a further simplification, we exclude the ACK box for the moment.

We assume that the arrival of messages to the simple network is Poisson. Strictly speaking this is not true when there is a limitation on storage which would affect the central processor. However, as a practical matter, The central processor is so fast compared to the rest of the components as to be transparent. Its effect is to route incoming messages and to reject messages with errors. We assume that this routing is probabilistic.

The network that results from the foregoing simplifications is the open network consisting of the output channel buffer and the time-out box, shown in Figure 11.11. Recall that in Section 3.10 we showed that a service

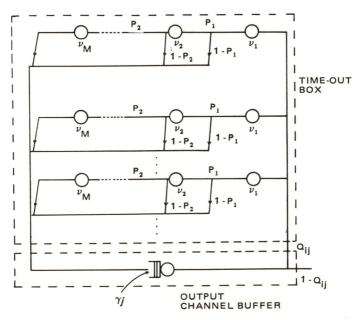

Figure 11.11. Portion of store-and-forward node.

distribution which has a rational Laplace transform can be represented by a multistage network. This representation is used in Figure 11.11 for each of the servers in the infinite server queue representing the time-out box. There are a total of M stages for each of the servers; the service time in each stage is exponentially distributed with mean value $1/\nu_i$. After each stage a message may depart the time-out box with probability P_i. The average service time in the output channel buffer is $1/\mu_j$ seconds. The arrival rate from the central processor is Poisson with average $\gamma_j, j = 1, 2, \ldots, O(i)$ messages per second. If the total number of messages in the two-node network is equal to some maximum value, newly arrived messages are not admitted into the network. We assume that messages that are not admitted are lost. After residence in the output channel buffer, messages are routed to the time-out box with probability Q_{ij}. The traffic equations giving the flow into portions of the network are easily found from observation. The flow into the output channel buffer is denoted as Ω_j and the flow into the ith stage of the time-out box is denoted as ω_j. We have

$$\Omega_j = \sum_{i=1}^{M-1} \omega_i(1 - P_i) + \omega_M + \gamma_i \qquad (11.21a)$$

$$\omega_1 = Q_{ij}\Omega_j \qquad (11.21b)$$

$$\omega_{i+1} = \omega_i P_i, \qquad i = 1, 2, \ldots, M - 1 \qquad (11.21c)$$

The state of the network in Figure 11.11 is the $(M + 1)$-dimensional vector $(n, k_1, k_2, \ldots, k_M)$, where n is the number of messages in the output channel buffer and k_i is the number of messages in the ith stage of the time-out box, $i = 1, 2, \ldots, M$. As in our previous study of networks of queues, we consider changes in an incremental interval. Because of the limited scope of the model, there are a limited number of events that can take place. A message can depart any stage of the time-out box and join the output channel buffer. Similarly, a message can depart the output channel buffer and join the time-out box or depart the system entirely. Finally, an external message may arrive to the output channel buffer. We may write the equilibrium equation as

$$
\left[\mu_i + \gamma_i(S) + \sum_{i=1}^{M} k_i \nu_i \right] P(n, k_1, k_2, \ldots, k_M)
$$

$$
= Q_{ij} \mu_j P(n + 1, k_1 - 1, \ldots, k_M) + \gamma_j(S) P(n - 1, k_1, k_2, \ldots, k_M)
$$

$$
+ \sum_{i=1}^{M-1} \nu_i [1 - P_i][k_i + 1] P(n - 1, k_1, \ldots, k_i + 1, \ldots, k_M)
$$

$$
+ \nu_M [k_M + 1] P(n - 1, k_1, \ldots, k_M + 1)
$$

$$
+ \sum_{i=1}^{M} \nu_i P_i [k_i + 1] P(n, k_1, \ldots, k_i + 1, k_{i+1} - 1, \ldots, k_M) \quad (11.2.2)
$$

Notice that k_i messages in the ith stage implies that the departure rate is $k_i \nu_i$. We understand, of course, that there can be no departures from an empty queue. In equation (11.22) the term $\gamma_i(S)$ indicates that arrivals depend upon the state of the system. As in the one-dimensional case, state-dependent arrivals are used to model finite storage. When the total number of messages is at a specified upper limit, then $\gamma_j(S) = 0$; otherwise the rate is γ_j messages/sec.

The local balance equations for this network are

$$
\mu_j P(n, k_1, k_2, \ldots, k_M) = \Omega_j P(n - 1, k_1, k_2, \ldots, k_M) \quad (11.23a)
$$

$$
k_i \nu_i P(n, k_1, k_2, \ldots, k_M) = \omega_i P(n, k_1, k_2, \ldots, k_i - 1, \ldots, k_M),
$$

$$
i = 1, 2, \ldots, M \quad (11.23b)
$$

The solution to equations (11.23a) and (11.23b) is

$$
P(n, k_1, \ldots, k_M) = P(0) \left(\frac{\Omega_j}{\mu_j} \right)^n \prod_{i=1}^{M} \rho_i^{k_i} / k_i! \quad (11.24)
$$

where $P(0)$ is a normalizing constant which ensures that the probabilities sum to 1 and where $\rho_i = \omega_i/\nu_i$, $i = 1, 2, \ldots, M$. We shall consider the calculation of $P(0)$ in due course. That equation (11.24) is a solution to the equilibrium equation (11.22) can be shown by substitution into (11.22) and application of the traffic equations (11.21a)–(11.21c). This is the same procedure as in Chapter 10.

Our interest is not so much the number of messages in individual stages as the total number in the time-out box. The form of the distribution allows a simple answer. Consider, for example, the joint distribution when there are only two stages in the time-out box:

$$P(n, k_1, k_2) = P(0) \left(\frac{\Omega_j}{\mu_j}\right)^n \frac{\rho_1^{k_1} \rho_2^{k_2}}{k_1! \, k_2!} \tag{11.25a}$$

Summing over k_1 and k_2 such that $k_1 + k_2 = K$, we find that

$$P(n, k_1 + k_2 = K) = P(0) \left(\frac{\Omega_j}{\mu_j}\right)^n \sum_{k=0}^{K} \frac{\rho_1^k}{k!} \frac{\rho_2^{K-k}}{(K-k)!}$$
$$= P(0) \left(\frac{\Omega_j}{\mu_j}\right)^n (\rho_1 + \rho_2)^K / K! \tag{11.25b}$$

Now let $K = \sum_{i=1}^{M} k_i$. By induction it can be shown that the joint distribution of n and K is given by

$$P\left(n, \sum_{i=1}^{M} k_i = K\right) = P(0) \left(\frac{\Omega_j}{\mu_j}\right)^n \rho_T^K / K! \tag{11.26}$$

where $\rho_T = \sum_{i=1}^{M} \rho_i$. Consider now the term ρ_T in equation (11.26). From equations (11.21a)–(11.21c) we have

$$\rho_T = \sum_{i=1}^{M} \omega_i/\nu_i = \omega_1 \sum_{i=1}^{M} \left(\prod_{j=1}^{i-1} P_j\right) \bigg/ \nu_i = \omega_1 \bar{m}_T \tag{11.27}$$

Notice that ω_1 is the input rate to the time-out box and $\bar{m}_T$ is the mean processing time of a message in the time-out box. Thus equation (11.27) shows that the distribution of the total number in the time-out box is a function only of the mean and not of the distribution of the processing time.

The message arrival rates in equations (11.26) and (11.27) can be expressed in terms of the input rate. From equations (11.21a)–(11.21c) we have

$$\Omega_j = \gamma_j/(1 - Q_{ij}) \tag{11.28a}$$

and

$$\omega_1 = \gamma_j Q_{ij}/(1 - Q_{ij}) \qquad (11.28b)$$

The form of the results obtained so far allows us to derive the probability distribution of message occupancy for the whole node.

We begin with a single branch. By going through the same steps as above, we can show that the joint probability of n messages in the output channel buffer and K messages in the time-out and ACK boxes of the jth branch of the node is

$$P(n, K) = P(0)\left(\frac{\Omega_j}{\mu_j}\right)^n [\bar{m}_T \gamma_j Q_{ij}/(1 - Q_{ij}) + \bar{m}_A \gamma_j]^K / K! \qquad (11.29)$$

where $\bar{m}_A$ is the average time spent in the ACK box and γ_j is the flow in messages per second through the ACK box. The application of a convolution such as that in equation (11.25b) provides this result. In the sequel we shall find it convenient to use the definition $R_j = \bar{m}_T \gamma_j Q_{ij}/(1 - Q_{ij}) + m_A \gamma_j, j = 1, 2, \ldots, O(i)$.

Up to this point we have found the probability distribution for the number of messages in a single branch of the node. However, we are interested in the probability distribution of the total number of messages in the whole node. In order to find this, we consider the flows within the node. We represent the total arrival rate to the node in messages per second as Γ_i. The probability that messages are routed by the central processor to the jth output line is P_{ij}. Also some of these messages are discarded because of the detection of a channel error. We assume that this event occurs with probability E_i. The flow in the jth branch is then

$$\gamma_j = \Gamma_i P_{ij}(1 - E_i) \qquad (11.30)$$

We bear in mind that the arrival rate depends upon the number of messages in the node in that there can be no arrival when there are already a maximum number of messages present. The joint distribution of the number of messages in each of the other branches may be found. The total number of messages in all of the time-out and the ACK boxes is simply the same convolution operation that is done in equation (11.25b). For the central processor and the output channel buffers, the product form obtains. The result is by now familiar. The probability of $n_j, j = 1, 2, \ldots, O(i)$ messages in the output channel buffers, n_0 messages in the central processor, and K messages in the time-out and the ACK boxes is then

$$P(n_0, n_1, \ldots, n_{O(i)}, K) = P(0)\left(\frac{\Gamma_i}{\mu_0}\right)^{n_0} \prod_{j=1}^{O(i)} \left(\frac{\Omega_j}{\mu_j}\right)^{n_j} R_T^K / K! \qquad (11.31)$$

where $1/\mu_0$ is the mean service time in the central processor and $R_T = \sum_{j=1}^{O(i)} R_j$.

The pertinent restriction on storage is for the whole node. Accordingly, we calculate the probability of there being a total of M_j messages in the entire node. A difficulty with this computation arises in connection with the number of messages in the central processor and the output channel buffers. In contrast to the time-out and the ACK boxes, there is no simple expression for the probability distribution for the total number when a constraint is involved. The problem is the same as that encountered in closed networks of queues: there are too many possible combinations. The approach to this problem is a variation of the   convolution algorithm presented in Section 11.4.1.

We begin with a definition of the term $f(n)$, which has an obvious connection with the probability of n messages in the central processor and the output channel buffers:

$$f(n) = \begin{cases} 1, & n = 0 \\ \sum_{T(n)} \prod_{j=0}^{O(i)} \left(\frac{\Omega_j}{\mu_j}\right)^{n_j}, & n \neq 0 \end{cases} \tag{11.32}$$

where $T(n)$ is the set of $n_0, n_1, \ldots, n_{O(i)}$, such that $\sum_{j=0}^{O(i)} n_j = n$. $f(n)$ is evaluated by the techniques of Section 11.4.1. A table similar to Table 11.1 can be found for $f(n)$. A second term, $p(N, k)$, is based on a convolutional operation:

$$p(N, x) = \begin{cases} 1, & N = 0 \\ \sum_{n=0}^{N} f(n)x^{N-n}/(N - n)!, & N > 0 \end{cases} \tag{11.33}$$

By comparison with equation (11.31) we have for the probability of K messages in node i

$$P(K) = P(0)p(K, R_T) \tag{11.34}$$

Since there can be no more than M_i messages in the node, the probabilities $P(0), P(1), \ldots, P(M_i)$ must sum to one, allowing us to calculate $P(0)$. We have

$$P(0) = 1 \bigg/ \sum_{K=1}^{M_i} p(K, R_T) \tag{11.35}$$

The probability of blocking is given by

$$B_i = P(M_i) \tag{11.36}$$

where M_i is the maximum number of messages allowed in node i.

11.5.3. The Blocking Network

Having found the probability of blocking for a node for a given amount of traffic into the node, we consider the entire network in this section.[18] As in Chapter 10, we may write for the flow of information within the network the traffic equation

$$\Lambda_i = \lambda_i + \sum_{j=1}^{N} P_{ji} \Lambda_j \tag{11.37}$$

where λ_i is newly generated message traffic at node i. We emphasize that this is the actual flow of information and does not take into account retransmission due to error and blocking. The probability that a message suffers a detectable error on the channel between nodes i and j is denoted as E_{ij}. A transmission may fail because of channel error or because of blocking in the receiving node. The probability of this event is given by

$$Q_{ij} = 1 - (1 - E_{ij})(1 - B_j) \tag{11.38}$$

where B_j is the probability of blocking in the receiving node. We assume that successive transmissions are independent, and, as a result, the total number of transmissions is geometrically distributed. In terms of total flow, including retransmissions, input to node i can be written

$$\Gamma_i = \lambda_i/(1 - B_i) + \sum_{j=1}^{N} \Lambda_j P_{ji}/(1 - Q_{ji}) \tag{11.39}$$

From equation (11.36) and its antecedents and from equation (11.39), we have a set of nonlinear, implicit equations which we represent as

$$B_i = F(B_1, B_2, \ldots, B_{O(i)}), \qquad i = 1, 2, \ldots, N \tag{11.40}$$

For convenience, in writing equation (11.40) we have suppressed all dependence on arrival and service rates. The set of nonlinear equations represented by (11.40) can be solved by means of a variation of the Newton–Raphson method. (For details of this calculation see Ref. 18.) From these quantities one could calculate such quantities as the average number of messages in the central processor, the output channel buffers, and the time-out boxes. From Little's formula the average delay can be found. Note that residence in the ACK box signifies completed transmission and does not contribute to delay.

11.5.4. Buffer Allocation

A problem analogous to the capacity allocation problem considered in the previous chapter is that of buffer allocation. A form of this problem is to allocate capacities to the various nodes of the network so as to minimize the total storage required subject to the constraint that the blocking probability be less than some value, ε, for each of the nodes in the network. Succinctly stated this is

$$\min M_i \qquad \text{for } B_i \leq \varepsilon$$

The following buffer assignment algorithm has been shown to yield results that are near optimum under several different criteria:

1. Initiate by setting $B_i = \varepsilon$ and $M_i = 1$ for $i = 1, 2, \ldots, N$.
2. Calculate traffic flows Γ_i and Ω_i from equations (11.28), (11.30), and (11.39).
3. Calculate $B_i, i = 1, 2, \ldots, N$ from equations (11.21a)–(11.21c), (11.28), (11.30), and (11.31).
4. If $B \leq \varepsilon$ then fix the value of J_i. Otherwise set $J_i = J_i + 1$ and go to step 2.
5. The algorithm terminates when $B_i \leq \varepsilon$ for all $i = 1, 2, \ldots, N$.

These results have been applied to the 19-node network shown in Figure 11.1. The nodes of this network are connected by full duplex lines of various speeds. The routing is fixed with flow apportioned to balance traffic within the network. The sort of results that are attainable are shown in Figure 11.12, where the maximum blocking over all of the nodes of the network is shown as a function of the average number of messages that can be stored in each node with the normalized load as a parameter. Two storage assignment techniques are considered, equal capacity in all of the nodes and the assignment obtained in the algorithm presented above.

11.5.5. Flow Control by Input Buffer Limitation

The results of the previous section can be applied to a flow control technique which limits the buffering available to newly arrived traffic in favor of traffic already in the network.[19] Accordingly, we split the traffic into two classes, transit and new. The model of the node is that analyzed

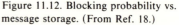

MAXIMUM NODAL BLOCKING PROBABILITY

— EQUAL ASSIGNMENT
··· BGR ALGORITHM
$\alpha = 0.9$

10^{-2}
10^{-3}
10^{-4}
10^{-5}
10^{-6}
10^{-7}

0.3   0.5   0.7

0   20   40   60

AVERAGE NUMBER OF
BUFFERS PER NODE, N

Figure 11.12. Blocking probability vs.
message storage. (From Ref. 18.)

in the previous section. We define the same sort of quantities as in the previous section with the superscripts T and N to indicate transit and new, respectively. The transit and the new arrival rates to node i are Γ_i^T and Γ_i^N, respectively. Recognizing that routing and error rate can differ for the two classes, we have for the flows in each of the branches

$$\gamma_j^T = (1 - E_j^T) P_{ij} \Gamma_j^T \tag{11.41a}$$

$$\gamma_j^N = (1 - E_j^N) P_{ij} \Gamma_j^N, \qquad j = 1, 2, \ldots, O(i) \tag{11.41b}$$

The service rates in the central processor and the output channel buffers are μ_0^T and μ_0^N and γ_j^T and γ_j^N, $j = 1, 2, \ldots O(i)$, respectively. The mean residence times in the time-out and the ACK boxes are $\bar{m}_T^T$ and $\bar{m}_T^N$ and m_A^T and m_A^N, respectively. Let n_0^T and n_0^N denote the numbers of messages of both classes in the central processor. The numbers of messages of both types in the output channel buffer branch j are n_j^T and n_j^N, $j = 1, 2, \ldots, O(i)$. Finally the number of messages in all of the time-out and the ACK boxes are K^T and K^N. Using the same techniques as in Sections 11.3.2 and 11.5.2, it can be shown that the joint distribution of the quantities is

$$P(n_0^T, n_1^T, \ldots, n_{O(i)}^T; n_0^N, n_1^N, \ldots, n_{O(i)}^N; K^T; K^N)$$

$$= P(0) \left(\frac{\Gamma_i^T}{\mu_0^T} \right)^{n_0^T} \left(\frac{\Gamma_i^N}{\mu_0^N} \right)^{n_0^N} (n_0^T + n_0^N)! / (n_0^T! n_0^N!)$$

$$\times \prod_{j=0}^{O(i)} (\Omega_j^T / \mu_j^T)^{n_j^T} (\Omega_j^N / \mu_j^N)^{n_j^N} \{ (n_j^T + n_j^N)! / (n_j^T! n_j^N!)$$

$$\times [(R^T)^{K^T} / K^T!][(R^N)^{K^T} / K^N!] \} \tag{11.42}$$

where

$$R^T = \sum_{j=1}^{O(i)} \gamma_j^T \bar{m}_T^T Q_{ij}^T / (1 - Q_{ij}^T) + \bar{m}_A^T \gamma_i^T$$

and

$$R^N = \sum_{j=1}^{O(i)} \gamma_j^N \bar{m}_T^N Q_{ij}^N / (1 - Q_{ij}^N) + \bar{m}_A^N \gamma_j^N$$

See equations (11.5), (11.26), and (11.31). The term $P(0)$ is a constant such that the probabilities sum to one.

As in previous sections, our interest is in the total number of messages of either type that are present in any part of the node. In particular, we are interested in the joint distribution of the new and the transit messages, which we write $P(K^T, K^N)$. This quantity can be found by means of the convolutional technique presented earlier. The basic principles are the same. The only real difference is that there is a restriction on two random variables.

We assume the total number of messages of either type that can be accommodated by the node is J and the maximum number of new messages is J^N. We assume that the transient message may take up all of the storage, while the entry of new messages is restricted. This restriction controls the flow of new messages entering the system. Transit messages are blocked when the storage space is filled, i.e., $K^T + K^N = J$. The probability of this event is

$$B^T = \sum_{k=0}^{J} P(k, J - k) \tag{11.43}$$

Notice that $P(k, j) = 0$ for $j > J^N$. New messages are blocked when the node contains the maximum allowable number of new messages. This event occurs with probability

$$B^N = B^T + \sum_{k=0}^{J - J^N} P(k, J^N) \tag{11.44}$$

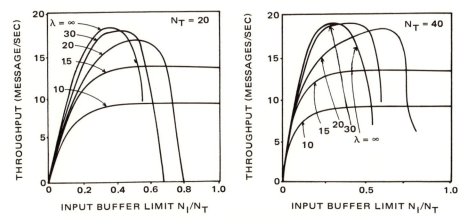

Figures 11.13. Throughput vs. input buffer limit. (From Ref. 19.)

The results have been applied to what is termed a uniform network. In this case it is assumed that all nodes have the same blocking probability for transit messages. This is a somewhat pessimistic assumption since congestion may be spread uniformly throughout the network. The parameters of this network are as follows:

- Three output branches
- Average time in central processor: 0.002 sec
- Average message length: 100 bits
- Line speed: 9600 bps
- Average time-out delay: 0.6 sec
- Average acknowledgment delay: 0.12 sec
- Routing probabilities

$$P_{i1}^T = 0.4(1 - P_{i4}^T) \qquad\qquad P_{ij}^N = 0.3(1 - P_{i4}^N), \qquad j = 2, 3$$

$$P_{i1}^N = 0.4(1 - P_{i4}^N) \qquad\qquad P_{i4}^T = 0.25$$

$$P_{ij}^T = 0.3(1 - P_{i4}^T), \qquad j = 2, 3 \qquad P_{i4}^N = 0.6$$

The assumption of a uniform network allows one to calculate a nonlinear equation for the blocking probabilities. Results for this example are shown in Figures 11.13a and 11.13b, where the throughput, defined to be $(1 - B^N)$, is shown as a function of the ratio J^N/J^T with Γ^N as a parameter. As we see there are broad optimum values of the ratio.

References

1. M. Gerla and L. Kleinrock, "Flow Control Protcols, *Computer Network Architectures and Protocols*, P. E. Green, Jr., editor, Plenum Press, New York (1982); also Special Issue *IEEE Transactions on Communications*, April (1980).
2. M. Reiser, "Performance Evaluation of Data Communication Systems," *Proceedings of IEEE*, **70**(2), 171–196, February (1982).
3. A. S. Tannenbaum, *Computer Networks*, Prentice-Hall, Englewood Cliffs, New Jersey (1981), pp. 167–177.
4. D. E. Carlson, "Bit-Oriented Data Link Control," *Computer Network Architectures and Protocols*, P. E. Green, Jr. editor, Plenum Press, New York (1982).
5. M. Easton, "Batch Throughout Efficiency of ADCCP/HDLC/SDLC Selective Reject Protocols," *IEEE Transaction Communications*, **COM-28**(2), 187–195, February (1980).
6. J. Labetoulle and G. Pujolle, "HDLC Throughput and Response Time for Bidirectional Data Flow with Nonuniform Frame Sizes," *IEEE Transactions on Communications*, **COM-30**(6), 405–413, June (1981).
7. W. Bux, K. Kummerle, and H. L. Tuong, "Balanced HDLC Procedures: A Performance Analysis," *IEEE Transactions on Communications*, **COM-28**(11), 1889–1898, November (1980).

8. A. J. LeMoyne, "Networks of Queues—A Survey of Equilibrium Analysis," *Management Science*, **24**(4), 464–481, December (1977).

9. F. Baskett, K. M. Chandy, R. R. Muntz, and F. G. Palacios, "Open, Closed, and Mixed Networks of Queues with Different Classes of Customers," *Journal of the ACM*, **22**(2), 248–260, April (1975).

10. M. C. Pennotti and M. Schwartz, "Congestion Control in Store-and-Forward Tandem Links," *IEEE Transactions on Communications*, **COM-23**(12), 1434–1443, December (1975).

11. J. P. Buzen, "Computational Algorithms for Closed Networks with Exponential Servers," *Communications of the ACM*, **16**, 527–531, September (1973).

12. M. Reiser and H. Kobayashi, "Numerical Solution of Semiclosed Exponential Server Queueing Networks," *Proceedings of the 7th Asilomar Conference on Circuits Systems and Computers*, November (1973), pp. 308–312.

13. M. Reiser and S. S. Lavenberg, "Mean Value Analysis of Closed Multichain Queueing Networks," *Journal of the ACM*, **22**, 313–322, April (1980).

14. M. Reiser, "A Queueing Network Analysis of Computer Communications Networks with Window Flow Control," *IEEE Transactions on Communications*, **COM-27**(8), 1199–1209, August (1979).

15. K. M. Chandy and C. H. Sauer, "Computational Algorithms for Product Form Queueing Networks," *Communications of the ACM*, **23**(10), 573–583, October (1980).

16. M. Reiser, "Mean Value Analysis and Convolution Method for Queue Dependent Servers in Closed Queueing Networks," *Performance Evaluation*, **1**(1), 7–18, January (1981).

17. P. J. Schweitzer and S. S. Lam, "Buffer Overflow in a Store-and-Forward Node," *IBM Journal of Research and Development*, **20**, 542–550 (1976).

18. S. S. Lam, "Store-and-Forward Requirements in a Packet Switching Network," *IEEE Transactions on Communications*, **COM-24**(4), 394–403, April (1977).

19. S. S. Lam and M. Reiser, "Congestion Control of Store-and-Forward Networks with Input Buffer Limits: An Analysis," *IEEE Transactions on Communications*, **COM-27**(1), 127–134, January (1979).

Exercises

11.1. Consider a network consisting of three nodes among which five messages circulate. The network forms a closed ring such as the network of Figure 11.7. Assume that there is no external traffic. Assume also that the departure rate from queue 0 is 1 message/sec and the departure rate from the two other queues is 2 messages/sec.

(a) What is the probability distribution of the number of messages in queue 0?

(b) What is the mean number of messages in this queue?

11.2. For the network in Exercise 11.1, repeat part (b) using the mean value analysis discussed in Section 11.4.3.

11.3. Although general closed networks of queues were not considered in the text, the results apply in a straightforward way. Consider the four-node network shown in Figure 11.14. Messages are routed probabilistically as shown. For simplicity assume that the service time of messages in queue i is $i \times 10^{-3}$ sec. Assume also that there are only three messages circulating in the network.

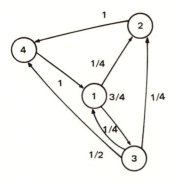

Figure 11.14. Network with probabilistic routing.

(a) What is the probability distribution of the number of message in queue 1?
(b) What is the mean number of messages in this queue?
(*Hint*: The first step is to calculate the proportions among the quantities γ_i, $i = 1, 2, 3, 4$.)

11.4. For the network in Exercise 11.3, repeat part (b) using the mean value analysis discussed in Section 11.4.3.

11.5. Consider the network of Figure 11.7 with external traffic when each of the nodes contains more than one exponential server with an FCFS discipline.
(a) What is the state space for this network?
(b) Show that the product form solution holds for this network.

11.6. Repeat Exercise 11.5 for the case where each node contains an infinite number of servers. Assume that the Laplace transform of each service density is a rational function.

11.7. Suppose that exponentially distributed messages having a mean value of 1000 bits arrive to a message switching node at a Poisson rate with average 75 messages/sec. There are two 9600-bps lines out of the node which share the load equally. Suppose that the central processor requires 0.1 msec to handle a message. Suppose also the time-out and the acknowledgment time are 30 and 20 msec, respectively. Finally, the probability of a message being successfully transmitted is 0.9.
(a) Write down an expression for the numbers of messages in each part of the node. (See Figure 11.10.)
(b) Find the distribution of the total number of messages in the node.
(c) Find the average number of messages in the node.

Routing–Flow Allocation

12.1. Introduction

As stated in the previous chapter, the two techniques that are used to control congestion within a network are flow control and routing. Having considered flow control we now turn to routing. The goal of routing is to spread the flow throughout the network so as to avoid congestion. Since we are interested in the minimization of congestion, flow control in conjunction with routing must also be considered. As we shall see presently there are models in which routing and flow control can be considered in the same theoretical framework.

Routing strategies must respond to changes in the topology of the network or to the traffic arriving at the network. Topological changes may be due to the failures of links or nodes or the addition of new links to the network. Topological changes also occur frequently in certain mobile radio systems. In commercial systems spanning several time zones, there will be variations in traffic patterns as the business day progresses. In systems with a limited number of sources, significant changes in traffic may occur as large users come on and go off.

There are a number of ways to categorize routing techniques: virtual circuit versus datagram implementation, static versus dynamic response to changing conditions, and centralized versus distributed control.† The virtual circuit implementation refers to the establishment of what is called a logical circuit between a source destination pair each time there is a data call. A packet that is part of a call is so identified in its address field. If a node knows the call number of a packet, tables within the node give the next node on the itinerary. The logical channel or virtual circuit is analogous to the physical circuit in the traditional voice network. In most practical

---

†Surveys of routing are contained in Refs. 1, 2, and 3. We have found the first two particularly helpful in preparing this chapter.

networks there is more than one route from the origin to the destination node. In establishing a virtual circuit the alternative paths must be compared. The path chosen for a call remains the same for its duration. In the datagram implementation the address field of a packet gives only the destination node of the packet. All packets with the same destination are treated the same by a node without respect to origin or call establishment. If there are alternate paths to the destination, successive packets from the same source may go by different routes.

The basic advantage of the virtual circuit implementation is that control of flow is much more under the control of the originating node. There is no possibility of packets being delivered out of sequence, for example. The drawback to the virtual circuit implementation as compared to datagram is that datagram can respond more rapidly to changing conditions. If, for example, there is a change in the nature of the traffic entering the system, routing assignments can be changed at each of the nodes of the network. It is not necessary to wait until the establishment of a new call in order to change routes.

The routing algorithms that we shall consider operate in what has been called a quasistatic environment, i.e., no sudden changes and no prolonged excursions from the mean values. In a quasistatic environment the relatively slow variations in traffic allow the routing algorithm to adapt so that near optimum performance is attainable for most of the time. We shall call the routing techniques that we consider quasi-static. Contrasting routing strategies are the so-called "dynamic" strategies, which respond to instantaneous system states. In Chapter 2 the call routing technique for the voice network is dynamic since it responds to trunks being busy. For data networks the corresponding dynamic technique puts messages on line having the least filled output buffers. At this writing dynamic routing procedures are not well understood. The potential danger of dynamic routing strategies is instability.[3] Most studies have been carried out by means of simulation rather than analysis. The results of these studies are that dynamic routing is beneficial only over a narrow range of moderate loading.[4] The difficulty with simulation studies is that their scope is limited. An approach to the analytical difficulties presented by dynamic routing is the diffusion approximation.[30,31] In the case of greatest interest, heavy loading, the network queues are described by a diffusion equation. This approximation allows the calculation of queue dynamics when messages are routed to the outgoing link with the shortest queue. More detailed treatment of this approach is beyond our scope

As we shall see, routing strategies are determined by calculations which are based on link characteristics such as traffic volume, delay, and generalized distance. In centralized control the link parameters are passed through a central point where all the necessary computations take place. The problem with centralized control is that channel capacity, which may be used to alleviate congestion in heavily loaded systems, is used up by overhead transmission. In addition to having high overhead, the delay through a large network may be so high that control information is obsolete before it is used. The alternative to centralized control is distributed control, in which routing strategies at nodes are based solely on information at adjacent nodes and links. Distributed control reduces overhead and can respond rapidly to local variations. The problem with distributed control is that local optimization may be suboptimum from a global point of view. Also, as we shall see, in distributed systems frequently more total computations are necessary than centralized systems. The tradeoff between centralized versus distributed control systems really lies in the relative values of communications costs versus computational costs.

12.2. Routing Model

In a theoretical consideration of routing in a packet switched network the important characteristics of the network are embodied in the topology, the traffic matrix, the link capacities, and propagation delays. We shall assume that the network has N nodes and L links. It is convenient to characterize the topology by the sets of links that impinge upon a node. Let $I(i)$ and $O(i)$, $i = 1, 2, \ldots N$, denote, respectively, the sets of links leading into and out of node i. In Figure 12.1, for example, $I(2) = \{2, 3, 5\}$ and $O(2) = \{4, 6, 8\}$. The element γ_{ij} of the traffic matrix $\Gamma = \{\gamma_{ij}\}$ is the average flow originating at node i destined for node j in data units per second. For reasons we shall make clear shortly, a widely used measure of performance in packet switched networks is average packet delay. Recall from equation (10.35) that the expression for average delay depends upon the link capacities $C_1, C_2, \ldots, C_L$ and the link propagation delays $P_1, P_2, \ldots, P_L$.

There are two equivalent ways that a routing strategy may be characterized, link oriented and path oriented. Superficially they are analogous to

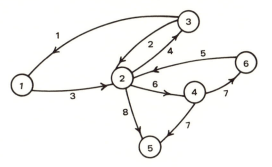

Figure 12.1. Six-node network.

the datagram–virtual circuit implementation discussed in the foregoing. In the link oriented characterization, each node maintains a table indicating the outgoing links for each destination node. There may be alternate routes, in which case the node keeps track of $\phi_{jl}(i)$, the proportion of traffic at node i destined for node j which is to be routed over link l. Clearly, $\sum_{l \in 0(j)} \phi_{jl}(i) = 1$. The alternative characterization of routing is with respect to paths. Between each origin–destination pair within the network there are $\Pi(i,j)$ paths some of which may have links in common. We denote by $\Theta_k(i,j)$ the proportion of traffic between nodes i and j which is routed over path k. Again the proportions must add up to one: $\sum_{k=1}^{\Pi(i,j)} \Theta_k(i,j) = 1$. The resemblance between datagram and the virtual circuit implementation here is only superficial since it is possible to express a path routing in terms of a link-by-link routing and vice versa.

As we said earlier, the average delay is used most often as the measure of performance in routing strategies. As we saw in our study of networks of queues in Chapter 10 under certain specific assumptions the average delay of a message can be written

$$\bar{T}(\mathbf{I}) = \frac{1}{\alpha} \sum_{l=1}^{L} T_l(I_l) = \frac{1}{\alpha} \sum_{l=1}^{L} \left(\frac{I_l}{C_l - I_l} + I_l d_l \right) \tag{12.1}$$

In deriving (12.1) from equation (10.35) we find it convenient to make the substitution $\Lambda_l P_l = \Lambda_l \bar{m}(P_l / \bar{m}) = I_l d_l$.

From the point of view of application to packet-switched networks the most troublesome assumption is that packet lengths are exponentially distributed. Packets are of constant lengths or are of a limited number of lengths. However, it has been found empirically that even though the measure given in equation (12.1) may not be the true average delay, its minimization leads to good network performance in a global sense.† This is not surprising in view of the general characteristics of the equation. At light loading, $C_l \gg I_l$, the cost in terms of delay increases with the load in a linear fashion. As the loading increases the cost escalates rapidly until at saturation, $I_l = C_l$, it is infinite. If there is a point of high congestion on a single link in the network the cost can be very large. From a purely mathematical point of view the function given in equation (12.1) has the desirable properties of being separable‡ and convex.§ As we have seen in

†This property of queueing models has been observed in other contexts as well.[5]
‡A function is separable if it is the sum of functions each of which depends on single independent variables, i.e., of the form $\sum f_i(x_i)$.
§A function is convex if in any interval $x_1 \leqslant x \leqslant x_2$

$$f(x) \leqslant \frac{(x - x_1)f(x_2) - (x_2 - x)f(x_1)}{x_2 - x_1}$$

(see Figure 12.8 for an illustration of convexity).

Chapter 10 in connection with capacity assignment problems, there are other tractable measures of performance, but equation (12.1) is simpler and yields similar global performance.

A packet switched network is part of the class of multicommodity flow networks with a commodity being identified with each origin–destination pair.[6,7] In the multicommodity flow problems, the usual objective function to be maximized is the total throughput $\sum_{i=1}^{N} \sum_{j=1}^{N} \gamma_{ij}$. There is no penalty for congestion when flow is close to capacity. Although the optimization techniques we shall consider in the sequel can handle this objective function, it is not appropriate for packet-switched networks.

In equation (12.1) the delay is expressed in terms of link flows. The delay can just as well be expressed in terms of path flows.[8] Recall that the total flow between nodes i and j is γ_{ij} data units per second and the total number of paths are $\Pi(i, j)$. We define

$$\delta(k, l) = \begin{cases} 1 & \text{if path } k \text{ contains link } l \\ 0 & \text{otherwise} \end{cases}$$

Link flows can be written in terms of path flows

$$\begin{aligned}
I_l &= \sum_{i=1}^{N} \sum_{j=1}^{N} \gamma_{ij} \sum_{k=1}^{\Pi(i,j)} \Theta_k(i, j)\delta(k, l) \\
&= \sum_{i=1}^{N} \sum_{j=1}^{N} \sum_{k=1}^{\Pi(i,j)} J_k(i, j)\delta(k, l), \qquad l = 1, 2, \ldots, L
\end{aligned} \tag{12.2}$$

between nodes i and j, where $J_k(i, j)$ is the flow in data units per second between nodes i and j which is routed over the kth path.

Equation (12.2) may be substituted into equation (12.1) to express average delay in terms of the path flows $J_k(i, j)$. We express this as

$$\bar{T} = \sum_{l=1}^{L} \bar{T}_l \left(\sum_{i=1}^{N} \sum_{j=1}^{N} \sum_{k=1}^{\Pi(i,j)} J_k(i, j)\delta_{kl} \right) \tag{12.3}$$

where $\bar{T}_l(I_l)$ is the average delay on link l.

12.3. Shortest-Path Algorithms

Many theoretical and practical routing algorithms can be solved by means of shortest-path algorithms. In this case we assume that queueing delay is negligible; $C_1, C_2, \ldots, C_L$ in equation (12.1) are assumed to be unbounded. We may write [see equation (12.1)]

$$\bar{T} = \frac{1}{\alpha} \sum_{l=1}^{L} I_l d_l \qquad (12.4)$$

$\bar{T}$ is minimized, by choosing paths for each commodity so that the sum of the propagation delays over the paths are minimized. This may be seen simply by decomposing the path delays in equation (12.4) into the sum of link delays. Since there is no constraint on link capacity we may consider each path independently. If there is more than one path, each with the same delay, the flow should be divided equally among the paths.

The performance measure expressed in equation (12.4) may be applied more broadly: d_l, $l = 1, 2, \ldots, L$ may be construed as a generalized distance or cost for using the link; the routing should be such that the total cost is minimized. For example, the cost per unit of bandwidth may be a function of length of the line. The cost may also be related to reliability. Suppose, for example, F_l is the probability of link l failing. An appropriate measure might be obtained by assigning to each link the weight $d_l = -\log(1 - F_l)$. If all of the links have the same weight, the solution to the shortest-path problem is to choose paths traversing the smallest number of links. In the sequel we shall assume that whatever the weights represent they are non-negative.

12.3.1. Centralized Shortest-Path Algorithm

The first algorithm we consider finds the minimum distance between a particular node and all other nodes in the network.[9,10] In a practical application the given node may be a central computer with which terminals at the other nodes interact. When these paths have been found we shall have a tree spanning all the nodes which is routed at the central node. Moreover, since these paths are minimum weight the tree is what is called a minimum spanning tree. Clearly there is a connection here with the topological design of networks which will be considered in Chapter 13.

In the algorithm that we consider, we grow an intermediate network step by step from the central node by adding nodes that are adjacent to the network and minimum distance to the central node. At each step we update the contents of the intermediate network and the distances from each node to the central node. Let $I = \{\cdot\}$ indicate the contents of the intermediate network; let d_{ij} be the distance of the link between nodes i and j, and let $D(j)$ be the total distance from node j to the central node through nodes inside the intermediate network. We designate node 1 as the central node and T as the total network of N nodes. The steps of the algorithm are as follows:

1. Initialize by setting $I = \{1\}$ and

$$D(i) = \begin{cases} d_{i1}, & \text{if node } i \text{ is adjacent to node } 1 \\ \infty, & \text{otherwise} \end{cases}$$

2. Among the nodes outside the intermediate network, choose the one with the smallest value of $D(\cdot)$.
3. Append the node found in step 2 to the network I.
4. For nodes adjacent to that found in step 2 recompute the values of $D(i)$. Record the new paths.
5. If all nodes are in the intermediate network the algorithm is complete; otherwise go to step 2.

This shortest-path algorithm is illustrated by the network shown in Figure 12.2. The lengths of the links are as indicated and all links are assumed to be two-way. The steps of the optimization algorithm are shown in Figures 12.3a–12.3e by showing the growth of the intermediate networks.

It is not difficult to show that this algorithm converges and does indeed give shortest paths. We add a node to the intermediate network at each step and there is no iteration on nodes already in the network. From the principle of optimality† an optimum path is composed of optimum subpaths. The algorithm is simply a construction of optimum subpaths.

12.3.2. A Distributed Shortest Path Algorithm

A drawback to the algorithm presented above is that it calls for central processing since distances of the nodes to the intermediate network must be gathered together and compared. There is a distributed algorithm that accomplishes the same task.[10] In this distributed algorithm information need only be exchanged between adjacent nodes. At each step of the algorithm each node updates and stores two numbers: the minimum distance to the central node and the preferred node which is an adjacent node on the optimum path to the central node. Let $A(i)$, $i = 1, 2, \ldots, N$ be the set of nodes adjacent to node i. As is the previous algorithm $D(i)$, $i = 1, 2, \ldots,$

†See Chapter 10, Section 10.6.2.

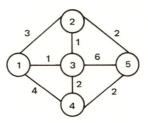

Figure 12.2. Six-node network.

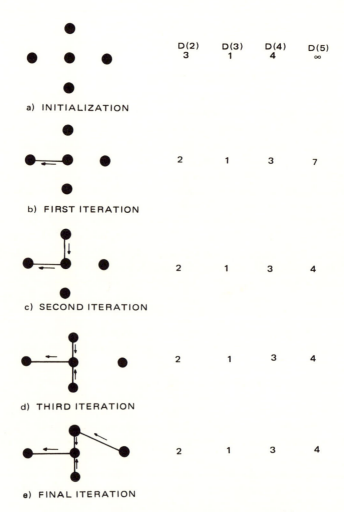

Figure 12.3. (a)–(e) Centralized shortest-path algorithm.

N is the current minimum distance to the central node and $d_{i,j}$, $i, j = 1$, $2, \ldots, N$ is the length of the link from node i to node j. The steps of the algorithm are

1. Initialize by setting $D(1) = 0$ and
   $D(i) = \infty$, $i = 2, 3, \ldots, N$.
2. At each node i ($i = 2, \ldots, N$) search among adjacent nodes to find a shortest path, i.e.,

$$D(i) = \min_{j \in A(i)} [D(j) + d_{ji}]$$

3. Store the path length and the adjacent node found in step 2.
4. If no further changes occur terminate the algorithm; otherwise go to step 2.

The operation of the algorithm is illustrated in Figures 12.4a–12.4c for the network shown in Figure 12.2. Again it is assumed that node 1 is the central node and that the links are full duplex. At each step the preferred nodes are as indicated by the arrows. In carrying out the example in Figure 12.4 it is assumed that nodes update in numerical order. With a different ordering the intermediate steps are different but the final result is the same.

The distributed shortest-path algorithm converges under a condition even weaker than all links having positive weights. A directed cycle in a network is a closed loop within the network. A directed cycle has negative weight provided a message can travel around the loop incurring negative cost. If a network has no negative cycles then the distributed algorithm converges to the shortest path. The convergence of this algorithm may be shown quite simply. If, at any step in the algorithm, $D(k) < \infty$ for $k \neq 1$, then node k has a preferred node, say j, such that $D(k) \geq D(j) + d(k, j)$ and $D(j) < \infty$. Since there is a preferred direction here, at some step there was equality $D(k) = D(j) + d(k, j)$, while $D(j)$ may be reduced to produce momentary inequality. If $D(k)$ were also reduced later, either node j is not a preferred node or equality holds again. Since the network is finite there are two possible results from following a path of preferred nodes: either the central node is reached or a repeated pattern of nodes is followed. Suppose that at every step of the algorithm and for every node k such that

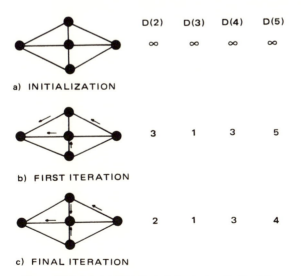

	D(2)	D(3)	D(4)	D(5)
a) INITIALIZATION	∞	∞	∞	∞
b) FIRST ITERATION	3	1	3	5
c) FINAL ITERATION	2	1	3	4

Figure 12.4. (a)–(c) Distributed shortest-path algorithm.

$D(k) < \infty$ we follow a path reaching the central node. Let the sequence of preferred nodes be denoted $k = n_1, n_2, \ldots, n_l = 1$. From the description of the algorithms we have

$$D(n_{i-1}) \geq D(n_i) + d(n_{i-1}, n_i), \qquad i = 2, \ldots, l$$

Summing along the sequence of inequalities we have

$$
\begin{aligned}
D(k) &\geq \sum_{i=2}^{l} d(n_{i-1}, n_i) + D(1) \\
&\geq \sum_{i=2}^{l} d(n_{i-1}, n_i)
\end{aligned}
\qquad (12.5)
$$

The algorithm terminates since the path lengths bounded from below (no cycling) and the $D(k)$ are monotone decreasing by the terms of the algorithm. When the algorithm terminates there must be equality in (12.5). Now suppose that at termination there were a shorter chain from node k to the central node. Let the sequence of nodes be denoted $k = n'_1$, $n'_2, \ldots, n'_m = 1$. For this chain

$$D(n'_m) + \sum_{i=2}^{m} d(n'_{i-1}, n'_i) < D(k)$$

But since the algorithm has terminated we must have

$$D(n_i) \leq D(n_{i-1}) + d(n_{i-1}, n_i) \qquad (12.6)$$

Summing over (12.6) gives a contradiction.

Let us now consider the second possibility, a cycle. We have a sequence of nodes $n_i, n_2, \ldots, n_j = n_1$ forming a directed cycle. Now suppose node n_l was the last node to choose a new preferred node. Immediately prior to this step we had

$$D(n_l) > D(n_{l+1}) + d(n_l, n_{l+1})$$

$$D(n_{l-1}) \geq D(n_l) + d(n_{l-1}, n_l)$$

Let $D'(n_{l-1}), D'(n_l), \ldots$, denote the distance after a new preferred node has been chosen. We have

$$D'(n_{l-1}) > D(n_l) + d(n_{l-1}, n_l) \qquad (12.7)$$

Suppose we sum the inequalities in (12.7) around the directed cycle. Since one of them is a strict inequality, we must have

$$\sum_{i=2}^{j} d(n_{i-1}, n_i) < 0$$

But under our assumption we cannot have directed cycles of negative weight.

The computational complexity of the two shortest-path algorithms depends upon the topology of the network. However, we can obtain estimates under worst case assumptions. Suppose that the network is fully connected, i.e., there is a link between every pair of nodes. The centralized algorithm goes through N steps adding a node to the intermediate network at each step. At each step on the order of N computations must be performed leading to a computational complexity on the order of N^2. The distributed algorithm converges after at most $N - 2$ iterations. At each of the iterations each of the nodes must check its connection to every other node. The computational complexity is then on the order of N^3. One can consider the choice between the two algorithms to be determined by the relative costs of communications and computations. Each of the nodes in the distributed algorithm does about the same amount of work as the processor in the centralized algorithm. However, the communications costs for the distributed algorithm are less. It seems that computational costs are coming down faster than communications costs. If present trends continue, distributed algorithms will be more attractive than centralized.

12.3.3. Changes in Topology

In all of these algorithms a central concern is the reaction to topological changes due to the breakdown of network links or the addition of components. This aspect of routing has been explicitly addressed in an algorithm devised by Merlin and Segal.[11] In this algorithm the structure is imposed by control messages that are alternatively passed up and down a tree rooted at a designated central node and spanning all the nodes of the network. Initially this tree is arbitrary, but as the algorithm progresses the tree is composed of preferred nodes. This term is used in the same sense as in the distributed algorithm above. The route from any node to the central node is preferred nodes giving a shortest path. Each step of the algorithm begins with an up cycle in which the central node broadcasts a control message to all its adjacent nodes. Upon receipt of control messages each node computes the delay to the central node and passes this information on to its adjacent nodes. From its neighbors each node receives their distances to the central node. For each neighbor the length of the path to the central node is computed. The minimum of these distances is stored until the distance to the preferred node is received on the down cycle. The minimum over all adjacent nodes, preferred or otherwise, for which information has been received is computed. This number is broadcast to all adjacent nodes *except* the preferred node. In this fashion distance information propagates up the tree away from the root at the central node toward the leaves. In the second half of the iteration information on preferred nodes propagates down the tree. When a node has received distance information from all adjacent nodes the minimum distance is sent to the current preferred node. After this point a new preferred node is computed as necessary. Presumably control messages going up the tree are differentiated from messages going down the tree.

A slight change in the algorithm is necessary in order to respond to changes in topology either through the addition or the deletion of a link. The route-updating cycles described in the preceding paragraph are numbered. The cycle number is incremented only when there is a change in topology. Nodes adjacent to the link that is added or deleted detect this change and generate control messages. The node down-tree from the link in question sends the message to the central node, where a new cycle is initiated. If one of the links making up the tree of preferred nodes fails, the node up-tree from the failed link sends a control message to the node that prefers it. This message is propagated up the tree. Each node receiving the message reinitializes by setting its preferred node to nil and the distance to the central node to infinity. If there is a path to the central node these nodes will receive distance information from adjacent nodes. After a node has received information from all neighboring nodes, it chooses a preferred node by finding the minimum distance to the central node. The node then sends the minimum distance to all neighbors.

Consider the ten-node network shown in Figure 12.5. Initially the optimum routings to the central node, node 1, are as shown. Now suppose that the link between nodes 7 and 8 fails. Control messages are sent down-tree by node 7 and up-tree by node 8. Nodes 6, 8, 9, and 10 reset their routing parameters. In the next cycle node 6 will be the first of this subset to receive distance information from node 5. After several iterations the new routing shown in Figure 12.6 will be established.

12.3.4. Extensions

In the foregoing we have found the shortest paths between a central node and all other nodes of the network. A number of variations are possible.† For example, one may wish to find the shortest paths between all possible pairs of nodes. Of course this can be found by the algorithms

---

†For a review of classical shortest-path algorithms see Ref. 12.

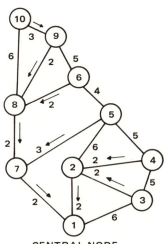

Figure 12.5. Ten-node network—before.   **CENTRAL NODE**

we have studied with each of the nodes acting in turn as a central node. A more efficient algorithm based on work by Warshall[13] has been found by Floyd.[14] It is estimated that the repeated application of the centralized algorithm considered above would result in an increase of computational complexity of about 50%.

Another alternative is to find the second shortest path between a pair of network nodes.[15] Paths that do not have the same set of nodes are assumed to be different. Successful algorithms for this problem are a systematic search of deviations from shortest paths.

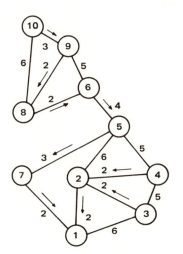

Figure 12.6. Ten-node network—after.

12.4. Capacity Constraints

We turn now to the consideration of routing problems where the link capacities are finite. Since links are shared, one cannot consider traffic between different source–destination pairs independently. The coupling between different kinds of traffic is embodied in the equations for conservation of flow and total flow. Let $I_l^{(i,j)}$ denote the flow in data units per second on link l of the traffic between nodes i and j. At each node n of the network we have the following conservation of flow

$$\sum_{l \in I(n)} I_l^{(i,j)} - \sum_{l \in O(n)} I_l^{(i,j)} = \begin{cases} -\gamma_{ij}, & n = i \\ \gamma_{ij}, & n = j \\ 0, & \text{otherwise} \end{cases} \qquad (12.8)$$

where $I(n)$ and $O(n)$ are, respectively, the sets of links into and out of node n.

By summing over all source–destination pairs the total flow in each of the links is obtained:

$$I_l = \sum_{i=1}^{N} \sum_{j=1}^{N} I_l^{(i,j)}, \qquad l = 1, 2, \ldots, L \qquad (12.9)$$

By the very definition of capacity we have the constraint on network flows

$$I_l \leq C_l, \qquad l = 1, 2, \ldots, L \qquad (12.10)$$

Equations (12.8), (12.9), and (12.10) form a set of linear constraints. A set of flows is called feasible if it satisfies these constraints. We denote the set of feasible flows as F. The set F is convex, meaning that if the flows I, $J \in F$ then $\lambda I + (1 - \lambda)J \in F$ for all $0 \leq \lambda \leq 1$. This property of the set of feasible flows is shown by simple substitution into the linear constraints.

Network optimization problems consist of maximizing or minimizing an objective function, F, over the convex set of feasible flows. For example, we mentioned earlier that the classic multicommodity flow problem is to maximize the throughput of the network

$$S = \sum_{i=1}^{N} \sum_{j=1}^{N} \gamma_{ij} \qquad (12.11)$$

The optimum solution consists of the commodity flows in each of the links $I_l^{(i,j)}$, $i, j = 1, 2, \ldots, N$, $l = 1, 2, \ldots, L$. These optimum flows can be realized by apportioning flow in a node onto the appropriate outgoing link. For node n, $n = 1, 2, \ldots, N$, the proportion of flow on link $l \in D(n)$ is $I_l^{(i,j)} / \sum_{l \in O(n)} I_l^{(i,j)}$. As in Chapter 11 the proper apportionment can be achieved through probabilistic routing.

12.4.1. Linear Programming Solution

Maximization of the total flow as given in equation (12.11) subject to the constraints in equations (12.8)–(12.10) is a linear programming problem.[16,17] The classic form of the linear programming problem is to maximize a linear combination of the variables $x_1, x_2, \ldots, x_k$, i.e.,

$$T = \sum_{i=1}^{k} c_i x_i \tag{12.12}$$

subject to a set of linear constraints:

$$\sum_{i=1}^{k} \sum_{j=1}^{l} a_{ij} x_i \leq b_j, \qquad j = 1, 2, \ldots, l \tag{12.13a}$$

$$x_i \geq 0, \qquad i = 1, 2, \ldots, k \tag{12.13b}$$

where the c_i, $i = 1, 2, \ldots, k$, the b_j, $j = 1, 2, \ldots, l$, and the a_{ij}, $i = 1, 2, \ldots, k$, $j = 1, 2, \ldots, l$ are given constants. The maximization problem can be converted to a minimization problem simply by changing the sign of the constants c_i. The inequality constraints in (12.13) can be changed into equality constraints by adding the slack variables $s_j \geq 0$, $j = 1, 2, \ldots, l$ to each of the inequalities in (12.13). The optimization is then carried out over the augmented set of variables $x_1, \ldots, x_k, s_1, \ldots, s_l$.

A solution to the linear programming problem is said to be feasible if it satisfies the set of constraints in (12.13). Since these constraints are linear it is not difficult to show that the set of feasible solutions forms a convex polyhedron in k-dimensional space. In the discussion following equations (12.8)–(12.10) we showed convexity for feasible flows. The reasoning is the same here. It can be shown that the linear form of equation (12.12) is maximized at extreme points of this polyhedron. The optimization problem is solved by means of the *simplex technique* devised by Danzig. The technique is an efficient means of searching the extreme points of the set of feasible solutions for a maximum. The linear programming problem is illustrated on Figure 12.7. Linear programming is a standard technique in operations research. A number of software packages are available to find optimal solutions.

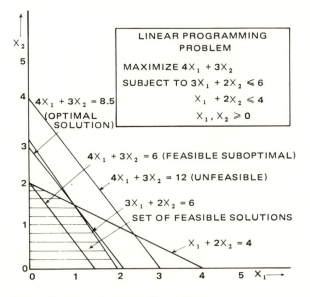

Figure 12.7. Linear programming problem in two dimensions.

The correspondences for the flow allocation problem are over the set $I_l^{(i,j)}$, $l = 1, 2, \ldots, L$, $i, j = 1, 2, \ldots, N$ the sum

$$S = \sum_{i=1}^{N} \sum_{n=1}^{N} \left[\sum_{l \in I(n)} I_l^{(i,n)} - \sum_{l \in O(n)} I_l^{(n,i)} \right]$$

is maximized subject to the equality constraints

$$\sum_{l \in I(n)} I_l^{(i,j)} - \sum_{l \in O(n)} I_l^{(i,j)} = 0, \qquad n \neq i, j$$

The exact variables in each of these equations depends upon the topology through the sets $I(n)$ and $O(n)$, $n = 1, 2, \ldots, N$.

The linear programming tool can also be employed in the routing problem where the objective function to be minimized is given in equation (12.1) and the constraints on flow are given by equations (12.8) and (12.10). Now the obvious difficulty here is that the cost function in equation (12.1) is a nonlinear function in the variables I_l, $l = 1, 2, \ldots, L$. However, the fact that the cost is a separable function allows us to circumvent this problem by piecewise linearization.[18] We define the subvariables x_{mn}, $m = 1, 2, \ldots, L$, $n = 1, 2, \ldots, K_m$ on the intervals $0 \leq x_{mn} \leq \delta_{mn}$. The flows in the links are expressed in terms of these subvariables:

$$I_m = \sum_{j=1}^{K_m} x_{mj}, \qquad m = 1, 2, \ldots, L \qquad (12.14)$$

The delay can be approximated by means of a linear combination of the subvariables (see Figure 12.7). Define

$$\Delta_{mn} \triangleq \sum_{k=1}^{n} \delta_{m_k}, \qquad m = 1, 2, \ldots, L, \qquad n = 1, 2, \ldots, K_m$$

In the interval $(\Delta_{mn-1}, \Delta_{mn})$ we may write

$$\frac{I_m}{C_m - I_m} \cong \sum_{k=1}^{n} \alpha_{mk} x_{mk}, \qquad m = 1, 2, \ldots, L \qquad (12.15)$$

where $\Delta_{m0} = 0$. The quantity α_{mn} is the slope of the piecewise approximation in the interval $(\Delta_{mn-1}, \Delta_{mn})$. The approximation can be made as accurate as we please by increasing the number of subvariables, i.e., increasing K_m, $m = 1, 2, \ldots, L$.

From equations (12.1) and (12.15) we have a cost function which is a linear combination of the subvariables. Equations (12.8), (12.9), (12.10), and (12.14) form a set of linear constraints in the variables x_{mn}, $m = 1, 2, \ldots, L$, $n = 1, 2, \ldots, K_m$ and $I_l^{(i,j)}$, $i, j = 1, 2, \ldots, N$, $l = 1, 2, \ldots, L$. Since the cost function is separable, each individual term can be approximated in this fashion with no cross terms. Since each of the terms in the summand of the cost function is convex, the slope α_{mn} in equation (12.15) is non-decreasing with n (see Figure 12.8). This ensures that the optimum set of subvariables yields a reasonable solution. For all $m = 1, 2, \ldots, L$, all solutions must be of the form

$$x_{mn} = \delta_{mn}, \qquad n < k$$

$$0 \leqslant x_{mn} \leqslant \delta_{mn}, \qquad n = k \qquad (12.16)$$

$$x_{mn} = 0, \qquad n > k$$

A solution other than that represented in (12.16) cannot be optimum since the x_{mn} could be adjusted to reduce the cost function while keeping the total link flows constant [see equations (12.14) and (12.15)].

There are two fundamental drawbacks to the solution of routing by piecewise linearization and linear programming. In order to obtain a good

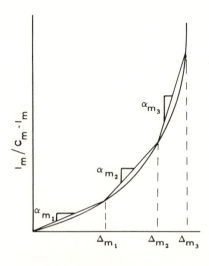

Figure 12.8. Piecewise linear approximation.

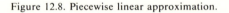

approximation to the objective function, a number of subvariables must be introduced for each link in the network. For networks of even moderate size this leads to a problem of very high dimensionality. Although efficient programs are available, the cost of finding solutions could get out of hand. The second difficulty is that the technique is totally centralized. Given the traffic matrix, γ_{ij}, $i, j = 1, 2, \ldots, N$ and the connectivity through the sets $I(i)$ and $O(i)$, the optimum routings are calculated at some central point. These optimum routings are then dispatched to the appropriate nodes. As pointed out earlier, in a dynamic network environment, the communications overhead may obviate all of the potential gains from optimal routing. In the next section we shall consider a technique for determining routings which is computationally efficient and which, while centralized, points the way toward decentralized techniques.

12.4.2. Flow Deviation Method

As in the previous section we shall assume that the problem is to minimize the average delay as given in equation (12.1) subject to the conservation of flow constraints expressed in equations (12.8)–(12.10). Another approach to this problem is what is called *flow deviation*, which is essentially a gradient technique suited to the optimization of network flows. We remind the reader that the set of feasible network flows, i.e., the set of flows that satisfy equations (12.8)–(12.10), form a convex set. The objective function in equation (12.1) is a convex function of link flow. Since link flows can be expressed directly in terms of path flows, the delay is also a convex function of path flows [see equations (12.2) and (12.3)]. The following lemma gives necessary and sufficient conditions for a minimum of a convex function on a convex set.†

Lemma. Let $F(x_1, x_2, \ldots, x_M)$ be a real differentiable, convex function on an M-dimensional space Ω^M and let C^M be a convex set on this space. The function $F(x_1, x_2, \ldots, x_M)$ is minimum at $(x_1^*, x_2^*, \ldots, x_M^*) \in C^M$ if and only if

$$\sum_{i=1}^{M} \frac{\partial F}{\partial x_i}(x_1^*, x_2^*, \ldots, x_M^*)(x_i - x_i^*) \geq 0, \qquad \forall (x_1, x_2, \ldots, x_M) \in C^M$$

$$(12.17\text{a})$$

where $\partial F(x_1^*, x_2^*, \ldots, x_M^*)/\partial x_i$ denotes the partial derivative with respect to x_i evaluated at the point $(x_1^*, x_2^*, \ldots, x_M^*)$.

Equation (12.17a) can be expressed in vector notation as

$$\Delta F(\mathbf{X}^*)(\mathbf{X} - \mathbf{X}^*)^T \geq 0, \qquad \forall \mathbf{X} \in C^M \qquad (12.17\text{b})$$

where $\Delta F(\mathbf{X}^*)$ is the gradient of F evaluated at $\mathbf{X} = (x_1, \ldots, x_n) = (x_1^*, x_2^*, \ldots, x_n^*) = \mathbf{X}^*$ and T denotes transpose. The proof of this lemma is as follows. Assume that $F(\mathbf{X})$ is minimum at $\mathbf{X}^* \in C^M$, where C^M is the set of feasible network flows. Now for every $\mathbf{X} \in C^M$ consider the function of the scalar variable $\lambda \in (0, 1)$, $G(\lambda) = F(\lambda \mathbf{X} + (1 - \lambda)\mathbf{X}^*)$. We point out that $\lambda \mathbf{X} + (1 - \lambda)\mathbf{X}^* \in \mathcal{F}$. On the interval $0 \leq \lambda \leq 1$, $G(\lambda)$ is minimum at $\mathbf{X} = \mathbf{X}^*$ therefore

$$\frac{dG(\lambda)}{d\lambda} = \sum_{i=1}^{M} \frac{dF}{\partial x_i}(x_1^*, x_2^*, \ldots, x_n^*)(x_i - x_i^*) = \Delta F(\mathbf{X}^*)(\mathbf{X} - \mathbf{X}^*)^T \geq 0$$

We have necessity, now let us show sufficiency. Suppose that $\Delta F(\mathbf{X}^*)(\mathbf{X} - \mathbf{X}^*) \geq 0$, $\forall \mathbf{X} \in C^M$ but $F(\mathbf{X}^*)$ is not minimum. Then there is another point $\mathbf{X}' \in C$ such that $F(\mathbf{X}') < F(\mathbf{X}^*)$. Now consider points along the line $\lambda \mathbf{X}' + (1 - \lambda)\mathbf{X}^* \in C^M$, $0 \leq \lambda \leq 1$. Again we define a function of the scalar $H(\lambda) = F(\lambda \mathbf{X}' + (1 - \lambda)\mathbf{X}^*)$. There is a contradiction since $dH(\lambda)/d\lambda \geq 0$ by assumption but $H(1) < H(0)$.

We apply this lemma over the convex set of path flows. We emphasize path flows over link flows because we have more direct control over them. Deviations from the optimum flows are in terms of variations in path flows. By the standard rules of differentiation the partial derivative of delay with respect to a path flow is equal to the sum of the derivatives over each of

†The development presented here is similar to that in Ref. 8.

the links in the path

$$\frac{\partial \bar{T}}{\partial J_k(i,j)} = \sum_{l=1}^{L} \delta(k,l) W_l \qquad (12.18a)$$

where $\delta(k,l)$ is as in equation (12.2) and where W_l is the derivative of link delay with respect to link flow [see equation (12.1)]:

$$W_l = \frac{d}{dI_l} \left(\frac{I_l}{C_l - I_l} + I_l d_l \right)$$

$$= \frac{C_l}{(C_l - I_l)^2} + d_l \qquad (12.18b)$$

Notice that in equation (12.18) we have expressed the partial derivative of link delay as the sum of the weights of links making up a path [see equation (12.5)]. We can think of this as the generalized length of a path. From the foregoing lemma we see that a necessary and sufficient condition for the delay to be minimized for path flows $J_k^*(i,j)$, $i,j = 1, 2, \ldots, N$, $k = 1, 2, \ldots, \Pi(i,j)$ is that

$$\sum_{i=1}^{L} \sum_{j=1}^{L} \sum_{k=1}^{\Pi(i,j)} \frac{\partial \bar{T}}{\partial J_k^{(i,j)}} (J_k(i,j) - J_k^*(i,j)) \geq 0 \qquad (12.19)$$

for all feasible path flows. This requires that for each origin–destination pair (i,j) we have

$$\sum_{k=1}^{\Pi(i,j)} \sum_{l=1}^{L} \delta(k,l) W_l^*(J_k(i,j) - J_k^*(i,j)) \geq 0, \qquad \forall J_k(i,j) \in \mathcal{F} \quad (12.20)$$

where W_l^* indicates evaluation of the derivative at the flows $J_k^*(i,j)$ [see equation (12.18b)]. Equation (12.20) implies that

$$\min_{\mathcal{F}} \sum_{k=1}^{\Pi(i,j)} \sum_{l=1}^{L} \delta(k,l) W_l^* J_k(i,j) \geq \sum_{k=1}^{\Pi(i,j)} \sum_{l=1}^{L} \delta(k,l) W_k^* J_k^*(i,j) \quad (12.21)$$

where the minimization is carried out over the set of feasible path flows, $\mathcal{F}$. Equation (12.21) shows that all of the paths for which $J_k^*(i,j) > 0$ must be minimum length. Suppose it were otherwise; then one could vary $J_k(i,j)$ over $\mathcal{F}$ so that the left-hand side of equation (12.21) is less than the right—a contradiction. The optimum path between nodes i and j can be found by use of one of the shortest-path algorithms discussed in an earlier section of this chapter with the generalized link lengths W_l^*.

The preceding suggests that starting with a feasible flow, the flow should be shifted incrementally to minimum path lengths. The flow deviation method is a way of doing this which can be shown to converge to the optimum set of flows. The method is an algorithm which iterates a set of feasible network flows. Let $J_k^{(n)}(i, j)$, $i, j = 1, 2, \ldots, N$; $k = 1, 2, \ldots, \Pi(i, j)$ be a set of feasible network flows at the nth iteration. For these flows the generalized link lengths, w_i, are calculated from equation (12.18b). For these generalized lengths find the set of path flows $\tilde{J}_k(i, j)$, $i, j = 1, 2, \ldots, N$, $k = 1, 2, \ldots, \Pi(i, j)$, which minimizes the sums of the distances for all paths and source–destination pairs [equation (12.19)]. We let the network flow be $(1 - \lambda)J_k^{(n)}(i, j) + \lambda\tilde{J}_k(i, j)$, for each value of i, j, and k. We emphasize that this is the flow on all paths between all source–destination pairs. The parameter λ is varied so as to minimize the average delay in the network. This calculation involves finding the link flows from equation (12.2) and substituting into equation (12.1). This calculation is carried out over a range of values of λ and numerical techniques used to find the optimum value which we designate as λ^*. We shall consider these techniques momentarily. At the beginning of the next iteration the network flows are set to

$$J_k^{(n+1)}(i, j) = (1 - \lambda^*)J_k^{(n)}(i, j) + \lambda^*\tilde{J}_k(i, j),$$

$$i, j = 1, 2, \ldots, n, \qquad k = 1, 2, \ldots, \Pi(i, j) \tag{12.22}$$

The iteration continues from this point. In order to find the optimum value, λ^* in equation (12.22) a centralized computation is necessary. We begin with a description of the mathematical steps that are involved. Subsequently the implementation of these steps in a distributed fashion will be discussed. Again we begin with the sets of flows $J_k^{(n)}(i, j)$ and $\tilde{J}_k(i, j)$, $i, j = 1, 2, \ldots, n$; $k = 1, 2, \ldots, \Pi(i, j)$ representing, respectively, the current iteration and the flows over the minimum incremental paths. We then calculate the corresponding link flows $I_l^{(n)}$ and $\tilde{I}_l$, $l = 1, 2, \ldots, L$ and form the set of feasible flows $(1 - \lambda)I_l^{(n)} + \lambda\tilde{I}_l$, $l = 1, 2, \ldots, L$. The next conceptual step is a Taylor series expansion of average delay around $\lambda = 0$ [see equation (12.1)]:

$$\bar{T}((1 - \lambda)\mathbf{I}^{(n)} + \lambda\tilde{\mathbf{I}})$$

$$= \sum_{l=1}^{L} [\bar{T}_l(I_l^{(n)}) + \lambda\bar{T}_l'(I_l^{(n)})(\tilde{I}_l - I_l^{(n)}) + \lambda^2\bar{T}''(I_l^{(n)})(\tilde{I}_l - I_l^{(n)}) \tag{12.23}$$

where $\mathbf{I}^{(n)}$ and $\tilde{\mathbf{I}}_l$ are L-dimensional vectors of link flows, $I_l^{(n)}$ and $\tilde{I}_l$, $l = 1, 2, \ldots, L$, and the prime and double prime indicate first and second derivatives, respectively. The value of λ to be used in the iteration is found by minimizing the right-hand side of equation (12.23) with respect to λ.

This is simply carried out by differentiating with respect to λ and setting the result equal to zero. We find

$$\lambda^+ = -\frac{\sum_{l=1}^{L} T_l'(I_l^{(n)})(\tilde{I}_l - I_l^{(n)})}{2\sum_{l=1}^{L} T_l''(I_l^{(n)})(\tilde{I}_l - I_l^{(n)})^2} \tag{12.24}$$

We are guaranteed that the quantity λ^+ given in equation (12.24) is positive. The flows $\tilde{I}_l$, $l = 1, 2, \ldots, L$ minimize the incremental distance through the network [see equation (12.4)] and the denominator in equation (12.24) is positive. The difficulty is that it can be greater than one. We simply take the value of λ^* to be used in equation (12.23) to be

$$\lambda^* = \min(1, \lambda^+) \tag{12.25}$$

If the objective function to be minimized is given by equation (12.1) it can be shown that the algorithm converges even if the initial feasible flow is quite far from the optimum flow.

The implementation of the algorithm in a distributed fashion begins with each node broadcasting the current flows on all its outgoing links, I_l, $l \in O(i)$, $i = 1, 2, \ldots, N$. Presumably this could be done over the last set of paths for which the incremental flow was minimum. Each node then calculates the first and second derivatives $\bar{T}_l'(I_l^{(n)})$ and $\bar{T}_l''(I_l^{(n)})$ for all $l = 1, 2, \ldots, L$. With the values of $\bar{T}_l'(I_l^{(n)})$ as generalized link distances each node can calculate the minimum deviation path from it to all other nodes. This is a straightforward application of the shortest-path algorithms we described earlier. Along these paths it transmits the current value of γ_{ij}, $i, j = 1, 2, \ldots, N$, the total flow between it and the destination node. Should there by more than one path between an origin–destination pair the quantity $J_k(i, j)$ is transmitted along the kth path, $k = 1, 2, \ldots, \Pi(i, j)$ [see equation (12.2)]. Each node then can compute the quantity $\tilde{I}_l$ for each of its output links. The differences $\tilde{I}_l - I_l^{(n)}$ is then broadcast to all other nodes. Again a spanning tree to all nodes with the broadcasting node at the root would be sufficient for this task. With this information each node can compute the new value of λ^* from equations (12.24) and (12.25) and the new link flows $I_l^{(n+1)}$ from equation (12.23).

There are other centralized and distributed algorithms, but from our point of view the centralized and the distributed algorithm that we have considered has the virtue of being relatively easy to explain.[8,21–23] There are also algorithms that are oriented toward link flows rather than path flows. The advantages of these other algorithms is faster convergence to the optimum and lower communication and processing costs. In the quasi-static environment where the network is attempting to track slow variations in traffic and topology, these advantages can be important since less of the network resources are needed.

12.5. Flow Control and Routing

In the previous chapter we studied techniques for controling the flow of messages into a network in order to avoid congestion. When capacity is limited a significant part of the routing strategy is the avoidance of congestion. The average delay, being a convex function of link flow, would serve to spread the flow of data throughout the network. In view of this common goal there should be coordination of routing and flow control strategies. In this section we shall show that, in the quasistatic environment, end-to-end flow control can be considered in the same mathematical framework as routing.[24,25] The flow control strategy can be part of an optimization procedure in the same fashion as routing.

The first step in the formulation of an optimization problem yielding the flow control strategy is the development of a suitable objective function. The flow into the network at node i destined for node j is γ_{ij} data units per second [see equation (12.8)]. In the terminology of telephone traffic engineering this is the load that is carried by the network. Under a flow control strategy a larger amount of traffic may be offered but deferred or rejected because of congestion. The window mechanism discussed in Chapter 11 provides a means for reducing the carried load in the network. Let us denote the offered load corresponding to γ_{ij} by γ_{ij}^0. The difference between γ_{ij}^0 and γ_{ij} represents what the customer desires from the network and the actual throughput. In order to derive a routing strategy we shall take user dissatisfaction to be the measure of performance. It is inevitable that such a measure of performance is somewhat arbitrary in its formulation. However, as we pointed out earlier even the average delay expression may not be correct, although it is useful as a measure of performance. As in the case of average delay we shall choose an objective function of the form

$$P_{ij}(\gamma_{ij}) = \left(\frac{a_{ij}}{\gamma_{ij}}\right)^{b_{ij}} \tag{12.26}$$

where a_{ij} and b_{ij} are positive constants which are chosen for each origin–destination pair (i, j). The larger a_{ij} and b_{ij} are the more sensitive the system will be to the control of flow through the reduction of $\gamma_{ij} \cdot P_{ij}(\gamma_{ij})$. The objective function in equation (12.26) can be written so as to resemble the objective functions in the routing problem. We define $K_{ij} \triangleq \gamma_{ij}^0 - \gamma_{ij}$ as the amount of overflow traffic. Substituting into equation (12.26) we obtain

$$P_{ij}(\gamma_{ij}) = \left(\frac{a_{ij}}{\gamma_{ij}^0 - K_{ij}}\right)^{b_{ij}} \qquad (12.27)$$

We see from (12.20b) that the user dissatisfaction is a convex function of K_{ij} with infinite dissatisfaction when $K_{ij} = \gamma_{ij}$. This is very much the same as the delay in each of the links of the network. This similarity suggests that we treat K_{ij} as the maximum allowable flow in a fictitious direct link between origin i and destination j. Controlling the flow into the network can be viewed as diverting flow onto the fictitious link. We form the augmented objective function [see equation (12.1)]

$$\bar{T} = \frac{1}{\alpha} \sum_{l=1}^{L} \left(\frac{I_l}{C_l - I_l} + I_l d_l\right) + \sum_{i,j=1}^{L} \left(\frac{a_{ij}}{\gamma_{ij}^0 - K_{ij}}\right)^{b_{ij}} \qquad (12.28)$$

The optimization problem proceeds in a similar fashion as in Section 12.4 for the augmented cost function.

12.6. Routing in Practice

Several packet-switched networks are currently in operation. These furnish useful insights into the operation of routing algorithms. Although routings are based to varying degrees on traffic, nothing like the algorithms developed in Section 12.4 have been used in practice.

Perhaps the greatest innovation with respect to routing is the ARPA network.† Since the nature of the ARPA network is to some extent experimental, it is fitting that entirely new techniques were applied. In all implementations of routing algorithms in the ARPA network shortest-path routing has been used (see Section 12.3). Each node in the network maintains sets of shortest paths to each destination. In the first version each node estimates the delay on outgoing links by counting the number of packets waiting in outgoing buffers.[26] A distributed shortest path algorithm similar to that discussed in Section 12.3 was used to establish paths between origin–destination pairs. This routing information was exchanged between nodes as often as 2/3 sec. The difficulty was that this method was subject to oscillations due to a positive feedback effect. The basic problem is that the generalized distances on the links are directly related to queueing delay and are a function of traffic levels. In an analysis of a similar routing strategy in a ring network it has been shown that the routing can alternate between clockwise and counterclockwise flow.[3] The oscillatory effect has been reduced in the ARPA network simply by adding a bias factor which causes the network to choose shortest-length paths. There has been a recent com-

†A description of the ARPA network is contained in Section 2.6 of Chapter 2.

plete revision of the routing technique in the ARPA network.[27] One of the significant changes incorporated in the new algorithm is to average the estimate of delay over 10-sec intervals. In this case all components of delay such as transmission time and propagation are taken into account. If there is a significant difference from previous measurements, the new value of delay is broadcast through the network. Minimum distance paths through the network are found by application of an algorithm similar to those considered in Section 12.3. Experiments with the new routing algorithm indicate a rapid response to topological changes without the oscillatory behavior that characterized the previous algorithm.

The TYMNET is a packet-switched network which has been in operation since 1970.[28] The network consists of over 300 nodes connected in the mesh topology so there is more than one path between pairs of nodes. For the most part the network uses telephone facilities in constructing links between nodes. The link speeds range from 2400 bits per second to 9600 bits per second. The paths within the network are on a virtual circuit basis, with the paths being determined by one of four centralized processors. Again a shortest-path algorithm is used.[29] In this case the generalized distances or weights are assigned to links by taking several factors into account. For example, lower weights are assigned to higher-speed lines. Also weights are added to a link if it becomes overloaded.

References

1. M. Schwartz and T. E. Stern, "Routing Techniques used in Computer Communication Networks," *IEEE Transactions on Communications* **COM-28**(4), 539–553, April (1980).
2. H. Rudin, "On Routing and Delta Routing a Taxonomy and Performance Comparison for Packet Switched Networks," *IEEE Transactions on Communications* **COM-24**(1), 43–59, January (1976).
3. D. P. Bertsekas, "Dynamic Behavior of a Shortest-Path Routing Algorithm of the ARPANET Type," *International Symposium on Information Theory*, Grignano, Italy, June (1979).
4. H. Rudin and H. Müller, "More on Routing and Flow Control," *Proceedings of the National Telecommunication Conference* (1979), pp. 34.5.1–34.5.9.
5. J. Spragins, "Analytical Queueing Models," *Computer*, April (1980).
6. L. R. Ford and D. R. Fulkerson, *Flows in Networks*, Princeton University Press, Princeton, New Jersey (1962).
7. T. C. Hu, *Integer Programming and Network Flows*, Addison-Wesley, Reading, Massachusetts (1970).
8. D. P. Bertsekas, "Notes on Optimal Routing and Flow Control for Communication Networks," MIT report No. LIDS–1169, December (1981).
9. E. W. Dijkstra, "A Note on Two Problems in Connection with Graphs," *Numer. Math.*, **1**, 269–271 (1959).
10. A. V. Aho, J. E. Hopcroft, and J. D. Ullman, *Design and Analysis of Computer Algorithms*, Addison-Wesley, Reading, Massachusetts (1974).
11. P. M. Merlin and A. Segall, "A Fail-Safe Distributed Routing Protocol," *IEEE Transactions on Communications*, **COM-27**(9), 1280–1287, September (1979).

12. S. E. Dreyfus, "An Appraisal of Some Shortest-Path Algorithms," *Operations Research*, **17**, 395–412 (1969).

13. S. Warshall, "A Theorem on Boolean Matrices," *Journal of the ACM*, **9**, 11–12 (1962).

14. R. W. Floyd, "Algorithm 97, Shortest Path," *Communications of the ACM*, **5**, 345 (1962).

15. W. Hoffman and R. Pavley, "A Method for the Solution of the Nth Best-Path Problem," *Journal of the ACM*, **6**, 506–514 (1959).

16. G. B. Danzig, *Linear Programming and Extensions*, Princeton University Press, Princeton, New Jersey (1962).

17. G. Hadley, *Linear Programming*, Addison-Wesley, Reading, Massachusetts (1964).

18. H. Frank and J. Frisch, "Planning Computer-Communication Networks," *Computer Communication Networks*, N. Abramson and F. Kuo, editors, Prentice-Hall, Englewood Cliffs, New Jersey (1973).

19. L. Fratta, M. Gerla, and L. Kleinrock, "The Flow Deviation Method: An Approach to Store-and-Forward Communication Network Design," *Networks*, **3**, 97–133 (1973).

20. D. G. Cantor and M. Gerla, "Optimal Routing in a Packet-Switched Computer Network," *IEEE Transactions on Computers* **C-23**(10), 1062–1069, October (1974).

21. D. P. Bertsekas, "On the Goldstein–Levitin–Poljak Gradient Projection Method," *IEEE Transactions on Automatic Control* **AC-21**, 174–184 (1976).

22. D. P. Bertsekas, E. M. Gafni, and R. G. Gallager, "Second Derivative Algorithms for Minimum Delay Distributed Routing in Networks," to be published, *IEEE Transactions on Communications* (1984).

23. R. G. Gallager, "A Minimum Delay Routing Algorithm Using Distributed Computation," *IEEE Transactions on Communications*, **COM-25**(1), 73–85, January (1977).

24. S. J. Golestaani, "A Unified Theory of Flow Control and Routing in Data Communication Networks," LIDS report No. TH-983, MIT, January (1980).

25. R. G. Gallager and S. J. Golestaani, "Flow Control and Routing Algorithms for Data Networks," *Proceedings of the Fifth International Conference on Computer Communication ICCC-80*, Atlanta, October (1980), pp. 779–784.

26. J. M. McQuillan, "Adaptive Routing for Distributed Networks," BBN report No. 2831, May (1974).

27. J. M. McQuillan, "The New Routing Algorithm for the ARPANET," *IEEE Transactions on Communications*, **COM-28**, 711–719, May (1980).

28. L. Tymes, "TYMNET—A Terminal-Oriented Communications Network," Spring Joint Computer Conference, *AFIPS Conference Proceedings*, **38**, 211–216 (1971).

29. A. Rajaraman, "Routing in TYMNET," *European Computing Conference*, London, England, May (1978).

30. G. J. Foschini, "On Heavy Traffic Diffusion Analysis and Dynamic Routing in Packet-Switched Networks," *Computer Performance*, K. M. Chandy and M. Reiser, editors, North-Holland, Amsterdam (1977).

31. G. J. Foschini and J. Salz, "A Basic Dynamic Routing Problem and Diffusion," *IEEE Transactions on Communications*, **COM-26**(3), 320–327, March (1978).

Exercises

12.1. For the ten-node network shown in Figure 12.9 find the shortest paths from all nodes to node 1 using the centralized algorithm of Section 12.3. Assume all links are full duplex with the distances indicated.

12.2. Repeat Exercise 12.1 for the distributed algorithm of Section 12.3.

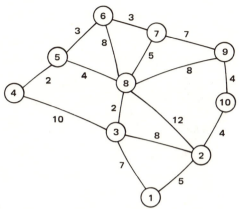

Figure 12.9. Ten-node network.

12.3. Suppose that after the routings found in the previous two exercises have been established, the link between nodes 3 and 8 breaks down. Show the steps necessary to establish a new routing.

12.4. Suppose that the five-node network shown in Figure 12.10 has the traffic matrix shown below:

			Origin		
Destination	1	2	3	4	5
1	—	50	40	40	40
2	50	—	40	30	30
3	40	40	—	50	40
4	40	30	50	—	50
5	40	30	40	50	—

All the flows are in kbps. Assume that routing is shortest path in terms of the number of links. When there are two or more shortest paths the traffic is divided equally. What are the flows in each of the links?

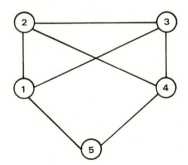

Figure 12.10. Five-node network.

12.5. Now suppose that all of the links are full duplex and have a capacity of 100 kbps.

(a) Set up the conservation of flow equations.

(b) Write down a piecewise linear approximation to the average delay in the network.

(c) Find the optimum flow allocation using linear programming. This step will require machine computation.

(d) Assuming a solution to part (c), what are the probabilistic routings so that the proper link flows are maintained?

12.6. For the five-node network shown in Figure 12.10, find the optimum flows by means of the flow deviation technique.

Network Layout and Reliability

13.1. Introduction

In all of our previous work, we considered the performance of networks, the exact topologies of which were known. In this chapter we shall move one step back, so to speak, and consider the layout of networks which, broadly defined, minimize costs under a set of user requirements. Pedagogy is the primary reason for postponing the discussion of this topic until the very last chapter of the book. The material in this chapter is a distinct departure since the underlying mathematical models are different from the previous chapters of the book. Much of our previous discussion is based of queueing theoretic models, whereas the material in this chapter is based on circuit theory, in particular graph theory.† Moreover, as we shall see, some of the techniques used in this chapter rely on results of previous chapters. The postponing of the discussion of layout techniques has had little impact on our development. In many applications, the topology is determined by factors other than line costs. In local area networks, for example, topology may be determined by the performance of an accessing technique.

Much of the discussion in this chapter is conducted within the framework of graph theory. A graph may be defined as a collection of vertices and edges in which the edges connect the vertices to one another. We shall consider the edges to be undirected so that an edge is specified by the pair of vertices it connects without regard to order. In conformity with the rest of the book, we use the terms "node" and "link" rather than "vertex" and "edge" or "branch," respectively. These latter terms are more common in graph theory. For the same reason we shall use the term "network" rather than "graph" in the remainder of our discussion. As in

---

†We have found Refs. 1 and 2 most helpful in our study of graph theory.

the previous chapter, a path is the sequence of links traversed in going from one node to another. A closed path goes back to the original node.

In the typical network layout problem, we are given the locations of N points. In general terms, the objective of our study is to find a network with nodes at the given points such that the links connecting the nodes to one another have minimum total distance. Along with this basic requirement are certain constraints which particularize the approaches used in problem solution.†

In applications of the technique, the given set of points are locations of terminals or processors and the links are transmission lines. Of the four classes of networks that we discussed in Chapter 2, the material in this chapter is most relevant to CATV networks and to telecommunications, networks using land lines. In these systems line costs are largely a function of distance and they usually are a sizable fraction of total system cost. In contrast, for satellite systems cost is distance independent.

In local area networks the currently prevalent topologies are the bus and the ring. Given a set of terminal locations, the ring or bus with the minimum line cost could be found by means of variations of the traveling salesman algorithm.[6-8] However, at the present state of the technology this is not a pressing problem since in local area networks line costs are a small fraction of the total cost.

Closely related to the layout problem are problems of reliability. Network configurations that provide connectivity in the face of link and node failures are considered. In some cases the network layout techniques can be used in reliability studies. In this case the length of a link can be a generalized quantity representing link reliability.

13.2. Trees

In a number of computer communications applications terminals are connected to a central point by means of multipoint lines. We have encountered such systems in Chapter 7 in our discussion of polling. The resulting multipoint network forms what is called a tree in graph theory. A tree can be defined as a network which as no closed paths and for which there is a unique path connecting any pair of nodes. An example of a tree network is shown in Figure 13.1. We may define a branch of a tree as a subset of a tree which is itself a tree. In Figure 13.1 the links $(6, 10)$, $(10, 11)$, and $(10, 12)$ form a branch. From the point of view of our presentation, the advantage of beginning our discussion with the tree structure is that there

---

†In preparing the material in the sequel, we have benefited greatly from several survey papers on the subject.[3-5]

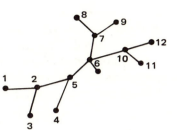

Figure 13.1. A tree network.

are no complications due to alternate routing. As we shall see this is not true for mesh networks where there is a relationship between routing and network layout.

13.2.1. Minimum Spanning Trees

The minimum spanning tree (MST) is the tree connecting a given set of nodes with the least total link length. We encountered the idea of a tree with minimum length in Chapter 12 when we found the shortest paths from a particular node to all other nodes. The difference between the two approaches is illustrated in Figures 13.2a and 13.2b. We have three points with the distance matrix shown. In Figure 13.2a, the minimum distances from node A are shown whereas in Figure 13.2b the MST for the three points is given.

We begin by considering the MST when there is no requirement on the network other than simple connectivity. The minimum spanning tree

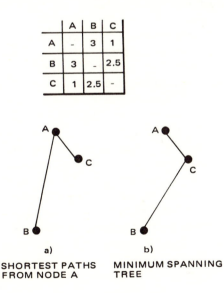

	A	B	C
A	-	3	1
B	3	-	2.5
C	1	2.5	-

a)

SHORTEST PATHS
FROM NODE A

b)

MINIMUM SPANNING
TREE

Figure 13.2. (a) Shortest path and (b) minimum spanning tree.

for a given set of points can be found by an algorithm† consisting of a repeated set of actions on what are called isolated nodes and subnets. A node is said to be isolated if it is unconnected to any other node. A subnet is simply a set of nodes which are connected to one another. The minimum spanning tree is found by repeating the following steps in arbitrary order until all the nodes are connected together:

- ◦ Connect an isolated terminal to its nearest neighbor, i.e., the node that is closest to it.
- ◦ Connect a subnet to the nearest node, i.e., the node closest to any of the nodes of the subnet.

A realization of the algorithm which is useful from the point of view of machine implementation is to begin by designating one of the nodes as the central node. The central node is then connected to the node closest to it. To the subnetwork consisting of these two nodes we add the node that is closest to it. This step of adding closest, isolated nodes to the subnetwork continues until all of the nodes are in the subnetwork. It can be shown that this algorthm leads to a unique minimum.

The proof that the algorithm leads to the MST rests on two necessary conditions:

- ◦ Every node in a minimum spanning tree is directly connected to at least one closest node.
- ◦ Every subnet is connected to at least one nearest neighbor by a shortest link.

The proof of the necessity of these conditions is shown by contradiction. If a network violates either of these conditions, a new network with shorter total distance can be generated. The steps of the algorithm conform to the necessary conditions.

We now apply the Prim algorithm to a particular case. In Table 13.1 the distances between pairs of points in a set of seven points is shown. For this set the succession of steps leading to a minimum spanning tree is illustrated in Figure 13.3.

The complexity of the algorithm can be evaluated by estimating the number of computations it requires as a function of the number of network nodes, N. At each step the minimum distances between isolated nodes and the subnet are computed. Since there are $N - i$ isolated nodes at the ith step of the algorithm, this involves $N - i$ comparisons. After an isolated node is added to the network, the distances to isolated nodes must be recomputed. This last step requires $N - i - 1$ comparisons. Adding over the n steps of the algorithm, we find that the total number of steps is N^2.

†The algorithm we present was devised by Prim.[9] For an alternative approach, see Ref. 10.

Table 13.1. Distance Matrix—Seven-Node Network

	A	B	C	D	E	F	G
A	—	4.0	7.3	9.6	4.4	7.4	9.2
B	4.0	—	2.6	5.7	2.0	4.5	5.0
C	7.3	2.6	—	2.4	5.0	6.0	2.7
D	9.6	5.7	2.4	—	6.7	6.8	2.8
E	4.4	2.0	5.0	6.7	—	3.0	7.7
F	7.4	4.5	6.0	6.8	3.0	—	8.6
G	9.2	5.0	2.7	2.8	7.7	8.6	—

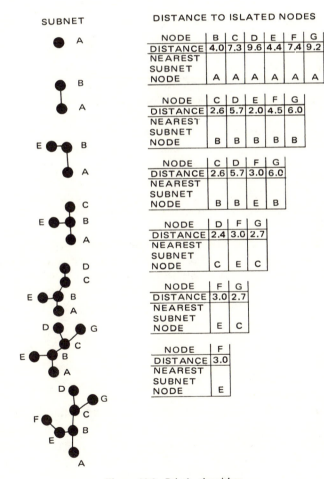

Figure 13.3. Prim's algorithm.

The MST algorithm can also be used to design more reliable networks. Suppose that, instead of the distance between points, we are given the probability that a link between a pair of points will fail. If we assume that links fail independently of one another, the probability of at least one node in a tree failing is $1 - \prod_{l=1}^{L} (1 - p_l)$, where L is the number of network links and p_l is the probability of the lth link failing. The problem is to find the tree that minimizes the probability of tree failure. As in the case of Euclidean distance, at the ith step we have a subnet consisting of i nodes. The tree failure probability resulting when each of the isolated nodes is added to the subnet is found. A new subnet is formed from the minimum.

13.2.2. Capacity Constraints

In a typical application of the tree topology, traffic flows between remote stations and a central processor. In terms of line length alone, the MST algorithm that we have been considering would find the optimum configuration for any central node. However, there is no guarantee that the capacities of the links are adequate to carry the traffic. In order to prevent the overloading of any of the links, we place a constraint on the volume of traffic that may flow in a link. For the sake of simplicity we shall assume that all existing links have the same capacity, C bps.

Reliability considerations may also impose a limitation on the number of nodes that may be located on the branch of a tree. If there were no such limitation, the failure of a single link could isolate an unacceptably large number of nodes. Both the constraint on the total traffic in a link and the constraint on the number of nodes in a branch can be handled in the same fashion.

Optimum constrained MST algorithms tend to be variations of *branch and bound* techniques. In this context, the term "branch" indicates the splitting of paths as alternative solutions are explored. The costs found on previous paths furnish a bound. A path violating the bound is abandoned. The application of the branch and bound technique to the constrained MST problem is based in part on the following theorem.[11]

Theorem. Suppose that an unconstrained MST over N nodes contains the links $(j_1, 1), (j_2, 1), \ldots, (j_k, 1)$, i.e., nodes $j_1, j_2, \ldots, j_k$ are directly connected to the central processor at node 1. There exists a constrained MST over the N nodes which include these same links.

We point out that, in order to satisfy the constraints, the constrained MST may have links to the central node other than those mentioned in the theorem. The proof of the theorem is based on the following observations.†
A branch of a constrained MST is an unconstrained MST over a subset of

---

†It is our intention here to establish plausibility. For the detailed proof see Ref. 11.

the N network nodes. The number of nodes in the subset is such that the constraints of the problem are satisfied. If link $(j_1, 1)$ is part of an unconstrained MST over all N nodes, it must be part of an unconstrained MST over a subset. Notice that if nodes and the links leading to them are removed from an unconstrained MST, the remaining networks are MSTs over the remaining nodes.

The algorithm for the constrained MST problem begins with the derivation of the unconstrained MST for all N points. An example for this algorithm is given in Figure 13.4 for the requirement given in Tables 13.1 and 13.2. The reader may wish to consult these tables while examining the algorithm. If the constraints are satisfied, we have an optimum configuration. Even if the constraints are not satisfied, we have made progress, for by Theorem 1 the links connected to the central node are part of the ultimate solution. The remainder of the algorithm consists of partitioning the set of possible solutions into smaller and smaller subsets. Each subset is the set of solutions under constraints involving the inclusion and exclusion of certain links. At each iteration of the algorithm a lower bound on the total length for each subset is computed. The algorithm terminates when the configuration representing the lower bound of a subset satisfies the constraints.

In order to describe the algorithm in detail, certain terminology and notation must be defined. The established links of a subset are those links which are present in every element of the subset. The disallowed links of

SUBSET	ESTABLISHED LINKS	DISALLOWED LINKS	LOWER BOUND
s(1, 1)	(E, F)	NONE	16.7
s(2, 1)	(E, F), (A, F), (B, E)	NONE	20.1
s(2, 2)	(E, F), (A, F)	(B, E)	22.1
s(3, 1)	(E, F), (A, F), (B, E), (B, C)	NONE	∞
s(3, 2)	(E, F), (A, F), (B, E)	(B, C)	22.5
s(3, 3)	(E, F), (A, F)	(B, E)	22.1
s(4, 1)	(E, F), (A, F), (B, E), (C, E)	(B, C)	∞
s(4, 2)	(E, F), (A, F), (B, E)	(B, C), (C, E)	23.5
s(4, 3)	(E, F), (A, F)	(B, E)	22.1
s(5, 1)	(E, F), (A, F), (B, E)	(B, C), (C, E)	23.5
s(5, 2)	(E, F), (A, F), (B, C)	(B, E)	22.1
s(5, 3)	(E, F), (A, F)	(B, C), (B, E)	24.5
s(6, 1)	(E, F), (A, F), (B, E)	(B, C), (C, E)	23.5
s(6, 2)	(E, F), (A, F), (B, C), (A, B)	(B, E)	∞
s(6, 3)	(E, F), (A, F), (B, C)	(B, E), (A, B)	22.6
s(6, 4)	(E, F), (A, F)	(B, C), (B, E)	24.5

Figure 13.4. Branch and bound example.

**Table 13.2. Traffic Volume—Seven-Node
Network**

Node	Average traffic volume (kbps)
A	45
B	20
C	10
D	10
E	25
G	5

a subset are present in no members of the subset. The links of a subset which are neither established nor disallowed are called free links. At the ith iteration the state of the algorithm is indicated by the notation $s(i, 1)$, $l(i, 1)$, $s(i, 2)$, $l(i, 2); \ldots ; s(i, k_i)$, $l(i, k_i)$, where k_i is the total number of subsets partitioning the set of solutions, $s(i, j)$ is the jth subset as defined by the sets of established and disallowed links. The term $l(i, j)$ indicates the lower bound on the total length of the jth subset.

The first step of the algorithm is to find the unconstrained MST for the set of points at hand. If the unconstrained MST is a feasible solution— i.e., it satisfies all of the constraints—it is the optimum solution. Otherwise, the algorithm is initialized by defining $s(1, 1)$ as the set of all solutions for which the links to the central node in the unconstrained MST are the only established links. $l(1, 1)$ is the length of the unconstrained MST. It follows from Theorem 1 that the complementary set to $s(1, 1)$ cannot contain an optimum solution and we eliminate it from consideration. $s(1, 1)$ is split into two subsets by making a free link established in one set and disallowed in the other. Also the lower bound for each of these new sets is calculated by finding the MST over all N nodes for a given set of established and disallowed links. If a subset has no feasible solution, it is eliminated from further consideration by setting its lower bound equal to infinity. (The details of these calculations will be treated in a moment.) The new sets and lower bounds are designated $s(2, 1)$ and $s(2, 2)$ and $l(2, 1)$ and $l(2, 2)$, respectively. At the $i + l$th step of the algorithm one finds the set $s(i, j)$ for which $l(i, j)$ is minimum, $j = 1, 2, \ldots, k_i$. If the MST which gives the lower bound for the set is feasible, it is the optimum solution. If not the set is split by designating a free link as either established or disallowed. The appropriate labels are assigned to the new subsets and bounds and the algorithm continues.

For each iteration of the algorithm an MST is found under certain constraints on links. This is done by means of an MST algorithm such as that presented earlier with the lengths of established links set at zero and disallowed links at infinity. Free links retain their normal values. The lower bound is the length of this "artificial" tree plus the sum of the lengths of the established links. The algorithm can be speeded up by the device of enlarging the set of disallowed links in this MST calculation. There may be certain links which are always part of unfeasible solutions. For example, the flow from nodes connected by established links may cause flow which is at or near saturation on certain links. Any links which contribute to that flow should be disallowed. Moreover, if the flow from nodes connected by established links saturates one or more links, then no member of the subset is feasible. In this case we set the lower bound eaual to infinity.

In Figure 13.4 an example for the constrained MST algorithm is worked out using the same set of points as in Table 13.1. As before we assume that node F is the central node. The average traffic volume from the outlying nodes to the central node is as shown in Table 13.2. It is assumed that the capacity of each of the links is 50 kbps. We assume that there is no constraint on the number of nodes that may reside in a branch. The steps of the algorithm are shown in Figure 13.4. On the second step of the algorithm we recognize that link (A, F) should be an established link for all solutions. If node A is connected to any other node, some link saturates. The process of splitting a set by making established and disallowed links is indicated by the arrows in Figure 13.4. The optimum solution is shown in Figure 13.5. Later developments have improved upon this algorithm.[12,13]

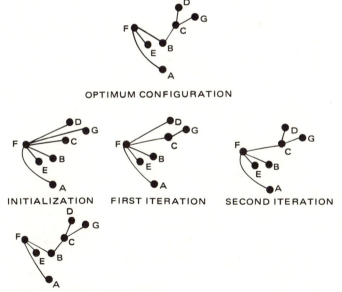

Figure 13.5. Esau–Williams algorithm.

13.2.3. Esau–Williams Algorithm

While the algorithm that we have just discussed obtains an optimum, it requires too much computation when the number of nodes is even of moderate size, $N = 40$, for example. However, several algorithms have been devised which yield solutions which are close to the optimum in fewer iterations. One of these is the Esau–Williams algorithm.[14] N remote terminals are to be connected to a central processor. Initially all of these terminals are assumed to have a dedicated line to the central processor. The repeated step of the algorithm is to calculate the maximum saving in line cost which may be realized by connecting a single one of these terminals to another terminal rather than directly to the central processor. This may be carried out in two substeps. For terminal i, $i = 1, 2, \ldots, N$, one computes the saving in line cost when it is connected to the terminals $j \neq i$. A connection is not allowed if it violates a capacity constraint. The maximum saving over all i is then found. The algorithm terminates when no improvement can be found.

The operation of the Esau–Williams algorithm is illustrated in Figure 13.5 for the same set of points as in Tables 13.1 and 13.2. Again it is assumed that F is the central processor. On the first iteration the maximum saving, 5.9 units of line length, is realized by connecting G to C. In the second iteration the saving is 4.4 units. In the last iteration the saving is 3.4 units. While it is true that terminal A is quite far from the central processor and offers potential saving, connecting it to any of its neighbors saturates the lines.

It happens in the seven-node example we have considered that the optimum branch and bound technique and the suboptimum Esau–Williams technique give the same solution. Of course this will not always be the case. Comparisons of suboptimum techniques with the optimum indicate that the suboptimum techniques yield networks whose costs are close to the optimum, typically within 10%, in far fewer computations.[5,7]

13.2.4. Concentrator Locations

In all of our treatment of tree networks we have assumed that only the given set of points could be nodes of the network. However, by allowing additions to the original set, line costs can be saved. A well-known example of this is shown in Figure 13.6. The length of the MST is 2 units. By adding what is called a Steiner point to the original set of three points, the network cost is reduced to 1.732 units. In telecommunications applications Steiner points would correspond to concentrators. At these points traffic from individual terminals would be multiplexed onto a transmission line to the central processor. The TDM techniques studied in Chapter 5 could well be used at this point.

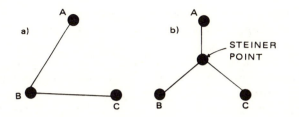

Figure 13.6. Steiner tree. (a) Minimum spanning tree; (b) Steiner tree.

The general concentrator problem is to minimize total cost including line and concentrator costs. Let c_{ij} be the cost of connecting terminal i to a concentrator at point j and let d_j be the cost of using a concentrator at point j. If there are N terminals and M concentrators, we may express the total cost as

$$T = \sum_{j=1}^{M} \sum_{i=1}^{N} x_{ij}c_{ij} + y_j d_j \qquad (13.1)$$

where

$$x_{ij} = \begin{cases} 1, & \text{if terminal } i \text{ is connected to a concentrator at point } j \\ 0, & \text{otherwise} \end{cases}$$

and where

$$y_j = \begin{cases} 1, & \text{if a concentrator is at point } j \\ 0, & \text{otherwise} \end{cases}$$

If a terminal may be connected to only one concentrator, we have the constraint

$$\sum_{j=1}^{M} x_{ij} = 1, \qquad i = 1, 2, \ldots, N$$

The problem then is to minimize the total cost subject to constraints on line and concentrator capacity. These latter constraints may include limitations on the total volume of traffic that can be handled or on the number of terminals that may be connected. If at most k terminals can be connected to a concentrator, we have the constraint

$$\sum_{i=1}^{N} x_{ij} \leq k, \qquad j = 1, 2, \ldots, M \qquad (13.2)$$

Under this general formulation, the problem is difficult, requiring a great deal of computational power.† We therefore seek a simplification. Suppose that the number of concentrators and their locations are known. The only problem then is to assign terminals to concentrators. An algorithm which gives an optimum is known. This algorithm is of interest because it is similar to a number of others. The algorithm is centered on the $N \times M$ matrix whose elements are the costs c_{ij}, $i = 1, 2, \ldots, N$, $j = 1, 2, \ldots, M$. We shall assume that the constraint is in the number of terminals that can be connected to a concentrator. [See equation (13.2).] The algorithm begins at the first row where the lowest cost concentrator for the first terminal is chosen. This step is repeated in turn for rows $2, 3, \ldots, N$ with a check to be sure that the constraint of equation (13.2) is satisfied. Now in any of these rows the lowest cost concentrator may be full due to prior selections. In this case no immediate selection of a concentrator is made for that particular terminal. The initial step of the algorithm ends after each of the N rows have been examined and whatever concentrators could be chosen have been chosen. Clearly the current assignment of terminals depends upon the order in which the rows were examined.

The next step is to return to the first row where a selection has not been made. Consider the lowest-cost assignment which does not violate the constraint. This assignment would yield a feasible, but not necessarily optimum, solution. Alternatives are examined in a systematic fashion. For the next lowest cost assignment there are k prior assignments of terminals to that concentrator. The gain in changing one of these prior assignments in favor of terminal l is calculated. The change that gives the largest positive gain is made. If there is no positive gain, no change is made. This step is repeated for each of the rows for which no assignment was made on the first iteration. The algorithm terminates when assignments have been made for all of the terminals.

The algorithm is worked out in Table 13.3 for the case of six terminals and four concentrators with the costs of connection as shown. The cost matrix is as shown. The element in the ith row and jth column is the cost of connecting terminal i to concentrator j. When a terminal is tentatively assigned the appropriate column is marked. The final minimal cost is 21 under the constraint of at most two terminals per concentrator.

13.3. Distributed Networks

The network topologies that we have considered to this point in the chapter have been suited to local distribution where traffic from a limited number of terminals is conveyed to a central processor. In this section we consider networks operating over a wide area. Packet and message switching

---

†For a summary of work in this area see Ref. 3.

Table 13.3. Concentrator Connection Algorithm

First iteration				Row three				Row four			
_6_	8	9	10	_6_	8	9	10	6	8	_9_	10
_2_	3	6	9	2	_3_	6	9	2	_3_	6	9
4	6	8	12	_4_	6	8	12	_4_	6	8	12
2	3	8	9	2	3	8	9	_2_	3	8	9
8	6	_1_	3	8	6	_1_	3	8	6	_1_	3
9	_2_	5	5	9	_2_	5	5	9	_2_	5	5

networks of this sort handle traffic from a range of sources in a flexible manner. For example routing and flow control can adapt to changes in traffic patterns. Such networks may form a backbone network tying together the central processors accessed by local distribution networks.

Since these networks carry traffic from a variety of sources over a wide area, reliability is of primary concern. One may to obtain a measure of reliability is to require that there be more than one path between all source–destination pairs in the network. (Notice that for the topologies we have considered previously in this chapter, there is only one such path.) The topology that results from this requirement may be called the mesh topology and the networks themselves are called distributed networks. We have seen an example of such a network in Figure 11.1.

The basic topological design problem begins with a traffic matrix indicating the flows between the source–destination pairs of the network. The objective is to choose links and link capacities so as to minimize the cost of the network subject to constraints on connectivity and performance. A reasonable measure of performance is average delay such as computed in Section 10.5 of Chapter 10.

The design of distributed networks draws from material that we have considered in previous chapters. Of particular importance is routing, considered in Chapter 12. As we have seen, optimum routing seeks to spread traffic throughout a network in order to optimize a particular cost criterion, e.g., average delay. Clearly routing and topology cannot be considered in isolation from one another.

For any reasonable number of nodes the number of possible network configurations is astronomical since any node can be connected to any number of other nodes. There are no known optimum techniques other than brute force search, which is out of the question for any network of interesting size. We shall present a particular suboptimum technique presently. The method is similar to the others that are available. All of the presently available methods are heuristic and have the same basic structure.†

†For a summary of these techniques, see Refs. 3–5.

A starting topology which satisfies the constraints is generated. This can be done by a combination of systematic and random procedures. The initial solution is changed slightly, by adding and dropping links, for example. If there is a decrease in cost, new routings are calculated for the new configuration and the constraints are checked. This operation is repeated on the new configuration until no improvement in performance can be obtained by the perturbation. The solution is then a local minimum which depends upon the starting configuration. The next step is to generate a new initial configuration and to derive a new local minimum. The process continues until no improvement is discerned. There are no hard and fast rules for the stopping point. Much depends upon the experience of the designer.

The effectiveness of the technique rests in large measure on the program implementing it. A key component of this program is the means of changing the current network since this is an operation that is repeated many times. Therefore it must be economical in terms of computer resources and must lead to a wide range of topologies. Again experience is important.

13.3.1. The Cut Saturation Algorithm

A design method that has been found to be successful is the cut saturation algorithm,[3] which is based on certain basic concepts of circuit theory.[1] A cut between two nodes is the set of links whose removal disconnects the nodes. For example, in Figure 13.7 possible cuts for nodes A and F are links AB and AC or links BD, CD, and EF. The sum of the capacities of the links of the cut is the capacity of the cut. The cut with the lowest capacity between a pair of nodes is called the minimum cut. A basic theorem of circuit theory is the Min Cut–Max Flow theorem, which states that the maximum flow between a pair of nodes cannot exceed the capacity of the minimum cut between the nodes. Now suppose that the traffic level in every link in the cut is at the capacity of the link. The only way the flow can be increased is by increasing the capacity of one of the links in the cut.

These circuit theoretic concepts suggest the following algorithm, which optimizes network cost with respect to throughput. A basic assumption is that all of the links have the same capacity. At the beginning of an iteration of the algorithm, we have a feasible network. The first step is to determine a saturated cutset. The links of this network are ordered according to the

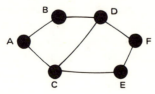

Figure 13.7. Simple mesh network.

volume of traffic they carry. Links are removed in sequence from the network, beginning with the most saturated, until two parts of the network are disconnected. We emphasize that this removal is only conceptual and has the purpose of finding the point of limitation to the throughput of the network. The next step of the algorithm consists of adding and deleting links between the two parts of the network separated by the saturated cut set. In order to provide diversity, added links are placed between nodes which had no prior direct links. Wherever possible end points of the new links are placed at least two links away from the end points of prior links. If a network is below the desired throughput or connectivity, links are only added. If the network is fully connected but costly, links can be deleted from the cut. It is reasonable to remove the most costly, least used link. Let d_i, C_i, and f_i be, respectively, the cost, the capacity, and the flow for link i. We calculate the quantity $d_i(C_i - f_i)/C_i$ for each link in the cut in order to determine the link to be deleted. When the network has near the desired throughput a link may be added and a link deleted in the same step. The same criteria as for separate additions and deletions are used.

After the additions and deletions have been completed optimal routing to minimize delay for the altered network is found. The techniques studied in Chapter 12, in particular the flow deviation method, can be employed in this step. The routing completes an iteration. The algorithm then returns to the determination of the saturated cutset.

The algorithm can be initiated either with a tree spanning the set of nodes or with a fully connected network. In the former case we begin with additions; in the latter with deletions.

The complexity of this algorithm, exclusive of routing, goes as the sum of the squares of the number of nodes and the number of links in the final design. Computations on typical networks have shown that the cut saturation algorithm performs at least as well as alternative techniques.

13.4. Network Reliability

As we stated above, distributed networks are designed so that more than one path exists between the source–destination pairs of the network. However, even with this redundancy multiple failures can cause network inoperability. In this section we consider techniques for assessing this event. Our study will be more in the nature of a survey than other areas that we have considered in this book. An in-depth study would require far more basic circuit theory than we have available.†

† For tutorials on network reliability see Refs. 15–17.

The basic approaches to network reliability may be classed under two broad categories: deterministic and random. In the deterministic approach a question that has been studied is, how many links must fail in a given network in order for the network to become disconnected? In the probabilistic approach it is assumed that links and node fail with certain probabilities. The question is, what is the probability of the network becoming disconnected? We shall concentrate on the probabilistic approach. This approach seems to be more relevant to communications networks. The deterministic approach is more in the realm of circuit theory.

13.4.1. Probability of Disconnect

A number of measures of performance have been considered in connection with the probabilistic approach. We shall consider others, but we begin with the simplest measure, which is the probability of at least one node in the network becoming disconnected. For simplicity we speak of this as the probability of the network becoming disconnected. The classical analysis of Moore and Shannon[18,19] allows bounds to be calculated.

Let L and N denote the number of links and nodes, respectively. We begin the analysis of network reliability with the assumption that individual links fail independently of one another with probability $p > 0$. We assume that the probability of node failure is zero. Let $C(k)$ denote the number of ways that a network under consideration can be disconnected when k links are operational. The probability of any particular set of k operational links is $p^{L-k}(1-p)^k$. Summing over all value of k we find that the probability of a network becoming disconnected is

$$f(p) = \sum_{k=0}^{L} C(k)p^{L-k}(1-p)^k \tag{13.3}$$

The key to this computation is of course the term $C(k)$. Consideration of this term leads to upper and lower bounds for $f(p)$. We begin with the observation that in order to connect N nodes at least $N-1$ links are required. If there are fewer links the network will be disconnected. We have $C(k) = \binom{L}{k}$ for $k = 0, 1, 2, \ldots, N-2$. The network can just as well be disconnected for a larger number of links, but ignoring these gives a lower bound

$$f(p) \geq \sum_{k=0}^{N-2} \binom{L}{k} P^{L-k}(1-p)^k$$

$$= \sum_{l=L-N+2}^{L} \binom{L}{l} p^l(1-p)^{L-l} \tag{13.4}$$

Consider now the upper bound. Let B be the minimum number of links that must be deleted for the network to be disconnected. Clearly $C(L - i) = 0$ for $i = 0, 1, 2, \ldots, B - 1$. Now the network may not be disconnected for $i = B, B + 1, \ldots, L$, but we form an upper bound by ignoring these possibilities. We have

$$f(p) \leq \sum_{k=B}^{L} \binom{L}{k} p^k (1 - p)^{L-k} \tag{13.5}$$

Further refinements of these bounds are possible. When there are only $N - 1$ links, the network connecting the N nodes is a tree. Therefore $C(N - 1)$ is the number of trees that can connect N nodes. This latter is a known quantity.[20] We may then add a term to the lower bound to obtain

$$f(p) \geq C(N - 1) p^{L-N+1}(1 - p)^{N-1} + \sum_{l=L-N+2}^{L} \binom{L}{l} p^l (1 - p)^{L-l} \tag{13.6}$$

In consideration of the upper bound, we note that B, the minimum number of links to disconnect, is often a small quantity; consequently the term $C(L - B)$ may be found by simple enumeration. We may then refine the lowest term in the upper bound to obtain

$$f(p) \leq \sum_{k=B+1}^{L} \binom{L}{k} p^k (1 - p)^{L-k} + C(L - B) p^B (1 - p)^{L-B} \tag{13.7}$$

For values of p close to 1, $f(p)$ is close to the lower bound and for p near 0, $f(p)$ is close to the upper bound. These results can be extended to the case where node as well as links have nonzero probability of failure.

Beyond this rudimentary beginning, work in reliability has gone in several directions. A number of criteria, other than network disconnect, have been used to evaluate network reliability.[17] A criterion that has commanded a great deal of attention is the probability that all paths between a particular pair of nodes are interrupted. Under the foregoing assumptions on link failures this can be written

$$g(p; A, B) = \sum_{k=0}^{L} CS(k; A, B) p^k (1 - p)^{L-k} \tag{13.8}$$

where A and B are the nodes in question and where $CS(k; A, B)$ indicates the set of cuts between A and B consisting of k links. As defined earlier, a cut is a set of links whose loss separates the nodes.

An algorithm which finds $CS(k; A, B)$ efficiently thereby allowing an exact calculation has been devised.[21] The algorithm consists of a search along the paths between the two nodes. Notice that the sets of links incident to either nodes are cuts. Again these results can be extended to the case of node and link failures. A more general approach which finds other measures of node connectivity has been found. An example of such measures is the expected number of pairs of node-pairs that can communicate with one another.

In the foregoing we have considered reliability criteria which focus on connectivity. Loss of network connectivity constitutes a hard failure. However, even in the absence of a hard failure, the loss of network links may cause network performance to be unsatisfactory. In spite of flow control and routing, the loss of network nodes and links will cause congestion in the remaining facilities thereby increasing delay. In view of these considerations, it is appropriate that the effect of link and node failures on throughput and delay be studied. The performance of the network can be found for each set of node and link failures. Under our assumptions on the independence of failures, the probabilities of each of the states can be calculated. Performance averaged over the states can then be found. The difficulty of this approach is that calculations are required for all network states. In any reasonable size network this calculation is intractable. An alternative approach is to find bounds on performance based on the subset of most probable states.[22]

In the analyses that have been discussed above, it is assumed that failures are independent. In many applications this is a significant shortcoming. In the telephone plant, for example, local loops share the same bundle. If the bundle is cut, links which are diversified from an electrical point of view are lost. Further, as we have seen in Chapter 2, a number of channels may be multiplexed on the same carrier facilities. The reader may well wonder if studies of this aspect of reliability have appeared in the literature. The answer is "yes".[23–25]

References

1. H. Frank and I. T. Frisch, *Communication, Transmission and Transportation Networks*, Addision-Wesley, Reading, Massachusetts (1971).
2. S. Even, *Graph Algorithms*, Computer Science Press, Rockville, Maryland (1979).
3. R. Boorstyn and H. Frank, "Large-Scale Network Topological Optimization," *IEEE Transactions on Communications*, **COM-25**(1), 29–47, January (1977).
4. H. Frank and W. Chou, "Topological Optimization of Computer Networks," *Proceedings of the IEEE*, **60**, 1385–1397, November (1972).
5. M. Gerla and L. Kleinrock, "On the Topological Design of Distributed Computer Networks," *IEEE Transactions on Communications*, **COM-25**(1), 48–60, January (1976).
6. S. Lin, "Computer Solutions of the Traveling Salesman Problem," *Bell System Technical Journal*, **44**, 2245–2269 (1965).
7. R. E. Gomory, "The Traveling Salesman Problem," *Proceedings of the IBM Scientific Computing Symposium on Combinatorial Problems* (1966).

8. E. M. Reingold, J. Nievergelt, and N. Deo, *Combinational Algorithms Theory and Practice*, Prentice-Hall, Englewood Cliffs, New Jersey (1977).

9. R. C. Prim, "Shortest-Connection Networks and Some Generalizations," *Bell System Technical Journal*, **36**, 1389–1401 (1957).

10. J. B. Kruskal, "On the Shortest Spanning Subtree of a Graph and the Traveling Salesman Problem," *Proceedings of the American Mathematical Society*, **7** (1956).

11. K. M. Chandy and R. A. Russel, "The Design of Multipoint Linkages in a Teleprocessing Tree Network," *IEEE Transactions on Computers*, **COM-21**, 1062–1066, October (1972).

12. K. M. Chandy and T. Lo, "The Capacitated Minimum Spanning Tree," *Networks*, **3**(2), 173–182 (1973).

13. D. Elias and M. J. Ferguson," Topological Design of Multipoint Teleprocessing Networks," *IEEE Transactions on Communications*, **COM-22**(11), 1753–1762, November (1974).

14. L. R. Esau and K. C. Williams, "A Method for Approximating the Optimal Network," *IBM Systems Journal*, **5**, 142–147 (1966).

15. H. Frank and I. T. Frisch, "Analysis and Design of Survivable Networks," *IEEE Transactions on Communication Technology*, **COM-18**(5), 501–520, October (1970).

16. R. S. Wilkov, "Analysis and Design of Reliable Computer Networks," *IEEE Transactions on Communications*, **COM-20**(3), 660–678, June (1972).

17. M. O. Ball, "Computing Network Reliability," *Operations Research*, **27**(4), 823–838, July–August (1979).

18. E. F. Moore and C. E. Shannon, "Reliable Circuits Using Less Reliable Relays," *Journal of the Franklin Institute*, **262**, Pt I, 191–208 (1956).

19. R. Van Slyke and H. Frank, "Network Reliability Analysis, Part I," *Networks*, **1**, 279–290 (1972).

20. R. G. Busacker and T. L. Saaty, *Finite Graphs and Networks*, McGraw-Hill, New York (1965).

21. E. Hansler, G. K. McAuliffe, and R. S. Wilkov, "Exact Calculations of Computer Network Reliability," *AFIPS Proceedings*, **41** (1972).

22. V. O. K. Li and J. A. Silvester, "Performance Analysis of Networks with Unreliable Components," to be published *IEEE Transactions on Communications*.

23. J. Spragins, "Dependent Failures in Data Communication Systems," *IEEE Ttansactions on Communications*, **COM-25**(15), 1494–1499, December (1977).

24. S. N. Pan and J. Spragins, "Dependent Failure Reliability Models for Tactical Communications Networks," *Proceedings of the International Conference on Communications* (1983), pp. 765–771.

25. Y. F. Lam and V. O. K. Li, "A Failure Model and Reliability Evaluation for Networks with Dependent Failures," to be published *IEEE Transactions on Communications*.

Exercises

13.1. Find the minimum spanning tree for the set of points whose distances from one another are given in Table 13.4.

13.2. We wish to design a tree spanning five nodes that is maximally reliable. Suppose that the probability of the failures of links between pairs of nodes is given in Table 13.5.

13.3. For the distance between pairs of nodes given in Table 13.1, find the constrained MST when the constraint is that no more than three nodes should be on the same branch. Again assume that all flow is into node *G*. Do this two ways: (a) the branch and bound algorithm, (b) the Esau–Williams algorithm.

Table 13.4. Distance Matrix—Seven-Node Network

	A	B	C	D	E	F	G
A	—	4.5	6.0	4.0	7.5	8.5	13.0
B	4.5	—	4.0	8.5	6.5	9.5	10.5
C	6.0	4.0	—	8.0	3.0	7.5	7.0
D	4.0	8.5	8.0	—	7.0	5.0	13.0
E	7.5	6.5	3.0	7.0	—	5.0	6.0
F	8.0	9.5	7.5	5.0	5.0	—	10.5
G	13.0	10.5	7.0	13.0	6.0	10.5	—

Table 13.5. Failure Probabilities—Five-Node Network

	A	B	C	D	E
A	—	0.02	0.01	0.03	0.04
B	0.02	—	0.01	0.02	0.02
C	0.01	0.01	—	0.01	0.03
D	0.03	0.02	0.01	—	0.02
E	0.04	0.02	0.03	0.02	—

13.4. Consider the distance matrix given in Table 13.4. Suppose that a central processor is located at node G. All links have capacity 9.6 kbps. Assume that the traffic generated at each of the nodes is 3.0 kbps. Find the MST using the branch and bound algorithm and the Esau–Williams algorithm.

13.5. For the mesh network shown in Figure 13.8, what are the cuts between nodes A and J?

13.6. For the network shown in Figure 13.7, calculate the upper and lower bound for the probability of the network becoming disconnected as a function of p, the probability of link failure.

13.7. Repeat Exercise 13.6 for the network shown in Figure 13.8.

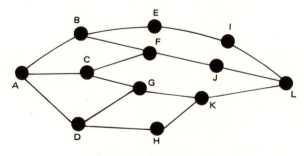

Figure 13.8. Mesh network.

Review of Probability Theory

In this appendix we review the basic concepts of probability theory. This review is not intended to be adequate for the reader encountering the subject for the first time. For a complete treatment the reader is directed to one of the many excellent texts on the subject.†

A.1. Axioms of Probability

Basic set theory forms the foundation for the definition of probability. We define Ω as the set of all possible outcomes of an experiment, e.g., 1, 2, 3, 4, 5, 6 in the toss of a die. We define the set of events A. An *event* is defined to be a subset of the set of all experimental outcomes, e.g., odd numbers in the toss of a die. The elements of A are subsets of Ω. On the set of events we define the following set operations:

1. Complementation: A^c is the event that event A does not occur.
2. Intersection: $A \cap B$ is the event that events A and B occur.
3. Union: $A \cup B$ is the event that events A or B occur.
4. Inclusion: $A \subset B$ event A occurring implies event B occurs.

The set of events, A, is closed under these operations. Thus if A and B are events then A^c, B^c, $A \cup B$, $A \cap B, \ldots$, are also events. For example, if in the toss of a die, $\{1, 4, 5\}$ and $\{1\}$ are events, so are $\{2, 3, 6\}$, $\{1, 2, 3, 6\}$, $\{2, 3, 4, 5, 6\}$, $\{4, 5\}$, $\varnothing$ (empty or null set), and Ω. Two sets of events are said to be disjoint if they have no common elements, i.e., events A and B are disjoint if $A \cap B = \varnothing$.

Let $P(A)$ denote the probability of event A. The probability of event A is a function on the set of events which satisfies the following axioms:

†At the end of this appendix are listed the three probability texts with which we are most familiar.

A.I   There is a nonempty set of experimental outcomes, Ω, and, $\mathscr{A}$, a set of events defined over the set of outcomes.

A.II   For any event $A \in \mathscr{A}$, $\Pr(A) \geq 0$.

A.III For the set of all possible experimental outcomes, Ω, $\Pr(\Omega) = 1$.

A.IV   If the events A and B are disjoint then $P(A \cup B) = P(A) + P(B)$.

A.V   For countably infinite sets $A_1, A_2, A_3, \ldots$, such that $A_i \cap A_j = \varnothing$ for $i \neq j$ we have

$$P\left(\bigcup_{i=1}^{\infty} A_i\right) = \sum_{i=1}^{\infty} P(A_i)$$

From these axioms all of the properties of the probability can be derived. A partial list of these properties is as follows:

1. $P(A) \leq 1$ for any event $A \in \mathscr{A}$;
2. $P(A^c) = 1 - P(A)$, where A^c denotes the complement of A;
3. $P(A \cup B) = P(A) + P(B) - P(A \cap B)$, for arbitrary A and B;
4. $P(A) \leq P(B)$ for $A \subset B$.

A.2. Conditional Probability

The idea of the probability of an event can be extended to establish relationships between events. We define the *conditional* probability

$$P(A/B) = \frac{P(A \cap B)}{P(B)} \tag{A.1}$$

We term $P(A/B)$ the probability of event A conditioned on the occurrence of event B. It can be shown that $P(A/B)$ is a valid probability inasmuch as it satisfies the axioms. The events A and B are said to be *independent* if $P(A \cap B) = P(A)P(B)$. From equation (A.1) this implies that $P(A/B) = P(A)$, meaning that the occurrence of event B has no bearing on the probability of event A.

Consider now a set of events which partition the set of experimental outcomes, if

$$\bigcup_{i=1}^{n} A_i = \Omega \tag{A.2a}$$

and

$$A_i \cap A_j = \varnothing, \qquad i \neq j \tag{A.2b}$$

We say that the sets $A_1, A_2, \ldots, A_n$ partition the space. We can write any event B in terms of the disjoint events $A_1, A_2, \ldots, A_n$:

$$B = \bigcup_{i=1}^{n} (A_i \cap B) \tag{A.3a}$$

From axiom A.IV we have

$$P(B) = \sum_{i=1}^{n} P(A_i \cap B) \tag{A.3b}$$

This is the *law* of *total probability*, which is of considerable utility in the text. The application of this law leads to *Bayes rule*, which states that

$$P(A_i/B) = \frac{P(A_i)P(B/A_i)}{\sum_{i=1}^{n} P(A_i)P(B/A_i)} \tag{A.4}$$

A.3. Random Variables—Probability Distributions and Densities

A *random variable* is a function on the set of experimental outcomes mapping the experimental outcomes onto the real line. *Discrete random variables* are mapped onto a countable set of points on the real line, possibly infinite. *Continuous random variables* are mapped into an interval on the real line. Discrete or continuous random variables may be characterized by their *probability distribution functions*, which are defined as

$$F_X(x) \triangleq P[X \leq x] \tag{A.5}$$

Thus the probability distribution function evaluated at x is the probability of a set of experimental outcomes which map into the interval $(-\infty, x)$.

From the basic axioms of probability the following properties for the probability distribution function may be shown: $F_X(-\infty) = 0$, $F_X(\infty) = 1$, and $F(X_1) \leq F(x_2)$ if $x_1 \leq x_2$. From the probability distribution function one can calculate the probability of an event lying in an interval

$$P[x_1 < X \leq x_2] = F_X(x_2) - F_X(x_1), \qquad x_1 \leq x_2 \tag{A.6}$$

For a *discrete* random variable the probability distribution function is a sequence of steps. The height of each step is the probability of the random variable assuming a particular value (see Figure A.1). From equations (A.5) and (A.6), we have

$$P[X = x] = F_X(x) - F_X(x^-) \tag{A.7}$$

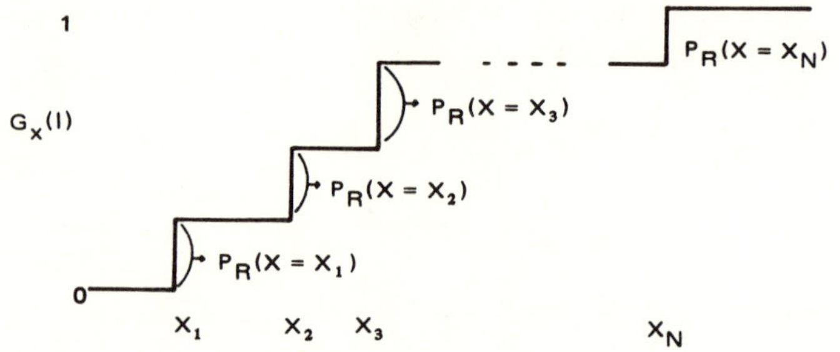

Figure A.1. Probability distribution function, discrete random variable.

where

$$x^- = \lim_{\varepsilon \to 0} x - \varepsilon, \qquad \varepsilon > 0$$

The probabilities $P(X = x_i)$, $i = 1, 2, \ldots, N$, where $x_1, x_2, \ldots, x_N$ are all possible values of X, serve as an alternate characterization of the random variable. From the axioms of probability we have

1. $P[X = x_i] \geq 0, \qquad i = 1, 2, \ldots, N$
2. $P[(X = x_i) U(X = x_j)] = P[X = x_i] + P[X = x_j], \qquad i \neq j$
3. $\sum_{i=1}^{N} P[X = x_i] = 1$

In the text three types of discrete random variables play a prominent role in the text. For the *binomial* distribution

$$P[X = k] = \binom{n}{k} p^k (1 - p)^{n-k}, \qquad k = 0, 1, \ldots, n \qquad \text{(A.8a)}$$

where $0 \leq p \leq 1$ and the positive integer n are parameters. The *Poisson* distribution is given by

$$P[X = k] = \frac{\lambda^k e^{-\lambda}}{k!}, \qquad k = 0, 1, 2, \ldots \qquad \text{(A.8b)}$$

where $\lambda \geq 0$ is a parameter. Finally we have the *geometric* distribution in which

$$P[X = k] = Q^k (1 - Q), \qquad k = 0, 1, \ldots \qquad \text{(A.8c)}$$

where $0 \leq Q \leq 1$.

It is an easy exercise to demonstrate that the probabilities in each of these cases sum to one.

For a *continuous* random variable the probability distribution function is a continuous monotonically nondecreasing function. (See Figure A.2.) In this case the random variable may be characterized by the *probability density function*, which is defined as

$$f_X(x) \triangleq \frac{dF_X(x)}{dx} \qquad (A.9a)$$

or

$$F_X(x) = \int_{-\infty}^{x} f_X(e)\, dx \qquad (A.9b)$$

The properties of the probability distribution function imply the following properties for the density function: $f_X(x) \geq 0$ for all x and $\int_{-\infty}^{\infty} f_X(x)\, dx = 1$. Although the distribution function and the density function may be defined for discrete random variable, they find greater use in connection with continuous random variables. By way of illustration we cite three prominent examples of continuous random variables. (See Figure A.3.) First of all we have the Gaussian or normally distributed random variables which has density function

$$f_X(x) = \frac{e^{-(x-\mu)^2/2\sigma^2}}{(2\pi)^{1/2}\sigma}, \qquad -\infty < x < \infty \qquad (A.10a)$$

where μ and σ are parameters.

The *exponentially* distributed random variable has density function

$$f_X(x) = \begin{cases} 0, & x < 0 \\ \lambda\, e^{-\lambda x}, & x \geq 0 \end{cases} \qquad (A.10b)$$

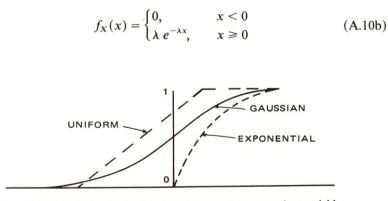

Figure A.2. Probability distribution functions, continuous random variables.

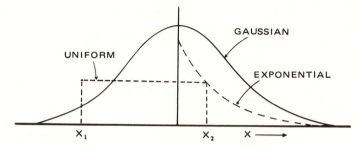

Figure A.3. Probability density functions, continuous random variables.

where λ is a parameter. Finally given x_1 and x_2, with $x_1 \leq x_2$, as parameter, the *uniform* distribution is

$$f_X(x) = \begin{cases} 1/(x_2 - x_1), & x_1 \leq x \leq x_2 \\ 0, & \text{otherwise} \end{cases} \qquad \text{(A.10c)}$$

The probability distribution function for each of these random variables can be found from equation (A.9b).

There are applications where a mixed random variable is encountered. the probability is spread over an interval as for a continuous random variable but there are points of concentration as for a discrete random variable. In this case the probability distribution has jumps at the points of concentration represented by unit steps

$$F_X(x) = \sum_{i=1}^{N} P_i U(x - x_i) + G_X(x)$$

where P_i are the probabilities and $G_X(x)$ is a continuous function. The probability density may be represented in terms of Dirac delta functions

$$f_X(x) = \sum_{i=1}^{N} P_i \delta(x - x_i) + g_X(x)$$

A.4. Joint Distributions of Random Variables

In this section we consider relations between two or more random variables. We define the *joint* probability distribution function of two random variables X and Y as

$$F_{XY}(x, y) \triangleq P[X \leq x, Y \leq y], \qquad -\infty < x, y < \infty \qquad \text{(A.11)}$$

where x and y are real numbers. the random variables may represent different mappings onto the real line from the same space of experimental outcomes. the properties of the joint density function are

$$F_{XY}(-\infty, -\infty) = 0, \qquad F_{XY}(\infty, \infty) = 1,$$

$$F_{XY}(x_1, y) \leq F_{XY}(x_2, y) \qquad \text{for } x_1 \leq x_2$$

and

$$F_{XY}(x, y_1) \leq F_{XY}(y, y_2) \qquad \text{for } y_1 \leq y_2$$

The joint probability density function of the random variables X and Y is defined as

$$f_{XY}(x, y) \triangleq \frac{\partial^2 F_{XY}(x, y)}{\partial x \, \partial y}, \qquad -\infty < x, y < \infty \tag{A.12}$$

In analogy with the one-dimensional case we have the following properties for the joint density function:

$$f_{XY}(x, y) \geq 0_i, \qquad -\infty < x, y < \infty \quad \text{and} \quad \int_{-\infty}^{\infty} dx \int_{-\infty}^{\infty} dy \, f_{XY}(x, y) = 1$$

The marginal distribution and density functions, when they exist, may be calculated from the joint functions. We have

$$F_X(x) = F_{XY}(x, \infty) \tag{A.13a}$$

$$F_Y(y) = F_{XY}(\infty, y) \tag{A.13b}$$

$$f_X(x) = \int_{-\infty}^{\infty} f_{XY}(x, y) \, dy \tag{A.13c}$$

$$f_Y(y) = \int_{-\infty}^{\infty} f_{XY}(x, y) \, dx \tag{A.13d}$$

Two random variables are independent if

$$F_{XY}(x, y) = F_X(x) F_Y(y) \tag{A.14a}$$

or equivalently in terms of probability density functions

$$f_{XY}(x, y) = f_X(x) f_Y(y) \tag{A.14b}$$

For random variables which are not independent the concepts of conditional distribution and density functions come into play. We define the conditional distribution function

$$F_{X/Y}(x/y) = \frac{P(X \le x, Y \le y)}{P(Y \le y)} = \frac{F_{XY}(x, y)}{F_Y(y)} \qquad \text{(A.15a)}$$

The events here is the probability that $\{X \le x\}$ given that $Y \le y$. We may also define the conditional density of the random variable X as

$$f_{X/Y}(x/y) = \frac{f_{XY}(x, y)}{f_Y(y)} \qquad \text{(A.15b)}$$

This is the probability density of X conditioned on the event $Y = y$.

Although we have discussed joint density functions, joint distribution functions, and independence in connection with two random variables, these same concepts apply in a straightforward way to three or more random variables.

A.5. Expectation of a Random Variable—Moments

The distributions of random variables are characterized by a number which is called the *expectation* or the *mean value* of a random variable, which is defined to be

$$E[X] \triangleq \sum_{i=1}^{\infty} x_i P(X = x_i) \qquad \text{(A.16a)}$$

for discrete random variables and

$$E[X] \triangleq \int_{-\infty}^{\infty} x f_X(x) \, dx \qquad \text{(A.16b)}$$

for continuous random variables.

The expectation of a random variable which can be expressed as a function of another random variable, X, i.e., $E[Y]$, where $Y = g(X)$, can be found from the distribution function of X. In the discrete case we have

$$E[Y] = E[g(X)] = \sum_{i=1}^{\infty} g(x_i) P[X = x_i] \qquad \text{(A.17a)}$$

and in the continuous case

$$E[Y] = E[g(X)] = \int_{-\infty}^{\infty} g(x)f_X(x)\, dx \qquad \text{(A.17b)}$$

The most useful functions in terms of characterizing random variables are of the form $Y = X^k$. The kth moment of a random variable is $E[X^k]$ and the kth central moment is $E[(X - E[X])^k]$. The *variance* of a random variable is the second central moment:

$$\text{Var}(X) \triangleq E[(X - E[X])^2] = E[X^2] - (E[X])^2 \qquad \text{(A.18)}$$

For the random variables cited above, it can be shown that the means and the variances are as shown in Table A.1. Notice that in all of these cases if the form of the distribution, e.g., Gaussian, is known, then knowledge of the mean and the variance allows the complete distribution to be found. In the cases of the Poisson, geometric, and exponential distributions only the mean is required. From the properties of expectation the mean and the variance of a linear transformation follow immediately:

$$E[aX + b] = aE[X] + b \qquad \text{(A.19a)}$$

$$\text{Var}(aX + b) = a^2\,\text{Var}(X) \qquad \text{(A.19b)}$$

If the joint probabilities of two random variables are known, joint moments may be calculated. In the discrete and the continuous cases we have, respectively,

$$E[XY] = \sum_{i=1}^{\infty} \sum_{j=1}^{\infty} x_i y_j P(X = x_i, Y = y_j) \qquad \text{(A.20a)}$$

Table A.1. Means and Variances

Distribution	Mean	Variance
Binomial (A.8a)	nP	$nP(1 - P)$
Poisson (A.8b)	λ	λ
Geometric (A.8c)	$Q/(1 - Q)$	$Q/(1 - Q)^2$
Gaussian (A.10a)	μ	σ^2
Exponential (A.10b)	$1/\lambda$	$1/\lambda^2$
Uniform (A.10c)	$(x_2 - x_1)/2$	$(x_2 - x_1)^2/3$

and

$$E[XY] = \int_{-\infty}^{\infty} dx \int_{-\infty}^{\infty} dy \, xy f_{XY}(x, y) \tag{A.20b}$$

This joint first moment is called the *correlation* or the *autocorrelation* of the random variables X and Y. The *covariance* or the *autocovariance* is defined as

$$\begin{aligned}
\text{Cov}\,(X, Y) &= E[(X - E[X])(Y - E[Y])] \\
&= \sum_{i=1}^{\infty} \sum_{j=1}^{\infty} (x_i - E[X])(y_j - E[Y]) \\
&\quad \times P[X = x_i, Y = y_j] \qquad \text{(discrete case)} \\
&= \int_{-\infty}^{\infty} dx \int_{-\infty}^{\infty} dy \,(x - E[X])(y - E[Y]) \\
&\quad \times f_{XY}(x, y) \qquad \text{(continuous case)}
\end{aligned} \tag{A.21}$$

We say that two random variables are uncorrelated if $E[XY] = E[X]E[Y]$ or equivalently $\text{Cov}\,(X, Y) = 0$. When random variables are independent they are of necessity uncorrelated. However, it is only for Gaussian random variables that uncorrelatedness implies independence. Since taking the expectation of a random variable is a linear operation, the expected value of the sum of two random variables is simply the sum of the expected values:

$$E[X_1 + X_2] = E[X_1] + E[X_2] \tag{A.22}$$

This holds even if the random variables are not independent. When two random variables are uncorrelated the variance of the sum is equal to the sum of the variance:

$$\text{Var}\,(X_1 + X_2) = \text{Var}\,(X_1) + \text{Var}\,(X_2) \tag{A.23}$$

The distribution of sums of independent random variables can be found by means of convolution. Let $Y = X_1 + X_2$. If X_1 and X_2 are discrete random variables then

$$P[Y = k] = \sum_{i=-\infty}^{\infty} P[X_1 = i]P[X_2 = k - i] \tag{A.24a}$$

For continuous random variables we have

$$f_Y(y) = \int_{-\infty}^{\infty} dx\, f_{X_1}(x) f_{X_2}(y - x) \qquad \text{(A.24b)}$$

when $f_Y(y)$, $f_{X_1}(x)$, and $f_{X_2}(x)$ are the appropriate probability density functions.

A.6. Probability-Generating Functions and Characteristic Functions

Frequently it is more convenient to express distributions in terms of transforms. This is the case in queueing theory, for example. The *probability-generating function* of the discrete random variable X is defined as

$$X(Z) \triangleq E[Z^X] = \sum_{i=0}^{\infty} Z^i P[X = i] \qquad \text{(A.25)}$$

where Z is a complex variable. The probability-generating function has an obvious relationship to the Z transform of the sequence $P[X = i]$, $i = 0, 1, 2, \ldots$. The probability-generating function contains all of the information that the probability distribution does. One can be obtained from the other. A noteworthy property of the probability-generating function is that it is analytic on the unit disk. Note that

$$|X(Z)| \leq \sum_{i=0}^{\infty} |Z|^i P[X = i] \leq \sum_{i=0}^{\infty} P[X = i] = 1 \qquad \text{(A.26)}$$

Given the probability-generating function of a random variable the moments of the random variable can be easily found. For the first moment we have

$$E[X] = \frac{dX(Z)}{dZ}\bigg|_{Z=1} = \sum_{i=0}^{\infty} iZ^{i-1} P[X = i]\big|_{Z=1} = \sum_{i=0}^{\infty} iP[X = i]$$

Higher moments can be found from successive differentiation and manipulation. For example, we find

$$E[X^2] = \frac{d^2 X(Z)}{dZ^2}\bigg|_{Z=1} + \frac{dX(Z)}{dZ}\bigg|_{Z=1}$$

From equation (A.24a) and the definitions of generating functions it can be shown that the generating functions of the sum of independent random variables is the product of the individual generating function; i.e., if $Y = X_1 + X_2$ then

$$Y(Z) = X_1(Z)X_2(Z) \qquad \text{(A.27)}$$

where $X_1(Z)$ and $X_2(Z)$ are the probability-generating functions of X_1 and X_2, respectively. For the continuous random variable, X, we define the *characteristic function* to be

$$\phi_X(\omega) = E[e^{j\omega x}] = \int_{-\infty}^{\infty} dx \, e^{jx\omega} f_X(x) \qquad \text{(A.28a)}$$

and

$$j = \sqrt{-1}$$

where ω is real. The properties of the characteristic function are similar to those of the probability-generating function. The characteristic function and the probability density functions are Fourier transform pairs. Given the characteristic function, the density function is given by

$$f_X(x) = \frac{1}{2\pi} \int_{-\infty}^{\infty} \phi_X(\omega) \, e^{-j\omega x} \alpha\omega \qquad \text{(A.28b)}$$

The moments of the random variable X can be found in an even more straightforward fashion:

$$\left. \frac{d^k \phi_X(\psi)}{d\omega^k} \right|_{\omega=0} = \int_{-\infty}^{\infty} dx \, x^k f_X(x) = j^k E[X^k] \qquad \text{(A.29)}$$

If the random variables X_1 and X_2 are independent, then the characteristic function of $Y = X_1 + X_2$ is

$$\phi_Y(\omega) = \phi_{X_1}(\omega)\phi_{X_2}(\omega) \qquad \text{(A.30)}$$

where $\phi_{X_1}(\omega)$ and $\phi_{X_2}(\omega)$ are the characteristic functions of X_1 and X_2, respectively.

Closely related to the characteristic function of a random variable is the Laplace transform of its probability density function. For a random variable X with probability density function $f_X(x)$ we have

$$\mathscr{X}(s) \triangleq \int_0^{\infty} e^{-st} f_X(t) \, dt \qquad \text{(A.31)}$$

$\mathcal{X}(s)$ is analytic in the right-half plane. If, as is frequently the case in queueing theory, X is a positive random variable, then

$$\mathcal{X}(s) = E[e^{-sx}] \tag{A.32}$$

In this case the relation between the characteristic function and the Laplace transform is

$$\mathcal{X}(-j\omega) = \Phi_X(\omega)$$

Moments of the random variable can be calculated from the Laplace transform. From equation (A.31) we have

$$\left.\frac{d^j\mathcal{X}(s)}{ds^j}\right|_{s=0} = \int_0^\infty (-t)^j f_X(t)\, dt = (-1)^j E[X^j] \tag{A.33}$$

If random variables X_1 and X_2 are independent then the Laplace transform of the density function of $Y = X_1 + X_2$ is given by

$$\mathcal{Y}(s) = \mathcal{X}_1(s)\mathcal{X}_2(s) \tag{A.34}$$

where $\mathcal{X}_1(s)$ and $\mathcal{X}_2(s)$ are the Laplace transforms of the density functions of X_1 and X_2, respectively.

   In queueing theory it is frequently the case that answers are obtained in the form of the Laplace transform of a density function. The probability density can be obtained by taking the inverse transform

$$f_X(t) = \frac{1}{2\pi}(P)\int_{-\infty}^\infty e^{st}\mathcal{X}(s)\, d\omega \tag{A.35}$$

where $S = \sigma + j\omega$ and σ is chosen so that the integrand $f_X(t)\,e^{-\sigma t}$ is absolutely integrable from 0 to ∞. Since $f_X(t)$ is the density of a random variable we only require that $\sigma \geq 0$.

A.7. Bounds and Limit Theorems

   It is often the case that exact expressions for quantities are difficult to obtain, but certain inequalities give insight. The best known of these is the *Chebychev inequality*, which states that

$$P[X \geq a] \leq \frac{E[g(x)]}{g(a)} \tag{A.36a}$$

where $g(x)$ is a non-negative even measurable function which is increasing on $[0, \infty]$. A case which is of particular interest is

$$P(|X - E[x]| \geqslant \varepsilon) \leqslant \frac{\text{Var}\,(X)}{\varepsilon^2} \tag{A.36b}$$

The Chebychev inequality may be used to say something about sums of independent random variables. Let $Y_n = (1/n) \sum_{i=1}^{n} X_i$, where X_i, $i = 1, 2, \ldots$, are independent identically distributed random variables with mean μ and variance σ^2. From equations (A.13) and (A.16) we have

$$E[Y_n] = \mu \quad \text{and} \quad \text{Var}\,Y_n = \sigma^2/n$$

From the Chebychev inequality

$$\lim_{n \to \infty} P(|Y_n - \mu| > \varepsilon) = 0.$$

This result shows that the arithmetic average approaches the mean of the distribution with probability 1. This is known as the *strong law* of *large numbers*. A related result is the central limit theorem: Let $S_n \triangleq \sum_{i=1}^{n} X_i$. The distribution of S_n approaches the Gaussian form as $n \to \infty$.

Bibliography

W. B. Davenport, *Probability and Random Processes*, McGraw-Hill, New York (1970).

W. Feller, *An Introduction to Probability Theory and its Applications*, John Wiley, New York (1950).

A. Papoulis, *Probability Random Variables and Stochastic Processes*, McGraw-Hill, New York (1965).

Review of Markov Chains

In this appendix we shall review the basic properties of Markov chains. Since this is only a review, no detailed proofs will be given.† Markov chains are members of the class of random processes which assume a countable set of values and which change state at regularly spaced intervals. Markov chains are characterized by a certain memorylessness in the state transitions; the probability distribution of the state after the next transition depends only on the present state and not on the succession of states that led up to the present state.

B.1. Example: Bernoulli Trials

Bernoulli trials provide an example of Markov chains. On each trial there is success with probability Q independent of the outcomes of past trials. We define the state on the Nth trial to be the accumulated number of successes. Let S_i denote the total number of successes after the ith trial. The probability distribution of the state after the $(N + 1)$st trial conditioned on the previous states is given by

$$P(S_{N+1} = l_{N+1}|S_1 = l_1, \ldots, S_N = l_N) = P(S_{N+1} = l_{N+1}|S_N = l_N) \quad \text{(B.1)}$$

The unfolding of the process in this case in governed by the state transition probability given in equation (B.1). We shall be returning to this example in order to illustrate other properties of the Markov chain.

A Markov chain is a random process which assumes a countable set of values and which changes state at regularly spaced points of time. The process is characterized by an initial state and by a transition probability

---

†There are a number of texts that treat Markov chains. At the end of this appendix we cite four with which we are most familiar.

with the memorylessness property given in equation (B.1). We define the state transition probability as

$$P_i[l_i|l_{i-1}] \triangleq P[S_i = l_i|S_{i-1} = l_{i-1}] \tag{B.2}$$

where S_{i-1} and S_i are the states at adjacent transition points. Let $P_0(k) = P(S_0 = k)$ denote an initial probability distribution of states. From the law of total probability [see equation (A.3b)] we have

$$P[S_N = l_N] = \sum_{l_0} \sum_{l_1} \sum_{l_{N-1}} P[S_0 = l_0, S_1 = l_1, \ldots, S_{N-1} = l_{N-1}, S_N = l_N]$$

$$= \sum_{l_0} \sum_{l_1} \sum_{l_{N-1}} P_0 P_1[l_1|l_0] P_2[l_2|l_1] \cdots P_N[l_N|l_{N-1}] \tag{B.3}$$

The subscript on P in equations (B.2) and (B.3) indicates that the transition probability may change with time. For a *homogeneous* Markov chain there is no time dependence and the transition probability is a function only of the states. In this case we denote the probability of transition from state i to state j by P_{ij}. Again Bernoulli trials offer a pertinent example. We can consider the Markov chain as the accumulation of successes on each trial. For successive trials, we have the state transition probabilities $P_{ii} = 1 - Q$ and $P_{ii+1} = Q$, where Q is the probability of success. If the Markov chain is defined to be the number of successes accumulated in trials spaced k trials apart, the state transition probabilities are given by

$$P_{ij} = \begin{cases} \binom{k}{j-1} Q^{j-i}(1-Q)^{k-j+i}, & i \leq j \\ 0, & i > j \end{cases} \tag{B.4}$$

Now suppose that the time at which we observe the number of successes remains fixed but the number of trials between these observation times increases without limit while Q approaches zero in such a way that the average rate of successes $Q = \lambda$ remains constant. The number of successes is governed by the Poisson distribution. We have

$$P_{ij} = \begin{cases} (\lambda T)^{j-i} e^{-\lambda T}/(j-i)!, & i \leq j \\ 0, & i > j \end{cases} \tag{B.5}$$

B.2. State Transition Matrix

A convenient representation for the states in a homogeneous Markov chain is the state transition probability diagram. The possible states in the chain are connected by directed arcs which are weighted by the probability of going from one state to another. In Figure B.1 we show the state transition probability diagram for Bernoulli trials where the spacing between sampling points is $k = 2$ [see equation (B.4)]. Notice that in Figure B.1 the sum of the weights on arcs out of a state must be one. We include transitions into the same state.

If there are a finite number of states, state transitions may be represented by the state transition matrix whose elements are the state transition probabilities

$$P \triangleq \begin{vmatrix} P_{11} & P_{12} & \cdots & P_{1n} \\ P_{21} & P_{22} & \cdots & P_{2n} \\ \vdots & & & \\ P_{n1} & P_{n2} & \cdots & P_{nn} \end{vmatrix} \qquad (B.6)$$

Since the elements in the rows of P sum to one, it is called a stochastic matrix. If a_i is the probability of state i at time zero the probability of state j after one trial is

$$a_j^{(1)} = \sum_{i=1}^{n} P_{ij} a_i, \qquad j = 1, 2, \ldots, n \qquad (B.7a)$$

or in matrix notation

$$A^{(1)} = PA \qquad (B.7b)$$

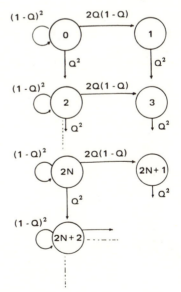

Figure B.1. State transition probability diagram.

where A and $A^{(1)}$ are column vectors with elements $a_1, a_2, \ldots, a_n$ and $a_1^{(1)}$, $a_2^{(1)}, \ldots, a_n^{(1)}$, respectively. Equations (B.7a) and (B.7b) follow directly from equation (B.7). After n trials we have

$$A^{(n)} = P^n A \tag{B.8}$$

where the ith elements of the column vector $A^{(n)}$ is the probability of being in state i after n trials. An example of a state transition matrix is (see Figure B.2)

$$P = \begin{vmatrix} 1/6 & 1/2 & 0 & 1/3 \\ 1/4 & 0 & 1/2 & 1/4 \\ 0 & 0 & 1 & 0 \\ 0 & 1/4 & 3/4 & 0 \end{vmatrix}$$

The transition matrix after two trials is

$$P^2 = \begin{vmatrix} 11/12 & 1/6 & 1/2 & 13/12 \\ 1/24 & 3/16 & 11/16 & 1/12 \\ 0 & 0 & 1 & 0 \\ 1/16 & 0 & 7/8 & 1/16 \end{vmatrix}$$

The process continues for as many trials as we please. There is an interesting feature of the example illustrated in Figure B.2. If state 3 is reached on a trial, on all successive trials the chain remains in state 3. For obvious reasons such a state is called an *absorbing state*. Notice that every other state (1, 2, 4) can go into state 3 with nonzero probability after at least two trials. After many trials the probability of state 3 will be close to one and the probability of the other states negligible. There will be negligible change on each trial after enough trials have taken place. This can be seen by substituting

$$A = \begin{pmatrix} 0 \\ 0 \\ 1 \\ 0 \end{pmatrix}$$

into equation (B.7b).

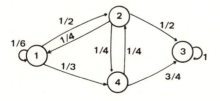

Figure B.2. Markov chain with an absorbing state.

B.3. Steady-State Distribution

The probability distribution of the states after a large number of trials is of considerable interest. As we shall see, if the state transition matrix is of the right form a *steady-state* distribution exists. This steady-state distribution does not necessarily imply an absorbing state. Basically the existence of steady-state solutions depends on the connectivity of states. We define $P_{ij}^{(n)}$ to be the probability of going from state i to state j in n trials; $P_{ij}^{(n)}$ is the element in the ith row and the jth column of the matrix P^n in equation (B.8). We define $P_{ii}^{(0)} = 1$ and $P_{ij}^{(0)} = 0$, $i \neq j$. We say that state j is accessible from state i if $P_{ij}^{(n)} > 0$ for some values of n. If two states i and j are accessible from each other we use the notation $i \leftrightarrow j$. In the example of Figure B.2 we have $1 \leftrightarrow 2$, $1 \leftrightarrow 4$, and $2 \leftrightarrow 4$. However, since 3 is an absorbing state $3 \nleftrightarrow 1$, $3 \nleftrightarrow 1$, and $3 \nleftrightarrow 4$. A set of states C is called *closed* if no state outside C can be reached from a state inside C. An absorbing state is a closed set with only one member. A Markov chain is called *irreducible* if there exist no closed sets other than the set of all states. Since there is an absorbing state in the example in Figure B.2, the Markov chain that the state transition probability diagram represents is not irreducible. In Figure B.3 we show a slightly modified diagram which does represent an irreducible Markov chain. General Markov chains can be decomposed into one or more irreducible chains.

The long-term properties of the Markov chain depend upon the recurrence of states. Because of the memorylessness of the Markov chain each time a particular state, say j, recurs after a number of trials we are in the same position in terms of future evaluation. This is called a recurrent event. The probability of returning to state j after l steps is $p_{ii}^{(l)}$. For each state j we define its *period*, $d(j)$, as the greatest common divisor of all the integers $l \geq 1$ for which $p_{jj}^{(l)} > 0$. If $p_{ii}^{(l)} = 0$ for all $l \geq 1$, we define $d(j) = 0$. In Figure B.3. for example, we have $d(j) = 1$, $j = 1, 2, 3, 4$. A Markov chain for which each state has period one is called *aperiodic*. The next concept that we consider is the *first return* to a state. Let $f_{ij}^{(l)}$ be the probability that, given that state i occurred on the zeroth trial, it occurs again for the first

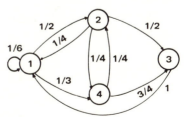

Figure B.3. Irreducible Markov chain.

time on the *l*th trial. We define $f_{jj}^{(0)} = 0$ for consistency. In Figure B.3, for example, $f_{11}^{(1)} = 1/6, f_{11}^{(2)} = 1/8, f_{11}^{(3)} = 25/48. \ldots$ The events of the first return on trials 1, 2, ... are disjoint events, and by the basic axioms of probability

$$P[\text{eventual return to state } j] = \sum_{l=1}^{\infty} f_{jj}^{(l)} \le 1, \qquad j = 1, 2, \ldots \quad (B.9)$$

If there is equality in (B.9) for some *j*, then we say that the state *j* is *persistent*.

The probability of return to a state, not necessarily the first return, can be expressed in terms of first return probabilities. Consider the event that state *i* occurs at the *l*th trial given that *i* occurred on the zeroth trial. It may be that state *i* occurred a number of times in the intervening trials. Each pattern of occurrence constitutes a disjoint event. We may write

$$P_{jj}^{(l)} = \sum_{i=0}^{l} P[\text{first return on } i\text{th trial, return on } l\text{th trial}]$$

$$= \sum_{i=0}^{l} P[\text{return on } l\text{th trial}|\text{first return on } i\text{th trial}] \quad (B.10)$$

$$\times P[\text{first return on } i\text{th trial}]$$

$$= \sum_{i=0}^{l} p_{jj}^{(l-i)} f_{jj}^{(i)}, \qquad l \ge 1$$

Recall that we have defined $f_{jj}^{(0)} = 0$ and $p_{jj}^{(0)} = 1$. The key to writing equation (B.10) is the memorylessness property of Markov chains. Define the following generating functions for $|z| < 1$

$$P_j(z) \triangleq \sum_{l=0}^{l} P_{jj}^{(l)} z^l \quad (B.11a)$$

and

$$F_j(z) \triangleq \sum_{l=0}^{\infty} f_{jj}^{(l)} z^l \quad (B.11b)$$

Summing both sides of equation (B.10) we have

$$\sum_{l=1}^{\infty} p_{jj}^{(0)} z^l = p_j(z) - 1 = \sum_{l=1}^{l} z^l \sum_{i=0}^{\infty} f_{jj}^{(l)} p_{jj}^{(l-1)} = P_j(z) F_j(z)$$

or

$$P_j(z) = \frac{1}{1 - F_j(z)} \quad (B.12)$$

It is not difficult to see that if a state of a Markov chain with first passage probabilities $f_{jj}^{(l)}$ is persistent then $\lim_{z \to 1} F_j(z) = \sum_{l=0}^{\infty} f^{(l)} = 1$. Furthermore, a necessary and sufficient condition for a state to be persistent is

$$\lim_{z \to 1} P_{jj}(z) = \infty$$

A state is called transient if $\sum_{l=0}^{\infty} f_{jj}^{(l)} < 1$. A necessary and sufficient condition for a transient state is $\sum_{l=0}^{\infty} p_{jj}^{(l)} < \infty$. It is not difficult to show that $\sum_{n=0}^{\infty} p_{ij}^{(l)} < \infty$ for this case. The *mean recurrence* time for a state is

$$\mu_j = \sum_{l=1}^{\infty} l f_{jj}^{(l)}$$

A state j is a *persistent null state* if $\mu_j = \infty$. It can be shown that a necessary and sufficient condition for a persistent null state is $\sum_{l=1}^{\infty} p_{jj}^{(l)} = \infty$ but $\lim_{l \to \infty} p_{jj}^{(l)} = 0$. It follows directly that for a persistent null state

$$\lim_{l \to \infty} p_{ij}^{(l)} = 0 \qquad (B.13)$$

A state j has period $t > 1$ if $p_{jj}^{(n+1)}$ only for trials $t, 2t, 3t, \ldots$. If j is persistent and aperiodic then

$$\lim_{l \to \infty} p_{ij}^{(l)} \sum_{l=0}^{\infty} f_{ij}^{(l)} / \mu_j \qquad (B.14)$$

where $f_{ij}^{(l)}$ is the probability of reading state j from state i for the first time on trial l. It can also be shown that

$$\lim_{l \to \infty} p_{jj}^{(l)} = 1/\mu_j \qquad (B.15)$$

For example, for the null state $\mu_j = \infty$ and $\lim_{l \to \infty} p_{jj}^{(l)} = 0$. Now if a state j is persistent and periodic with period t then

$$\lim_{l \to \infty} p_{jj}^{(lt)} = t/\mu_j \qquad (B.16)$$

Persistent states that are neither periodic states nor null states are called *ergodic* states.

Armed with these definitions two important theorems on Markov chains can be stated. These theorems give the key to finding the steady-state distribution of a Markov chain.

Theorem B.1. In an irreducible Markov chain all states belong to the same class. They are all transient, all persistent null states or all persistent non-null states. In all cases they have the same period. Moreover, every state can be reached from every other state.

In every chain the persistent states can be divided uniquely into closed sets. From any state of one of these sets all other states in that set can be reached and no state outside the set can be reached. In addition to the closed sets the chain may contain transient states in general. From this transient state a closed set of states may be reached.

Examples. In the example of Figure B.2 state 3 is a set of closed states. State 1 is a transient state. This can be seen from the fact that the series $f_{11}^{(l)}$, $l = 1, 2, \ldots$ is dominated by 2^{-l} and $\sum_{l=1}^{\infty} 2^{-l} = 1$. In the example of Figure B.3 all of the states are persistent.

Corollary. In a Markov chain with finitely many states there exist no null states and not all states may be transient states.

Theorem B.2. An irreducible aperiodic Markov chain belongs to one of the following two classes:

(a) The states are either all transient or all null states; in this case $\lim_{l=0} p_{ij}^{(l)} = 0$ for all i, j and a steady-state distribution does not exist.

(þ) All states are ergodic:

$$\lim_{l \to \infty} p_{ij}^{(l)} = 1/\mu_k > 0 \tag{B.17}$$

In this case $1/\mu_k$ is the unique steady-state distribution. If for an arbitrary distribution $v_1, v_2, \ldots, v_n$ we have

$$v_k = \sum_{j=1}^{n} v_j p_{jk}, \qquad k = 1, 2, \ldots. n \tag{B.18}$$

then for any initial distribution $a_1, a_2, \ldots, a_n$ we have

$$\lim_{l \to \infty} \sum_{l=1}^{n} a_j p_{jk}^{(l)} = v_k = 1/\mu_k, \qquad k = 1, 2, \ldots, n$$

Thus the steady-state distribution is independent of the initial condition. In order to find the steady-state distribution given the state transition matrix we solve equation (B.18) together with the normalizing condition

$$\sum_{k=1}^{n} v_k = 1 \qquad \text{(B.19)}$$

In matrix form equation (B.18) can be written

$$V = PV \qquad \text{(B.20)}$$

where V is the column vector with elements $v_1, v_2, \ldots, v_n$. We recognize that V is an eigenvector of the matrix P.

We apply this to the example of Figure B.3. The state transition matrix is

$$P = \begin{vmatrix} 1/6 & 1/2 & 0 & 1/3 \\ 1/4 & 0 & 1/2 & 1/4 \\ 1 & 0 & 0 & 0 \\ 0 & 1/2 & 3/4 & 0 \end{vmatrix}$$

From equations (B.18) and (B.19) we have

$$\tfrac{1}{6}v_1 + \tfrac{1}{4}v_2 + v_3 = v_1$$

$$\tfrac{1}{2}v_1 + \tfrac{1}{4}v_4 = v_2$$

$$\tfrac{1}{2}v_2 + \tfrac{3}{4}v_4 = v_3$$

$$\tfrac{1}{3}v_1 + \tfrac{1}{4}v_2 = v_4$$

$$v_1 + v_2 + v_3 + v_4 = 1$$

The solution to these equations is $v_1 = 0.358$, $v_2 = 0.223$, $v_3 = 0.243$, and $v_4 = 0.175$ as can be verified by simple substitution.

In our work we shall not meet Markov chains with only four states. In practical problems there are a large number of states so it is often not practical to obtain solutions by hand, and machine computation is necessary.

Bibliography

W. Feller, *An Introduction to Probability and Its Applications*, Vol. 1, John Wiley, New York (1957).

S. Karlin and H. M. Taylor, *A First Course in Stochastic Processes*. Academic Press, New York (1975).

D. R. Cox and H. D. Miller, *The Theory of Stochastic Processes*, Methuen, New York (1965).

L. Kleinrock, *Queueing Systems*, Vol. 1: *Theory*, John Wiley, New York (1975).

Index